T0333899

FINANCIAL SYSTEMS AND ECONOMIC GROWTH

Throughout much of the twentieth century, economists paid little heed to the role of financial intermediaries in procuring a beneficial allocation of capital. But by the end of the century some financial historians had begun to turn the tide, and the phrase 'finance-growth nexus' became part of the lexicon of modern economics. Recent experience has added another dimension in that countries with broader, deeper and more active financial systems might be prone to financial crises, particularly if regulatory structures are inadequate. In this book, Peter L. Rousseau and Paul Wachtel have gathered together some of today's most distinguished financial historians to examine this finance-growth nexus from historical and modern perspectives. Some essays examine the nexus in a particular historical or cross-country context. Others, in the light of recent experience, explore the expanded nexus of finance, growth, crises, and regulation.

Peter L. Rousseau is Professor of Economics at Vanderbilt University, Tennessee and secretary-treasurer of the American Economic Association. He is a macroeconomist and economic historian who studies the role of financial markets and institutions in growth and development. He has published extensively in leading economic journals, including the *Journal of Political Economy*, the *Journal of Monetary Economics*, the *Journal of Financial Economics* and the *Journal of Economic History*.

Paul Wachtel is Professor of Economics at New York University's Stern School of Business. He has published extensively on macroeconomics, monetary policy, and central banking. He is the co-editor of *Comparative Economic Studies* and a consultant to the Central Bank of Croatia.

STUDIES IN MACROECONOMIC HISTORY

Series Editor: Michael D. Bordo, *Rutgers University*

Editors:
Owen F. Humpage, *Federal Reserve Bank of Cleveland*
Christopher M. Meissner, *University of California, Davis*
Kris James Mitchener, *Santa Clara University*
David C. Wheelock, *Federal Reserve Bank of St. Louis*

The titles in this series investigate themes of interest to economists and economic historians in the rapidly developing field of macroeconomic history. The four areas covered include the application of monetary and finance theory, international economics, and quantitative methods to historical problems; the historical application of growth and development theory and theories of business fluctuations; the history of domestic and international monetary, financial, and other macroeconomic institutions; and the history of international monetary and financial systems. The series amalgamates the former Cambridge University Press series *Studies in Monetary and Financial History* and *Studies in Quantitative Economic History*.

Other books in the series:

Øyvind Eitrheim, Jan Tore Klovland, and Lars Fredrik Øksendal, *A Monetary History of Norway, 1816–2016* (2016)

Jan Fredrik Qvigstad, *On Central Banking* (2016)

Michael D. Bordo, Øyvind Eitrheim, Marc Flandreau, and Jan F. Qvigstad, Editors, *Central Banks at a Crossroads: What Can We Learn from History?* (2016)

Michael D. Bordo and Mark A. Wynne, Editors, *The Federal Reserve's Role in the Global Economy: A Historical Perspective* (2016)

Owen F. Humpage, Editor, *Current Federal Reserve Policy Under the Lens of Economic History: Essays to Commemorate the Federal Reserve System's Centennial* (2015)

Michael D. Bordo and William Roberds, Editors, *The Origins, History, and Future of the Federal Reserve: A Return to Jekyll Island* (2013)

Michael D. Bordo and Ronald MacDonald, Editors, *Credibility and the International Monetary Regime: A Historical Perspective* (2012)

Robert L. Hetzel, *The Great Recession: Market Failure or Policy Failure?* (2012)

Tobias Straumann, *Fixed Ideas of Money: Small States and Exchange Rate Regimes in Twentieth-Century Europe* (2010)

Forrest Capie, *The Bank of England: 1950s to 1979* (2010)

Aldo Musacchio, *Experiments in Financial Democracy: Corporate Governance and Financial Development in Brazil, 1882–1950* (2009)

Claudio Borio, Gianni Toniolo, and Piet Clement, Editors, *The Past and Future of Central Bank Cooperation* (2008)

Robert L. Hetzel, *The Monetary Policy of the Federal Reserve: A History* (2008)

Caroline Fohlin, *Finance Capitalism and Germany's Rise to Industrial Power* (2007)

John H. Wood, *A History of Central Banking in Great Britain and the United States* (2005)

Gianni Toniolo (with the assistance of Piet Clement), *Central Bank Cooperation at the Bank for International Settlements, 1930–1973* (2005)

Richard Burdekin and Pierre Siklos, Editors, *Deflation: Current and Historical Perspectives* (2004)

Pierre Siklos, *The Changing Face of Central Banking: Evolutionary Trends since World War II* (2002)

Michael D. Bordo and Roberto Cortés-Conde, Editors, *Transferring Wealth and Power from the Old to the New World: Monetary and Fiscal Institutions in the 17th through the 19th Centuries* (2001)

Howard Bodenhorn, *A History of Banking in Antebellum America: Financial Markets and Economic Development in an Era of Nation-Building* (2000)

Mark Harrison, Editor, *The Economics of World War II: Six Great Powers in International Comparison* (2000)

Angela Redish, *Bimetallism: An Economic and Historical Analysis* (2000)

Elmus Wicker, *Banking Panics of the Gilded Age* (2000)

Michael D. Bordo, *The Gold Standard and Related Regimes: Collected Essays* (1999)

Michele Fratianni and Franco Spinelli, *A Monetary History of Italy* (1997)

Mark Toma, *Competition and Monopoly in the Federal Reserve System, 1914–1951,* (1997)

Barry Eichengreen, Editor, *Europe's Postwar Recovery,* 1996

Lawrence H. Officer, *Between the Dollar-Sterling Gold Points: Exchange Rates, Parity and Market Behavior* (1996)

Elmus Wicker, *Banking Panics of the Great Depression* (1996)

Norio Tamaki, *Japanese Banking: A History, 1859–1959* (1995)

Barry Eichengreen, *Elusive Stability: Essays in the History of International Finance, 1919–1939* (1993)

Michael D. Bordo and Forrest Capie, Editors, *Monetary Regimes in Transition* (1993)

Larry Neal, *The Rise of Financial Capitalism: International Capital Markets in the Age of Reason* (1993)

S. N. Broadberry and N. F. R. Crafts, Editors, *Britain in the International Economy, 1870–1939* (1992)

Aurel Schubert, *The Credit-Anstalt Crisis of 1931* (1992)

Trevor J. O. Dick and John E. Floyd, *Canada and the Gold Standard: Balance of Payments Adjustment under Fixed Exchange Rates, 1871–1913* (1992)

Kenneth Mouré, *Managing the Franc Poincaré: Economic Understanding and Political Constraint in French Monetary Policy, 1928–1936* (1991)

David C. Wheelock, *The Strategy and Consistency of Federal Reserve Monetary Policy, 1924–1933* (1991)

Financial Systems and Economic Growth

Credit, Crises, and Regulation from the 19th Century to the Present

Edited by

PETER L. ROUSSEAU

Vanderbilt University

and

PAUL WACHTEL

Leonard N. Stern School of Business, New York University

CAMBRIDGE
UNIVERSITY PRESS

University Printing House, Cambridge CB2 8BS, United Kingdom

One Liberty Plaza, 20th Floor, New York, NY 10006, USA

477 Williamstown Road, Port Melbourne, VIC 3207, Australia

4843/24, 2nd Floor, Ansari Road, Daryaganj, Delhi – 110002, India

79 Anson Road, #06–04/06, Singapore 079906

Cambridge University Press is part of the University of Cambridge.

It furthers the University's mission by disseminating knowledge in the pursuit of education, learning, and research at the highest international levels of excellence.

www.cambridge.org
Information on this title: www.cambridge.org/9781107141094
10.1017/9781316493281

© Cambridge University Press 2017

First published 2017

Printed in the United States of America by Sheridan Books, Inc.

A catalogue record for this publication is available from the British Library.

Library of Congress Cataloging in Publication Data
Names: Rousseau, Peter L., 1961– editor. | Wachtel, Paul, 1945– editor.
Title: Financial systems and economic growth : credit, crises, and regulation from the 19th century to the present / edited by Peter L. Rousseau, Vanderbilt University and Paul Wachtel, Leonard N. Stern School of Business, New York University.
Description: New York : Cambridge University Press, 2017. | Series: Studies in macroeconomic history
Identifiers: LCCN 2016041216 | ISBN 9781107141094 (hardback)
Subjects: LCSH: Economic development. | Finance, Public. | Monetary policy. | Banks and banking. | BISAC: BUSINESS & ECONOMICS / Development / Economic Development.
Classification: LCC HD82 .F4577 2017 | DDC 332–dc23
LC record available at https://lccn.loc.gov/2016041216

ISBN 978-1-107-14109-4 Hardback

In appreciation of Richard Sylla's many contributions to economic and financial history.

Contents

Contributors

Michael D. Bordo is the Board of Governors Professor of Economics and director of the Center for Monetary and Financial History at Rutgers University as well as a research associate of the National Bureau of Economic Research and a member of the Shadow Open Market Committee. He is the editor of the series, Studies in Macroeconomic History, for Cambridge University Press and has published a wealth of articles and books on monetary economics and monetary history. Previously, Dr. Bordo held many academic positions including at Cambridge, where he was Pitt Professor of American History and Institutions. He has also spent time as a visiting scholar at the International Monetary Fund, the Federal Reserve Banks of St. Louis and Cleveland, and more. Dr. Bordo holds a B.A. from McGill University, and an M.S. in economics from the London School of Economics. He received a Ph.D. from the University of Chicago.

Charles W. Calomiris is the Henry Kaufman Professor of Financial Institutions at Columbia Business School, the Director of Columbia Business School's Program for Financial Studies and of the PFS Initiative on Finance and Growth in Emerging Markets, and a professor at Columbia's School of International and Public Affairs. His research spans the areas of banking, corporate finance, financial history and monetary economics. He is a distinguished visiting fellow at the Hoover Institution, a fellow at the Manhattan Institute, a member of the Shadow Open Market Committee and of the Financial Economists Roundtable, and is a research associate of the National Bureau of Economic Research. He has served on numerous other committees, including the Advisory Scientific Committee of the European Systemic Risk Board, the U.S. Congress's International Financial Institution Advisory Commission, the Shadow Financial Regulatory Committee, and the Federal Reserve

System's Centennial Advisory Committee. He is co-managing editor of the *Journal of Financial Intermediation*. Dr. Calomiris received a B.A. in economics from Yale, and a Ph.D. in economics from Stanford.

Mark Carlson is a senior economic project manager in the Division of Monetary Affairs at the Federal Reserve Board of Governors. In addition to contributing to staff efforts supporting monetary policy at the Federal Reserve, he has worked on issues related to financial stability and to developments in the commercial banking sector. His research focuses on understanding financial crises, particularly historical episodes such as the banking crises of the 1930s and the panics of the National Banking Era, and on understanding the impact of such crises on financial intermediation. Dr. Carlson's work has been published in the *Journal of Political Economy*, the *Journal of Money, Credit and Banking*, the *Journal of Financial Economics*, and *Explorations in Economic History*. Dr. Carlson has also held the position of senior economist at the Bank for International Settlements. He received his Ph.D. from the University of California, Berkeley.

Niall Ferguson, M.A., D. Phil., is a senior fellow at the Hoover Institution, Stanford University. He has published fourteen widely acclaimed books, including *The World's Banker: The History of the House of Rothschild*, which won the Wadsworth Prize for Business History and was also short-listed for the Jewish Quarterly/Wingate Literary Award and the American National Jewish Book Award. Dr. Ferguson is a regular con-tributor to television and radio on both sides of the Atlantic. In 2003 he wrote and presented a six-part history of the British Empire for the UK's Channel 4. The accompanying book, *Empire: The Rise and Demise of the British World Order and the Lessons for Global Power*, was a bestseller in both Britain and the United States. In 2004 *Time Magazine* named him one of the 100 most influential people in the world. Dr. Ferguson is a member of the board of trustees of the New York Historical Society. His many prizes and awards include the Benjamin Franklin Prize for Public Service (2010) and the Hayek Prize for Lifetime Achievement (2012). He is Managing Director at Greenmantle LLC and serves on the Board of Directors of Affiliated Managers Group, Inc., a global asset management company.

Marc Flandreau is professor of international history and international economics at the Graduate Institute, Geneva. His work focuses on the history of credit, information, and finance. He has widely published on the history of the international monetary system, exchange-rate regimes, public finance, monetary unions, rating agencies, financial journalism, white-collar criminality, investment banking, and financial crises. Previously, Dr. Flandreau held teaching and research positions at the Centre National de la Recherche Scientifique and at Sciences Po, and has held visiting positions at many universities including Stanford, Berkeley, Princeton, Yale, and the University of Tokyo, as well as in the research departments of the International Monetary Fund and the Bank for International Settlements. He was president of the Economic History Society from 2007 to 2009, and has served on the editorial boards of the *Journal of Economic History*, the *Economic History Review*, and the *European Review of Economic History*. Dr. Flandreau holds a European Doctorate in Quantitative Economics, which is a Ph.D. awarded jointly by the London School of Economics, EHESS in Paris, the University of Bonn, and the University of Louvain.

Christopher M. Meissner is professor of economics at the University of California, Davis. His research focuses on the economic history of the international economy, and his articles have appeared in the *American Economic Review*, the *Journal of Development Economics*, the *Journal of Economic History*, the *Journal of International Economics*, and the *Journal of Monetary Economics*. He has held visiting positions at Harvard, INSEAD, the International Monetary Fund, and the Paris School of Economics. In 2006 he was the Houblon-Norman Fellow at the Bank of England. Dr. Meissner is also a research associate at the National Bureau of Economic Research in the Development of the American Economy program. Previously, Dr. Meissner was on the Faculty of Economics at Cambridge University. He received his Ph.D. from the University of California, Berkeley.

Peter L. Rousseau is professor of economics and professor of history at Vanderbilt University, as well as the secretary-treasurer of the American Economic Association. Dr. Rousseau is a macroeconomist and economic historian who studies the role of financial markets and institutions in growth and development. He is particularly interested in the monetary history of the United States and Europe and in how financial markets assist in spreading transformative technological changes through an economy. He has published in various economic journals, including the *Journal of Political Economy*, the *Review of Economics and Statistics*, the *Journal of Monetary Economics*, the *Journal of Financial Economics*, and the *Journal of Economic History*. Dr. Rousseau received his Ph.D. from New York University.

Paul Wachtel is professor of economics at New York University's Stern School of Business where he is currently the Academic Director of the program in Business and Political Economy. His primary areas of research include monetary policy, central banking, and financial sector reform in economies in transition. He is the author of several books, including *Banking in Transition Economies: Developing Market Oriented Banking Sectors in Europe*. His research has been published in numerous journals, including, most recently, *The Journal of Finance, Economic Inquiry, Journal of Banking and Finance, Comparative Economic Studies*, and the *Journal of Money Credit and Banking*. He is the co-editor of *Comparative Economic Studies* and the program chair for the Dubrovnik Economic Conferences. He has been a research associate at the National Bureau of Economic Research, a senior economic advisor to the East West Institute, and a consultant to the Bank of Israel, the IMF and the World Bank. Dr. Wachtel received his B.A. from Queens College and his M.A. and Ph.D. degrees from the University of Rochester.

John Joseph Wallis is professor of economics at the University of Maryland and a research associate at the National Bureau of Economic Research. His work as an economic historian focuses on the interaction of political and economic development, with particular interest in how patterns of economic institutions change over time and specifically how patterns of economic institutions interact with political institutions in a way that make both economic and political institutions sustainable over time. Most of his work has been in American history, but over the last decade Dr. Wallis has begun working on contemporary development problems around the world. His interests span economics, institutional economics, political economy, economic history, development economics, political science, history, anthropology, sociology, and cognitive psychology. Dr. Wallis received his B.A., M.A., and Ph.D. degrees from the University of Washington.

Eugene N. White is Distinguished Professor of Economics at Rutgers University and a research associate at the National Bureau of Economic Research. His recent research focuses on the evolution of bank supervision in the United States from the 19th century to the present, the housing market boom of the 1920s, stock market booms and crashes, the microstructure of securities markets in Europe and America, and the management of financial crises by the Banque de France and the Bank of England in the 19th century. He is the editor of a series on financial and economic history for Yale University Press. Dr. White received an A.B. from Harvard

University, a B.A. from Oxford University, and M.A. and Ph.D. degrees from the University of Illinois at Urbana-Champaign.

Robert E. Wright is the Nef Family Chair of Political Economy at Augustana University. An economic and financial historian and acclaimed author or co-author of more than twenty books, Dr. Wright's research focuses on the roles of financial policies, institutions, and markets in the economic performance of the early United States. Previously, Dr. Wright was a clinical associate professor of economics at New York University's Stern School of Business, and a guest curator for the Museum of American Finance. His most recent books include *Genealogy of American Finance* (2015, with Richard Sylla) and *The Poverty of Slavery* (2017). Dr. Wright received a B.A. in history from Buffalo State College, and M.A. and Ph.D. degrees from the State University of New York at Buffalo.

Discussants at the Conference

Larry D. Neal, University of Illinois Urbana-Champaign
Hugh Rockoff, Rutgers University
Mary Tone Rodgers, State University of New York at Oswego
Moritz Schularick, University of Bonn
George D. Smith, New York University
Peter Temin, Massachusetts Institute of Technology
Gianni Toniolo, Duke University
David Weiman, Barnard College
David C. Wheelock, Federal Reserve Bank of St. Louis

Introduction

Peter L. Rousseau and Paul Wachtel

The early 1990s saw a resurgence of interest in studies relating financial development and financial systems to modern growth within and across countries (King and Levine 1993; Demetriades and Hussein 1996; Rousseau and Wachtel 1998), and a vibrant literature now brings a wide range of regional and firm-level information to bear in exploring relationships between financial and real activity as well as the underpinnings of financial development itself. The success of this literature is undeniable, yet a less sanguine undercurrent continues to question whether the policy prescriptions informed by such studies are too simple and whether a "one-size-fits-all" approach to financial development can be as harmful to growth in some cases as it can be helpful in others (Rioja and Valev 2004; Rousseau and Wachtel 2011).

Interestingly, economic and financial historians made these same observations decades ago. Raymond W. Goldsmith's 1969 book *Financial Structure and Development*, for example, while often receiving only passing mention in reference lists of research articles using modern data and techniques, is deeply representative of the economic history tradition that views a balanced combination of data and narrative as the path to better understanding of not just whether but how financial factors influence growth. Other pioneers such as John G. Gurley and Edward S. Shaw (1955), and later Ronald I. McKinnon (1973), taking viewpoints primarily from development economics, emphasized how institutional change can loosen bottlenecks that impede the smooth flow of credit that is so crucial for modernization.

Prior to these contributions, research in financial history and in financial economics preceded along largely independent tracks. Business historians devoted attention to institutional history and particularly the role of banks, whereas earlier economists interested in development paid relatively little attention to financial institutions. Rather, studies of

1

economic growth emphasized resource availability, trade, and technological change. For example, U.S. economic growth was traditionally attributed to the abundance of land and the immigration of talented human resources. The role of institutions generally and financial institutions specifically was just not part of the discussion.

The integration of financial and economic history emerged in the research of Richard Sylla and a few others. Sylla's work on post-colonial American economic growth demonstrated how important the early emergence of financial institutions was for the gradual acceleration of growth in the United States. In particular, the financial innovations envisioned and implemented by Alexander Hamilton, the nation's first Secretary of the Treasury, created an institutional structure that allowed the United States to become the world's dominant economic power by the time of World War I (Sylla 1998). Earlier scholars underestimated the complexity, modernity, and size of the early U.S. financial system.

From the very start of his career, Sylla put a research spotlight on the role of banks in American economic growth (Sylla 1969, 1972). A broad explanation of the role of the financial sector in the modernization and development of economies is found in Sylla (2002); Rousseau and Sylla (2005) provide an econometric demonstration of the finance-growth nexus in the early United States that shows that the American growth spurt started with the financial reforms of the 1790s and not much later (i.e., in the 1820s or even after the Civil War), which was the generally accepted view among historians. Although Sylla's scholarly contributions are largely on the American experience, his research introduced the next generation of economic historians to a new paradigm.

The essays in this volume range in topic from the American colonial experience to important twentieth-century financial sector institutions and contemporary issues. In every instance, the essays echo the ideas about the role of the financial sector introduced by Richard Sylla. The title of this book – *Financial Systems and Economic Growth* – reflects both the subject of the contributions collected here and the theme of Sylla's career and his influence on the economics profession.

The chapters were prepared for a conference held at the Stern School of Business, New York University, on March 27–28, 2015. The occasion for the conference was the retirement of Richard Sylla, the Henry Kaufman Professor of the History of Financial Institutions and Markets. Dick Sylla is in many respects the godfather of much contemporary research on the history of American financial institutions and the role of finance in the historical development of the American economy, the subject of many of the papers in this volume. The influence of his seminal work on the historical role of finance in American development can be seen in all of the contributions to this volume, which we briefly summarize here.

In Chapter 1, Michael D. Bordo and Christopher M. Meissner start with a review of the incidence of financial crises around the world from the time that reliable data begin to become available early in the nineteenth century to the present. "Growing Up to Stability? Financial Globalization, Financial Development and Financial Crises" also provides in-depth case studies for four nineteenth-century emerging markets: Argentina, Australia, Canada, and the United States. Their central question is why some countries learn from experience (i.e., grow up to stability) and others do not. The importance of the question is self-evident in light of the evidence that relates financial stability and development to economic growth. Some nations are able to access international capital markets and harness the funds for development while others are prone to repeated financial crises, which inhibit development and increase economic volatility.

Bordo and Meissner examine the crisis experiences of countries with available data and active participation in international markets, and place them into three groups. The first are the "leaders," which exhibited financial stability and development early on. This group includes Belgium, France, Germany, the Netherlands, Switzerland, and Great Britain. Countries in the second group, the "learners," were often colonial off-shoots that experienced bumps in the road but learned from their crisis experiences to develop stable financial institutions. This group includes Australia, Canada, New Zealand, and the United States, as well as Denmark, Japan, Norway, and Sweden. Finally, a third group of countries are the "non-learners" or "repeat offenders," which experience repeated crises over long periods of time that inhibit financial development and economic growth. This group includes Argentina, Brazil, Chile, Greece, Italy, Portugal, and Spain.

In the golden age of globalization – the period from 1880 until World War I – the leaders had the deepest financial markets and highest growth rates. The learners had more frequent crises but experienced deepening financial markets and rapid growth as compared to the non-learners, which tended to bounce from boom to bust and experience periods of secular decline. Later in the twentieth century, the learners grew more rapidly than the leaders, and the non-learners lagged far behind. Countries in all three groups experience financial crises, but the likelihood of crisis experience declines the longer a country goes without a crisis. Thus, the learners use the crisis experience to develop stable financial systems whereas the non-learners experience frequent crises throughout their history.

Among the case studies, U.S. financial history is particularly revealing. The nation came into existence with a debt crisis and the first of many banking crises. Banking crises, some large, others small, occurred first in 1792 and most recently in 2007–2009. Currency crises stemmed from the operations of the bimetallic standard and later the gold standard, and persisted until the gold window was closed in 1971. Throughout these crisis experiences, Bordo and Meissner show a continued history of government responses and innovation in policy making that remedied problems without inhibiting private sector financial development. That is not to say that the United States did not make institutional mistakes, such as the Federal Reserve's repeated missteps during the Great Depression.

The United States was not the only distinguished learner. Bordo and Meissner suggest that Canada was the most successful in institutional learning with respect to banking crises. It adopted early on a model of nationwide branch banking and responded to problems with successive pieces of banking legislation that improved the soundness of the system and avoided any incidence of systemic banking crisis.

It is not easy to take general lessons away from Bordo and Meissner about why certain countries are learners and others are repeat offenders, as a dense nexus of factors seem to come into play in generating financial stability. Yet their contribution, by drawing heavily upon on the literature on institutions, suggests that the countries with successful financial development also saw greater political stability, adherence to the rule of law, well-defined property rights, and more democratic political systems.

Their discussion is complemented by the econometric analysis in Chapter 2 by Peter L. Rousseau and Paul Wachtel. In "Episodes of Financial Deepening: Credit Booms or Growth Generators?" we explore the influence of economic crises on the finance-growth nexus with historical data for seventeen countries from 1870 to 1929. This is the period when banks and other financial institutions developed rapidly in many countries. Earlier work (Wachtel and Rousseau 1995; Rousseau and Wachtel 1998; Rousseau and Sylla 2003) shows that financial deepening in this period was associated with economic growth. Yet it is also a period when many countries experienced financial crises, including serious banking and debt crises, which affected the operation of the financial system.

The main theme of Chapter 2 is that financial deepening has a dual role: it can provide the financial sector impetus for growth or it can lead to credit booms that sometimes end in systemic crises and economic downturns. These dual roles – the Jekyll-and-Hyde nature of credit deepening – have usually been discussed in separate strands of the literature. There is a literature on the finance-growth nexus (King and Levine 1993; Rousseau and Wachtel 1998) and an historical literature on crises (Reinhart and Rogoff 2009; Schularick and Taylor 2012). A connection between the two strands was suggested in Rousseau and Wachtel (2011), which examines data for the last fifty years. We found that the strength of the finance-growth nexus weakened in the last decade of the twentieth century and suggest that the reason might be the increased incidence of financial crises. The long-term impact of financial deepening on economic growth is muted when a country experiences a financial crisis. In this chapter, we examine the relationship between episodes of financial deepening and systemic financial crises.

Financial deepening episodes are defined as years where the ratio of broadly defined money (M2) to gross domestic product (GDP) increases by at least 30 percent over the previous ten years. There are sixty-one such episodes in our sample (1870–1929) and forty-nine systemic financial crises during the same period. About one-half of the financial crises are associated with a deepening episode, and about two-thirds of the deepening episodes are not associated with a financial crisis.

We conduct the analysis using cross-country regressions similar to those found in earlier work on finance and growth. Our econometric specification distinguishes the effects of those episodes of financial deepening that end in a crisis from those that do not. Thus, the results illustrate how expansions in credit affect the operation of the finance-growth nexus. We find that episodes of financial deepening, if not taken to the excesses that end in financial crises, enhance links between financial depth and growth. That is, the effects of credit deepening on growth are enhanced during credit booms that are not associated with crisis and diminished in crisis-boom periods compared to other periods. Thus, episodes of credit deepening are beneficial except when they are associated with financial crises.

In addition to the econometric evidence, the chapter includes brief discussions of crisis and deepening episodes in some of the countries. The descriptions of historical experiences are consistent both with our econometric evidence and the narratives offered by Bordo and Meissner in Chapter 1, suggesting that countries can learn from crisis experiences and benefit from continued financial deepening.

Chapter 3 takes an in-depth look at several aspects of U.S. financial sector development. In "Financing U.S. Economic Growth, 1790–1860," Robert E. Wright begins by observing that historians did not develop a serious interest in early financial development until the 1970s. Late-twentieth-century changes in the global financial structure due to the erosion of Depression-era financial repression and the end of the Bretton Woods regime resulted in rapid change, which in turn piqued interest in earlier periods of rapid financial change. The United States entered the nineteenth century with six interconnected elements of a modern financial system in place due to the political stability that came with the adoption of the federal Constitution and with the financial innovations introduced by Alexander Hamilton in the early years of the republic (Rousseau and Sylla 2003). Consequently, the United States enjoyed a stable unit of account, a central bank, a banking sector, an insurance sector, securities markets and, finally, as Wright emphasizes, a for-profit corporate business sector. With these foundations in place, economic and financial institutions developed rapidly in the early nineteenth century.

Wright uses a publicly available database that he constructed with Richard Sylla on "U.S. Corporate Development 1790–1860" (http://reposi tory.upenn.edu/7) to illustrate the extent of financial sector development in the antebellum period and its influence on economic development. The astounding feature of the U.S. economy was the rapid appearance of large numbers of chartered corporations in every industrial sector. From 1790–1860, charters were granted to 1,636 corporations in the extractive sector; 2,122 in insurance; 10,775 transportation companies; 3,566 manu-facturing firms; 1,165 construction companies; and 692 service companies.

The importance of chartered companies is twofold. First, a charter facilitated the raising of capital on the nascent financial markets. Second, companies utilized the growing banking sector to conduct business. Going beyond the aggregate data, Wright cites many examples of the interactions between the financial sector and the business sector, which financed innovation and expansion in agriculture, manufacturing, and transporta-tion. He argues that the complex financial structure allowed for risk sharing and diversification that resulted in high levels of capital formation and rapid economic growth. Despite some elements of financial fragility (i.e., more than occasional financial panics and the failure to renew the central bank charter twice), the financial infrastructure (payments mechanisms, capital markets, and others) was sufficiently resilient to serve the growing business sector. The antebellum United States had a surprisingly modern economy and sophisticated financial system.

Chapter 4, "Banks and Democracy" by John Joseph Wallis, also focuses on U.S. institutions. The essay discusses the political institutions governing banking in the United States as well as the larger interaction of political and economic development in the period from 1790 until the start of the Civil War. The antebellum period is characterized by rapid development of both economic institutions in the United States (as Wright demonstrates in Chapter 3) and by the emergence of a populist democracy. Wallis is very interested in banks and notes, particularly the connection between free banking and America's free-wheeling democracy that earlier historians have mentioned. Some attribute free banking to the constitutional era while others attribute it to Jacksonian populism. Wallis argues that the Jackson era unleashed an unfettered financial system that allowed almost anyone to establish a bank and, in the process, promoted economic development. He emphasizes the importance of egalitarian democracy (as opposed to elite democracy) in the development of the banking system. Thus, American economic development is not rooted in the ideas of the founding generation about a governmental system that balances the equality of different privileged groups, but rather is rooted in a system where rules are impersonal and opportunity is open to all. Free banking (and one would suppose the spread of the limited liability corporation described by Wright) is the economic manifestation of the development of American democracy. Populist democracy, banks, and economic growth go hand in hand in Wallis's interpretation.

Wallis emphasizes the importance of rules. There was extensive rule making about banking at the state level through the early nineteenth century, and many reforms came about because of problems in the banking sector. The rule making, however, was largely done in the context of free entry and other democratic sensibilities, which led to efforts to restrain and control groups privileged in the earlier system. As a result, the interaction of democracy and banking worked well to encourage financial and economic development.

The next chapter brings us forward to the twentieth century and another period when the interactions of political and economic institutions are of interest. Although far removed in time from Wallis's focus on the antebellum era, Chapter 5 also focuses on the influence of political developments on economic institutions and its impact on the economy. The cold war (1947–1991) has not yet been a subject of much interest to economic historians, but Niall Ferguson's contribution in Chapter 5 is likely to change that. In "Financial Systems, Economic Growth, and Globalization in the Era of the Cold War," Ferguson poses two puzzles about the world economy in this critical period. The first is why the United States continued to grow as rapidly as it did when defense expenditures were high and burdensome. The second is that while the world was under the cloud of potential Armageddon throughout this period, the U.S. economy grew rapidly.

Ferguson takes issue with the conventional view of the economic consequences of the cold war as epitomized by Paul Kennedy's *The Rise and Fall of the Great Powers*, which was published in 1987 as the cold war was drawing to a close. Kennedy argued that the burden of maintaining military prowess would crowd out productive investment, place a drain on America's finances, and ultimately lead to the eclipse of the great power. Importantly, Ferguson points out that the United States had uniquely deep and wide capital markets and access to global finance as well, which made it able to absorb the increases in defense spending in the later stages of the cold war under President Reagan. Indeed, the economy that did not benefit from a robust financial structure was the Soviet Union's, which sank under its military burden and inability to allocate capital efficiently. Ferguson suggests a parallel to the wars between Britain and France in the eighteenth century. The *ancient regime* fell because, like the Soviet Union, it did not have the financial wherewithal to compete.

To illustrate the nature of the cold war as an actual war, Ferguson draws attention to the "doomsday clock" that was published in the *Bulletin of the Atomic Scientists* and was widely followed at the time. It hovered around midnight throughout the period and came closest in the early 1950s and the mid 1980s. Many people expected that a world war with nuclear weapons employed (which would have been devastating to all involved) would occur. The paradox is that a golden age of economic growth occurred in the midst of these enormous risks. The implication is that once the risks were removed with the end of the cold war, individuals would have greater optimism about the future and saving should increase. Similarly, the chapter considers evidence that war risk or cold war politics affected asset allocations and interest rates and finds none to be compelling. Ferguson's answer to this puzzle is that the possibility of a third world war was an incalculable uncertainty so people naturally focused on imaginable and calculable risks.

To support this hypothesis, Ferguson turns to the writings of Siegmund Warburg, a British financier whose firm, S. G. Warburg, grew rapidly in the early postwar years. Warburg was a student of world politics who was thoroughly aware that the cold war brought the threat of societal disintegration. But he and his generation, according to Ferguson, conducted business as if the threat did not exist.

Twenty-five years down the road, the cold war has almost receded from memory. It was a period of unexpected economic prosperity because robust financial markets enabled Western nations to fight off cold war threats from the Soviet Union; indeed, Warburg's philosophy that one could lead an active business life despite those unimaginable threats seems to have prevailed.

In Chapter 6, Marc Flandreau draws our attention to an important interwar episode during which political and economic events interacted. "Reputation, Regulation and the Collapse of International Capital Markets, 1920–1935" analyzes the shift in financial power from London to New York in the 1920s and the influence of the New Deal in the 1930s on international finance.

After World War I, the center for underwriting in the global bond market moved from the merchant bankers in London to the investment bankers in New York. London markets suffered from the U.K.'s postwar economic situation – unemployment, balance of payments problems, and instability. As a result, in a short period of time, the New York underwriters gained the prestige and experience that enabled them to dominate the global markets. Nevertheless, the international issuance of bonds virtually disappeared in the financial and banking crises of the early 1930s. In a conventional view, the New Deal policy responses to the crisis were efforts to stem its spread with crisis interventions (such as the bank holiday) and legislative responses (such as the Glass-Steagall Act). Flandreau examines the tensions between the Roosevelt administration and the banking community and suggests that the New Deal might have been the cause of the shutdown of international markets rather than a response to it. In this view, policy changes inhibited the bankers and made it more difficult for them to use their prestige in risky underwriting activity. As a result, the bankers retreated and the foreign debt markets collapsed. These experiences shaped the development of the modern (post–World War II) bond markets where impersonal bond ratings supplanted the personal involvement of bankers.

The final two chapters return to specific episodes in U.S. banking history that are of particular interest because of the strong lessons that can be drawn for contemporary problems. In Chapter 7, Eugene N. White examines an earlier episode during which the Federal Reserve (or at least one of its regional banks, the Federal Reserve Bank of Atlanta) acted boldly to stem the spread of a systemic crisis. In Chapter 8, Charles W. Calomiris and Mark Carlson reach back to the national banking era and find many precursors to what we now call macro prudential regulation.

A full exposition of the "lender of last resort" function of a central bank dates back more than 100 years to Bagehot (1873), but for much of recent history it did not get much attention. Particularly in the United States, post–Great Depression reforms such as deposit insurance and institutional developments (e.g., the market for federal funds) made the lender of last resort function seem an anachronism. Of course, interest in the proper role and use of the Fed's lending facilities to the banking system came roaring back after the 2007–2009 financial crisis. Most observers agree that central banks should flood the markets with liquidity in a time of crisis, but whether there should be constraints on the support given to individual financial institutions is hotly debated.

Eugene White's chapter, "Protecting Financial Stability in the Aftermath of World War I: The Federal Reserve Bank of Atlanta's Dissenting Policy," describes an early episode in the Fed's history when one district bank used the lender of last resort function vigorously to maintain the stability of the banking system. In the 1920–1921 recession, the Federal Reserve Bank of Atlanta acted on its own and, contrary to the deflationary policies of the Federal Reserve Board, chose to lend to district banks that were severely affected by the decline in the price of cotton. The recessionary shock in 1920–1921 was particularly severe in the cotton-producing area of the Atlanta Fed district. Although the term *systemic risk* would not have been known to the board of the Atlanta Fed, White argues that they understood the concept. Declines in the value of collateral assets could lead to bank failures, fire sales, further declines in asset prices, and a systemic crisis. The Atlanta Fed responded by borrowing gold reserves from other district banks thus enabling it to increase its lending.

In the early years of the Fed, district banks managed discount lending individually, and often the discount rate would differ from district to district. However, the extent to which the Atlanta Fed adopted its own policy approach in this period was not known until White delved into the minutes of the board of directors of the Federal Reserve Bank of Atlanta, which clearly express the bank's intention to use its lending and redis-counting authority to assist weak banks and protect financial stability. We do not know whether other district banks considered the possibility of more aggressive lending or expressed similar concerns with financial stability because, with the exception of Atlanta, the minutes of the district banks boards are not available to the public.

The fifty years of the national banking era in the United States (from the Civil War to the founding of the Fed, 1863–1913) are often viewed as a period when a fragmented banking system was poorly regulated and consequently experienced repeated banking panics. In "Rediscovering Macro-Prudential Regulation: The National Banking Era from the Perspective of 2015," Charles Calomiris and Mark Carlson take a new look at the period and conclude that banking regulation under the national banking system might have been more effective than previously thought. Specifically, bank examiners exhibited concern for systemic risks in the system more than a century before the term came into use. Calomiris and Carlson base their conclusions on a study of a sample of the national bank examiner's reports in the 1890s, as well as other documents.

Calomiris and Carlson examine several contemporaneous discussions of the role of bank examination in the national banking era such as an 1880 report of the Comptroller of the Currency and a 1914 unpublished internal study by the newly created Federal Reserve Board that discussed the pre-Fed examination process. In both of these instances, the authors find considerable emphasis on the idea that the role of bank examination is not just to judge the solvency of individual banks but also to maintain the payments system and trust among banks so that panics and sudden withdrawals can be avoided.

The chapter takes a detailed look at a sample of bank examination reports for 206 banks in 37 medium-sized cities around the country during the 1890s. The reports include extensive data on balance sheets, ownership structure, and management. It ends with a recapitulation that provides the examiner's estimate of losses and necessary write downs, and a narrative description of the condition of the bank and recommendations regarding measures that should be taken if the bank was having difficulties.

Even though there were no requirements regarding the minimum ratio of capital to assets, bank examinations paid careful attention to the risk-taking behavior of banks and placed limits on real estate lending, which was viewed as an undiversifiable risk in local markets. Further macro prudential concerns were evident from the concern for cash holding (particularly by larger banks), the limits on real estate lending, and the public disclosures of key information. Based on this sample, the authors argue that bank supervision in the later years of the National Banking Act was effective and contributed to the systemic health of the U.S. banking system.

With its broad coverage of financial systems from the earliest days of the American republic through the cold war, a volume of this nature surely omits important aspects of the process through which financial development and financial systems affect real sector outcomes. Rather, it offers a set of observations about how various financial system innovations, and particularly those in the United States, fit into a broader story of financial market evolution that leaves us in the present. That present involves financial systems which operate within nations that remain vulnerable to credit booms, financial crises, and considerable uncertainty stemming from macroeconomic and geo-political risks. Despite these perennial problems, however, the inescapable conclusion remains that well-developed financial systems and innovations therein have served nations well as engines of growth throughout modern history – indeed, so well that the return to an alternative state of financial stagnation and low economic performance is beyond serious discussion. Richard Sylla's ability to drive these points home is his legacy to the economics profession, and the chapters that follow speak to the lasting value of his ideas.

References

Bagehot, Walter. (1873). *Lombard Street: A Description of the London Money Market*. London: Henry S. King & Co.

Demetriades, Panicos, and Khaled Hussein. (1996). "Does Financial Development Cause Growth? Time Series Evidence from 16 Countries." *Journal of Development Economics* 51(2):387–411.

Goldsmith, Raymond W. (1969). *Financial Structure and Development*. New Haven, CT: Yale University Press.

Gurley, John G., and Edward S. Shaw. (1955). "Financial Aspects of Economic Development." *American Economic Review* 45(4):515–538.

Kennedy, Paul. (1987). *The Rise and Fall of Great Powers: Economic Change and Military Conflict from 1500 to 2000*. New York: Vintage Books.

King, Robert G., and Ross Levine. (1993). "Finance and Growth: Schumpeter Might Be Right." *Quarterly Journal of Economics* 108(3):717–737.

McKinnon, Ronald I. (1973). *Money and Capital in Economic Development*. Washington, DC: The Brookings Institution.

Reinhart, Carmen M., and Kenneth S. Rogoff. (2009). *This Time Is Different: Eight Centuries of Financial Folly*. Princeton, NJ: Princeton University Press.

Rioja, Felix, and Naveen Valev. (2004). "Does One Size Fit All? A Reexamination of the Finance and Growth Relationship." *Journal of Development Economics* 74(2):429–447.

Rousseau, Peter L., and Richard Sylla. (2003). "Financial Systems, Economic Growth, and Globalization." In M. D. Bordo, A. M. Taylor, and J. G. Williamson (eds.), *Globalization in Historical Perspective*, pp. 373–413. Chicago: University of Chicago Press.

Rousseau, Peter L., and Richard Sylla. (2005). "Emerging Financial Markets and Early U.S. Growth." *Explorations in Economic History* 42(1):1–26.

Rousseau, Peter L., and Paul Wachtel. (1998). "Financial Intermediation and Economic Performance: Historical Evidence from Five Industrialized Countries." *Journal of Money, Credit and Banking* 30(4):657–678.

Rousseau, Peter L., and Paul Wachtel. (2011). "What Is Happening to the Impact of Financial Deepening on Economic Growth?" *Economic Inquiry* 49(1):276–288.

Schularick, Moritz, and Alan M. Taylor. (2012). "Credit Booms Gone Bust: Monetary Policy, Leverage Cycles, and Financial Crises, 1870–2008." *American Economic Review* 102(2):1029–1061.

Sylla, Richard. (1969). "Federal Policy, Banking Market Structure, and Capital Mobilization in the United States, 1863–1913." *Journal of Economic History* 29(4):657–686.

Sylla, Richard. (1972). "American Banking and Growth in the Nineteenth Century: A Partial View of the Terrain." *Explorations in Economic History* 9:197–227.

Sylla, Richard. (1998). "U.S. Securities Markets and the Banking System, 1790–1840." *Federal Reserve Bank of St. Louis Review* 80:83–98.

Sylla, Richard. (2002). "Financial Systems and Economic Modernization." *Journal of Economic History* 62(2):277–292.

Wachtel, Paul, and Peter L. Rousseau. (1995). "Financial Intermediation and Economic Growth: A Historical Comparison of the United States, United Kingdom, and Canada." In M. D. Bordo and R. Sylla (eds.), *Anglo-American Financial Systems: Institutions and Markets in the Twentieth Century*, pp. 329–381. New York: Irwin Professional Publishing.

1

Growing Up to Stability? Financial Globalization, Financial Development, and Financial Crises

Michael D. Bordo and Christopher M. Meissner

An important literature on comparative long-run economic growth focuses on financial development. This work in economic history strongly complements the extensive empirical research by King and Levine (1993) and many others who have established a strong connection between financial development and subsequent economic growth. Rousseau and Sylla (2003) develop the concept of financial revolutions. They argue – based on the history of the Netherlands, Great Britain, the United States, France, Germany, and Japan – that these countries grew rapidly after financial revolutions which created "good" financial systems. Such systems have five key components: sound public finance and public debt management, a stable monetary regime, a banking system, a central bank, and well-functioning securities markets.

Financial development in the past three centuries has also been accompanied by two other complementary important phenomena: financial globalization and financial crises. *Financial globalization* is a term for the opening up of international capital markets and the export of capital from advanced to emerging countries. More recently financial globalization has seen capital flowing in both directions (from poor to rich and rich to poor) with very high gross flows being the hallmark of the last two decades. Capital inflows to capital-scarce regions have long been crucial to the economic development of the recipient countries. Financial crises (banking, currency, and debt) also became more of an issue along with each successive wave of financial development and globalization. Recently it has

We thank Peter Rousseau, Paul Wachtel, Gianni Toniolo, and participants at the conference at the Stern School of Business, New York University, March 27–28, 2015, for comments. Remaining errors are attributable to the authors.

been argued that capital inflows often lead to an expansion of bank lending, which can create an asset price boom (especially in real estate), an asset price bust, and a financial crisis (Borio, James, and Shin 2014). In this essay, we focus on the interface between financial development, globalization, and financial crises. We are also interested in the prospects and determinants of the learning required to make policies to harness finance for growth while avoiding financial instability. In our case studies, we concentrate primarily on the years from the early nineteenth century to 1914, with a focus on the first era of globalization. However, we also explore these issues in the twentieth century to some degree. We ask several questions:

1. Why were some emerging markets able to access international capital markets and successfully use these funds to finance their development?
2. Why are some countries hit by financial crises which delay their development and increase economic volatility?
3. Why have some countries been able to avoid financial crises altogether?
4. Why have some countries learned from their crisis experience and developed ways to reduce the likelihood and impact of financial crises while others have not?

In sum, the question we ask is "Why have some countries learned to grow up to financial stability and others have not?"

In this essay, we provide a comparative survey of financial crisis experience in emerging markets and leading countries from the nineteenth century into the twentieth century. We complement this evidence with case studies on four emerging countries – the United States, Canada, Australia, and Argentina – which were all recipients of capital flows and which experienced significant financial development but had very different experiences with financial crises and policy changes in the wake of these major events.

Overview: Capital Flows, Financial Crises, and Financial Development

International capital flows have a long history, but they increased significantly beginning in the 1820s. With the advent of the telegraph in the 1840s and other advances in transportation and communication, capital flows progressively increased. The period 1870–1914 was the first era of globalization. This era was characterized by the rapid growth of international trade, extensive international financial integration, and massive international migration comparable to the present era of globalization (Bordo, Taylor, and Williamson 2003). Key elements of this era were adherence to the gold standard and stable exchange rates, political stability attributable to Pax Britannica, and the balance of power; it was an era of limited government involvement in the economy. During this period, many of today's advanced countries were essentially emerging market economies. Many also went through financial revolutions (Rousseau and Sylla 2003).

Financial globalization raises real economic growth in emerging market countries, but it is also often accompanied by financial crises (sudden stops, currency crises, banking crises, and sovereign debt defaults).[1] Indeed there has been considerable recent debate on whether financial integration contributes to growth or whether positive growth effects were negated by financial crises. Gourinchas and Jeanne (2006) argued that capital flows had limited effects on growth.[2] Others have argued that net capital flows aid growth and that crises only have temporary effects (Tornell and Westerman 2005; Bordo and Meissner 2011).

Bordo and Meissner (2011) found that the British Dominions and Northern Europe did better than Southern Europe and Latin America in absorbing capital flows and avoiding financial crises or learning from them. The British Dominions and Northern European countries were more financially developed, and based on their development and institutional arrangements, they learned from their financial crisis experience to improve their institutions and policies. Crises could not be eliminated, but their frequency and severity seems to have been reduced when comparing these countries to a set that included Argentina, Brazil, Chile, and Greece, among others. In addition, regulatory and legislative efforts in these countries usually attempted, at the very least, to redress the deficiencies that caused the last crisis. Whereas regulators might be accused of "fighting the last war," such a strategy in a complex world may be better than no or only cosmetic reform (Hubbard 2013).

---

[1] Sudden stops are large turnarounds in capital flows or sharp declines in the current account deficit. Currency crises involve sharp changes in nominal exchange rates and speculative attacks or "runs" on currencies. Banking crises are systemic events involving bank failures for a significant portion of the nation's banking system. Debt crises occur when sovereign borrowers significantly alter the original terms of their debt obligations. We survey the comparative causes of these crises over the long run in the working paper version of this chapter available from the National Bureau of Economic Research as Working Paper No. 21287.

[2] Also see Henry (2007) and Brooks et al. (2004).

Other countries (e.g., Argentina, Brazil, Chile, and Greece), to cite some extreme examples, faced two centuries of capital inflows, asset booms and busts, and recurrent financial crises whose origins and causes were strikingly similar from one crisis to the next. Sovereign debt crises were a particular problem, but currency instability and banking crises also were quite prevalent. In many instances, minimal efforts at reform were undertaken, and quite often policy change was superficial such that subsequent crises unfolded in dramatically similar ways. Outcomes such as high inflation or hyperinflation, debt default, and financial system collapse were common and remain so until today.

The successful countries were more financially developed and had the following attributes: political stability, competitive political systems, lower income inequality, adherence to the rule of law, well-defined property rights, and democracy. There is, of course, an extensive literature on the origins and impacts of the institutional environment (North and Weingast 1989; Engerman and Sokoloff 1997; Rajan and Zingales 2003; Acemoglu, Johnson, and Robinson 2005; North, Wallis, and Weingast 2009; Calomiris and Haber 2014). Relatively little attention has been paid, however, to the impact these institutions had on the ability to learn from financial meltdowns and hence on long-run financial stability.

To illustrate the process of growing up to financial stability, and of learning and adapting while under the pressure of finicky financial markets, we propose a two-pronged approach. First we look at the data on long-run incidence of crises for different groups of countries. We then turn to a small set of case studies to compare the experience of three learners (Australia, Canada, and the United States) who had varying degrees of success as well as one potential learner (Argentina) that has demonstrated itself to be a non-learner. We will show that political institutions, the constitutional framework, legal traditions, and property rights seem to shape how the economic landscape might respond to financial crises.

Empirical Evidence on Crises over the Long Run

In this section, we study historical crisis chronologies to highlight differences across countries in crisis frequency and recurrence. Based on the long-run record, we inductively classify countries into three groups to illustrate the long-run record on financial stability. One group could be considered "leaders" in terms of institutional outcomes, financial development, and stability. This group includes Belgium, France, Germany, the Netherlands, Switzerland, and Great Britain/the U.K. A second group might be termed "learners." These were historically settler colonies, but they worked their way up the economic ladder from the ranks of the emerging markets of the day to first-class citizens in terms of financial stability and development. This set includes Australia (or its component colonies prior to 1901), Canada (its component colonies prior to 1867), Denmark, Japan, New Zealand, Norway, Sweden, and the United States. Finally, a third group of "non-learners" or "repeat offenders" includes Argentina, Brazil, Chile, Greece, Italy (post-1861 only), Portugal, and Spain. These countries form a representative sample of reasonably sized nations that have been independent over the long run and which have had significant engagement with international capital markets or market access.

In Figures 1.1.A, 1.1.B, and 1.1.C, we present evidence on financial development as measured by the population-weighted averages of the ratio of broad money to gross domestic product (GDP) for these three groups of countries from 1880 to circa 1995.[3] In the period 1880 to 1913, the leaders show the highest ratios and the steadiest growth rates. In the same period, the learners make great progress, though they show some evidence of instability particularly centered around the mid-1880s and the 1907 period – moments of great international financial stress. The non-learners show a boom and bust in the 1890s leading to a secular decline up to World War I. The interwar period illustrates greater levels of similarity in these ratios with the non-learners having the lowest levels in most years. Since the United States is included in the learners category, it is not surprising to see that this group posts the highest values. By the post–World War II period, the learners have clearly taken the lead in terms of financial development with high and stable ratios. The countries we classify as leaders are in second place, although a comeback is evident at the tail end driven by the United Kingdom and financial deregulation in the 1980s. Finally the non-learners are behind. The gap between the first two groups increases from the 1980s, beginning with the debt crises of the 1980s. As in the post-1890s period, these ratios show a secular decline in the wake of major financial crashes.

In Figure 1.2, we present the sample probability that a country would experience a financial crisis of any kind (banking, currency, twin, or debt) in each of four periods (1880–1913, 1919–1939, 1945–1972, and 1973–2011).

---

[3] There are missing data on the ratio of money to GDP for France and Germany from 1990 to 1997. For similar reasons, our series for the learners ends in 1994 and for the non-learners in 1995.

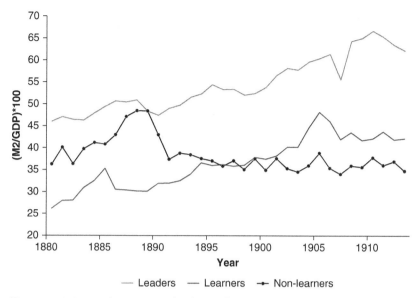

Figure 1.1.A Ratio of M2 to GDP for three subsets of countries, 1880–1914.

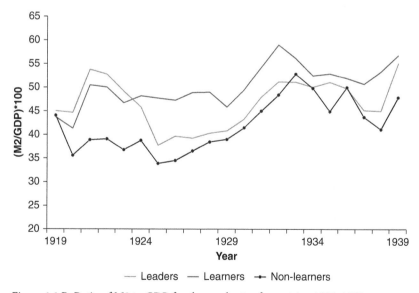

Figure 1.1.B Ratio of M2 to GDP for three subsets of countries, 1919–1939.

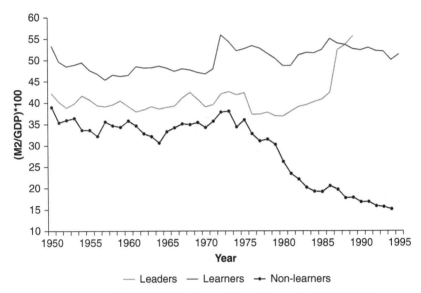

Figure 1.1.C Ratio of M2 to GDP for three subsets of countries, 1950–1997.
Notes: These figures show the population-weighted average ratio of broad money (M2) to GDP. Data are from Bordo et al. (1999). Leaders include Belgium, France, Germany, the Netherlands, Switzerland, and Great Britain/the U.K. Learners include Australia (or its component colonies prior to 1901), Canada, Denmark, Japan, New Zealand, Norway, Sweden, and the United States. Non-learners include Argentina, Brazil, Chile, Greece, Italy, Portugal, and Spain.

This value is calculated as the total number of country years in which countries in each of the country subsets is in the first year of a financial crisis divided by the total number of country years within that subsample.[4] We see significant heterogeneity among the groups. Two facts emerge from this figure. First, the non-learners have always, with the exception of the interwar period, had a greater likelihood of experiencing a crisis. In both periods of globalization, a clear ranking emerges with the leaders having the lowest probabilities, the learners occupying the middle range, and the non-learners having the highest values. If we pool all years, we find the probabilities are 0.068, 0.061, and 0.118, respectively. We cannot reject that the means across the first two groups are different, but we can reject that the mean of the

---

[4] Data are taken from several sources. For banking, currency, and twin crises between 1880 and 1997, we rely on Bordo et al. (2001). For banking and currency crises post-1997, we rely on Laeven and Valencia (2013). For debt crises and banking crises prior to 1880, we rely on Reinhart (2010). For Greece 1825–2012, we rely on Lazaretou (2012).

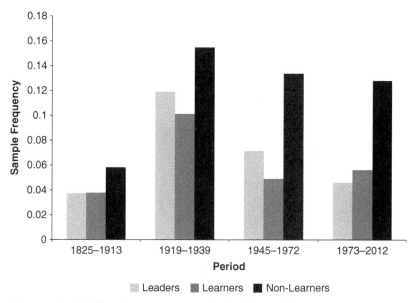

Figure 1.2 Probability of experiencing any kind of financial crisis, 1825–2012.
Notes: The probability of experiencing a crisis is calculated as the ratio of the number of country years in which countries in each subsample are in the first year of a banking, currency, twin, or debt crisis to the total number of country years within the period. Leaders include Belgium, France, Germany, the Netherlands, Switzerland, and Great Britain/the U.K. Learners include Australia (or its component colonies prior to 1901), Canada (its component colonies prior to 1867), Denmark, Japan, New Zealand, Norway, Sweden, and the United States. Non-learners include Argentina, Brazil, Chile, Greece, Italy (post-1861 only), Portugal, and Spain.

non-learners is different from that of the leaders (p-value = 0.07) and the learners (p-value = 0.05).

Figure 1.3 pools across all years and breaks the sample by category and type of crisis. In every category, the non-learners have a higher sample likelihood of having a financial crisis. In some cases, such as banking crises, these means are not too dissimilar. Pooling across years, we cannot reject equality of means by category for banking, currency, and twin crises. For debt crises, we can reject the hypothesis that the frequencies are similar in the non-learners and in the other two categories.

Figures 1.4.A, 1.4.B, 1.4.C, and 1.4.D reveal differences across categories by period for each type of crisis. Figure 1.4.A shows that with the exception of the period 1825–1913, the non-learners were more likely to have banking crises. This group of countries is the only group to have such crises in the so-called quiet period 1945–1972. As regards the lower frequency prior

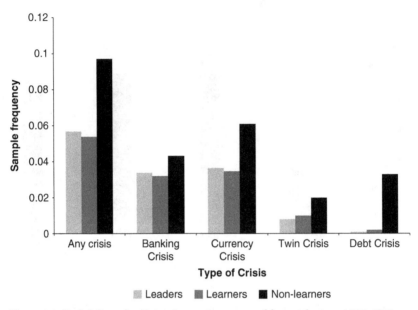

Figure 1.3 Probability of experiencing various types of financial crises, 1825–2012.
Notes: The probability of experiencing a crisis is calculated as the ratio of the number of country years in which countries in each subsample are in the first year of either a banking, currency, twin, or debt crisis or any kind of crisis to the total number of country years within the period. Leaders include Belgium, France, Germany, the Netherlands, Switzerland, and Great Britain/the U.K. Learners include Australia (or its component colonies prior to 1901), Canada (its component colonies prior to 1867), Denmark, Japan, New Zealand, Norway, Sweden, and the United States. Non-learners include Argentina, Brazil, Chile, Greece, Italy (post-1861 only), Portugal, and Spain. Each probability is calculated for all years between 1825 and 2012.

to 1913, we believe that two forces may be at work. First, some of the non-learners' banking crises in the period 1825–1880 have yet to be identified by economic historians. It may also be the case that at low levels of financial development, when the formal banking sector is small and capital markets are not highly integrated, countries may not be as prone to financial crises. To have a financial crisis, a country must have a financial sector by definition, and these countries were at very primitive stages in their monetary development prior to the 1870s.

In Figure 1.4.B, we note that the non-learners always have a higher propensity for a currency crisis with the exception of the 1930s. The rise and decline in the probability of currency crises in the leading and learning countries is attributable to the problems highlighted by Eichengreen (1992) in the interwar period. In the postwar period, imbalances were

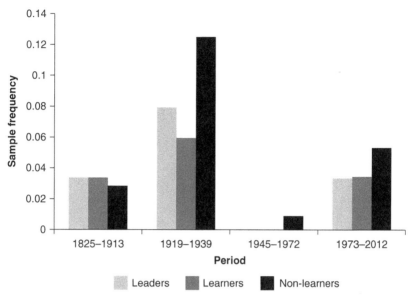

Figure 1.4.A Probability of experiencing a banking crisis, by period, 1825–2012.

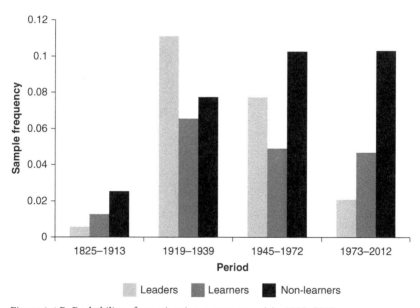

Figure 1.4.B Probability of experiencing a currency crisis, 1825–2012.

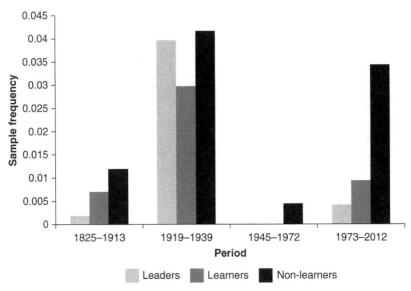

Figure 1.4.C Probability of experiencing a twin crisis, 1825–2012.

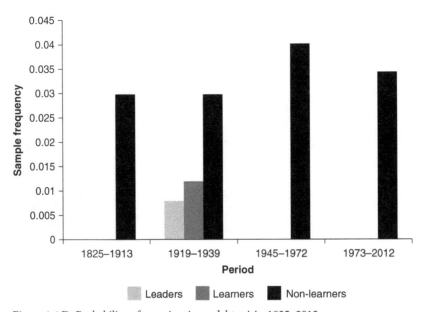

Figure 1.4.D Probability of experiencing a debt crisis, 1825–2012.
Notes: The probability of experiencing a crisis is calculated as the ratio of the number of country years in which countries in each subsample are in the first year of each type of crisis to the total

a nontrivial problem. The data display some learning in the leading two groups of countries as these nations have moved to floating exchange rates or more solid pegs such as currency union in Europe.

Figure 1.4.C shows that twin crises emerged as a major problem for all countries in the 1930s. Although the non-learners have not progressed much in the post-1972 period compared to the levels seen in the 1930s, the other two groups of countries have made some progress since the 1930s, albeit unevenly, with a trough in the 1945–1972 period and a slight rise post-1972. Finally, Figure 1.4.D suggests that sovereign debt crises are recurrent in the non-learners. In the other two groups, only a handful of defaults are recorded, and those are associated with the Great Depression (Germany in 1933, Australia in 1932 in a debt conversion, and the United States in 1933 with the abrogation of the gold clause).[5]

Figures 1.5 and 1.6 zoom in and show the record on financial crises for a select set of countries. Each bar represents a particular kind of crisis, and its width records the duration of the crisis.[6] It is notable that banking crises are historically extremely rare events in Canada and Australia. The United Kingdom shows a number of banking crises prior to 1866 but a long, quiet period associated with substantial learning that took place in the wake of the Overend-Gurney crisis of 1866. From this period onward, the Bank of England acted deftly in accordance with Bagehot's rule. Only two more crises are recorded in the subsequent 145 years. Canada stands alone among these seven countries in terms of its ability to avoid banking crises.

Caption for Figure 1.4 (cont.)

number of country years within the period. Twin crises occur when a banking crisis and a currency crisis affect a country within a span of two years. In Figure 1.4.D, the absence of a bar signifies that no debt crisis occurred within the period. Leaders include Belgium, France, Germany, the Netherlands, Switzerland, and Great Britain/the U.K. Learners include Australia (or its component colonies prior to 1901), Canada (its component colonies prior to 1867), Denmark, Japan, New Zealand, Norway, Sweden, and the United States. Non-learners include Argentina, Brazil, Chile, Greece, Italy (post-1861 only), Portugal, and Spain.

[5] One could include the defaults of the Allies on the war debts with the United States and others. The Allies argued that it was understood that repayment was conditional on German payments of reparations. This is admittedly a gray area. The same could be said for the United States and Australia's voluntary conversion.

[6] Duration for banking, currency, and twin crises was defined by Bordo et al. (2001) as the number of years from the start of the crisis until GDP began growing at its pre-crisis trend rate. The duration of debt crises is measured as the number of years until a definitive settlement and restructuring occurs.

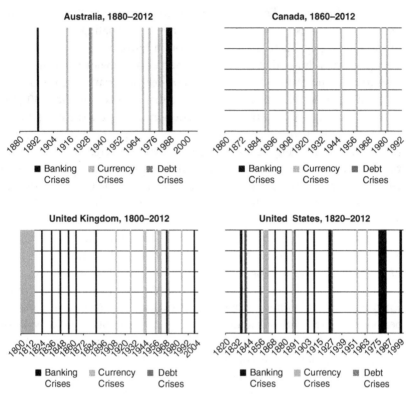

Figure 1.5 Long-run frequency of crises for four countries.

Note: Bars represent the incidence of a given type of crisis. The width represents the time in years until a country resumed growing at its precrisis trend as in Bordo et al. (2001).

The United States, as we detail later in this chapter, undertook some learning but faced significant setbacks along the way.

Currency crises are visible in the first set of countries, but the nature and frequency of these crises is almost surely different from the record in Figure 1.6 for the non-learners. The United States has been the weakest performer in some respects, but Canada has also faced pressure. Notably the United Kingdom maintained currency stability for the greater portion of the nineteenth century. It is very likely that this contributed to London's financial preeminence, but it may also be the case that being a financial center helped ensure currency stability by providing a deep and liquid financial system.

In Figure 1.6, three non-learners (Argentina, Brazil, and Chile) show patterns consistent with our previous figures. Debt crises predominate. In

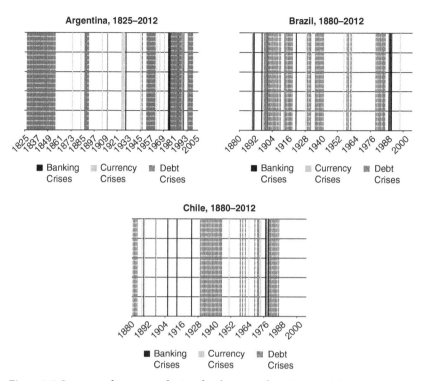

Figure 1.6 Long-run frequency of crises for three non-learning countries.

this case, we also can see the length of time until settlement of default is often quite high and much higher compared to the few debt crises evident in Figure 1.5. The period between 1973 and 2012 also presents itself as a highly unstable period for these three countries in the Southern Cone of South America.

In Figure 1.7, we present Kaplan-Meier non-parametric survivor curves for our three subsets of countries over the long run. The survivor curve gives the probability that a country within the subset (or set of countries) would experience a financial crisis *after* a given numbers of years since the last crisis. If there is evidence of successful learning, then the survivor curves should shift out over time as the time between crises lengthens. Also the higher the survivor curve within a period, the less likely a country is to quickly relapse into another crisis. Analysis time here runs over four periods: period 1 (1825–1913), period 2 (1919–1939), period 3 (1945–1972), and period 4 (1973–2012). For the top two sets of countries, the ranking for highest survivor curves is period

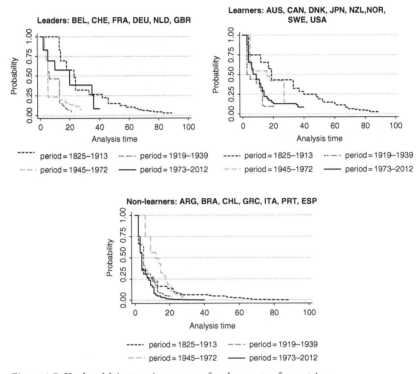

Figure 1.7 Kaplan-Meier survivor curves for three sets of countries.
Note: Figures show the Kaplan-Meier non-parametric survivor function for three sets of countries. The curve represents the empirical likelihood that a country will have any kind of financial crisis in *T* years' time after the last crisis.

1, period 4, period 2, and then period 3. Period 2, the Great Depression years, and the period 3, the Bretton Woods period, are very close in crisis frequency. The Bretton Woods period after 1950 was largely tranquil in these countries, so the closeness to the Depression years is associated with the currency crises and devaluations of the 1945–1950 period. However, nations in the leaders set of countries largely learned to avoid these crises later in the Bretton Woods period.

The panel pertaining to the learners shows a two-steps forward, one-step back dynamic. The first period has the highest survivor curve. The interwar period represents a major shift downward. Following that, the Bretton Woods period has a survivor curve akin to that in the first wave, whereupon the recent period sees a shift downward. While these countries were not crisis free, there is some evidence of a learning dynamic. For the non-learners, most of the survivor curves lie on top of each other for all periods, suggesting there is not much change. The exception perhaps is the Bretton Woods period, where the curve has shifted out somewhat.

We can also compare within-period survivor curves across groups of countries. In nearly all periods, the survivor curves for the leaders are higher than those of the learners, which are themselves higher than for the non-learners. One large difference is visible in period 4 – the most recent period. For the non-learners, there is a 75 percent chance that a country would experience a crisis prior to 10 years since the last crisis. This probability is significantly lower for the leaders, standing at less than 40 percent. In the learners' panel, the figure is 50 percent. From this we conclude that while few countries can avoid crises, the upper two panels (the leaders and the learners) seem to have a lower likelihood of relapsing than the bottom panel of countries (the repeat offenders).

Case Studies

In this section, we study the cases of four emerging countries in the pre–World War I era. In some cases, we extend the story into the twentieth century. Each country had a different political and institutional history, and each had a different response to the waves of capital flows and financial crises of the era. As will be seen, some did better than others and learned from their crisis experience, and others did not. The four cases are the United States, Canada, Australia, and Argentina. We study the crisis history of these countries and try to infer the learning process. For each country, we focus on their history of banking, currency, and debt crises.

The United States

Banking Crises
The U.S. Constitution of 1787 gave the Congress the power "to coin money and regulate the value thereof," but it did not explicitly give the federal government the power to begin chartering commercial banks. That was left to the states. Alexander Hamilton, the first secretary of the treasury, chartered the First Bank of the United States amid protest from populists and states' rights advocates. In many ways, it was modeled after the Bank of England. It was established as a bank of issue, as the government's bank to help it fund its debt and also to make loans to the private sector to promote commerce. It was allowed to have branches in every state. It may also have been an early lender of last resort. It was well capitalized and had considerable financial power. Extensive opposition to the First Bank by the

Jeffersonians led to the revocation of its charter in 1811. A brief chaotic period followed when the United States chartered a large number of banks and contributed to the inflation of the War of 1812. The Second Bank was chartered in 1816 to stabilize the country's finances, to unify the currency, and to act as a lender of last resort. In the first four decades of the republic, the number of banks chartered by the states grew rapidly, and there were banking panics in 1792 and 1811. Sylla, Wright, and Cowen (2009) argue that the crisis of 1792 was effectively headed off by Bagehot-style (Bagehot 1873) lender-of-last-resort actions by Alexander Hamilton and the First Bank.

The Second Bank was undermined and transformed into an emasculated state bank in the 1830s by Andrew Jackson, an ardent populist and opponent of centralized federal financial power. For the next 80 years, there was no federally chartered institution to act as lender of last resort or provide other central banking functions that had been performed by the two Banks of the United States and which were common at the time in Europe.

After the demise of the Second Bank, the states controlled the creation of commercial banks. Most states adopted free banking laws, which greatly eased entry to provide credit to the rapidly growing country (Rockoff 1974). The banking system – characterized by a plethora of undercapitalized unit banks issuing notes of varying quality, a prohibition on interstate banking, and weak oversight – was easily subject to local/regional shocks that led to numerous bank failures, some fraud, and a series of banking panics (1837, 1839, 1857, and 1861).

During the Civil War, when the southern states who had most vociferously opposed a federal presence in banking were absent, Congress created the national banking system to help finance the war, but also to create a uniform note issue and improve upon the flawed payments mechanism of the pre–Civil War banking system, under which a myriad of state bank notes circulated at varying rates of discount. It was also supposed to reduce the incidence of banking panics by requiring national banks to have higher capital and reserve ratios and to be stringently regulated. In some respects, it could be viewed as an example of institutional learning from the earlier experience of banking crises.

Under the national banking system, the federal government chartered unit national banks, which issued U.S. government bond–backed notes. This created a uniform currency and a viable payments system. But the national banking system also had serious flaws, which made it crisis prone.

The flaws included the persistence of unit banking (Calomiris and Haber 2014), the inverted pyramid of reserve-holding and credit which linked the stock market to the banking system and created a source of systemic risk, and a strong seasonal in money market interest rates which made the system crisis prone (Bordo and Wheelock 2013). The most serious flaw was the "inelasticity of high powered money" (i.e., there was no lender of last resort to quickly meet the demand for high-powered money in the face of a banking panic).

In addition, the inability of the unit banking system to provide sufficient credit to finance the growth of large enterprises led to the development of securities markets and non-bank financial intermediaries (i.e., unregulated shadow banks such as trust companies) which in turn became sources of systemic risk (Rockoff 2014). The national banking system competed with the state banking systems after the Civil War. The latter made a comeback as these institutions could lend against real estate. The regulatory environment varied substantially across states, but at the same time, regional and local financial markets were tied to the national market via the New York money market, correspondent bank networks, and reserve pyramiding.

The national banking era had three serious banking panics (1873, 1893, and 1907) and four minor crises. Private sector innovations helped allay the minor panics – clearinghouse loan certificates pooled the resources of the member banks and provided emergency currency (Gorton 1985). The U.S. Treasury also did some limited LLR (lender of last resort) actions as did J. P. Morgan in 1893 and 1907, but these interventions were insufficient to allay the panics, which finally ended after the suspension of convertibility of deposits into currency.

The Crisis of 1907 – "the straw that broke the camel's back" – led to a successful movement toward reform of the U.S. financial system. The Aldrich–Vreeland Act of 1908 institutionalized the clearinghouse loan certificates into National Currency Associations. It also created the National Monetary Commission to recommend on the creation of a U.S. style central bank. A secret meeting at Jekyll Island, Georgia, in 1910 led to a blueprint for a new central bank in the Warburg Plan. The Warburg Plan became the Aldrich bill in 1912, which after some modifications became the Federal Reserve Act in 1913 (Bordo and Wheelock 2011).

The Federal Reserve system was made up of twelve regional Federal Reserve banks, coordinated by the Federal Reserve Board in Washington, DC. The Fed was designed to serve as a lender of last resort, smooth the seasonal short-term interest rates, manage the gold standard, and conduct countercyclical monetary policy. The Fed was able to smooth the seasonal interest rate and moderate the business cycle (Miron 1988) in its initial two decades of operation. It also may have prevented banking panics by its discount rate policy (Gorton and Metrick 2013). In that sense, considerable institutional learning was accomplished.

However, going beyond the Golden Age, major flaws in the design of the Federal Reserve Act, which did not appear in the relatively benign conditions of the 1920s, led to the Great Contraction in 1929–1933. These include the real bills doctrine (Meltzer 2003), structural flaws (Friedman and Schwartz 1963), adherence to the gold standard (Eichengreen 1992), and an inadequate discount window (Bordo and Wheelock 2011). The Fed failed to prevent a series of banking panics in 1930–1933, which turned a serious recession into the Great Depression.

The debacle of the Great Contraction led to major institutional adaptation and learning. The newly elected Franklin D. Roosevelt blamed the Fed and the banks for the Depression. Major legislation in 1933 and 1935 increased the power of the Federal Reserve Board relative to the regional Reserve banks and created federal deposit insurance and many regulations on the banking system. These reforms ushered in four decades of financial stability and financial repression. The Great Inflation of the 1960s and 1970s, largely a consequence of Fed policies (Bordo and Orphanides 2013), undermined the New Deal regulations and led to a return to banking instability. By the 1980s, deregulation and lax oversight in some instances led to significant losses in the savings and loan industry and several other hiccups such as the run on Continental Illinois in 1984. "Too big to fail," further deregulation, a number of new financial innovations, and a rogue shadow banking sector led to the crisis of 2007–2008. That crisis was centered in the shadow banking system, where maturity mismatch in the repo markets led to an "invisible" banking panic that eventually spilled over into the commercial banking sector.

Currency Crises

Since 1791, the United States was on the specie standard (gold and silver bimetallism). There were no currency crises until the Civil War in 1861, when it became apparent that the Treasury would issue fiat money to finance the war and that it would threaten specie convertibility. A run on the specie reserves of the New York commercial banks and then on the Treasury led to a suspension of convertibility in December, and the United States went on the Greenback standard and a floating exchange rate. Resumption to the specie standard (de facto gold) at the prewar parity occurred on January 1, 1879, following a vociferous political debate between the advocates of hard money (a return to specie at the original parity) and the advocates of soft money (either staying on the fiat money regime, resumption at a devalued parity, or bimetallism at a mint ratio below the rapidly rising world silver price of gold).

The specie standard that was restored was de facto a gold standard because silver had been undervalued at the mint since the gold discoveries of the 1840s; moreover, convertibility of the standard silver coin had been removed by the Currency Act of 1873 (i.e., the "Crime" of 1873). By 1879, following massive silver discoveries in Colorado and Nevada, which reduced the market value of silver to the point where silver would have begun to enter the currency supply, a new debate started between those who advocated "Free Silver" and those who advocated that the United States be on the gold standard. The passage of the Bland Allison Act in 1878 and the Sherman Silver Purchase Act in 1890 greatly increased the share of silver in the U.S. monetary base. This led to a run on the Treasury's gold reserves in January 1895, when speculators became concerned that the United States would be forced to abandon the gold standard. The Treasury was rescued by a syndicate organized in February 1895 by J. P. Morgan and August Belmont (two prominent investment bankers) that would market U.S. Treasury bonds in Europe in exchange for gold to be transferred to the Treasury (Garber and Grilli 1986).

The Gold Standard Act of 1900 put the United States on a de jure gold standard at $20.67 per ounce and ended bimetallism. The outbreak of World War I in the summer of 1914 led to a massive global scramble for liquidity and gold. A major banking panic and currency crisis was headed off by Treasury Secretary McAdoo and the newly formed Federal Reserve (Silber 2007); the United States did not suspend gold convertibility, while virtually every country in the world did. However, in September 1917, after the United States entered the war, an embargo was placed on gold exports in order to preserve gold reserves. The embargo was removed two years later.

The Fed pursued a very expansionary monetary policy during World War I, and this led to high inflation. After hostilities ceased in November 1918, high inflation continued. Following the removal of the gold embargo in June 1919, continued inflation led to a growing balance of payments deficit and a significant decline in the Fed's gold reserve ratio toward the legal limit. Fearing a possible attack on its reserves, the Fed shifted to a very tight monetary policy stance in early 1920, which both restored the gold reserves and led to the serious but short-lived recession of 1920–1921.

The next threat to the dollar was during the Great Contraction in September 1931, when the United Kingdom left the gold standard. This led to an attack on the dollar and a massive gold drain. The Fed reacted by raising its discount rate by 200 basis points in the midst of a banking panic. The gold reserves were protected, but the Depression deepened. A second attack on the dollar occurred in the winter of 1932–1933 in the midst of a massive banking panic which both involved attempts by the public to convert deposits into currency and attempts by both domestic residents and foreigners to convert dollars into gold. The run threatened the reserves of the New York Fed. One of Roosevelt's first actions following his inauguration was to suspend the gold standard in April 1933. The dollar was then devalued by 60 percent in January 1934, and the gold standard was officially restored at $35 per ounce. However, until World War II it became a managed gold standard (Friedman and Schwartz 1963).

After World War II, the United States became part of the Bretton Woods adjustable peg exchange rate system. Under the Bretton Woods Articles of Agreement, the United States would peg the dollar to gold at $35 per ounce and the rest of the world would peg their currencies to the dollar. Once the Western European countries adopted current account convertibility in December 1958, the Bretton Woods system evolved into a gold dollar standard, under which the rest of the world increasingly used dollars as international reserves. This created the Triffin Dilemma, which stated that as the outstanding amount of dollars held by the rest of the world increased relative to U.S. gold reserves, the likelihood of a run on the dollar would increase (Triffin 1960). In an attempt to prevent this from happening, the U.S. Treasury imposed capital controls and made other arrangements including the Gold Pool. The Federal Reserve created an extensive swap network with the central banks of other advanced countries (Bordo, Humpage, and Schwartz 2015). These policies were effective in protecting the gold reserves until the mid-1960s, when the Fed shifted to an inflationary policy to both reduce unemployment and finance growing fiscal deficits. A run on the dollar in 1968 led to the creation of a two-tiered gold market to insulate official gold reserves from private speculation. These arrangements quickly broke down, and when the United Kingdom and France began converting their outstanding dollars into gold in 1971, President Nixon closed the gold window on August 15. The Bretton Woods par value system ended in 1973, and most countries, including the United States, let their exchange rates float, which inaugurated the present system of managed floating.

Debt Crises

The United States began with a debt crisis. The Revolutionary War was financed by paper money (the Continental) and some Dutch and French debt to the states and the Congress. This debt was defaulted on. The Confederation (1782–1789) did not resolve the debt problem. Rather, it was resolved by Alexander Hamilton in his Stabilization Plan of 1790 after the Constitution was adopted. In this plan, the federal government assumed the states' debts at par and consolidated them into specie-denominated consols. The European creditors were paid in full in specie. The U.S. debt was to be serviced by import tariffs and excise taxes. A concerted effort to reduce debt and to rely as much as possible on domestic debt markets so that democratic politics would lead to an electorate vested in financial stability helped eliminate federal debt crises. The new U.S. debt issue proved to be so successful that within a few years, U.S. bonds sold in Europe at prices comparable to that of many European countries (Perkins 1994).

The next U.S. debt crisis in 1841 involved many of the states. In the first half of the nineteenth century, the federal government played only a minimal role. Its budget was no more than 1 percent of GDP. By contrast, the states were actively involved in developing infrastructure improvements (canals and later railroads), and much of this was financed by British capital inflows. The loans were made on the assumption that economic growth would generate the needed tax revenue to service the debt. The financial crises of 1837 and 1839 led to a serious recession that prevented ten states from being able to service their debt (Sylla, Wallis, and Grinath 2004). The federal government refused to bail out the states, leading them to default on their loans to the British. As a consequence, the United States was cut off from British capital (a sudden stop). This worsened the recession. Since then, most states adopted, by popular approval, balanced budget rules and other mechanisms to limit similar self-dealing and corruption. This represented major institutional learning.

After the Civil War, a number of Confederate states defaulted on their debt, but there was no federal bailout. In the twentieth century, Arkansas defaulted on some of its debt in 1936; again there was no federal bailout. Today states continue to borrow but at relatively low levels. Most states have balanced budget rules and ask their voters to approve any significant borrowing that is typically backed by dedicated revenue streams. There is no direct federal bailout, although the fiscal federal arrangement worked out in the 1930s has taken pressure off states in hard times.

Canada

Banking Crises

Canada adopted the Scottish banking system of note issuing branch banks with double liability and the real bills doctrine of short–term lending. The Bank of Montreal, first chartered in 1817, may have been modeled after the First Bank of the United States (Calomiris and Haber 2014). Other banks were chartered in later years. The Canadian banking system never experienced a banking panic, although there were a number of large bank failures such as the Bank of Upper Canada, which failed in 1866 (Bordo, Redish, and Rockoff 1994). The Bank of Upper Canada had engaged in real estate lending in a land boom and failed in the bust. In reaction, the Bank Act of 1871 made mortgage lending illegal.

The British North America Act of 1867 leading to confederation gave the federal government the power to charter banks. This is very different from the United States, where individual states chartered commercial banks. According to Calomiris and Haber (2014), the difference between the two countries reflected the different political bargains struck between the principal players in the "game of banks" (i.e., the government, the bankers, and the public). In the United States, where the Constitution gave the states the power to charter banks, the states' rights and populist forces controlled the political economy of banking from 1832 until the 1980s. This led to the predominance of unit banks and the prohibition of interstate branching. This created a weak, undercapitalized, and crisis-prone system. In contrast, the English and Scottish merchants dominated the banking industry and preferred central government control of banking. According to Calomiris and Haber, central government control of banking was done to prevent conservative French Canadian interests from blocking economic development.

In Canada, bank charters were renewed and reviewed every decade in successive bank acts, which became avenues to incorporate intervention. They enforced the "Grand Bargain", whereby the banks would deliver stability in exchange for government enforced barriers to entry (Bordo, Redish, and Rockoff 2015).

Large losses to note holders and deposit holders in the 1870s and 1880s also led to institutional learning. The Bank Act of 1890 authorized the creation of the Bank Circulation Redemption Fund in which each bank was required to contribute 5 percent of its average note circulation. This fund would protect note holders from losses.

Subsequent bank acts beginning in 1900 allowed and encouraged mergers within and between provinces. The merger movement in the next two decades, as had occurred in the United Kingdom a decade before, led to the creation of a small number of banks (ten) with nationwide branches by the eve of World War I. These banks developed a number of safeguards against failures; most notably, a consortium of banks would agree to take over the assets of a failing bank to protect its depositors and note holders.

The Canadian nationwide branch banking system provided a strong bulwark against both bank local and regional shocks, but it did not create a complete safeguard against nationwide liquidity shocks. Canada did not create a central bank until 1935, but a number of safeguards against global financial crises were developed beforehand. These included reserves in the New York money market, asset-backed notes, and the Bank of Montreal's on occasion acting as a quasi-lender of last resort by arranging lifeboat operations as had been done by the Bank of England in the Baring Crisis of 1890. The Canadian government first acted as a lender of last resort in the Crisis of 1907 by issuing dominion notes as an emergency currency. The Finance Act in 1914 created a discount window facility. When the Home Bank, a large Winnipeg bank, failed in 1923, its assets were assumed by the other banks without creating a panic. During the Great Depression, there were no bank failures or panics in Canada. Canada finally established a central bank, the Bank of Canada, in 1935 – not to provide financial stability or to fight the Depression, but because other commonwealth countries had adopted them (Bordo and Redish 1987).

Currency Crises

Canada was on the gold standard before 1914; there were no actual currency crises, but there were several periods of stress (Bordo et al. 2001). Canada left gold with the United Kingdom at the outbreak of World War I and returned to the gold standard in 1926 at the original parity. Canada left the gold standard in September 1931 after the United Kingdom left the gold standard, and the Canadian dollar floated until World War II, when it was pegged to the U.S. dollar. Canada joined the Bretton Woods system in 1945 at a parity of 90.9 (US) cents. The Canadian dollar was revalued to parity with the U.S. dollar in 1946. Then in 1949, it was devalued back to 90.9 cents after the United Kingdom devalued sterling. In the face of massive capital inflows from the United States at the start of the Korean War, Canada allowed the Canadian dollar to float in September 1950 in violation of the Bretton Woods articles. It returned to the par value system at a devalued peg of 92.5 cents in May 1962 after a speculative attack on the Canadian dollar in April, which ended with a rescue by the International Monetary Fund (IMF) and the United States

(Bordo, Dib, and Schembri 2010). It then left the Bretton Woods system in 1970 as the system was unraveling, and it has floated ever since.

Debt Crises

Canada did not have any debt crises in the pre-1914 era. In 1929, in the face of the collapse in world trade, Canada did not follow other commodity-producing countries and default on its debt. It maintained the servicing of its outstanding foreign debt in gold, but it stopped paying domestic debt holders in gold (Bordo and Redish 1990). Reinhart and Rogoff (2009) would categorize this as a domestic default.

The Canadian fiscal federal system, unlike the system in the United States, did not have a "no bailout clause." The provinces have always borrowed extensively on global markets and have relied on market discipline. In 1936, Alberta defaulted on its debt after rejecting the conditions of a federal bailout. In the 1980s and 1990s, a number of provinces ran large deficits and built up high debt to GDP ratios. This led to high-risk premia and downgrades by the credit rating agencies. In the 1990s, both the federal government and the provinces undertook a major fiscal retrenchment in the face of external pressure. Canada has had the strongest fiscal position of the G-10 ever since. These actions suggest significant policy and institutional learning and a persistent ability to avoid going over the brink with outright default.

Australia

Banking Crises

Like Canada, Australia adopted British/Scottish banking institutions including branch banking and the real bills doctrine (Davis and Gallman, 1999). The Australian trading banks relied heavily on British deposits in the nineteenth century. There were two types of banks: imperial banks that were headquartered in London and colonial banks that were headquartered in Australia with offices in London. Australia also had other types of non-bank financial intermediaries including building societies, mortgage banks, land banks, savings banks, and pastoral companies. Banking regulation came under the purview of the colonies by the 1860s. Typical restrictions included limited or double liability on capital, unlimited liability on note issue, and a limit on lending for real estate (Hickson and Turner 2002).

Australia experienced a massive land boom in the 1870s and 1880s in the face of rapid immigration and British demand for wool. Capital flows from

London funneled through the trading banks financed the building of cities and the extension of pastoral land. The trading banks funded the non-bank financial intermediaries that financed mortgages so that de facto they violated the real bills doctrine and they were exposed to a maturity mismatch. Hickson and Turner (2002) report that while real estate lending had long been banned or discouraged, the colony of Victoria removed this restriction in 1888.

The trading banks actively solicited deposits in England and Scotland, offering a higher rate of interest on savings accounts than the domestic British banks. In a sense, they fooled the British (mainly Scottish) savers into believing that the Australian banks were similar to the Scottish banks. The "Law of Gravity" kicked in the late 1880s when the terms of trade turned against Australian wool. The commodity boom of the 1880s (which was worldwide) led to the failures of many pastoral companies and mortgage companies in 1891–1892.

The crisis spread to the trading banks in 1892–1893 (the Mercantile Bank of Australia, the Federal Bank of Australia, and the Commercial Bank of Australia), leading to a full-fledged banking panic. Although the associated banks were supposed to pool the assets of the Melbourne banks to save banks from liquidity problems, they failed to do so for the Federal Bank. The government of Victoria tried to collaborate with the associated banks in Melbourne to save the Commercial Bank. While the forum reiterated its intentions, the Commercial Bank was soon also allowed to fail. In New South Wales, bank notes were given legal tender status to ease access to means of payment, and the government declared a five-day banking holiday (Bordo and Eichengreen 1999). Depositors were forced to exchange their demand and savings deposits for long-term deposits and debentures and hence lost liquidity.

British depositors also were caught by the crisis and pulled their funds from the Australian banks. In consequence, Australia was hit by a classic sudden stop of international capital, and Australia suffered a serious depression for much of the 1890s. This was aggravated by a severe drought.

In reaction to the crisis, unlike what occurred in the United States and Canada, the banks were not regulated by the government. The surviving banks retrenched heavily, raised their capital and liquidity ratios, and gave up mortgage lending. The colonial governments set up their own mortgage banks and thereby funded agricultural expansion and urban building.

Australia federated in 1901. The federation set up the Commonwealth Bank to help fund the government. It also competed with the trading banks for private business and had an advantage since its notes were not taxed.

It became more like a central bank over time and was eventually super-seded by the Reserve Bank of Australia, founded in 1959. During the 1930s, Australia suffered greatly from the Great Depression, although there were no bank failures or panics. The banks and the rest of the financial system were heavily regulated (as in the United States), and financial repression prevailed until the 1980s.

Currency Crises

Australia, like Canada, was on the gold standard, and effectively in a monetary union with Great Britain throughout the nineteenth century prior to the establishment of the Commonwealth Bank. There were no currency crises before 1914. Like the United Kingdom, Australia left the gold standard at the outbreak of World War I and returned to gold at the original parity in 1925. Australia was hard hit by the global collapse of commodity prices in the late 1920s and left the gold standard in 1929.

After World War II, Australia joined the Bretton Woods system and maintained pegs until 1983. It devalued its currency in 1949 along with Great Britain and experienced a currency crisis in 1971 (when the Bretton Woods system was in collapse) as well as in 1976, 1983, and 1985.

Debt Crises

Australia did not have any sovereign debt crises before 1914, but one of the states, New South Wales, defaulted in 1931. However, the federal govern-ment maintained debt service the next day (Reinhart and Rogoff 2009). The Australian Loan Council had been established in December 1927; it formalized state cooperation that had existed since World War I. It set limits on state borrowing at the national level. Cooperation via a gentlemen's agreement between national and subnational governments also kept the borrowing of the cities and municipalities in line (Grewal 2000). In addition, the Australian government forced conversion of its internal/domestic debt and implemented a voluntary loan conversion on its external debt in the 1930s.

Argentina

Banking Crises

Argentina has had a long history of banking instability: ten banking crises between 1880 and the present according to Reinhart and Rogoff (2009). The largest historic crisis was the Baring crisis in 1890. It precipitated a global financial crisis. Argentina in the 1880s was the largest borrower in terms of the share of GDP, and it accounted for almost half of British foreign lending. The crisis followed a foreign capital–induced land boom to develop the pampas. It was funded by a massive expansion of bank credit.

The explosion in bank credit was facilitated by the creation of the National Guaranteed Banking System in 1887. Under the law, banks were required to buy National Gold Bonds directly from the treasury as a requirement for note issue.[7] The banks raced to borrow as much as they could on foreign markets, mostly in London, and deposited the gold with the treasury. They could then use the banknotes as a basis for domestic bank credit expansion. After 1887, money creation surged (Cortes Conde 1989). The land price bust in 1889 led to a 50 percent decline in land prices. The Banco de la Nacion (Bank of the Nation), a quasi-central bank, found itself unable to pay its dividend, triggering a run. All banks suspended convertibility in the wake of this event. The peso fell by 36 percent against sterling in 1890 and by 37 percent in 1891.

To cope with the crisis, the government created the Bank of the Argentine Nation from the ruins of the old Bank of the Nation and other provincial banks. It took bad loans off their books while requiring the old banks to surrender their specie and bonds and declare a three-year moratorium on interest payments. The twin crisis led to a serious depression with real GDP falling by 15 percent. Underpinning this crisis and most of the others in the nineteenth and twentieth century was a faulty system of banking regulation.

Currency Crises

Argentina had nineteen currency crises between 1880 and the present. Before 1914 it, along with other Latin American countries, had considerable difficulty in adhering to the fixed parity of the gold standard. Between 1865 and 1914, Argentina was off gold in three episodes of suspension totaling twenty-four years (Bordo and Schwartz 1994). In each case, expansionary monetary and fiscal policy inconsistent with adherence to the peg was the culprit.

Gold convertibility in Argentina began after a failed attempt in 1863. Convertibility was suspended in May 1876 after several years of political unrest and rising government deficits. Convertibility was restored in 1883 but lasted only until January 1885, following a period of expansionary fiscal

---

[7] Della Paolera (1994) notes that banks in the U.S. National Banking System were to purchase government bonds on a secondary market.

policy. Inconvertibility was associated with lax fiscal policy leading to debt default in 1890. In 1899, convertibility was restored with the return to fiscal orthodoxy in 1896 and the establishment of a form of currency board. Argentina suspended convertibility in 1914 at the outbreak of World War I. It resumed convertibility at a changed parity in August 1927, and suspended again in 1929. Inconvertibility prevailed during the balance of the interwar period (Bordo and Schwartz 1994, p. 16). In the post–World War II period, Argentina like the other Latin American countries had high inflation, frequent currency crises, and devaluations.

Debt Crises

Argentina had two major debt crises before 1914. In 1825 Argentina, along with other Latin American countries, defaulted on British debt. Much of the capital flows were used to fund government expenditures on infrastructure. As in the case of the American states in 1841, when the economy didn't perform well enough to service the debt, defaults ensued. It took four decades before debt servicing began during which time there were no capital inflows.

The second major default occurred in 1890 along with the banking and currency crises already described. Much of the foreign capital flowed into fiscal expansion and growing fiscal deficits. The recession associated with the financial crisis led to a collapse in tax revenues. This was aggravated by the money-induced run-up in inflation, which made Argentina uncompetitive and reduced tax revenues.

The Province of Buenos Aires and the national government defaulted on their debt in 1890 as did the other provinces. This led to a sudden stop that lasted through the 1890s.

In January 1891, Argentina secured a 15 million pound sterling funding loan in London at 6 percent. As conditions, investors demanded that the government not incur additional liabilities for three years and that it retire 15 million pesos worth of notes in any year in which the gold premium exceeded 50 percent. Although this loan provided breathing space, by 1892 it was clear that the plan would not sustain the public finances. The Rothschilds orchestrated the "Romero fix" (Arreglo Romero) of 1893, which rescheduled Argentina's debt repayment plan. Under this agreement, Argentina was obligated to pay only half of its contractual obligations until 1901, when the amortization of principal resumed (Bordo and Eichengreen 1999, p. 51).

It is interesting to note that Argentina, nearly unique among Latin American countries, did not default during the Great Depression, although it did suspend the gold standard and it had heavy provincial borrowing. It may have been aided by heavy exchange controls. In the post–World War II period, Argentina defaulted five times; the latest episode began in 2001 and still has not been fully resolved (Reinhart and Rogoff 2009).

Conclusion

This chapter seeks to provide an answer to the question "Why did some countries learn to grow up to financial stability and others did not?" Our survey of the theory of financial crises in the context of history and our tabulations for the nineteenth and twentieth centuries, combined with the narratives of four countries, suggest that the answer is not so simple. The empirical evidence shows clear differences between "leaders," "learners," and "repeat offenders." The narratives based on four emerging countries back up the nomenclature of the last two categories.

The U.S. experience in banking is one of institutional and policy learning from financial crises. The process was not linear. It involved both progress and regression. The instability of the pre–Civil War period led to the institution of the National Banking System, which was an improvement in the sense that it created a uniform national currency and a safe payments system. However, there was retrogression, namely in the system's inability to deal with the bank panic problem. The creation of the Federal Reserve was a major institutional step forward to dealing with the banking panic problem. But the Fed failed during the 1930s. Progress on the bank stability front occurred with the New Deal reforms, but they in turn led to serious problems in the Great Inflation period which ultimately created "Too Big to Fail" and seeds of the 2007–2008 crisis.

Like the case of banking crises, there was nonlinear institutional/policy learning with respect to currency crises in the United States. The specie standard (gold) instituted in 1791 brought long-run price stability and sanctity of long-term contracts, but it had to be temporarily abandoned to efficiently finance the Civil War (Bordo and Kydland 1995). The United States returned to the specie standard after resumption in 1879, but uncertainty over the possible adoption of a silver standard led to a speculative attack on the dollar in 1895, which was offset by a private intervention. The Federal Reserve became the protector of the currency in 1914, successfully (with the Treasury) holding off a speculative attack in July 1914. It also did so in September 1931 at the expense of a banking panic. During Bretton Woods, the Fed and the U.S. Treasury preserved the dollar peg to gold for a decade but failed when the Fed changed its priorities from price stability to full employment and began monetizing the fiscal deficit. This led to a shift to floating exchange rates in the 1970s, and with some trial and error in the use of exchange market intervention, the Fed achieved price and exchange rate stability by the 1980s. With this innovation, currency crises were by definition assigned to the dustbin of history.

The United States was very successful in dealing with sovereign debt crises. Alexander Hamilton's Stabilization Plan in 1790 resolved the Revolutionary War debt default and put the country on a sound fiscal footing. However, the states ran into fiscal difficulties in the early 1840s and were not bailed out by the federal government, leading the states to default. From that experience, the states learned over the subsequent century to adopt balanced budgets, making themselves also models of fiscal probity.

Canada, of all of our countries, was the most successful in institutional learning with respect to banking crises. From the very beginning, it adopted the Scottish model of nationwide branch banking, which provided insurance against regional and local shocks that can produce banking panics. Through successive bank acts, innovations often responding to near miss–systemic events improved the soundness of the Canadian chartered banks, which have avoided systemic banking instability to the present day.

Canada also had a successful experience with respect to currency crises. It had none under the gold standard and only one during the Bretton Woods period. It was brought on in 1962 by the finance minister who wanted to end Canada's float and return it to its Bretton Woods peg. He announced that he would like to see the value of the Canadian dollar reduced, leading speculators to dump Canadian dollars. Since then, the government and the Bank of Canada have learned to let the exchange rate be determined by fundamentals.

Canada also had an excellent record with respect to avoiding debt crises. Moreover, it avoided a sovereign default in 1929 when most countries in the same league as Canada could not. Fiscal difficulties by several provinces in the 1980s led to a federal provincial compact in the 1990s that has made Canada one of the most fiscally prudent countries in the world.

The Australian experience with banking crises in the golden age was quite different from its sister dominion, Canada. Like Canada, its banking system was modeled on the Scottish system of nationwide branch banking, but Australia violated the prohibition on real estate lending, leading to the crisis of 1893. Institutional learning occurred via private sector retrenchment but also in the creation of new government financial institutions. Later, during the Great Depression, Australia followed the model of other countries of adopting extensive regulation and financial repression, which was only removed later than many other advanced countries. The Australian banking system, like that of Canada, avoided the 2007–2008 financial crisis.

The Australian experience with currency crises was different from Canada's. There were no crises in the golden age, but Australia ran into trouble during the Great Depression and Bretton Woods by following the example of the United Kingdom. Since the 1980s, Australia has deepened its financial markets and followed monetary rules toward price stability. Australia is no longer vulnerable to speculative attacks per se, but its currency does follow the vagaries of commodity markets.

Like Canada, Australia had an excellent record with respect to fiscal probity during the golden age, but there were some relatively small problems with the states during the Depression. Because the British pound sterling was devalued, Australia avoided some of the perils of currency mismatch. In addition, it was able to increasingly shift toward domestic debt and thereby strike better bargains with bondholders.

The difference between bank-based systems as in Canada and Australia versus market-based systems as in the United States may have mattered for financial stability. Restrictions on banking such as those in the United States, which led to a system of unit banks with a prohibition on interstate branching, created an environment ripe for instability. This can be compared to the Canadian nationwide branch banking system, which allowed for the interregional pooling of risk. As a consequence, the United States developed the shadow banking system (non-bank financial intermediaries) and extensive financial markets. This system was subject to periodic crises and instability.

Argentina's experience with banking crises was very different from the other countries. It had many more crises than the others. Its record of learning from crises was dismal. It did adopt institutions from other countries such as free banking, and it attempted to imitate the national banking system of the United States. But these institutions did not transfer well into the southern hemisphere, where substantive changes to the prototype policies were introduced, leading ultimately to a greater potential for instability (Della Paolera 1994).

Argentina's record with currency crises was also different and much more turbulent from those of the learners. It had a bad experience under the gold standard because it could not follow the monetary and fiscal orthodoxy consistent with a hard currency regime. Some learning did occur after the crisis of 1890, but by the 1930s Argentina had once again lost its ability to ensure stability when engaged with the global economy.

It had much worse problems in the late-twentieth-century regime of fiat money and high inflation. Finally, the Argentine experience with debt crises was also disastrous. There appears to be very little evidence of institutional learning. Many of the crises were repeats of the older ones combining hard pegs, currency and maturity mismatch, sudden stops, and lax regulatory environments.

In conclusion we ask, "How much did the four countries learn from their crises?" The United States did learn from its experience with crises but not enough to prevent their reoccurrence. One can characterize its experience as two steps forward and one step back. Canada had an exemplary record. It had adopted sound institutions from the beginning, and it always learned from its crisis/near-crisis experience. Its learning can be characterized as two steps forward, no steps back.

Australia was more like the United States. It can be characterized as two steps forward, one step back. Argentina was very different from the other three. It rarely learned from its crisis experience. Its experience can be characterized as no steps forward or even worse, as one step forward, two steps back.

What explains the experiences of the different countries? The extensive literature on institutions and economic performance suggests that the countries that financially developed successfully had greater political stability, adherence to the rule of law, well-defined property rights, and better democracy. The three successful countries that we describe certainly have these attributes. By contrast, Argentina has been deficient in all respects.

It would appear that the lesson from history is that financial stability is in part also determined by these forces.[8] This is natural since sound financial and monetary policies can minimize the problems inherent in a world of incomplete markets and maturity mismatch. These institutional determinants help in many ways. Political stability and rule of law can help avoid excessive rent seeking and limit corruption. Rule of law gives rise to better regulatory frameworks regardless of "legal origins" (Musacchio 2008). Democracy gives those aggrieved by the market externalities of financial instability a chance for redress via civil interaction and consensus. Political stability leads to longer time horizons in financial and political "markets," and it may also enhance the credibility of monetary authorities.

---

[8] Between 1945 and the 1970s, banking crises were largely regulated out of existence with financial repression. Limited international capital flows diminished the number of debt crises. However, currency crises did not disappear. Our research is more applicable to market-based economies without financial repression.

Financial crises can never be fully eliminated, and in the same way complex machines and complex systems cannot avoid occasional failure. In addition, the environment is never constant in an evolutionary sense. Financial market participants, as well as regulators, may act rationally, but market failures and unforeseen complexities make for new challenges analogous to the battle against constantly evolving pathogens that each living species faces. What we assert is that certain constellations of political, institutional, and economic variables increase the possibility that countries redress earlier failures and attempt to look ahead to avoid future crises.

We end with two final thoughts. Barry Eichengreen (2015, p. 324) argued that:

The experience of the 1930s suggests that radical reform is possible only in the wake of an exceptional crisis. Absent that crisis, business as usual remains the order of the day . . ... The problem starting in 2009, if it can be called a problem, was that policy makers managed, just barely, to prevent a 1930s-style crisis.

While there is much to agree with here, we do not think that the long-run record from the non-learners is totally consistent with this argument. Major crises rocked the non-learners over the last two centuries and yet reform was largely feeble. We suggest that although a large crisis is a necessary condition for significant reform and learning, institutions are also a key variable. In the absence of the factors we discuss earlier, large crises cannot alone spark major changes.

Second, following the insightful work of Reinhart and Rogoff (2009), the ironic mantra "This time is different" has become commonplace. We think the long-run record shows that less irony may be required. The crisis of 2007–2008 in the United States and other leading countries had its roots, as all crises do, in an environment of imperfect information and maturity mismatch (e.g., in the repo market). A number of contributing factors such as deregulation, misguided regulation, opportunism, overly loose monetary policy, global imbalances, and moral hazard probably enhanced the likelihood of a crisis. But given the supreme complexity and disagreement about the leading causes of the crisis in the literature to date, the facts that the repo market was largely undocumented by regulators and that historically unparalleled levels of securitization and financial innovation such as the credit default swap (CDS) and associated options were all present suggest that it would have been hard to foresee exactly how the crisis would unfold. Few observers believed it would be systemic in nature. Also, what can explain the fact that Australia, Canada, and New Zealand sat this crisis out despite their ostensible similarities to the United States and the United Kingdom? So much cannot be said for the real estate booms in Spain and Ireland or the excessive borrowing based on falsified national accounts that occurred in Greece. These crises bear much more similarity to previous crises as our selective analysis of the long run illustrates. The crises in Argentina in 2001, Brazil in 2002, and Latin America and Asia in the 1980s and 1990s bear a significant resemblance to previous crises despite "real time" optimism. What we conclude is that next time may very well be different in the leading countries, but in others it may not be so different.

References

Acemoglu, Daron, Simon Johnson, and James A. Robinson. (2005). "Institutions as a Fundamental Cause of Long-Run Growth." In P. Aghion and S. N. Durlauf (eds.), *Handbook of Economic Growth, Volume 1A*, pp. 386–472. Amsterdam: North Holland.

Bagehot, Walter. (1873). *Lombard Street: A Description of the London Money Market.* London: Henry S. King & Co.

Bordo, Michael D., Ali Dib, and Lawrence Schembri. (2010). "Canada's Pioneering Experience with a Floating Exchange Rate in the 1950s: (Hard) Lessons for Monetary Policy in a Small Open Economy." *International Journal of Central Banking* 6 (3):51–99.

Bordo, Michael D., and Barry Eichengreen. (1999). "Is Our Current Economic Environment Unusually Crisis Prone?" In D. Gruen and L. Gower (eds.), *Capital Flows and the International Financial System*, pp. 18–74. Canberra: Reserve Bank of Australia.

Bordo, Michael D., Barry Eichengreen, Daniela Klingebiel, and Maria Soledad Martinez-Peria. (2001). "Is the Crisis Problem Growing More Severe?" *Economic Policy* 16(32):52–82.

Bordo, Michael D., Owen F. Humpage, and Anna J. Schwartz. (2015). *Strained Relations: U.S. Foreign Exchange Operations and Monetary Policy in the Twentieth Century.* Chicago: University of Chicago Press.

Bordo, Michael D., and Finn E. Kydland. (1995). "The Gold Standard as a Rule: An Essay in Exploration." *Explorations in Economic History* 32(4):423–464.

Bordo, Michael D., and Christopher M. Meissner. (2011). "Foreign Capital, Financial Crises and Incomes in the First Era of Globalization." *European Review of Economic History* 15(1):61–91.

Bordo, Michael D., and Athanasios Orphanides. (2013). *The Great Inflation: The Rebirth of Modern Central Banking.* Chicago: University of Chicago Press.

Bordo, Michael D., and Angela Redish. (1987). "Why Did the Bank of Canada Emerge in 1935?" *Journal of Economic History* 47(2):405–417.

Bordo, Michael D., and Angela Redish. (1990). "Credible Commitment and Exchange Rate Stability: Canada's Interwar Experience." *Canadian Journal of Economics* 24 (1):357–380.

Bordo, Michael D., Angela Redish, and Hugh Rockoff. (1994). "The U.S. Banking System from a Northern Exposure: Stability vs. Efficiency." *Journal of Economic History* 54(2):325–341.

Bordo, Michael D., Angela Redish, and Hugh Rockoff. (2015). "Why Didn't Canada Have a Banking Crisis in 2008 (or in 1930, or 1907, or . . .)?" *Economic History Review* 68(1):218–243.

Bordo, Michael D., and Anna J. Schwartz. (1994). "The Specie Standard as a Contingent Rule: Some Evidence for Core and Peripheral Countries, 1880–1990." Working Paper No. 4860, National Bureau of Economic Research.

Bordo, Michael D., Alan M. Taylor, and Jeffrey G. Williamson (2003). *Globalization in Historical Perspective*. Chicago: University of Chicago Press.

Bordo, Michael D., and David C. Wheelock. (2013). "The Promise and Performance of the Federal Reserve as Lender of Last Resort 1914–1933." In M. D. Bordo and W. Roberds (eds.), *The Origins, History and Future of the Federal Reserve*, pp. 59–98. New York: Cambridge University Press.

Borio, Claudo, Harold James, and Hyun Song Shin. (2014). "The International Monetary and Financial System: A Capital Account Historical Perspective." Working Paper No. 457, Bank for International Settlements.

Brooks, Robin, Hali Edison, Manmohan S. Kumar, and Torsten Sløk. (2004). "Exchange Rates and Capital Flows." *European Financial Management* 10 (3):511–533.

Calomiris, Charles W., and Stephen H. Haber. (2014). *Fragile by Design: The Political Origins of Banking Crises and Scarce Credit*. Princeton, NJ: Princeton University Press.

Cortes Conde, Roberto. (1989). *Dinero, Dueda y Crisis: Evolucion Fiscal y Monetaria En La Argentina, 1862–1890*. Buenos Aires: Editorial Sudamericana Instituto Torcuata di Tella.

Davis, Lance E., and Robert E. Gallman. (2001). *Evolving Financial Markets and International Capital Flows: Britain, the Americas and Australia: 1865–1914*. Cambridge: Cambridge University Press.

Della Paolera, Gerardo. (1994). "Experimentos Monetarios y Bancarios en Argentina: 1861–1930." *Revista de Historia Económica* 12(3):539–590.

Drelichman, Mauricio, and Hans-Joachim Voth. (2011). "Lending to the Borrower from Hell: Debt and Default in the Age of Philip II." *The Economic Journal* 121 (557):1205–1227.

Eichengreen, Barry. (1992). *Golden Fetters*. Oxford: Oxford University Press.

Eichengreen, Barry. (2015). *The Hall of Mirrors*. Oxford: Oxford University Press.

Engerman, Stanley L., and Kenneth L. Sokoloff. (1997). "Factor Endowments, Institutional and Differential Paths of Growth among New World Economies: A View from Economic Historians of the United States." In S. Haber (ed.), *How Latin America Fell Behind: Essays in the Economic Histories of Brazil and Mexico*. Palo Alto: Stanford University Press.

Friedman, Milton, and Anna J. Schwartz. (1963). *A Monetary History of the United States*. Princeton, NJ: Princeton University Press.

Garber, Peter M., and Vittorio U. Grilli. (1986). "The Belmont-Morgan Syndicate as an Optimal Investment Banking Contract." *European Economic Review* 30(3):649–677.

Gorton, Gary. (1985). "Clearing Houses and the Origins of Central Banking in the United States." *Journal of Economic History* 45(2):277–283.

Gorton, Gary, and Andrew Metrick. (2013). "The Federal Reserve and Panic Prevention: The Roles of Financial Regulation and Lender of Last Resort." *Journal of Economic Perspectives.* 27(9):45–64.

Gourinchas, Pierre-Olivier, and Olivier Jeanne. (2006). "The Elusive Gains from International Financial Integration." *Review of Economic Studies* 72(3):715–741.

Grewal, Bhajan S. (2000). "Australian Loan Council: Arrangements and Experience with Bailouts." Working Paper No. R-397, Inter-American Development Bank Research Network.

Henry, Peter B. (2007). "Capital Account Liberalization: Theory, Evidence, and Speculation." *Journal of Economic Literature* 45(4):887–935.

Hickson, Charles R., and John D. Turner. (2002). "Free Banking Gone Awry: The Australian Banking Crisis of 1893." *Financial History Review* 9(2):147–167.

Hubbard, Glenn. (2013, September 12). "How to Stop the Next Financial Crisis: The Fed Might Be Our Last Great Hope." *The Atlantic.* Retrieved from www.theatlantic.com/business/archive/2013/09/how-to-stop-the-next-financial-crisis-the-fed-might-be-our-last-great-hope/279594.

King, Robert G., and Ross Levine. (1993). "Finance and Growth: Schumpeter Might Be Right." *Quarterly Journal of Economics* 108(3):713–737.

Laeven, Luc, and Fabian Valencia. (2013). "Systemic Banking Crises Database." *IMF Economic Review* 61(2):225–270.

Lazaretou, Sophia. (2012). "Financial Crises and Financial Market Regulation: The Long Record of an 'Emerger.'" In Y. Görmez, Ş. Pamuk, and M. İ. Turhan (eds.), *Monetary Policy during Economic Crises: A Comparative and Historical Perspective*, pp. 85–112. Ankara: SEEMHN and Central Bank of the Republic of Turkey.

Meltzer, Alan H. (2003). *A History of the Federal Reserve Volume I.* Chicago: University of Chicago Press.

Miron, Jeffrey A. (1988). "The Founding of the Fed and the Destabilization of the Post-1914 Economy." Working Paper No. 2701, National Bureau of Economic Research.

Musacchio, Aldo. (2008). "Can Civil Law Countries Get Good Institutions? Lessons from the History of Creditor Rights and Bond Markets in Brazil." *Journal of Economic History* 68(1):80–108.

North, Douglas C., John Joseph Wall, and Barry R. Weingast. (2009). *Violence and Social Orders: A Conceptual Framework for Interpreting Recorded Human History.* New York: Cambridge University Press.

North, Douglas C., and Barry R. Weingast. (1989). "Constitutions and Commitment: The Evolution of Institutions Governing Public Choice in Seventeenth Century England." *Journal of Economic History* 49(4):803–832.

Perkins, Edwin J. (1994). *American Public Finance and Financial Services, 1790–1815.* Columbus: Ohio State University Press.

Rajan, Raghuram G., and Luigi Zingales. (2003). *Saving Capitalism from the Capitalists.* New York: Crown Business.

Reinhart, Carmen M. (2010). "This Time Is Different Chart Book: Country Histories on Debt, Default, and Financial Crises." Working Paper No. 15815, National Bureau of Economic Research.

Reinhart, Carmen M., and Kenneth S. Rogoff. (2009). *This Time Is Different: A History of Financial Crises.* Princeton, NJ: Princeton University Press.

Rockoff, Hugh. (1974). "The Free Banking Era: A Reexamination." *Journal of Money, Credit and Banking* 6(2):141–167.

Rockoff, Hugh. (2014). "It Is Always the Shadow Banks: The Failures That Ignited America's Financial Panics." Rutgers University (mimeo).

Rousseau, Peter L., and Richard Sylla. (2003). "Financial Systems, Economic Growth and Globalization." In M. D. Bordo, A. M. Taylor, and J. G. Williamson (eds.), *Globalization in Historical Perspective*, pp. 373–416. Chicago: University of Chicago Press.

Silber, William L. (2007). *When Washington Shut Down Wall Street: The Great Financial Crisis of 1914 and the Origins of America's Monetary Supremacy.* Princeton, NJ: Princeton University Press.

Sylla, Richard, John Joseph Wallis, and Arthur Grinath, III. (2004). "Sovereign Default and Repudiation: The Emerging-Market Debt Crisis in the United States, 1839–1843." Working Paper No. 10753, National Bureau of Economic Research.

Sylla, Richard, Robert E. Wright, and David J. Cowen. (2009). "Alexander Hamilton, Central Banker: Crisis Management during the U.S. Financial Panic of 1792." *Business History Review* 83(1):61–86.

Tornell, Aaron, and Frank Westerman. (2005). *Boom-Bust Cycles and Financial Liberalization.* Cambridge, MA: MIT Press.

Triffin, Robert. (1960). *Gold and the Dollar Crisis: The Future of Convertibility.* New Haven, CT: Yale University Press.

2

Episodes of Financial Deepening: Credit Booms or Growth Generators?

Peter L. Rousseau and Paul Wachtel

A well-developed literature now recognizes that financial development plays an important role in promoting long-run growth.[1] Yet measures commonly used to gauge the extent of financial development, such as the ratio of broad money to output, also serve well as predictors of financial crises, especially when expressed as rapid changes in the ratio (Radelet and Sachs 1998; Terrones 2004; Schularick and Taylor 2012). History reinforces the second interpretation with account after account of credit booms and the accompanying monetary expansions leading to financial crashes and panics (Calomiris and Haber 2014).

These two parallel strands in the literature on financial development and the economic performance of countries have for the most part developed independently of one another. The first, the finance-growth nexus, focuses on the role of financial deepening in economic growth, while the second emphasizes the costly effects of financial crises that can follow from episodes of excessive leveraging and credit expansion. The two facets are particularly interesting because it is often difficult to distinguish one from the other.

The emphasis on financial crises, though certainly justified in the wake of the 2007–2009 disturbances and the obvious costs associated with them, may leave the impression that all credit expansions are unhealthy. Recent historical work such as Reinhart and Rogoff (2009) and Schularick and Taylor (2012) reinforce that conclusion. We examine whether there is also scope for virtuous episodes of credit expansion that spur growth and provide a countervailing force against crises. Rousseau and Wachtel

Research assistance from Filip Herceg is greatly appreciated.
[1] See, among many others, King and Levine (1993), Demetriades and Hussein (1996), Rousseau and Wachtel (1998), and Levine, Loayza, and Beck (2000).

(1998) offer evidence supporting this relationship in a study of five indus-
trializing countries (Canada, Norway, Sweden, the United Kingdom, and
the United States) covering the period from 1870 to 1929, but the sample
selection may limit the generality of the findings.[2] Cross-country studies
with many countries and data after 1960, such as King and Levine (1993),
show correlations from financial development to higher subsequent
growth rates, but it unclear whether the effects emerge from dynamics
within individual countries as the relevant theory indicates they should
(Gurley and Shaw 1955; Goldsmith 1969; McKinnon 1973), or whether
they are artifacts of omitted country characteristics that correlate with
financial development to yield a result dominated by variation across
countries (Wachtel 2001, 2011).

A connection between the two strands of the literature was suggested by
our panel study with data for the last fifty years (Rousseau and Wachtel
2011). We found that the strength of the finance growth nexus weakened in
the last decade of the twentieth century and suggested that the reason
might be the increased incidence of financial crises. The long-term impact
of financial deepening on economic growth is muted when a country
experiences a financial crisis.

In this chapter, we examine the financial "deepening" experiences of
seventeen economies from 1880 to 1929 to identify cases of growth-
enhancing expansions of credit.[3] The historical focus is useful because it
is believed that financial development can have its strongest effects in the
earlier stages of economic growth (Cameron 1963), and considering a
simpler global economy and nations that would be classified as emerging
markets by today's standards might shed light on the effects of credit
expansions in modern emerging and transitional economies. Our broad
scope of countries also serves to attenuate selection issues.

We conduct the analysis using cross-country regressions similar to
those in the seminal literature on finance and growth with some important
additional features. We identify episodes of financial deepening and distinguish the effects of those ending in a crisis from those that do not. This
allows us to illustrate how expansions in credit affect the operation of the
finance-growth nexus. We close by discussing some of the episodes of
beneficial deepening that appear in our sample.

---

[2] Rousseau (1999) provides similar evidence for Meiji-era Japan.
[3] The seventeen countries are Argentina, Australia, Brazil, Canada, Denmark, Finland,
France, Germany, Italy, Japan, the Netherlands, Norway, Portugal, Spain, Sweden, the
United Kingdom, and the United States.

Describing the Data

The analysis includes countries for which we have annual macroeconomic accounts dating back to at least 1880. Data for population, the broad money stock (M2), gross domestic product (GDP), the GDP deflator, imports, and exports are from worksheets underlying Bordo and Jonung (1987), Rousseau and Wachtel (1998), Rousseau (1999), and Obstfeld and Taylor (2000). For the dating of financial crises since 1870, we use the list from the online appendix of Schularick and Taylor (2012), which we adjust for Canada and the United Kingdom, and then add our own dates for two countries (Argentina and Brazil) which are not included in their sample.[4]

The ratio of M2 to GDP is our measure of financial development; it primarily reflects the size of a country's banking system. Ideally we would like additional measures of financial development, such as the ratio of private credit or stock market capitalization to GDP, but these aggregates are not available for a broad range of countries over the full period of our study.[5] The M2 to GDP ratio, of course, emphasizes the role of banks, which were the primary financial intermediaries at the time, and includes the provision of the transactions asset by both private-sector financial intermediaries and the government. Money creation by the private banking sector is a fundamental form of intermediation since bank liabilities are a way of holding savings, and bank assets are used to finance investment activity.

We convert output to real per capita values using population and the GDP deflator before computing growth rates.

[4] Schularick and Taylor (2012) use documentary descriptions of crisis events from Bordo et al. (2001) and Reinhart and Rogoff (2009) to date financial crises. Correspondence with Michael Bordo and our own reading of Bordo et al. (2001) suggest that Canada and the United Kingdom did not experience systemic financial crises between 1870 and 1929, and we adjust the list accordingly by removing financial crises for Canada in 1873, 1907, and 1923, and for the United Kingdom in 1873 and 1890. Our econometric findings are qualitatively identical when we use Schularick and Taylor's list without our adjustments.

[5] Schularick and Taylor (2012) build a dataset of bank loans for fifteen of the countries we study starting as early as 1870 in some instances, but the coverage across countries is not adequate for our purposes. In particular, the sample of loan data prior to 1900 is about one-third smaller than our M2 sample and would lead to the omission of many nineteenth-century crisis episodes. Given our interest in exploring relationships between financial development, financial crises, and growth going back well into the nineteenth century, we proceed with M2 as our financial aggregate. At the same time, we note that the annual series for bank loans and M2 have correlations greater than 0.9 for all fifteen countries common to our samples when calculated with the available common observations. We thank Moritz Schularick for making an updated version of the bank loan data available to us.

We determine episodes of financial deepening from our annual data for M2/GDP for each of the seventeen countries by rolling through the samples and computing for each country-year:

$$D_{i,t} = 1 \text{ if } F_{i,t}/F_{i,t-10} > 1.3, \text{ and}$$
$$D_{i,t} = 0 \text{ otherwise,}$$

where F represents the ratio of M2 to GDP, and the subscripts i and t index countries and individual years, respectively. In words, we begin by turning on a dummy variable indicating an episode of "financial deepening" in year t when the growth rate of M2/GDP over the previous ten years exceeds 30 percent. This implies an average annual deepening of about 2.7 percent over the decade. Deepening episodes can thus span multiple years when the ratio's ten-year growth rate remains above 30 percent in consecutive years. We also work with an alternative definition of a deepening episode based on computing for each country-year

$$D_{i,t} = 1 \text{ if } F_{i,t} - F_{i,t-10} > 0.2, \text{ and}$$
$$D_{i,t} = 0 \text{ otherwise.}$$

This criterion turns on a dummy variable for an episode of financial deepening in year t when the ratio of M2 to GDP (in percent) rises by more than 20 percentage points over the previous ten years. The use of these type of criteria to identify deepening episodes was hinted at by Jordà, Schularick and Taylor (2013, p. 9), who note that "three quarters of all episodes during which credit to GDP rose by 30 percentage points or more over a five-year period ended in a systemic crisis."

Determining whether a country is in the midst of a deepening episode at any point in time depends on criteria set by the researcher, and our strategy is no exception. For example, one year of extraordinary advance in ratio of M2 to GDP could trigger the dummy variable for as many as ten subsequent years, even if there was no deepening in the interim. As it turns out, however, our thresholds of 30 percent or 20 percentage point increases avoid this outcome, and we see very few lengthy episodes in the sample. This would not be the case if we lowered the thresholds. Our criteria therefore reflect a balance between finding too many or too few deepening episodes.

Table 2.1 lists both the systemic financial crises and the episodes of financial deepening for the seventeen countries. There were forty-nine systemic financial crises between 1870 and 1929. Six countries experienced crises in 1907 and four countries in 1893 and in 1921.

Table 2.1 *Financial Crises and Episodes of Financial Deepening*

		Episodes of Financial Deepening to 1929	
Country and Start of Credit Data	Systemic Financial Crises, 1870–1929	30 percent increase over last 10 years	20 percentage point increase over last 10 years
Argentina (1884)	1890	1905 1910–1911 1922	
Australia (1880)	1893	1894–1896 1899–1900	
Brazil (1880)	1891 1900	1890 1918 1921–1923	
Canada (1870)		1885 1892–1901 1917	
Germany (1880)	1873 1891 1901 1907	1890–1892 1894–1895 1898 1900 1902–1904 1906–1911	
Denmark (1850)	1877 1885 1908 1921	1860 1862–1864 1875–1890 1910 1918	1881 1886–1889 1918
Spain (1875)	1883 1890 1913 1920 1924	1885–1901 1917–1919 1921–1926	1918
Finland (1862)	1878 1900 1921	1872–1876 1886–1890 1892–1904 1911 1915	1873–1874 1889 1895–1904 1908 1910–1911 1914–1918
France (1851)	1882 1889	1861–1878 1909	
Italy (1872)	1873 1887 1893 1907 1921	1883–1884 1887–1889 1892 1919	

(continued)

Table 2.1 (*continued*)

		Episodes of Financial Deepening to 1929	
Country and Start of Credit Data	Systemic Financial Crises, 1870–1929	30 percent increase over last 10 years	20 percentage point increase over last 10 years
Japan (1878)	1882	1899	1906
	1900	1902	1910–1911
	1904	1904–1915	1917–1918
	1907	1917–1918	1923
	1913	1923	1928–1929
	1927	1929	
Netherlands (1850)	1893	1860–1861	1898
	1907	1867–1869	1918
	1921	1872–1873	
		1875–1881	
		1883–1884	
		1897–1902	
		1917–1918	
Norway (1865)	1899	1878–1888	1903–1904
	1922	1890	1906
		1901–1910	1908–1909
		1918	1918
		1921–1923	1921–1927
		1925–1926	
Portugal (1880)	1890	1914–1915	
	1920	1917–1923	
	1923		
Sweden (1870)	1878	1887–1888	1909
	1907	1909	
	1922		
USA (1850)	1873	1871–1872	
	1884	1874	
	1893	1887–1892	
	1907	1894–1895	
	1929	1906	
UK (1870)		1909	1909
		1921	

Note: See text for definitions of *financial crises* and *deepening episodes.* The years that data begin for broad money appear in parentheses in the first column, and episodes of financial deepening can be identified ten years afterward. Country *i* experiences an episodes in year *t* when the ratio of M2 to GDP rises by more than 30 percent (third column) or 20 percentage points (fourth column) over the previous ten years.

Table 2.2 *Financial Crises and Deepening Episodes by Decade*

Decade	Crises	Episodes of Financial Deepening (30 percent over last 10 years)	Episodes of Financial Deepening (20 percentage points over last 10 years)
1860s	–	5	0
1870s	6	7	1
1880s	7	8	3
1890s	10	13	2
1900s	12	11	7
1910s	2	14	8
1920s	12	8	3

Note: Data are not available to compute episodes of financial deepening for all countries in the 1860s, 1870s, 1880s, and 1920s. Crises are observed after 1870.

Using the 30 percent criterion, there are fifty-four episodes of financial deepening starting between 1880 and 1929, though twenty-five of these represent only a single year. Each country has at least one such episode. Since we require data on M2/GDP for at least ten past years to identify a deepening episode for a particular country in a given year, we go back as far as 1870 to compute the ten-year growth rates needed to determine episodes in the 1880s. Although data are unavailable for more than two-thirds of the countries in our sample before 1870, Table 2.1 shows another twelve episodes of financial deepening that begin prior to 1880.

We identify only twenty-four episodes of financial deepening that begin in 1880 or later using the 20 percentage point criterion, and thirteen of these represent a single year. Notably, nine of the seventeen countries (Argentina, Australia, Brazil, Canada, Germany, France, Italy, Portugal, and the United States) never experience a deepening using this criterion, and this seems unlikely given evidence for long-term financial deepening in Canada and the United States provided by Rousseau and Wachtel (1998). For this reason, we prefer the 30 percent criterion and focus on results that use it, leaving the alternate criterion for robustness checks.

Table 2.2 shows that both crises and deepening episodes are spread throughout the sample period.

Table 2.3 reports the frequency of deepening episodes (using the 30 percent criterion) and crises by country since 1870. The left column shows the number of times a financial crises occurred during a deepening episode, the center column indicates deepening episodes not associated with a crisis, and the right column indicates financial crises that occur outside of

Table 2.3 *The Incidence of Financial Crises and Deepening Episodes, 1870–1929*

Country	Crises with Deepening	Deepening without Crisis	Crises without Deepening
Argentina	0	3	0
Australia	1	1	0
Brazil	1	2	1
Canada	0	3	0
Denmark	2	2	2
Finland	1	3	2
France	0	2	2
Germany	3	3	0
Italy	2	2	2
Japan	3	4	1
Netherlands	0	5	3
Norway	1	6	1
Portugal	2	1	1
Spain	3	0	2
Sweden	0	2	3
UK	0	2	0
USA	3	2	2
Totals	**22**	**43**	**22**

Note: Table 2.3 uses only those years where data are available to identify both financial crises and deepening episodes. Deepening episodes are defined with the 30 percent criterion (third column of Table 2.1).

deepening episodes. There are as many financial crises that occur outside of deepening episodes in our sample as occur within them (twenty-two), and nearly two-thirds of deepening episodes do not involve a financial crisis. Since economic theory suggests that the relation between finance and growth is a dynamic one, it is natural that distinguishing between these two types of deepening episodes turns out to be central in the empirical models we estimate.

Table 2.4 reports average growth rates of real per capita GDP for the seventeen countries across five-year periods from 1880 to 1929 based on whether a financial deepening, crisis, or both a deepening and crisis occurs during the period.[6] The table shows that growth rates are much higher on

---

[6] Our econometric analysis uses the five-year periods as the unit of observation as is common in the literature. A country experiences a financial deepening in a given five-year period if at least one of the deepening spells indicated in Table 2.1 falls within the period, and similarly for the financial crises.

Table 2.4 *Average Real GDP Growth in Five-Year Periods, 1880–1929*

	Deepening with Crisis	Deepening without Crisis	Crises without Deepening	Other (No Crisis or Deepening)	All Periods
Growth rate in period	0.93	1.75	1.75	1.62	1.58
Growth rate in next period	2.92	1.59	1.67	1.06	1.83
Number of periods	21	52	16	62	151

Note: A country experiences a "deepening" if in any year within a given five-year period it records an increase of more than 30 percent in M2/GDP over the previous ten years. A country is defined to experience a "crisis" if it experiences a financial crisis at any time in a given five-year period. The table includes observations for which growth data are available and sufficient credit data to determine deepening episodes. Due to data availability, there are only 131 observations included in the second row.

average in periods of financial deepening that are not associated with a crisis than those that are (1.75 percent compared to 0.93 percent). Average growth is about the same when there is financial deepening but without crisis or a crisis period without financial deepening. In the subsequent five-year period, growth is most rapid following a period of deepening with crisis. Focusing on the financial crises, subsequent growth is more rapid after crises that are associated with a deepening than after crises occurring outside of a deepening (2.92 percent compared to 1.67 percent). Finally, growth rates during episodes of financial deepening without a crisis are higher than the average of 1.58 percent across all countries and five-year periods.

These statistics suggest a narrative in which episodes of financial deepening can promote growth if not taken to excess, but also that growth tends to recover rapidly after financial crises that follow credit booms. Given that financial deepening episodes are related to only about half of the financial crises in our sample (Table 2.3), this suggests that episodes of modest financial deepening may help to drive economic growth, and that taking them too far on occasion may be preferable to no deepening at all. In the following section, we develop an econometric framework that enables us to explore these hypotheses.

Econometric Findings

Our econometric methodology is a modified version of the cross-country growth regression developed by Barro (1991) and extended to the study of the finance-growth nexus by King and Levine (1993). The analysis covers five-year periods from 1880 to 1929 to impose a reasonable degree of balance across the panel of countries and to work with the sample data that are most reliable. The baseline regression has the form

$$\text{Growth } Y_{i,t} = \alpha_0 + \alpha Y_{i,t} + \beta F_{i,t} + \Phi_t + \mu_{i,t} \qquad (1)$$

where the dependent variable, *Growth* $Y_{i,t}$, is the average annual percentage growth rate of real per capita income over the five-year period t and $Y_{i,t}$ is the natural logarithm of the level of real per capita income in U.S. dollars in the first year of period t. $F_{i,t}$ is the average ratio of M2 to GDP over the five-year period, Φ_t are dummy variables for the five-year periods, and $\mu_{i,t}$ is the error term. We expect a negative coefficient on the log of initial income due to the tendency for growth rates to converge across countries and over time. In some regressions, we include an additional variable often found in this literature, the ratio of international trade (the sum of imports and exports) to GDP, which we expect to have a positive coefficient.[7]

We then augment the baseline with binary indicator variables for deepening episodes, financial crises, and their interactions with M2/GDP. We turn on the deepening indicator for a given country and five-year period if at least one of the years in the third column of Table 2.1 (financial deepening indicated by an increase in the M2/GDP ratio of at least 30 percent over ten years) falls within the period, and set the indicator for financial crises similarly using years in the second column of Table 2.1. Thus, each five-year period can be characterized as a crisis period, a deepening period, both a deepening episode and crisis period, or a period of neither deepening nor crisis. A little more than half of the five-year periods in the sample see a deepening and/or crisis; crisis periods account for one-quarter of all five-year observations and are about evenly divided between those associated with an episode of financial deepening and those that are not.

Table 2.5 presents instrumental variables estimates of equation (1), where we instrument the average ratios of M2 and international trade to

---

[7] The five-year periods are 1880–1884, 1885–1889, 1890–1894, 1895–1900, 1900–1904, 1905–1909, 1910–1914, 1915–1919, 1920–1924, and 1925–1929. The sample includes at least seven and up to ten observations for each of the seventeen countries. The missing five-year observations due to insufficient data for computing deepening episodes are: Argentina 1880–1884, 1885–1889, 1890–1894; Australia 1880–1884; 1885–1889; Brazil 1880–1884, 1885–1889; France 1915–1919, 1920–1924, 1925–1929; Germany 1880–1884, 1885–1889, 1915–1919, 1920–1924, 1925–1929; Japan 1880–1884; Portugal 1880–1884, 1885–1889; and Spain 1880–1884.

Table 2.5 *Instrumental Variables Growth Regressions, 1880–1929*

			Dependent Variable: Five-Year Average Growth Rate of Real Per Capita GDP (%)				
	(1)	(2)	(3)	(4)	(5)	(6)	(7)
Log real GDP per capita (USD)	-0.678**	-0.846***	-0.688**	-0.660**	-0.907***	-0.882***	-0.882***
	(0.314)	(0.316)	(0.324)	(0.313)	(0.316)	(0.317)	(0.318)
Ratio M2 to GDP	3.000***	3.412***	3.021***	2.967***	3.497***	3.447***	3.438***
	(1.091)	(1.086)	(1.115)	(1.087)	(1.083)	(1.081)	(1.119)
Crisis		-1.318**					
		(0.525)					
Deepening			-0.061				
			(0.451)				
Deepening – Crisis				0.526		0.399	0.400
				(0.348)		(0.343)	(0.345)
Deepening × Crisis					-1.870***	-1.772***	-1.768***
					(0.641)	(0.646)	(0.660)
Ratio international trade to GDP							0.013
							(0.439)
Period dummies	Yes	Yes	Yes	Yes	Yes	Yes	Yes
R^2	0.129	0.166	0.129	0.143	0.179	0.187	0.187
Observations	151	151	151	151	151	151	151

Notes: The table shows coefficients from instrumental variables regressions with data from available five-year periods between 1880 and 1929, with standard errors in parentheses. Five-year averages of M2/GDP and trade/GDP are instrumented by their values in the initial year of each period. "Deepening" is a binary variable set to unity if any year within a given five-year period sees an increase of more than 30 percent in M2/GDP over the previous ten years. "Crisis" is a dummy variable set to unity if a country experiences a financial crisis in a given five-year period. *, **, and *** denote statistical significance at the 10, 5, and 1 percent levels, respectively.

GDP in each five-year period by their values in the initial year of the period. The two-stage least squares estimates in effect extract the components of M2/GDP and trade/GDP that can be explained by their own past values and the other exogenous variables and then insert these fitted values into the actual (second stage) regression. We augment the baseline specification (column 1) with specifications where the binary variables for financial deepening episodes and financial crises enter directly (columns 2–7). The baseline indicates a positive coefficient for the initial value of the M2/GDP ratio that is significant at the 1 percent level. This is consistent with earlier findings by Rousseau and Sylla (2003) and relates a 10 percentage point increase in M2/GDP with a 0.3 percentage point increase in the rate of annual GDP growth. Column (2) indicates that financial crises have a direct and negative effect on growth that is statistically significant at the 5 percent level, with a financial crisis relating to a decline in annual per capita growth of 1.3 percentage points. Columns (3) and (4) find no significant direct effect of our deepening indicators on output growth. Columns (5) and (6) indicate that financial crises occurring during episodes of financial deepening have even more severe effects on growth than those occurring outside of them [compare to the crisis coefficient in column (2)]. Columns (4) and (6) indicate that episodes of financial deepening that occur without crisis have a positive effect on annual growth of about 0.4 percent, although the effects are barely larger than their standard errors. Finally, column (7) shows that the results are robust to the inclusion of the ratio of international trade (the sum of exports and imports) to GDP as an additional regressor, which turns out to be not statistically significant.

The lack of direct explanatory power for the financial deepening episodes in our sample indicates that any effects on growth are likely to be indirect. The proposition that these deepening episodes act through the M2 ratios themselves is reasonable because we might expect episodes of financial deepening to improve the efficacy of the finance-growth relationship so long as they are not excessive. We therefore turn next to specifications in which our binary variables are interacted with the M2 to GDP ratio.[8]

Table 2.6 reports instrumental variables regression results with interaction terms included. Column (1) repeats the baseline regression, but this

---

[8] Rousseau and Wachtel (2011) show the effects of both financial crises and liberalizations on the strength of the finance-growth nexus with panel data for the period 1960–2004.

Table 2.6 *Instrumental Variables Growth Regressions with Interaction Terms*

	Dependent Variable: Five-Year Average Growth Rate of Real Per Capita GDP (%)						
	(1)	(2)	(3)	(4)	(5)	(6)	(7)
Log real GDP per capita (USD)	-0.678**	-0.841***	-0.670**	-0.597**	-0.893***	-0.805**	-0.805***
	(0.314)	(0.308)	(0.331)	(0.311)	(0.314)	(0.316)	(0.317)
Ratio M2 to GDP	3.000***	4.282***	2.941**	2.498**	4.129***	3.606***	3.584***
	(1.091)	(1.136)	(1.319)	(1.101)	(1.136)	(1.172)	(1.221)
M2/GDP × Crisis		-2.858***					
		(0.905)					
M2/GDP × Deepening			0.071				
			(0.857)				
M2/GDP × (Deepening – Crisis)				1.416**		1.104*	1.107*
				(0.638)		(0.638)	(0.641)
M2/GDP × Crisis × Deepening					-3.134***	-2.767**	-2.753**
					(1.064)	(1.076)	(1.100)
Ratio international trade to GDP							0.028
							(0.435)
Period dummies	Yes	Yes	Yes	Yes	Yes	Yes	Yes
R^2	0.129	0.192	0.129	0.165	0.181	0.203	0.203
Observations	151	151	151	151	151	151	151

Note: See notes to Table 2.5.

time, column (2) adds an interaction of M2/GDP (instrumented by its initial value) with the crisis dummy. The coefficient on M2/GDP rises to more than four in this case, and the coefficient on the interaction term is negative and statistically significant at the 1 percent level. This suggests that financial crises also have negative effects on growth that operate through the finance-growth nexus. Specifically, the results in column (2) indicate that a 10 percentage point increase in M2 as a percent of GDP is associated with a 0.43 percentage point increase in the annual growth rates for a country that avoids financial crisis and just 0.14 percentage points (0.43 – 0.29) otherwise.

Columns (3) and (4) address episodes of financial deepening. Column (3) includes results with interactions of the deepening variable with M2/GDP and finds a positive coefficient that is not statistically significant. This might be expected as the dummy variable is turned on for all deepening episodes, including those associated with a financial crisis. When we remove those episodes associated with a financial crisis in column (4), the potential for rapid and beneficial financial deepening to enhance growth becomes clear with a coefficient on the interaction term that is significant at the 5 percent level. The coefficient indicates that the additional impact of a 10 percentage point increase in the M2 to GDP ratio on the annual growth rate is 0.14 percent when a country experiences an episode of deepening without a crisis. That is, the effect of a 10 percentage point deepening on annual growth is 0.39 percentage points (0.25 + 0.14) for crisis-free deepening episodes and 0.25 percentage points otherwise.

Column (6) of Table 2.6 shows that the effects of crisis-free deepening episodes persist even when we control for deepening episodes that end in a crisis, though the coefficient on the interaction term is now significant at only the 10 percent level. A ten percentage point deepening episode has a differential effect on growth in crisis-free and non-crisis-free booms; it is 0.39 percentage points higher in crisis-free booms (the difference between 0.11 and -0.28). Finally, column (7) indicates that the results are robust to the inclusion of the ratio of international trade (i.e., imports plus exports, instrumented by its initial values) to GDP in the specification.

Tables 2.7 and 2.8 repeat the analyses in Tables 2.5 and 2.6, but use 20 percentage point increases in M2 as a percent of GDP to define episodes of financial deepening. Even with this reduced set of deepening episodes (see Table 2.1), the findings are qualitatively very similar to those related to the broader 30 percent criterion.

Table 2.7 *Robustness of IV Growth Regressions to 20 Percentage Point Episodes of Financial Deepening, 1880–1929*

	Dependent Variable: Five-Year Average Growth Rate of Real Per Capita GDP (%)						
	(1)	(2)	(3)	(4)	(5)	(6)	(7)
Log real GDP per capita (USD)	−0.678**	−0.846***	−0.720**	−0.677**	−0.832***	−0.823***	−0.824***
	(0.314)	(0.316)	(0.332)	(0.312)	(0.319)	(0.318)	(0.319)
Ratio M2 to GDP	3.000***	3.412***	3.303**	2.556**	3.917***	3.471***	3.407***
	(1.091)	(1.086)	(1.357)	(1.127)	(1.177)	(1.222)	(1.261)
Crisis		−1.318**					
		(0.525)					
Deepening			−0.325				
			(0.749)				
Deepening – Crisis				0.710*		0.644	0.644
				(0.421)		(0.419)	(0.421)
Deepening × Crisis					−2.306**	−2.194**	−2.162*
					(1.096)	(1.093)	(1.108)
Ratio international trade to GDP							0.087
							(0.436)
Period dummies	Yes	Yes	Yes	Yes	Yes	Yes	Yes
R^2	0.129	0.166	0.129	0.148	0.154	0.170	0.170
Observations	151	151	151	151	151	151	151

Notes: The table shows coefficients from instrumental variable (IV) regressions using data averaged over five-year periods from 1880 to 1929, with standard errors in parentheses. The estimations are the same as in Table 2.5 except here "Deepening" is a binary variable set to unity if any year within a given five-year period sees an increase of more than 20 percentage points in M2/GDP over the previous ten years. As before, "Crisis" is a dummy variable set to unity if a country experiences a financial crisis in a given five-year period. *, **, and *** denote statistical significance at the 10, 5, and 1 percent levels, respectively.

Table 2.8 *Robustness of IV Growth Regressions with Interactions to 20 Percentage Point Episodes of Financial Deepening*

	Dependent Variable: Five-Year Average Growth Rate of Real Per Capita GDP (%)						
	(1)	(2)	(3)	(4)	(5)	(6)	(7)
Log real GDP per capita (USD)	−0.678**	−0.841***	−0.712**	−0.601*	−0.832***	−0.746**	−0.746**
	(0.314)	(0.308)	(0.338)	(0.311)	(0.317)	(0.318)	(0.319)
Ratio M2 to GDP	3.000***	4.282***	3.278**	2.347**	4.070***	3.374***	3.281**
	(1.091)	(1.136)	(1.504)	(1.132)	(1.188)	(1.254)	(1.297)
M2/GDP × Crisis		−2.858***					
		(0.905)					
M2/GDP × Deepening			−0.313				
			(1.046)				
M2/GDP × (Deepening − Crisis)				1.470**		1.272*	1.284*
				(0.691)		(0.694)	(0.697)
M2/GDP × Crisis × Deepening					−2.839**	−2.490*	−2.438*
					(1.278)	(1.280)	(1.296)
Ratio trade to GDP							0.117
							(0.436)
Period dummies	Yes	Yes	Yes	Yes	Yes	Yes	Yes
R^2	0.129	0.192	0.128	0.163	0.159	0.185	0.185
Observations	151	151	151	151	151	151	151

Note: See notes to Table 2.7.

Our regression results provide strong support for the finance-growth nexus among the seventeen economies in our sample starting in 1880.[9] Indeed, the results are very similar to those found with much larger groups of countries with data that begin about a century later. Many countries in our historical data experienced periods of rapid financial sector growth, particularly around the turn of the twentieth century. In addition, financial crises were common occurrences, with each county having on average three crises in the sixty-year period from 1870 to 1929. We find that the effects of credit deepening on growth are enhanced during credit booms that are not associated with crisis and diminished in crisis-boom periods compared to other periods. Thus, episodes of credit deepening are beneficial except when they are associated with financial crises.

Financial Deepening and Financial Crises

In this section, we discuss the relationship between financial development and the incidence of crises and booms in several of the countries in our sample. We characterize the historical record and show that it is often consistent with the broad picture suggested by our econometric findings. That is, deepening episodes are associated with economic growth, although the relationship is often muted by crises.

For the United States, Rousseau and Sylla (2005) offer evidence for a financial revolution in the half-century following the ratification of the Constitution in 1789 that changed the trajectory of growth in the initial years of the republic. Yet the econometric evidence for finance-led growth in the United States from 1870 to 1929 is even stronger than this (Rousseau and Wachtel 1998). The literature on the National Banking period often focuses on the system's deficiencies and the extent to which it left the nation vulnerable to financial crises, and indeed there were well-documented crises in 1873, 1884, 1893, and 1907. But the periods of financial deepening that we identify are no less striking. The resurgence of state banks outside of the national banking system and the shift toward deposit banking after 1880 led to rapid increases in the money stock and the amount of available credit over the years between the disturbances of 1884 and 1893 and then again in 1894–1895. By most accounts, the 1884 crisis was mild by nineteenth-century standards, and the nation quickly

---

[9] The findings are nearly identical when we estimate with ordinary least squares using initial values of M2/GDP and trade/GDP as explanatory variables in place of their contemporaneous five-year averages.

rebounded from the crisis in 1893. Overall, the period from 1870 to 1914 in the United States may have been punctuated by several financial crises, but the deepening that accompanied these episodes relates closely to the rapid growth that the nation experienced as the path of industrialization continued to press forward.

Canada took a somewhat different route to financial development than the United States, but the rise of its banking system and assets held by its financial intermediaries exhibits similar albeit somewhat muted trends over the same period. The key difference usually cited between the Canadian and U.S. systems is that Canadian banks were fewer in number but allowed multiple branches rather than the unit system that characterized banks in the United States from the start. Consolidation also led a decline in the number of Canadian banks from 70 in 1870 to only 13 by 1935. Did branching and consolidation reduce competition and lower efficiency? Bordo, Rockoff, and Redish (1994) show that Canadian banks actually achieved higher profit rates than U.S. banks over the period, but they also observe that the profits were accompanied by higher shares of loans to total assets. They proceed to point to Canada's banking stability as evidence that its more productive banks could promote growth while avoiding the negative consequences of financial crises.

Our lists of crises and episodes of financial deepening make it difficult to challenge this view. Even though Canada experienced some discomfort in 1873, 1907, and 1923, these events were not systemic crises and certainly were not comparable to the disturbances experienced by the United States in 1873 and 1907. Canada also had an extended episode of financial deepening in the 1890s that is among the longest in the sample and achieved a 3.7 percent growth average rate of per capita output over that episode. Annual growth averaged 2 percent in other years, and even that compares favorably with the 1.6 percent average growth rate achieved by the United States from 1880 to 1929. Remaining relatively crisis free as a banking system develops no doubt has its advantages.

The United Kingdom was the world's first great financial power, building upon early seventeenth-century Dutch innovation to launch a financial revolution with the founding of the Bank of England in 1694. The monopoly granted to the Bank on note issue, coupled with restrictions on the formation of banks as corporations with limited liability until 1825, produced a banking system that was likely sub-optimal in terms of size and the diffusion of banking services. But the system improved upon these earlier deficiencies and by the late nineteenth century had established many more banks and a host of other intermediaries (Sheppard 1971).

As the most mature financial system in our sample, the United Kingdom was crisis free from 1880 until the Great Depression, but it is perhaps not surprising that it also experienced few episodes of financial deepening according to our criterion. This is consistent with Cameron (1963), who argued that financial development is most effective in the earlier stages of a transition to modern growth.

The restoration of the Meiji dynasty in 1868 is often credited with ushering in the start of financial reforms that put Japan on a modern growth trajectory. Much of the credit for the sea change should probably go to Masayoshi Matsukata, Japan's finance minister at the time. Matsukata commuted rents traditionally paid in rice to the feudal nobility in favor of long-term government bonds in 1872, and then much like the United States some 90 years earlier, allowed the bonds to be tendered as capital for shares in the Bank of Japan when it was formed in 1879. Combined with a nationalization of banking in 1876 along the lines of the U.S. national banking system, these innovations generated markets to trade the government's debt and shares of the central bank as well as a system of banks to lodge the new monetary balances. The rise of development banks such as the Yokahama Specie Bank followed quickly. The credit boom generated by this activity apparently jump-started economic growth (Rousseau 1999), yet it ended in a spectacular inflation and crash in 1882. But with the seeds of modern markets in place, the nation was able to expand financially once again, with a continuous episode of financial deepening (according to our dating technique) from 1904 to 1915, which is among the longest in our sample. The fact that this deepening was actually punctuated by financial crises in 1907 and 1913 indicate just how resilient the burgeoning financial sector was to temporary disturbances. As such, Japan stands as a classic example of a financial revolution characterized by boom and bust cycles, yet this tumultuous path led the way to economic modernization.

One view of Swedish financial development is that mid-nineteenth-century Sweden was a poor country with a sophisticated financial system, much like the United States at the start of the century. In this view, the financial system along with a high level of education enabled the economy to take off rapidly in the second half of the century. Another view is that the banking system did not develop until commercial bank lending began to replace Riksbank credit after mid-century (Hansson and Jonung 1997). In this view, two significant financial sector developments toward the end of the century were contemporaneous with economic growth. Specifically, the Riksbank developed modern central banking functions, and the commercial banks replaced merchant banking houses as a source of credit. This latter interpretation is consistent with our data, which indicates a period of financial deepening in the late 1880s while the only nineteenth-century crisis occurred in 1878. Another distinguishing feature of Swedish financial sector development around the turn of the century was the emergence of strong links between banks and their industrial customers, which strengthened over time. In this sense, the dominant role of bank credit may have been destabilizing, and so Sweden experienced systemic crises in 1907 and 1921 (though the latter was the consequence of the post–World War I fall in output and ensuing deflation).

German economic growth in the three decades following political unification in 1871 was remarkable; the only comparable experience might be the growth of China in the last thirty years. Some of the institutions that support growth were in place prior to unification (e.g., railroads, the transportation infrastructure, education, and the craft system), but finance was not one of them. A uniform currency was introduced in 1873 and the central bank, the Reichsbank, was established three years later. A liberal discounting policy by the Reichsbank led to the rapid growth of universal commercial banks and an explosion of credit. By our criterion, Germany was experiencing a credit boom in all but six years in the period from 1880 to 1911. The banks grew from trade financing institutions into universal banks with large deposit bases that provided both short- and long-term financing to German industry, particularly the rapidly growing capital-intensive manufacturing firms. Thus it is not surprising that the banks developed the close ties to industrial firms that characterize the German economy to this day. Banks often maintained an equity interest in firms, and bank representatives served on supervisory boards, voting the shares of the bank as well as those that other shareholders had deposited with the bank.[10]

The link between financial deepening and crisis in Germany is weak. The country experienced a major crisis in 1873, just a few years after unification and before our econometric analysis begins. The young banking institutions had substantial exposures to securities and were affected by the business cycle downturn and falling asset prices. Interestingly, there were no major banking crises in the following years of rapid credit

---

[10] It is a matter of controversy whether Germany is an example of bank-led economic growth or whether the banking expansion occurred in response to demand from the industrial sector; see Burhop (2006) and Fohlin (2007).

expansion even though Germany had a largely free banking structure throughout this period. The crises on the list were either minor (e.g., the 1891 crisis was due to bank failures caused by fraudulent management) or caused by international shocks (e.g., 1907).

Argentina and Australia are two countries in our sample with similar experiences [see McLean (2006)]. Table 2.1 indicates that both experienced one financial crisis: 1890 in Argentina and 1893 in Australia. These crises were both similar and related. Investment booms were fueled by foreign investment, which dried up when asset prices fell. Further, the situation in Australia was affected by emerging-markets contagion from the Argentine crisis that preceded it. Argentina rebounded quickly from its crisis whereas Australia experienced a very slow recovery. The post-crisis boom in the M2-to-GDP ratio shown for Australia is due to the fall in GDP rather than a rise in credit. Episodes of credit deepening did occur in both countries in the first decade of the twentieth century, but this occurred simultaneously with more rapid growth.

Brazil's enormous land mass and strong ocean currents left it fragmented and isolated over much of its modern history, and its lack of financial development can be traced to a weak central government that emerged from these unfavorable initial conditions (Calomiris and Haber 2014). The government's regular practice of expropriating banking resources at times of need throughout its history rendered it difficult to raise banking capital or deposits, and inflationary finance was a ready tool when outright expropriation failed. A lack of a coordinated banking system was the result, and this led to a tumultuous boom and bust in the early 1890s that ended in yet another crisis in 1900. By the end of our sample period, the nation's financial system consisted primarily of a state-owned bank that directed much of its credit flows to the treasury and a declining share to private businesses (Musacchio 2009). Our 30 percent criterion identifies two episodes of financial deepening after 1914 (one in 1917–1918 and the other 1921–1923). Part of this identification is surely due to the lack of depth of financial intermediation; M2/GDP in 1910 was only 0.24, making a 30 percent increase to 0.31 over ten years not too great a feat, yet it is also interesting to observe that Brazil experienced robust growth in real per capita output of nearly 5.5 percent between 1915 and 1925.

While the preceding discussions are only suggestive and necessarily brief, they are largely consistent with our econometric finding that episodes of financial deepening are beneficial to growth when they are not associated with financial crises.

Conclusion

The role of financial deepening in economic growth is thought to be a dynamic process that acts through the expansion and increased intensity of banking and other financial services, yet modern cross-country studies do not capture this dynamic explicitly. We examine evidence of it in a sample of seventeen economies over the period from 1870 to 1929 – a time when many nations in our group might still be considered emerging markets. By identifying specific episodes of financial deepening in individual countries, we reach beyond standard relationships between initial financial conditions and subsequent growth to link the deepening episodes themselves to smoother operation of the finance-growth nexus. We find that episodes of financial deepening, if not taken to the excesses that end in financial crises, enhance links between the level of financial development and growth, thereby revealing the role for dynamics described by theory. An examination of financial crises and episodes of financial deepening in the broader context of historical narratives offers further evidence of the plausibility of the mechanisms we uncover.

Financial crises are indeed costly and well deserving of the emphasis they have recently received in the economics literature. At the same time, our chapter aims to serve as a timely reminder that crises and output losses are not the only outcomes associated with credit expansions. Rather, the other side of the coin – robust economic growth – is much brighter, and the past only reinforces its luster.

References

Bordo, Michael D., Barry Eichengreen, Daniela Klingbiel, and Maria Soledad Martinez-Perez. (2001). "Is the Crisis Problem Growing More Severe?" *Economic Policy* 16 (32):51–82.

Bordo, Michael D., and Lars Jonung. (1987). *The Long-Run Behavior of the Velocity of Circulation.* New York: Cambridge University Press.

Bordo, Michael D., Hugh Rockoff, and Angela Redish. (1994). "The U.S. Banking System from a Northern Exposure: Stability vs. Efficiency." *Journal of Economic History* 54(2):325–341.

Burhop, Carsten. (2006). "Did Banks Cause the German Industrialization?" *Explorations in Economic History* 43(1):39–63.

Calomiris, Charles W., and Stephen H. Haber. (2014). *Fragile by Design: The Political Origins of Banking Crises and Scarce Credit.* Princeton, NJ: Princeton University Press.

Cameron, Rondo. (1963). "Banking in the Early Stages of Industrialization: A Preliminary Survey." *Scandinavian Economic History Review* 11(2):117–134.

Demetriades, Panicos O., and Khaled A. Hussein. (1996). "Does Financial Development Cause Economic Growth? Time-Series Evidence from 16 Countries." *Journal of Development Economics* 51(2):387–411.

Fohlin, Caroline. (2007). *Finance Capitalism and Germany's Rise to Industrial Power.* New York: Cambridge University Press.

Goldsmith, Raymond W. (1969). *Financial Structure and Development.* New Haven, CT: Yale University Press.

Gurley, John G., and Edward S. Shaw. (1955). "Financial Aspects of Economic Development." *American Economic Review* 45(3):515–538.

Hansson, Pontus, and Lars Jonung. (1997). "Finance and Economic Growth: The Case of Sweden 1834–1991." *Research in Economics* 51(3):275–301.

Jordà, Òscar, Moritz Schularick, and Alan M. Taylor. (2013). "Sovereigns versus Banks: Credit, Crises, Consequences." Working Paper No. 19506, National Bureau of Economic Research.

King, Robert G., and Ross Levine. (1993). "Finance and Growth: Schumpeter Might Be Right." *Quarterly Journal of Economics* 108(3):717–737.

Levine, Ross, Norman Loayza, and Thorsten Beck. (2000). "Financial Intermediation and Growth: Causality and Causes." *Journal of Monetary Economics* 46(1):31–77.

McKinnon, Ronald I. (1973). *Money and Capital in Economic Development.* Washington, DC: Brookings Institution.

McLean, Ian W. (2006). "Recovery from Depression: Australia in an Argentine Mirror 1895–1913." *Australian Economic History Review* 46(3):215–241.

Musacchio, Aldo. (2009). *Experiments in Financial Democracy: Corporate Governance and Financial Development in Brazil, 1882–1950.* Cambridge: Cambridge University Press.

Obstfeld, Maurice, and Alan M. Taylor. (2000). *Global Capital Markets: Integration, Crises, and Growth.* Japan–US Center Sanwa Monographs on International Financial Markets. New York: Cambridge University Press.

Radelet, Steven, and Jeffrey D. Sachs. (1998). "The East Asian Financial Crisis: Diagnosis, Remedies, Prospects." *Brooking Papers on Economic Activity* 1:1–90.

Reinhart, Carmen M, and Kenneth S. Rogoff. (2009). *This Time Is Different: Eight Centuries of Financial Folly.* Princeton, NJ: Princeton University Press.

Rousseau, Peter L. (1999). "Finance, Investment, and Growth in Meiji-Era Japan." *Japan and the World Economy* 11(2):185–198.

Rousseau, Peter L., and Richard Sylla. (2003). "Financial Systems, Economic Growth, and Globalization." In M. D. Bordo, A. M. Taylor, and J. G. Williamson (eds.), *Globalization in Historical Perspective*, pp. 373–413. Chicago: University of Chicago Press.

Rousseau, Peter L., and Richard Sylla. (2005). "Emerging Financial Markets and Early U.S. Growth." *Explorations in Economic History* 42(1):1–26.

Rousseau, Peter L., and Paul Wachtel. (1998). "Financial Intermediation and Economic Performance: Historical Evidence from Five Industrialized Countries." *Journal of Money, Credit and Banking* 30(4):657–678.

Rousseau, Peter L., and Paul Wachtel. (2011). "What Is Happening to the Impact of Financial Deepening on Economic Growth?" *Economic Inquiry* 49(1):276–288.

Schularick, Moritz, and Alan M. Taylor. (2012). "Credit Booms Gone Bust: Monetary Policy, Leverage Cycles and Financial Crises, 1870-2008." *American Economic Review* 102(2):1029–1061.

Sheppard, David K. (1971). *The Growth and Role of U.K Financial Institutions, 1880–1962.* London: Methuen.

Terrones, Marco. (2004). "Are Credit Booms in Emerging Markets a Concern?" *World Economic Outlook* (April):147–166.

Wachtel, Paul. (2001). "Growth and Finance: What Do We Know and How Do We Know It?" *International Finance* 4(3):335–362.

Wachtel, Paul. (2011). "The Evolution of the Finance Growth Nexus." *Comparative Economic Studies* 53(3):475–488.

3

Financing U.S. Economic Growth, 1790–1860: Corporations, Markets, and the Real Economy

Robert E. Wright

National income statisticians and econometricians will continue to study precisely *when* and *where* real (price level adjusted) per capita income grew in the antebellum United States, but nobody doubts that it was about two and a half to three times higher on the eve of the Civil War than it had been at the new nation's founding just a lifetime before (Lindert and Williamson 2013). Scholars also generally agree on *how* real income growth occurred: relative political stability enabled development of the agricultural and transportation sectors, which freed up sufficient resources (people and land) to allow growth in the higher value-added manufacturing sector, the so-called Industrial Revolution. More difficult, as always, is determining *why* growth occurred.

This chapter, building on the econometric analysis in Rousseau and Sylla (2005), shows that the development of a modern financial *system* composed of six interconnected institutions – a stable unit of account, a central bank, a banking sector, an insurance sector, securities markets, and a for-profit corporate sector – triggered (was the proximate cause of) increases in per capita income in the early United States by aiding and stimulating investment in the agricultural, transportation, manufacturing, and other real sectors. The modern financial system, in turn, arose due to an improved system of governance that credibly committed to protect the lives, liberty, and property of a significant segment of the population, most literate white males (Acemoglu and Robinson 2012). Convinced that their governance reforms (independence from Britain followed by establishment of the Constitution) secured their basic civil rights, those Americans had powerful incentives to work harder and smarter, which of course improved their productivity (Madison 1792; Gallatin 1831).

The chapter first surveys how earlier generations of scholars characterized the early U.S. financial system and generally downplayed its relationship to American economic growth and development. The next section describes a more recent view, popularized by Edwin Perkins, Richard Sylla, and others, that attributes America's early growth to its governance and financial revolutions. With the aid of a new database of early corporate charters, the next four sections show how the financial system enabled and even spurred the more famous "revolutions" (really evolutions) in agriculture, transportation, and manufacturing, as well as the less intensively studied productivity improvements in the construction, utilities, and service sectors. The conclusion explains that while the antebellum financial system was imperfect in many ways, it was somewhat responsive to shocks. It also notes that other nations that developed economically prior to the twentieth century, from the Netherlands to Japan, experienced governance and financial revolutions prior to productivity increases in their real sectors, suggesting that the U.S. experience was not exceptional but rather an example of a standard developmental pattern.

Historiographical Background

Early scholars generally misconstrued or entirely missed the role of the financial system in early and antebellum America's governance, agricultural, transportation, and industrial revolutions. Before the disintegration of the Bretton Woods monetary system in the early 1970s, scholars generally ignored, downplayed, or underestimated the complexity, modernity, and size of America's early financial system – that is, banks, insurers, and securities markets and their interactions (Nettels 1962). Studies by Redlich (1947), Payne and Davis (1956), Hammond (1957), Fenstermaker (1965), and others made important contributions to scholars' understanding of early banks and banking, but they did not portray banks as part of a wider financial system that drove economic growth. Krooss and Blyn (1971, p. 37), in fact, *apologized* for the "failure" of financial intermediaries to make "a substantial contribution to the total economy," arguing that banks and insurers were "in the early stages of experiment." Even in the late antebellum period, they argued, new technologies, such as telegraphs and railroads, drove financial development rather than the reverse. Finance "comes of age" in their view only during and after the Civil War (p. 91). Davis et al. (1972) claimed that prior to 1828, "many bankers had little commitment to even the concept of reserves" (p. 347) and that "commercial banks were almost the only type of financial intermediary" (p. 349), and generally portrayed the early financial sector as primitive.

The limited role ascribed to finance in economic growth reflected both prevailing economic theory (Robinson 1952; Lucas 1988) and the realities of postwar financial policies, which were characterized by what some have termed "financial repression" (Turner 2014). To reduce the likelihood of a repeat of the rampant bank failures of the Great Depression, regulators restricted new entry into banking, capped the rate of interest that banks could pay to different types of depositors, separated investment and commercial banking activities, and limited bank mergers and de novo branching. Such policies limited competition and thus reduced incentives for risk taking by enabling bankers to earn relatively high returns without much exertion, innovation, or risk (D'Arista 1994). Moreover, international finance remained relatively unimportant during the postwar Bretton Woods system because the nations of the free world wanted fixed exchange rates and wide latitude in their domestic monetary policies, choices that effectively forced them to impose international capital controls (Obstfeld, Shambaugh, and Taylor 2005).

The Bretton Woods system of fixed exchange rates and capital controls came under increasing strain in the 1960s and broke down entirely in the early 1970s, leading to a rapid expansion in international banking and finance. At the same time, domestic inflationary pressures led to a variety of reforms that deregulated banking, insurance, and various financial markets, leading to a period of rapid development and growth of the financial sector that some scholars have termed "financialization" (Epstein 2006; Palley 2013). Instead of passively following developments in the real economy, especially the manufacturing sector, as the repressed postwar financial sector seemed to have done, the rapidly changing post–Bretton Woods financial system increasingly appeared to be a driver of economic growth, a notion fueled by Goldsmith (1969), McKinnon (1973), Shaw (1973), King and Levine (1993), and other proponents of what came to be called the finance-led growth hypothesis, who argued that modern financial systems stimulate growth by lowering the transaction costs of linking investors to innovators (intermediation), reducing asymmetric information (including adverse selection and moral hazard), increasing the efficiency of asset allocation, smoothing consumption over time, and other channels (for an overview, see Levine 1997 or Levine 2005).

Economic historians were of course part of that same change in the Zeitgeist, and unsurprisingly some began to scour history for examples of finance-led growth. While Cameron (1967), Neal (1990), and others concentrated on Europe, especially the Netherlands (Tracy 1985) and Great

Britain (Dickson 1967; Cottrell 1980), several hit upon the early United States. Lamoreaux (1994), for example, found that banks in eastern New England financed various commercial and industrial enterprises. Perkins (1994) broadly surveyed the early U.S. financial system and, although he underestimated the importance of early securities markets and insurers (pp. 282–324), he did argue that the "financial services" sector laid "the foundation for the future development of the American economic and political systems" by fostering "steady economic advancement" (p. 1). Following the lead of Schumpeter (1942), and applying the insights of Gerschenkron (1962), Trescott (1963), Cameron (1967), and others, Sylla (1972a, 1972b, 1976, 1977, 1982a, 1982b, 1985) was even more adamant about the causal link between the early U.S. financial sector, which he characterized as a true *system* (i.e., composed of interdependent parts), and economic growth.

To further establish the causal connection between finance and growth in the early United States, Sylla teamed up with other scholars to obtain grants from the National Science Foundation which funded the creation of three datasets that added considerable quantitative weight to his conclusions. The first, reported in Sylla, Legler, and Wallis (1987) and Wallis, Sylla, and Legler (1994), laid bare the link between state governments' respective sources of revenue and their incentives for promoting the banking industry. The second, reported in Sylla (1998) and Wright (2002b) and housed on EH.net (http://eh.net/database/early-u-s-securities-prices), demonstrated that the early United States was home to several efficient domestic securities markets that were linked to markets in Europe, especially London (Sylla, Wilson, and Wright 2006), and laid the basis for important econometric work such as Rousseau and Sylla (2005). The third database, reported in Wright and Sylla (2011), Wright (2014a), and herein, is housed at Penn Libraries (http://repository.upenn.edu/mead/7). It documents that before the U.S. Civil War (1861–1865), entrepreneurs chartered tens of thousands of business corporations – an order of magnitude more than early scholars had estimated (Wright 2014a, pp. 231–232).

Thanks to the work of those and other scholars (cited in the following paragraphs where appropriate), the economic growth of the early United States can now be convincingly attributed to a governance revolution (1787–1788), which established a new constitutional order that inspired the confidence of numerous entrepreneurs and investors at home and abroad, and a financial revolution (1789–1794) that rapidly assembled the six major components of a modern financial system: a stable unit of account, a central bank, a banking sector, an insurance sector, securities markets, and a for-profit corporate sector. The corporate sector included financial as well as many non-financial corporations, and is here considered part of the financial *system* (as opposed to the narrower financial sector) because all for-profit corporations engaged in corporate finance (i.e., the selling of shares and bonds, the obtaining of loans, the issuing of promissory notes, and so forth). The components of the modern financial system then interacted with agents in the real economy – in the agricultural, transportation, manufacturing, construction, utilities, and service sectors – to stimulate increased efficiency and hence higher per capita incomes.

America's Governance and Financial Revolutions

Scholars know that ratification of the U.S. Constitution in 1788 greatly increased confidence among business owners, entrepreneurs, and investors because numerous contemporaries explicitly said so and quantitative evidence supports their assertions. Manufacturing advocate, Treasury Department official, and early economic statistician Tench Coxe (1794, p. xi) claimed that "there was never applied, to the improvement and advancement of Pennsylvania, so great an aggregate of money as is employed directly or indirectly at the present time." He then listed a series of canals, river improvements, the Lancaster turnpike, bridges, and "mills, work-shops and dwelling houses in every town and every quarter of the state." "The actual situation of many parts" of the country, he asserted, was "nearly *the reverse* [emphasis in original] of what it was at times within the memory of children" (p. 1). It was all due, he believed, to the expectation that the new government would maintain "with sincerity and vigilance *the freedom of its citizens*, and with energy and firmness, *the rights of property*" [emphases in original] (p. 4). Many others concurred, including overseas investors (Stadnitski 1792; Opal 2008; Wright 2008).

Confidence in the new government spurred innovation and investment in the financial sector as well as in the real economy. Rapid financial modernization, in turn, aided the new government's stability, engendering yet more confidence. In 1789, when Alexander Hamilton became the nation's first Secretary of the Treasury, the new United States effectively enjoyed none of the six major components of a modern financial system: strong public finances and debt management, a known and stable unit of account; a central bank; a commercial banking *system*; mechanisms for sharing or trading risks; integrated securities markets; and numerous limited liability corporations (Sylla 2002, 2003). By the time Hamilton left office in early 1795, the new nation enjoyed all six [including derivatives markets (cf. Banner 1998)] and Dutch, British, and other European investors eagerly purchased American securities (Van Winter and Riley 1977; Wilkins 1989; Wright 2008) and lands (Stadnitski 1792; Brooks 1996).

Hamilton developed and steered to passage legislation that defined the dollar in terms of gold and silver (Wright 2005), encouraged the development of securities markets and corporations (Wright 2002a; Wright and Cowen 2006), including insurers (Wright and Kingston 2012), and established a central bank that could branch across state lines, act as a lender of last resort to the government or to the entire commercial sector during crises (Sylla, Wright, and Cowen 2009), and tie the nation's growing number of banks into a coherent system (Cowen 2000). Hamilton also funded the national debt through tariffs and import duties and assumed the debts of the several states, thereby fostering the development of liquid securities markets and binding the allegiance of bondholders – past, present, and prospective – to the nascent federal government (Wright 2008). We cannot know for certain if the Union would have come apart without Hamilton's funding and assumption programs, but many contemporaries (Coxe 1794) and historians (Cunningham 1987; Schoen 2010) believed that the young national government was quite fragile because of contentious issues such as slavery and tariffs (Einhorn 2006; Mason 2006). Tellingly, the men behind three important challenges to the Union – the Hartford Convention (1814–1815), the Nullification Crisis (1832–1833), and the Secession Crisis (1860–1861) – did not own appreciable sums of federal bonds (Wright 2008).

Of course the nation's early financial system did not arise fully formed from the head of Hamilton. Many other individuals were involved in the financial revolution, such as bankers Thomas Willing and Stephen Girard, financiers William Duer and Robert Morris, author-bureaucrat-merchant Tench Coxe, and Treasury Secretary Albert Gallatin (McCraw 2012; Wright and Cowen 2006). Scores of other important early financiers could be adduced, including serial corporate entrepreneur and investor Israel Thorndike (Forbes 1953), long-time U.S. Treasurer Michael Hillegas (Wright 2005), merchant banker William Bingham (Alberts 1969), entrepreneur and speculator John Nicholson (Arbuckle 1975), banker and insurance man Alexander Bryan Johnson (Todd and Sonkin 1977), and a slew of long-lived bank cashiers and insurance company presidents.

Moreover, the financial system Hamilton and the others founded continued to develop as financiers innovated in response to changing market and political conditions (Sylla 2001). The locus of innovation first centered in Philadelphia, but by the late 1830s it had shifted to New York (Wright 2005). Wall Street continues to symbolize American high finance today, but Manhattan never monopolized financial innovation in the United States, which has always been home to competitive regional securities exchanges (Wright 2002a, 2002b; Vitiello and Thomas 2010), money centers, investment funds (Allen 2015), and bank and insurance regulators. Overall, the early U.S. financial system was competitive and innovative even if parts of it, such as the unit banks that dominated some states, were relatively uncompetitive and fragile (Calomiris and Haber 2014). Competition between companies within an industry but also among industries (e.g., between life insurers and savings banks in the mortgage market) ensured that the financial system rebounded from macroeconomic and political shocks and that it evolved to meet the changing needs of each major economic sector, from agriculture to utilities.

Financing Farming and Other Extractive Industries

It has long been known that agriculture, "the spring of our commerce, and the parent of our manufactures" (Coxe 1794, p. 7), received indirect aid from a financial system purportedly dominated by merchants, men who exchanged the nation's agricultural surpluses for manufactured goods, mostly foreign at first but later increasingly domestic (e.g., cotton textiles). Until recently, however, scholars underestimated the importance of bank finance and insurance to America's agricultural evolution, the "modest annual growth in output per worker" (Weiss 1991, p. 14), and crop yields that took place over the first half of the nineteenth century.

Part of that productivity growth was due to mechanization, of course, that is, substituting machines for human and/or animal labor (Lindstrom 1978; Weiss 1991), but a surprising amount of it, up to half in fact, was driven by biological and cultural advances, to wit strains of grain better adapted to local climatic conditions, better pest management techniques, and more efficient fertilizing, planting, and sowing practices (Nettels 1962). As the transportation evolution discussed in succeeding paragraphs progressed, specialization [roughly into von Thunen rings, Lindstrom (1978) claimed] brought additional productivity gains in key crops such as cotton (Whartenby 1977), corn, and small grains (Rothenberg 1992; Craig 1993; Peskin 2003; Neem 2008), as well as in livestock, including beef cattle, dairy cattle, draft horses, goats, hogs, and sheep (Olmstead and Rhode 2008).

Certainly some early American farmers were rural rubes content to scratch out a bare subsistence, but many were ambitious men who wanted to accumulate wealth, men who were not content merely to maintain their absolute condition (Kulikoff 1992; Opal 2008). Climatic variability and the Red Queen problem, the fact that agriculturalists have to innovate simply to maintain yields in the face of rapidly evolving rusts, smut fungi, flies, midges, weeds, and other threats, means that most farmers would have been bankrupted if they did not have inexpensive methods for smoothing their incomes (Olmstead and Rhode 2002). Moreover, it is difficult to see how farmers in regions such as Northern Virginia, who switched from tobacco to grain in the late eighteenth and early nineteenth centuries, could have done so without some way of smoothing their incomes and mitigating other risks (Crothers 1999, 2001).

The percentage of farmers who enjoyed access to credit markets (as borrowers and/or as savers) in any given place and year is not known with precision, but likely it was usually closer to one hundred percent than to zero or even fifty. The interesting question is the terms by which farmers could borrow. Scholars who claim that early "banks served capitalists but ignored farmers" (Kulikoff 1992, p. 108) took complaints about a lack of banking facilities too seriously and charter stipulations that required banks to lend to farmers or other specific groups not seriously enough. Complaints about banks often came from men who had limited understanding of actual commercial practices or, more often, were fighting legislative battles to establish banks of their own in the period before general incorporation statutes (Hammond 1957; Papenfuse 1975; Wright 1997).

Early American agriculturalists indeed borrowed from banks. Coxe (1794, p. 352) claimed that banks by 1792, while still few, ministered to the "convenience, the necessities, and the interests of . . . the planter, the farmer, the merchant . . . the fisherman." Wright (1997, 2001) showed that rural banks such as the Bank of Utica regularly lent to farmers. Lockard (2000) showed that 28 percent of the people who borrowed from the Hampshire Bank of Northampton, Massachusetts between 1813 and 1837 were farmers and that they received 27 percent of the total sum lent. Farmers were 37 percent of all borrowers and received a third of all loans from the Franklin Bank in Greenfield, Massachusetts, between 1827 and 1829. The nearby Franklin Savings Institute lent almost 18 percent of its funds to farmers between 1838 and 1850. Farmers' share dropped to

14 percent between 1851 and 1860, but the total number of loans almost doubled and the total dollar volume of loans to farmers increased two and a half times. Between 1843 and 1860, the Northampton Institute for Savings of Northampton, Massachusetts lent 18 percent of its funds to farmers. Wang (2006) showed that by the 1840s, the Plymouth Bank lent about 7 percent of its funds to farmers (and another 9 to 10 percent to mariners, Massachusetts' farmers of the sea). The Worcester Bank also lent to agriculturalists (Brooke 1989). Bodenhorn (2000) showed that in the early 1850s, more than 10 percent of the loans of Branch & Company of Petersburg, Virginia went to agriculturalists.

According to Hammond (1957, p. 678), in 1840 a little less than half of the Bank of Indiana's loans went to merchants; the balance went to "manufacturers, mechanics, farmers" and miscellaneous others. But that is not to say that merchants received more than their seeming due as agriculturalists also borrowed from banks indirectly, via the factors, millers, and merchants who could extend farmers and planters credit because they had access to bank discounts by virtue of the superior cash flow characteristics of their businesses (Kilbourne 1995, 2006). Such indirect loans, of course, cost farmers more than borrowing directly from banks, which rationed on quantity due to usury laws and costly charters as well as asymmetric information (Wright 2002a). "Out of doors" markets, markets for informal person-to-person loans often made at usurious (illegally high) rates, appear to have been competitive. The complaint was always that "note shavers" were too common, not that they were difficult to find (Anon. 1837; Mayer 2010). Making usurious loans was technically illegal but not strenuously enforced. Ergo, if somewhat paradoxically, entry and exit into the market were unrestricted, so interest rates and other terms probably reflected rational expectations of the risks inherent in agricultural activities.

Agriculturalists also borrowed long term by mortgaging their land, livestock, and/or slaves (Kilbourne 1995, 2006). Lenders included individuals, insurers, and trust companies (Haeger 1981; Thornton 2007; Murphy 2010; Stickle 2011). Scholars have not tied specific agricultural loans to specific innovations in a systematic way, but they do not have to exert the effort because the proceeds of loans were fungible and the mere knowledge that one could smooth income over time, whether actually consummated or not, likely increased innovation and risk taking.

As Table 3.1 shows, few agriculturalists needed to incorporate their businesses, but securities markets supplemented banks in the financing of other extractive industries, most importantly the more than 1,300

Table 3.1 *Number and Capitalization of Specially Chartered Extractive Sector Corporations, 1790–1860*

Business Type	Number Chartered	Total Minimum Authorized Capital ($)
Agriculture	35	$1,395,000
Fishery	41	$2,251,000
Lumber	122	$1,563,500
Mining	1,322	$349,237,500
Quarry	116	$16,873,500
Totals	**1,636**	**$371,320,500**

Source: Richard Sylla and Robert E. Wright, "U.S. Corporate Development, 1801–1860," NSF SES Grant No. 0751577 (hereafter, Sylla and Wright database, which can be downloaded from http://repository.upenn.edu/mead/7).

mining corporations, nominally capitalized at almost $350 million, that received special charters prior to the Civil War. Banks also financed niche extractive industries, including the largely unincorporated Kanawha salt producers of western Virginia (Stealey 2000) and the whalers of New Bedford, Massachusetts (Wright 2011b). Whalers also obtained marine insurance, increasingly from incorporated insurers (Wright and Kingston 2012).

Agriculturalists did not benefit directly from marine insurance until the development of inland insurance in the early nineteenth century permitted them to insure produce in transit, which allowed them to ship to more distant markets with less risk. They also insured their property against fire – by forming specialized mutual farm insurers when necessary – and eventually against hail, wind, livestock theft, and other perils, including the death of their slaves. Agriculturalists, especially northern farmers, also insured their own lives in rapidly increasing numbers after 1820. It is a pernicious sociological myth that agriculturalists eschewed income protection. Young and/or leveraged farmers especially understood the risks that their premature death would pose for their families (Murphy 2010; Wright 2010).

Insurance constituted an important part of the financial system in its own right, one almost as important as commercial banking. Before the Civil War, more than 2,100 insurance companies chartered under special acts of incorporation and the combined initial capitalization of the almost 1,300 joint stock and hybrid (part joint stock, part mutual) specially incorporated insurers totaled between $212 million and $388 million

Table 3.2 *Number and Capitalization of Specially Chartered Insurance Corporations, 1790–1860*

Business Type	Number Chartered	Total Minimum Authorized Capital ($)
Insurance and banking	10	$2,257,500
Insurance, fire	782	$35,990,000
Insurance, general	411	$44,091,500
Insurance, health	25	$1,942,500
Insurance, life	87	$14,455,000
Insurance, livestock	23	$365,000
Insurance, marine	172	$24,905,000
Insurance, multiline	609	$88,945,000
Insurance, slave	3	$200,000
Totals	**2,122**	**$213,151,500**

Source: Sylla and Wright database.

(see Table 3.2). Specially incorporated banks were less numerous (1,564) but more highly capitalized ($445 million to $668 million) (Wright and Kingston 2012). Insurers also directly aided economic growth. In addition to serving as important intermediaries, they created significant positive externalities related to safety in the home, shop, and vessel (Wright 2010).

Importantly, early agriculturalists were a major class of investor. Savings allowed farmers and planters to assume greater risks in their agricultural pursuits by allowing them to smooth their incomes over time. In other words, instead of borrowing when a new strain of wheat or cotton did not take hold, or when they needed a new machine or piece of land, farmers could divest financial assets instead. In addition to lending to other individuals on note and mortgage (Rothenberg 1992; Kilbourne 1995, 2006), farmers and planters purchased corporate bonds and equities and government bonds. Careful study by Rothenberg (1992) showed that financial assets owned by agriculturalists at their death increased dramatically during the nation's first decades across all wealth levels except the poorest. By 1850, about 15 percent of total investor wealth at death was invested, on average, in corporate stocks and bonds, up from an average of less than 4 percent in 1800 (Sturm 1977).

Stock subscription lists tell a similar story (Wright 1997, 2001). Of the initial 100 investors in the Bank of Gettysburg, chartered in Pennsylvania in 1814, for example, fifty-three were farmers (Karmel 1999). Many of the subscribers in the Bank of Concord, chartered in Massachusetts in

1832, were described as "gentlemen farmers," that is, older, affluent agriculturalists (Patterson 1971, p. 20). Although Majewski (2006) did not attempt to identify the occupations of stockholders in Pennsylvania banks, the stockholders were so numerous, even in agricultural districts, that many must have been farmers. The same could be said of many of the thousands of stockholders in Maine's banks, manufacturers, and transportation companies in the 1830s and 1840s documented by Wright (2002b).

In sum, the modern financial system of the early United States greatly aided the extractive sector of the economy by providing farmers, fishers, miners, and such with a stable unit of account with which to conduct business, access to bank loans or other credit, a means to sell equity stakes in their businesses when appropriate, mechanisms for sharing income and property risks, and ways to save wealth in anticipation of temporary reductions in income or other shocks.

Transportation Finance

Agriculturalists, especially northern farmers, were also avid investors in transportation corporations, including bridges, canals, railroads, and turnpikes (Majewski 2000). Some of the return from such investments came in the form of coupon and dividend payments or securities price appreciation, and some came in the form of lower transportation costs, higher land values, and profits from construction contracts (Forbes 1953; Klein 1990; Klein and Majewski 1992). Merchants and land speculators invested in transportation companies for similar reasons, while others concentrated on direct investment returns (e.g., dividends), which were not as low as sometimes portrayed (Sanderlin 1946; Wright 2014c). In fact, before the Civil War, private investment in the transportation sector far outpaced public investment (Wright 2014b), which also leaned heavily on the financial system through the sale of bonds to savings banks and other investors at home and abroad (Olmstead 1976).

Insurance companies and banks also helped transportation companies (Wright 2001, 2002b). Lockard (2000), for example, showed that over a quarter of the money lent by Franklin Savings Institute of Greenfield, Massachusetts went to the Connecticut River Railroad Company. Bodenhorn (2000) showed that banks in both the North and South in the 1850s typically made loans to transportation companies, though in prudent sums of less than 5 percent of their total loan portfolios. Banks and insurers also bought transportation company securities, sometimes at the behest of state governments (Perkins 1994), but often to diversify their

Table 3.3 *Number and Capitalization of Specially Chartered Transportation Corporations, 1790–1860*

Business Type	Number Chartered	Total Minimum Authorized Capital ($)
Bridge	1,310	$33,471,855
Canal	404	$90,884,734
Dock	45	$5,055,500
Ferry	165	$6,782,400
Harbor	18	$804,000
Mixed	542	$118,333,683
Navigation	628	$133,042,500
Pier	11	$256,500
Plank road	931	$45,410,375
Railroad	2,503	$2,243,929,250
Telegraph	135	$6,875,128
Transportation	73	$10,936,000
Tunnel	4	$3,450,000
Turnpike	3,683	$119,265,719
Waterway improvement	213	$27,450,100
Wharf	110	$12,355,500
Totals	**10,775**	**$2,858,303,244**

Source: Sylla and Wright database.

securities portfolios (Wright 2002b). Many transportation companies, especially railroads but canals and others as well, issued bonds and almost all issued equity (Wright 2014a, b, c). As Table 3.3 shows, before the Civil War, 10,775 transportation companies of different sorts received special acts of incorporation and were authorized to raise more than $2.8 billion in capital.

Skeptics point out that many transportation companies never began operations or soon failed. That is true, but many did form and raised capital in securities markets. Between 1800 and 1821, more than 23,000 different investors in Pennsylvania alone owned toll bridge or turnpike stock (Majewski 2006). Moreover, the improvements in the transportation sector were very real as both costs and travel times dropped considerably for both passengers and freight (Ratner, Soltow, and Sylla 1993, p. 125). For example, the cost of shipping flour from Harpers Ferry, Virginia, sixty miles east to Washington, DC, fell from $1 to 7 cents per barrel, toll included, after the Chesapeake and Ohio Canal connected the two points in the early 1830s. Competition between that canal and the Baltimore and Ohio Railroad kept rates low and people and goods – agricultural, extractive, and manufactured – flowing. Tonnage doubled to more than 200,000 tons between 1850 and 1851 alone (Sanderlin 1946). Thousands of similar improvements substantially increased market size and enhanced efficiency (Taylor 1951).

Reductions in transportation costs and times wrought by bridges, canals, harbor facilities, railroads, steamboats, and turnpikes were crucial to agriculturalists because the improvements helped them to trade with the wider world more cheaply and quickly (Wright 2014a). Most improvements in time and costs were regional affairs, not national or sectional ones as once believed. Transportation improvements tied emerging and established urban areas to enlarged hinterlands, as was the case with Philadelphia (Lindstrom 1978) as well as Boston, New York, Baltimore, and emerging "western" cities such as Cincinnati and Louisville (Wade 1959; Wright 2009). Always important, the coasting trade also became more efficient through improvements in lighthouses, ships, tugs, and so forth, as well as the introduction of packet services (Coxe 1794). Before the Civil War, coastwise vessels, along with the Erie Canal–Great Lakes complex and the major river systems, not trunk railroads, tied together East and West, North and South.

Like the extractive sector, then, the transportation sector relied heavily on the young nation's modern financial system. Infrastructure corporations such as bridges, canals, railroads, and turnpikes received large initial investments provided by thousands of domestic and foreign investors active in the nation's equity and bond markets, as well as short-term operating loans made by banks. To thrive, the sector also needed, and received, insurance services and a stable unit of account and long distance payment system.

Investing in Industry

The transportation evolution, combined with the evolution in agriculture and the revolutions in governance and finance, made America's industrialization possible by reducing interest rates, country risk, and labor and transportation costs to the point that domestic manufacturers, sometimes with significant tariff protection and sometimes without, could compete against foreign manufacturers in many markets. The fact that palm-leaf hats were one of central Massachusetts's largest industries throughout the last three decades of the antebellum period is one indication of how far matters had progressed: palm leaves had to be imported from Cuba, and the quantity of lightweight palm-leaf hats produced (70,000 in 1837 alone) far exceeded local demand, so most were shipped to Boston and beyond, including the slave South (Brooke 1989).

With access to larger markets, artisans, mechanics, home manufacturers/farmers, and other proto-manufacturers, as well as merchants seeking to diversify their investment portfolios (Coxe 1794; Livesay and Porter 1972), expanded operations to tap scale economies (Wright 2002b, 2014a) and/or specialized to an extent impossible to achieve in a smaller market (Lindstrom 1978). Economies of scale did not entail building factories considered large by later standards but simply enlarging existing facilities such as those described in an 1815 bank loan application by soap boiler John Wirt:

> I ask the favour of inlargeing my accommodation as I have been making soap & candles in the small way & find it will answer well … will make from 3 to 4000 weight of soap per week if I can get Capitall to Lay in Stock (as quoted in Wright 2002b, p. 205).

Wirt had "Good workmen" as did other manufacturing establishments that found former farmers, shopkeepers, and artisans, children who no longer needed to work the family farm or shop, and/or immigrants willing to work for wages that they could afford to pay.

Other manufacturers, including Oliver Evans, opted to mechanize rather than to simply expand traditional operations (Coxe 1794; Ware 1924; Cochran 1979). By 1820, some American manufactured goods were already being exported, and exports grew, albeit modestly, between then and the Civil War (Peskin 2003). Industrial production for domestic markets grew much faster and was substantially larger (Davis 2004). By 1860, more than 140,000 manufacturers were in operation in the United States, with a total in excess of $1 billion in capital invested. The ten largest industries, by value added, were cotton; lumber; boots and shoes; flour; men's clothing; iron; machinery; woolens; carriages, wagons, and carts; and leather (Taylor 1951). The cotton, woolen, and iron industries were extremely competitive, which drove consumer prices down and created strong incentives to improve operating efficiency (Spalding 1963; Knowles 2013).

The notion that manufacturers received minimal help from the financial system is almost as well entrenched as the notion that agriculturalists did not receive bank loans (cf. Bodenhorn 2000 for a discussion). Douglass (1971, p. 251), for example, claimed that "capital accumulation in the New England companies came mostly from within the industry." In fact, manufacturers relied heavily on all major parts of the financial system. For starters, they used inland marine and fire insurance to protect their products and businesses from loss. The Pepperell Mill, for example, insured cotton in transit from the port of purchase to its facilities in Maine. Most manufacturers had to pay higher fire insurance premiums than other businesses did but that was because they posed higher risks until they began to adopt sundry safety measures (Knowlton 1948). When extant insurers resisted underwriting certain risks, so-called class mutuals (e.g., mutual mill insurers) arose to meet the demand. The interaction between insurers and insured led to the adoption of cost-efficient new safety and design features such as fire-resistant mills that kept blazes contained until workers could respond and put the fire out (Wright 2010).

Manufacturers also received short-term bank loans. Coxe (1794, p. 352) claimed that by 1792 banks ministered to the "convenience, the necessities, and the interests of ... the ship-builder, the manufacturer, and the mechanic." Lamoreaux (1994) showed that manufacturers in eastern New England formed their own banks and lent to themselves without compunction. In other places, outsider lending was more the norm, but manufacturers still received discounts (Wang 2006). Adams (1978) showed that for more than two decades some 10 to 15 percent of the depositors/borrowers in Stephen Girard's private bank in Philadelphia were artisans or mechanics. Wright (1997, 1999, 2001, 2002a) showed that banks such as the Bank of Utica, the Bank of Geneva, the Bank of Germantown, the Bank of New York, the Manhattan Company, and the Bank of North America regularly lent to artisans and mechanics.

In addition, Lockard (2000) showed that 20 percent of the entities that borrowed from the Hampshire Bank between 1813 and 1837 were artisans or manufacturers and that they received about 20 percent of the total sum lent. Borrowers included several ax makers, paper millers, and hatters, a broom maker, a tanner, a carding machine manufacturer, and a saddle and harness maker. Manufacturers and artisans constituted one in three borrowers in the Franklin Bank and received a third of all sums lent between 1827 and 1829. Loan recipients included tanners, iron works, a flaxseed oil producer, and a satinet manufacturer. The nearby Franklin Savings Institute lent 7 percent of its funds to artisans and manufacturers between 1838 and 1850, but their share increased to 10 percent between 1851 and 1860. Borrowers included grain, woolen, and saw mills, boot and shoe and cutlery manufacturers, and a baby carriage maker. Between 1843 and 1860, the Northampton Institute for Savings of Northampton, Massachusetts lent about 17 percent of its funds to artisans and manufacturers. Borrowers included sundry textile companies, a sash and blind manufacturer, and a brickyard. The Worcester Bank and other Worcester County banks "readily granted" loans to the many artisans and manufacturers of central Massachusetts (Brooke 1989), and the Plymouth Bank by the 1840s lent more than 27 percent of its loan funds to artisans and manufacturers (Wang 2006).

Moreover, Bodenhorn (2000) showed that in the early 1850s, more than 20 percent of the loans of Branch & Company of Petersburg, Virginia went to manufacturers. The Black River Bank of Watertown, New York, also regularly invested more than 10 percent of its loan portfolio in borrowers primarily engaged in manufacturing, while at the same time the Bank of Tennessee's branch in Memphis usually had 5 percent or more of its loan portfolio lent out to manufacturers (Bodenhorn 2000).

According to Knowlton (1948), the Pepperell Mill regularly received short- and medium-term (up to one year) loans from commercial, private, and savings bankers as well as from trusts (individuals and companies) and note brokers. In the two decades before the Civil War, some twenty commercial banks and several note brokerages throughout New England discounted the mill's accounts receivable to the tune of hundreds of thousands of dollars.

In addition, and against received wisdom, thousands of early manufacturers received help from the securities markets. Navin and Sears (1955) were right that relatively few industrials were listed on stock exchanges until late in the nineteenth century. Only about 100 appear in the Sylla, Wilson, and Wright antebellum securities database referenced earlier, which lists the prices of securities published in newspapers in Boston, New York, Philadelphia, and elsewhere. Before the Civil War, however, more than 3,500 manufacturers obtained special corporate charters and were authorized to raise almost $472 million in capital (see Table 3.4). They issued stock directly to investors, and the stock subsequently traded via the nation's ubiquitous over-the-counter markets and hence did not need to be listed on the exchanges or in the newspapers (Wright 2002a, b). Banks and insurers bought stock in early manufacturers, as did individual investors, including farmers (Davis 1958, 1960). Due to corporate governance strictures that limited stock watering, liquidity was largely one-sided: stockholders could sell whenever they wanted, but investors had to await the appearance of sellers before they could buy in (Spalding 1963; Wright 2002b, 2014).

Like agriculturalists, manufacturers also used the financial system to smooth their incomes by saving at times and diversifying their incomes

Table 3.4 *Number and Capitalization of Specially Chartered Manufacturing Corporations, 1790–1860*

Business Type	Number Chartered	Total Minimum Authorized Capital ($)
Alcohol	9	$860,000
Bricks	16	$1,025,000
Chemicals	21	$2,775,000
Copper	13	$3,720,000
Fertilizer	7	$145,000
Finished goods	182	$20,515,000
Firearms	28	$5,495,000
Foodstuffs	24	$2,915,000
Footware	31	$1,281,000
Glass	76	$6,940,000
Ice	29	$1,335,000
India rubber	20	$1,715,000
Iron	215	$26,677,250
Lead	12	$1,505,000
Lime	8	$252,500
Locomotive	38	$6,195,000
Lumber	28	$3,575,000
Machinery	52	$6,478,000
Metallurgy	67	$8,975,000
Mill	210	$10,189,900
Mixed	674	$112,119,000
Oil	12	$920,000
Paper	54	$3,523,300
Plaster	4	$310,000
Pottery	10	$1,011,000
Printing	21	$2,053,000
Salt	19	$2,128,000
Ships	18	$3,891,000
Steam engines	16	$1,935,000
Sugar	35	$7,240,000
Textiles	1,183	$180,360,850
Unknown	434	$43,593,500
Totals	**3,566**	**$471,653,300**

Source: Sylla and Wright database.

even during good times. Patterson (1971), for example, noted that artisans were stockholders in the Concord Bank. Majewski (2006) showed that artisans and manufacturers invested heavily in Philadelphia bank shares in the 1810s, and of course artisans and mechanics were well represented in savings banks, the poorer as depositors and the richer as borrowers (Payne and Davis 1956; Olmstead 1976).

Doubtless, then, the country's modern financial system was of crucial importance to the Industrial Revolution that began in earnest in the early nineteenth century (Davis 2004). Not all manufacturers incorporated and hence tapped the country's capital markets (Scranton 1983), but they all relied upon some combination of a stable unit of account, insurance, and bank credit (direct or indirect) to finance their value-added activities.

Construction, Utility, and Service Corporations

Few write about utilities or construction revolutions, perhaps because they are seen as part and parcel of industrial progress. As shown in Table 3.5, both sectors utilized the securities markets. Both needed and obtained insurance, primarily fire but also life in the case of the unincorporated construction contractors ubiquitous throughout the nation in the early national and antebellum periods (Rilling 2000). Like other artisans, those contractors received bank loans and were eager recipients of mortgages and, in places such as Philadelphia and Baltimore, ground rents, an early form of interest-only perpetual mortgage (Wright 2005).

The term *service revolution* is usually associated with the latter half of the twentieth century, but of course provision of various (nonfinancial)

Table 3.5 *Number and Capitalization of Specially Chartered Construction and Utilities Corporations, 1790–1860*

Business Type	Number Chartered	Total Minimum Authorized Capital ($)
Construction	193	$41,831,400
Dam	58	$2,120,000
Energy	19	$1,761,400
Gas	367	$37,072,000
Mixed	56	$19,701,625
Water	472	$26,434,530
Totals	**1,165**	**$128,920,955**

Source: Sylla and Wright database.

Table 3.6 *Number and Capitalization of Specially Chartered Service Corporations,*
1790–1860

Business Type	Number Chartered	Total Minimum Authorized Capital ($)
Cemetery	77	$413,900
Colonization	3	$1,030,000
Education	6	$215,000
Entertainment	35	$2,537,600
Fire protection	16	$15,000
Hospital	2	$75,000
Hospitality	90	$10,146,600
Hotel	322	$24,691,500
Library	6	$234,000
Livery	2	$3,000
Market	48	$6,091,500
Mercantile	35	$6,026,000
Mixed	9	$3,280,000
Museum	3	$360,000
Newspaper	5	$410,000
Park	6	$444,750
Salvage	7	$1,515,000
Scientific	2	$25,000
Warehouse	18	$1,363,000
Totals	**692**	**$58,876,850**

Source: Sylla and Wright database.

services is as old as the country itself. What is interesting is that before the
Civil War, some service providers, detailed in Table 3.6, were large enough
to benefit from special incorporation. While clearly third in importance to
the primary and manufacturing sectors, the service sector was already
growing, and some service providers were already in need of external
financing from securities markets. Many service companies, whether
incorporated or not, needed bank financing, insurance, and a stable monetary system in order to thrive.

Conclusion

Space limitations preclude full discussion of the reversals suffered by the
financial sector between Hamilton's financial revolution and the Civil War:

the closing of the first and second Bank of the United States in 1811 and 1836, respectively; the stress on the payments system and the instability of the unit of account caused by the suspension of specie payments during the War of 1812 and following the Panic of 1819 (Michener and Wright 2006); the corporate governance scandals of the 1820s (Hilt 2009); the complete repayment of the national debt in the 1830s (Wright 2008); and the financial panics of the 1830s, 1840s, and 1850s (Sylla 2007). The financial system, however, proved remarkably resilient as free banking replicated some of the functions of a central bank (Bodenhorn 2000, 2003), state and railroad debt supplanted federal government bonds in investment portfolios, and corporate governance adapted to evolving threats (Wright 2014a), among other changes. The U.S. financial system was never optimal; articles and books too numerous to list have explored its inefficiencies and infelicities. Such studies are important but should not detract from the main point of this chapter: that governments which protect the civil liberties of a substantial portion of their citizens create incentives that enable the emergence of modern financial systems which, in turn, stimulate productivity increases in the real economy, including the crucial agricultural, transportation, and manufacturing sectors, through channels such as intermediation, reduction of asymmetric information, and more efficient asset allocation.

Unfortunately, no state or section can be used to test the notion that finance provided the lynchpin of economic development. The South lagged the North in corporate development at first, but by the Civil War had come to a rough parity with it in per capita terms (Wright 2011a). Similarly, newer, western states soon also joined the "corporation nation" by chartering corporations, including banks and insurers as well as manufacturing, mining, service, transportation, and utilities companies, in prodigious quantities in per capita terms (Wright and Sylla 2011). Moreover, state-level income data is deficient over the entire period.

Comparisons with other nations, however, clearly reveal the importance of finance to growth. First, they show that the United States was not exceptional, that its economy grew for the same reasons that the economies of other early movers did: governance and financial revolutions. Canada, for example, lagged its southern neighbor economically until it experienced governance and financial revolutions of its own after the U.S. Civil War (Wright 2008). In fact, no early-developing nation, including the Netherlands, Great Britain, and Japan, developed economically without the aid of a modern financial system and its concomitant, a responsible government, and nations that failed to develop or maintain a modern financial system, such as Argentina, suffered severely as a consequence (Sylla 1999, 2003).

References

Acemoglu, Daron, and James A. Robinson. (2012). *Why Nations Fail: The Origins of Power, Prosperity, and Poverty*. New York: Crown.

Adams, Donald R. (1978). *Finance and Enterprise in Early America: A Study of Stephen Girard's Bank, 1812–1831*. Philadelphia: University of Pennsylvania Press.

Alberts, Robert C. (1969). *The Golden Voyage: The Life and Times of William Bingham, 1752–1804*. Boston: Houghton Mifflin Company.

Allen, David Grayson. (2015). *Investment Management in Boston: A History*. Boston: University of Massachusetts Press.

Anon. (1837). *A Familiar View of the Operation and Tendency of Usury Laws*. New York: John Gray.

Arbuckle, Robert D. (1975). *Pennsylvania Speculator and Patriot: The Entrepreneurial John Nicholson, 1757–1800*. University Park: Pennsylvania State University Press.

Banner, Stuart. (1998). *Anglo-American Securities Regulation: Cultural and Political Roots, 1690–1860*. New York: Cambridge University Press.

Bodenhorn, Howard. (2000). *A History of Banking in Antebellum America: Financial Markets and Economic Development in an Era of Nation-Building*. New York: Cambridge University Press.

Bodenhorn, Howard. (2003). *State Banking in Early America*. New York: Oxford University Press.

Brooke, John L. (1989). *The Heart of the Commonwealth: Society and Political Culture in Worcester County, Massachusetts, 1713–1861*. Amherst: University of Massachusetts Press.

Brooks, Charles E. (1996). *Frontier Settlement and Market Revolution: The Holland Land Purchase*. New York: Cornell University Press.

Calomiris, Charles W., and Stephen H. Haber. (2014). *Fragile by Design: The Political Origins of Banking Crises & Scarce Credit*. Princeton, NJ: Princeton University Press.

Cameron, Rondo. (1967). *Banking the Early Stages of Industrialization: A Study of Comparative Economic History*. New York: Oxford University Press.

Cochran, Thomas C. (1979). "An Analytical View of Early American Business and Industry." In J. R. Frese and J. Judd (eds.), *Business Enterprise in Early New York*, pp. 1–15. Tarrytown, NY: Sleepy Hollow Press.

Cottrell, Philip L. (1980). *Industrial Finance, 1830–1914: The Finance and Organization of English Manufacturing Industry*. London: Methuen.

Cowen, David J. (2000). *The Origins and Economic Impact of the First Bank of the United States, 1791–1797*. New York: Garland Publishing.

Coxe, Tench. (1794). *A View of the United States of America*. Philadelphia: William Hall.

Craig, Lee. (1993). *To Sow One Acre More: Childbearing and Farm Productivity in the Antebellum North*. Baltimore, MD: Johns Hopkins University Press.

Crothers, A. Glenn. (1999). "Public Culture and Economic Liberalism in Post-Revolutionary Northern Virginia, 1780–1820." *Canadian Review of American Studies* 29(3):61–90.

Crothers, A. Glenn. (2001). "Agricultural Improvement and Technological Innovation in a Slave Society: The Case of Early National Northern Virginia." *Agricultural History* 75(2):135–67.

Cunningham, Noble E. (1987). *In Pursuit of Reason: The Life of Thomas Jefferson.* New York: Ballantine Books.

D'Arista, Jane W. (1994). *The Evolution of US Finance, Volume II: Restructuring Institutions and Markets.* New York: M. E. Sharpe.

Davis, Joseph H. (2004). "An Annual Index of U.S. Industrial Production, 1790–1815." *Quarterly Journal of Economics* 119(4):177–215.

Davis, Lance E. (1958). "Stock Ownership in the Early New England Textile Industry." *Business History Review* 32(2):204–222.

Davis, Lance E. (1960). "The New England Textile Mills and the Capital Markets: A Study of Industrial Borrowing 1840–1860." *Journal of Economic History* 20(1):1–30.

Davis, Lance E. et al. (1972). *American Economic Growth: An Economist's History of the United States.* New York: Harper & Row.

Dickson, Peter G. M. (1967). *The Financial Revolution in England: A Study in the Development of Public Credit, 1688–1756.* London: Macmillan.

Douglass, Elisha P. (1971). *The Coming of Age of American Business: Three Centuries of Enterprise, 1600–1900.* Chapel Hill: University of North Carolina Press.

Einhorn, Robin. (2006). *American Taxation, American Slavery.* Chicago: University of Chicago Press.

Epstein, Gerald. (2006). *Financialization and the World Economy.* New York: Edward Elgar Publishing.

Fenstermaker, J. Van. (1965). *The Development of American Commercial Banking, 1782–1837.* Kent, OH: Kent State University Press.

Forbes, John. D. (1953). *Israel Thorndike, Federalist Financier.* New York: Exposition Press.

Gallatin, Albert. (1831). *Considerations on the Currency and Banking System of the United States.* Philadelphia: Carey & Lea.

Gerschenkron, Alexander. (1962). *Economic Backwardness in Historical Perspective: A Book of Essays.* New York: Frederick A. Praeger.

Goldsmith, Raymond W. (1969). *Financial Structure and Development.* New Haven, CT: Yale University Press.

Haeger, John D. (1981). *The Investment Frontier: New York Businessmen and the Economic Development of the Old Northwest.* Albany: State University Press of New York.

Hammond, Bray. (1957). *Banks and Politics in America: From the Revolution to the Civil War.* Princeton, NJ: Princeton University Press.

Hilt, Eric. (2009). "Rogue Finance: Life and Fire Insurance Company and the Panic of 1826." *Business History Review* 83(1):87–112.

Karmel, James. (1999). "Banking on the People: Banks, Politics, and Market Evolution in Early National Pennsylvania, 1781–1824." Ph.D. Diss., State University of New York, Buffalo.

Kilbourne, Richard H., Jr. (1995). *Debt, Investment, Slaves: Credit Relations in East Feliciana Parish, Louisiana, 1825–1885.* Tuscaloosa: University of Alabama Press.

Kilbourne, Richard H., Jr. (2006). *Slave Agriculture and Financial Markets.* London: Pickering & Chatto.

King, Robert G., and Ross Levine. (1993). "Finance and Growth: Schumpeter Might Be Right." *Quarterly Journal of Economics* 108(3):713–737.

Klein, Daniel B. (1990). "The Voluntary Provision of Public Goods? The Turnpike Companies of Early America." *Economic Inquiry* 28(4):788–812.

Klein, Daniel B., and John Majewski. (1992). "Economy, Community and Law: The Turnpike Movement in New York, 1797–1845." *Law & Society Review* 26(3):469–512.

Knowles, Anne K. (2013). *Mastering Iron: The Struggle to Modernize an American Industry, 1800–1868.* Chicago: University of Chicago Press.

Knowlton, Evelyn H. (1948). *Pepperell's Progress: History of a Cotton Textile Company, 1844–1945.* Cambridge, MA: Harvard University Press.

Krooss, Herman E., and Martin R. Blyn. (1971). *A History of Financial Intermediaries.* New York: Random House.

Kulikoff, Allan. (1992). *The Agrarian Origins of American Capitalism.* Charlottesville: University Press of Virginia.

Lamoreaux, Naomi. (1994). *Insider Lending: Banks, Personal Connections, and Economic Development in Industrial New England.* New York: Cambridge University Press.

Levine, Ross. (1997). "Financial Development and Economic Growth: Views and Agenda." *Journal of Economic Literature* 35(2):688–726.

Levine, Ross. (2005). "Finance and Growth: Theory and Evidence." In P. Aghion and S. N. Durlauf (eds.), *Handbook of Economic Growth, Vol. 1A*, pp. 865–934. New York: Elsevier North Holland.

Lindert, Peter H., and Jeffrey G. Williamson. (2013). "American Incomes Before and After the Revolution." *Journal of Economic History* 73(3):725–765.

Lindstrom, Diane. (1978). *Economic Development in the Philadelphia Region, 1810–1850.* New York: Columbia University Press.

Livesay, Harold C., and Glenn Porter. (1972). "The Financial Role of Merchants in the Development of U.S. Manufacturing, 1815–1860." *Explorations in Economic History* 9(1):63–87.

Lockard, Paul A. (2000). "Banks, Insider Lending and Industries of the Connecticut River Valley of Massachusetts, 1813–1860." Ph.D. Diss., University of Massachusetts, Amherst.

Lucas, Robert E., Jr. (1988). "On the Mechanics of Economic Development." *Journal of Monetary Economics* 22(1):3–42.

Madison, James. (1792). *Papers of James Madison.* William T. Hutchinson et al. (eds.), vol. 1, ch. 16, doc 23. Chicago: University of Chicago Press.

Majewski, John. (2000). *A House Dividing: Economic Development in Pennsylvania and Virginia before the Civil War.* New York: Cambridge University Press.

Majewski, John. (2006). "Toward a Social History of the Corporation: Shareholding in Pennsylvania, 1800–1840." In C. Matson (ed.), *The Economy of Early America: Historical Perspectives and New Directions*, pp. 294–316. University Park: Pennsylvania State University Press.

Mason, Matthew. (2006). *Slavery and Politics in the Early American Republic.* Chapel Hill: University of North Carolina Press.

Mayer, Robert. (2010). *Quick Cash: The Story of the Loan Shark.* DeKalb: Northern Illinois University Press.

McCraw, Thomas K. (2012). *The Founders and Finance: How Hamilton, Gallatin, and Other Immigrants Forged a New Economy.* Cambridge, MA: Belknap Press.

McKinnon, Ronald I. (1973). *Money and Capital in Economic Development.* Washington, DC: The Brookings Institution.

Michener, Ron, and Robert E. Wright. (2006). "Development of the U.S. Monetary Union." *Financial History Review* 13(1):19–41.

Murphy, Sharon A. (2010). *Investing in Life: Insurance in Antebellum America.* Baltimore, MD: Johns Hopkins University Press.

Navin, Thomas R., and Marian V. Sears. (1955). "The Rise of a Market for Industrial Securities, 1887–1902." *Business History Review* 29(2):105–138.

Neal, Larry. (1990). *The Rise of Financial Capitalism: International Capital Markets in the Age of Reason.* New York: Cambridge University Press.

Neem, Johann N. (2008). *Creating a Nation of Joiners: Democracy and Civil Society in Early National Massachusetts.* Cambridge, MA: Harvard University Press.

Nettels, Curtis P. (1962). *The Emergence of a National Economy, 1775–1815.* New York: Holt, Rinehart and Winston.

Obstfeld, Maurice, Jay Shambaugh, and Alan M. Taylor. (2005). "The Trilemma in History: Tradeoffs Among Exchange Rates, Monetary Policies, and Capital Mobility." *Review of Economics and Statistics* 87(3):423–438.

Olmstead, Alan L. (1976). *New York City Mutual Savings Banks, 1819–1861.* Chapel Hill: University of North Carolina Press.

Olmstead, Alan L., and Paul W. Rhode. (2002). "The Red Queen and the Hard Reds: Productivity Growth in American Wheat, 1800–1940." Working Paper No. 8863, National Bureau of Economic Research.

Olmstead, Alan L., and Paul W. Rhode. (2008). *Creating Abundance: Biological Innovation and American Agricultural Development.* New York: Cambridge University Press.

Opal, J. M. (2008). *Beyond the Farm: National Ambitions in Rural New England.* Philadelphia: University of Pennsylvania Press.

Palley, Thomas I. (2013). *Financialization: The Economics of Finance Capital Domination.* New York: Palgrave Macmillan.

Papenfuse, Edward C. (1975). *In Pursuit of Profit: The Annapolis Merchants in the Era of the American Revolution, 1763–1805.* Baltimore, MD: Johns Hopkins University Press.

Patterson, John A. (1971). "Ten and One-Half Years of Commercial Banking in a New England Country Town: Concord, Massachusetts, 1832–1842." Unpublished manuscript, Old Sturbridge Village, Sturbridge, MA.

Payne, Peter and Lance E. Davis. (1956). *The Savings Bank of Baltimore, 1816–1866: A Historical and Analytical Study.* Baltimore, MD: Johns Hopkins University Press.

Perkins, Edwin J. (1994). *American Public Finance and Financial Services, 1700–1815.* Columbus: Ohio State University Press.

Peskin, Lawrence A. (2003). *Manufacturing Revolution: The Intellectual Origins of Early American Industry.* Baltimore, MD: Johns Hopkins University Press.

Ratner, Sidney, James H. Soltow, and Richard Sylla. (1993). *Evolution of the American Economy: Growth, Welfare, and Decision-Making.* New York: Basic Books.

Redlich, Fritz. (1947). *Molding of American Banking: Men and Ideas.* New York: Hafner Publishing Co.

Rilling, Donna J. (2000). *Making Houses, Crafting Capitalism: Master Builders in Philadelphia, 1790–1850.* Philadelphia: University of Pennsylvania Press.

Robinson, Joan. (1952). *The Rate of Interest and Other Essays.* London: Macmillan.

Rothenberg, Winifred B. (1992). *From Market-Places to a Market Economy: The Transformation of Rural Massachusetts, 1750–1850.* Chicago: University of Chicago Press.

Rousseau, Peter L. and Richard Sylla. (2005). "Emerging Financial Markets and Early U.S. Growth." *Explorations in Economic History* 42(1):1–26.

Sanderlin, Walter S. (1946). *The Great National Project: A History of the Chesapeake and Ohio Canal.* Baltimore, MD: Johns Hopkins University Press.

Schoen, Brian D. (2010). *The Fragile Fabric of Union: Cotton, Federal Politics, and the Global Origins of the Civil War.* Baltimore, MD: Johns Hopkins University Press.

Schumpeter, Joseph A. (1942). *Capitalism, Socialism and Democracy.* New York: Harper & Row.

Scranton, Philip. (1983). *Proprietary Capitalism: The Textile Manufacture at Philadelphia, 1800–1885.* Philadelphia: Temple University Press.

Shaw, Edward S. (1973). *Financial Deepening in Economic Development.* New York: Oxford University Press.

Spalding, Robert V. (1963). "The Boston Mercantile Community and the Promotion of the Textile Industry in New England, 1813–1860." Ph.D. Diss., Yale University.

Stadnitski, Peter. (1792). *Advance Information on an American Land Speculation.* Amsterdam. Translated by R. W. G. Vail in University of Rochester Library Bulletin, vol. XXIV, no. 2 and 3 (Winter–Spring 1969).

Stealey, John Edmund III. (2000). *Kanawhan Prelude to Nineteenth-Century Monopoly in the United States: The Virginia Salt Combinations.* Richmond: Virginia Historical Society.

Stickle, Mark. (2011). "The Ohio Life Insurance and Trust Company: Eastern Capital and Mortgage Credit in Ohio, 1834–1845." Unpublished manuscript, Ohio State University.

Sturm, James L. (1977). *Investing in the United States, 1798–1893: Upper Wealth-Holders in a Market Economy.* New York: Arno Press.

Sylla, Richard E. (1972a). "American Banking and Growth in the Nineteenth Century: A Partial View of the Terrain." *Explorations in Economic History* 9(1):197–227.

Sylla, Richard E. (1972b). "The United States, 1863–1913." In R. Cameron (ed.), *Banking and Economic Development: Some Lessons of History*, pp. 232–262. New York: Oxford University Press.

Sylla, Richard E. (1976). "Forgotten Men of Money: Private Bankers in Early U.S. History." *Journal of Economic History* 36(1):173–188.

Sylla, Richard E. (1977). "Financial Intermediaries in Economic History: Quantitative Research on the Seminal Hypotheses of Davis and Gerschenkron." In R. Gallman (ed.), *Recent Developments in the Study of Business and Economic History*, pp. 55–80. Greenwich, CT: JAI Press.

Sylla, Richard E. (1982a). "Monetary Innovation in America." *Journal of Economic History* 42(1):21–30.

Sylla, Richard E. (1982b). "Monetary Innovation and Crises in American Economic History." In Paul Wachtel (ed.), *Crises in the Economic and Financial Structure*, pp. 23–40. Lexington, MA: D.C. Heath.

Sylla, Richard E. (1985). "Early American Banking: The Significance of the Corporate Form." *Business and Economic History* 14(1):105–123.

Sylla, Richard E. (1998). "U.S. Securities Markets and the Banking System, 1790–1840." *Federal Reserve Bank of St. Louis Review* 80(3):83–103.

Sylla, Richard E. (1999). "Emerging Markets in History: The United States, Japan, and Argentina." In R. Sato, R. V. Ramachandran, and K. Mino (eds.), *Global Competition and Integration*, pp. 427–446. Boston: Kluwer Academic Publishers.

Sylla, Richard E. (2001). "The United States: Financial Innovation and Adaptation." In M. D. Bordo and R. Cortes-Conde (eds.), *Transferring Wealth & Power from the Old to the New World: Monetary and Fiscal Institutions in the 17th through the 19th Centuries*, pp. 231–258. New York: Cambridge University Press.

Sylla, Richard E. (2002). "Financial Systems and Economic Modernization." *Journal of Economic History* 62(2):277–292.

Sylla, Richard E. (2003). "Financial Systems, Risk Management, and Entrepreneurship: Historical Perspectives." *Japan and the World Economy* 15(1):447–458.

Sylla, Richard E. (2007). "Reversing Financial Reversals: Government and the Financial System Since 1789." In P. Fishback et al. (eds.), *Government and the American Economy: A New History*, pp. 115–147. Chicago: University of Chicago Press.

Sylla, Richard, John B. Legler, and John J. Wallis. (1987). "Banks and State Public Finance in the New Republic, 1790–1860." *Journal of Economic History* 47(2):391–403.

Sylla, Richard, Jack W. Wilson, and Robert E. Wright. (2006). "Trans-Atlantic Capital Market Integration, 1790–1845." *Review of Finance* 10(4):613–644.

Sylla, Richard, Robert E. Wright, and David J. Cowen. (2009). "Alexander Hamilton, Central Banker: Crisis Management and the Lender of Last Resort in the US Panic of 1792." *Business History Review* 83(1):61–86.

Taylor, George R. (1951). *The Transportation Revolution, 1815–1860*. New York: Harper & Row.

Thornton, Tamara. (2007). "'A Great Machine' or a 'Beast of Prey': A Boston Corporation and Its Rural Debtors in an Age of Capitalist Transformation." *Journal of the Early Republic* 27(4):567–597.

Todd, Charles L., and Robert Sonkin. (1977). *Alexander Bryan Johnson: Philosophical Banker*. Syracuse, NY: Syracuse University Press.

Tracy, James D. (1985). *A Financial Revolution in the Habsburg Netherlands: Renten and Renteniers in the County of Holland, 1515–1565*. Berkeley: University of California Press.

Trescott, Paul B. (1963). *Financing American Enterprise: The Story of Commercial Banking*. New York: Harper & Row.

Turner, John D. (2014). *Banking in Crisis: The Rise and Fall of British Banking Stability, 1800 to the Present*. Cambridge: Cambridge University Press.

Van Winter, Pieter J., and James C. Riley. (1977). *American Finance and Dutch Investment, 1780–1805*. 2 vols. New York: Arno Press.

Vitiello, Domenic, and George E. Thomas. (2010). *The Philadelphia Stock Exchange and the City It Made*. Philadelphia: University of Pennsylvania Press.

Wade, Richard C. (1959). *The Urban Frontier: The Rise of Western Cities, 1790–1830*. Cambridge, MA: Harvard University Press.

Wallis, John, Richard E. Sylla, and John B. Legler. (1994). "The Interaction of Taxation and Regulation in Nineteenth Century U.S. Banking." In C. Goldin and G. D. Libecap (eds.), *The Regulated Economy: A Historical Approach to Political Economy*, pp. 122–44. Chicago: University of Chicago Press.

Wang, Ta-Chen. (2006). "Courts, Banks, and Credit Markets in Early American Development." Ph.D. Diss., Stanford University.

Ware, Norman. (1924). *The Industrial Worker, 1840–1860: The Reaction of American Industrial Society to the Advance of the Industrial Revolution*. Boston: Houghton Mifflin Co.

Weiss, Thomas J. (1991). "Long Term Changes in U.S. Agricultural Output Per Worker, 1800 to 1900." Historical Working Paper No. 23, National Bureau of Economic Research.

Whartenby, Franklee G. (1977). *Land and Labor Productivity in United States Cotton Production, 1800–1840*. New York: Arno Press.

Wilkins, Mira. (1989). *The History of Foreign Investment in the United States to 1914*. Cambridge, MA: Harvard University Press.

Wright, Robert E. (1997). "Banking and Politics in New York, 1781–1829." Ph.D. Diss., State University of New York, Buffalo.

Wright, Robert E. (1999). "Bank Ownership and Lending Patterns in New York and Pennsylvania, 1781–1831." *Business History Review* 73(1):40–60.

Wright, Robert E. (2001). *Origins of Commercial Banking in America, 1750–1800*. New York: Rowman & Littlefield.

Wright, Robert E. (2002a). *Hamilton Unbound: Finance and the Creation of the American Republic*. Westport, CT: Greenwood Press.

Wright, Robert E. (2002b). *The Wealth of Nations Rediscovered: Integration and Expansion in American Financial Markets, 1780–1850*. New York: Cambridge University Press.

Wright, Robert E. (2005). *The First Wall Street: Chestnut Street, Philadelphia, and the Birth of American Finance*. Chicago: University of Chicago Press.

Wright, Robert E. (2008). *One Nation Under Debt: Hamilton, Jefferson, and the History of What We Owe*. New York: McGraw-Hill.

Wright, Robert E. (2009). "Corporations and the Economic Growth and Development of the Antebellum Ohio River Valley." *Ohio Valley History* 9(1):47–70.

Wright, Robert E. (2010). "Insuring America: Market, Intermediated, and Government Risk Management since 1790." In L. C. de las Cagigas (ed.), *Encuentro Internacional Sobre la Historia del Seguro*, pp. 239–298. Madrid: Fundacion MAPFRE.

Wright, Robert E. (2011a). "Corporate Entrepreneurship in the Antebellum South." In S. Delfino, M. Gillespie, and L. Kyriakoudes (eds.), *Southern Society and Its Transformation, 1790–1860*, pp. 195–214. Columbia: University of Missouri Press.

Wright, Robert E. (2011b). "Governance and the Success of U.S. Community Banks, 1790–2010: Mutual Savings Banks, Local Commercial Banks, and the Merchants (National) Bank of New Bedford, Massachusetts." *Business History Online* 9(1):1–34.

Wright, Robert E. (2014a). *Corporation Nation*. Philadelphia: University of Pennsylvania Press.

Wright, Robert E. (2014b). "The Pivotal Role of Private Enterprise in America's Transportation Age, 1790–1860." *Journal of Private Enterprise* 29(2):1–20.

Wright, Robert E. (2014c). "Specially Incorporated Transportation Companies in the United States to 1860: A Comprehensive Tabulation and Its Implications." *Journal of Business and Economics* 5(7):972–989.

Wright, Robert E., and David J. Cowen. (2006). *Financial Founding Fathers: The Men Who Made America Rich.* Chicago: University of Chicago Press.

Wright, Robert E., and Christopher Kingston. (2012). "Corporate Insurers in Antebellum America." *Business History Review* 86(3):447–476.

Wright, Robert E., and Richard Sylla. (2011). "Corporate Governance and Stockholder/Stakeholder Activism in the United States, 1790–1860: New Data and Perspectives." In J. Koppell (ed.), *Origins of Shareholder Advocacy*, pp. 231–251. New York: Palgrave Macmillan.

4

Banks and Democracy

John Joseph Wallis

Richard Sylla is a pioneer in the study of the contributions made by financial development to the early history of the United States. This chapter focuses on a question close to his interests regarding the connection between political institutions governing banking and the larger interaction of political and economic development in the new nation from 1790 to 1860. Banks and finance played a direct role in economic development through their ability to mobilize capital. Banks played an equally important role in the development of the American structure of political economy, of how collectively govern-ment-enforced rules about who could form banks (and other organizations) changed over the early years of the nation's history. The United States was the first society to implement "free banking" institutions, where anyone meeting a minimum criteria was able to establish a bank.

A long tradition in American history regards the emergence of free banking as an institutional arrangement in the 1840s and 1850s as an outgrowth of the larger movement in American society toward egalitarian democracy. Within this tradition, one approach asserts that the ideas and beliefs that ultimately led to free banking, and indeed open access to many forms of economic, religious, and educational organizations, were already in place in the Revolutionary period. Pauline Maier's title, "The Revolutionary Origins of the American Corporation" captures the main idea. An alternative approach argues that a contest between elites and the masses over the shape of democracy took place in the first half century, with the masses eventually triumphing in the form of what is sometimes called "Jacksonian" egalitarian democracy (Wilentz 2005). Andrew Jackson may be the president least liked by financial historians for his

Helpful comments from Peter Rousseau, Paul Wachtel, Hugh Rockoff, Richard Sylla, David Weiman, and Eric Hilt improved this chapter. The errors remain my own.

opposition to the Second Bank of the United States and fractional reserve banking in general, but the political forces associated with his rise and their eventual triumph are a way to understand why the United States eventually allowed everyone to establish a bank and, in the process, unleashed the powerful capacity of an unfettered financial system to promote economic development.

This chapter questions both narratives and provides an alternative framework to explain both the rise of free banking and the larger issue of how economic and political development interacted to stimulate the rise of open access to the corporate form more generally. Because banking was so profitable and depended on public recognition of banks for contractual arrangements such as limited liability, banks played a central role in the development of government-enforced "impersonal rules" – rules that treated everyone the same (at least with respect to the formation of banks).

Since impersonal rules treat everyone the same, it is natural to assume that they emerge as social outcomes from a desire for equality. That underlies both of the traditional arguments for free banking and general incorporation. Either the democratic impulse that led to the Revolution inevitably produced government policies that treated people equally (Handlin and Handlin 1969; Maier 1992, 1993), or egalitarian democracy eventually triumphed over elite democracy (perhaps not inevitably) in the 1840s and 1850s (Wilentz 2005; Howe 2007). I begin with close attention to the ideas about equality held by the founding generation, as evidenced in the writing of Montesqueiu and Hume, and expressed by Hamilton and Madison in the founding era. Their ideas about equality involved the necessity for "balance" in the political system and were essentially ideas about a political equality of equally influential groups made up of economically unequal individuals. The founding generation worried about competition between elite groups, the outcome of which could be civil war, and they wanted balance between those groups.

As American democracy unfolded after 1790, intra-elite competition did not produce balance, but rather resulted in an unseemly and "corrupt" manipulation of economic privileges to consolidate political control. In many states, political coalitions and political parties limited who could obtain a bank charter in order to create political coalitions. American state governments moved to free banking and open access to the corporate form for financial institutions, not to ensure egalitarian democracy, but to prevent intra-elite competition from corrupting the political system altogether. Equality in the sense of free entry was not a goal; it was an instrumental institutional outcome incidental to making democracy stable and sustainable.

Many things changed between 1790 and 1850: ideas, institutions, markets, behavior, and firms. There was nothing inevitable about the institutional changes that enabled any citizen to form a bank or an organization for economic, religious, or educational purposes. Changes in the relationship between politics and economics occurred primarily at the state level, so the national level history that we usually tell misses important developments. By focusing on banks and democracy we can see clearly how political and economic forces interacted to produce development in early America.

Republican Ideas

Americans of the revolutionary and founding eras held ideas about the relationship between politics and economics that grew out of their experience as British citizens and colonial subjects. The ideas evolved as a criticism of the Whig government that dominated British politics after the Glorious Revolution of 1688. The ideas had older roots, but they took on a distinct tone in the eighteenth century as the British government grew in order to fight the long series of wars with France. Republican critics accused the Whig regime of corruption, the systematic manipulation of economic privilege to build a political coalition in the royal interest and to subvert the independence of the House of Commons. Americans revolted to save the British constitution from the British (Wood 1969). To both the surprise and disenchantment of the American founding generation, the new system of government and politics they designed turned out to be just as vulnerable to corruption as the British government they excoriated. On the intellectual side, my argument starts with republican theory, the ideological origins of the American Revolution (Bailyn 1967) and the Constitution (Wood 1969), and Hamilton's republican ideas (Rossiter 1964; Stourzh 1970).[1] A sophisticated version of republican ideas, taken from Hume (who influenced Hamilton), represents eighteenth-century republican principles of government, specifically of balance and equality.

---

[1] Republican theory has been the most studied subject in political and intellectual history, political theory, and political philosophy over the last sixty years. Its origins lay in the rediscovery of what the Whigs really meant in seventeenth- and eighteenth-century Britain. Bailyn's (1967) applications of these ideas to the origins of the American Revolution and Wood's (1969) to the formation of the second American constitution brought the issues to a prominence in American history that they have yet to yield. Pocock (1975, 1985) and the Cambridge school widened the inquiry to include political thought from the Middle Ages forward. The debate and investigation goes on (Skinner and van Gelderen 2002).

Traditional republican ideas did not carry all the way through to the 1840s. On the historical side, evidence on banking in the 1790s and early nineteenth century shows the predilection for corruption that early American politics clearly demonstrated. Banking history shows that neither balance nor equality between groups could be maintained under the original forms of republican governments created by the states. Competition between factions, à la Madison and Federalist Paper #10, could not be balanced even by the extended republic. It seemed that economic interests in the new American Republic were inevitably to be manipulated by political interests for political purposes.

Republican ideas about equality do not play a central role in the existing republican literature, which is notably concerned with problem of balance in a system of mixed government, but they are important for understanding how the founders thought. Bailyn's classic picture of republican theory in America still holds true. Republicans saw the revolution of 1688 as a triumph of mixed government in which the independence of the three parts of government – the king, the Lords, and the Commons – provided a defense of liberty and a bulwark against tyranny and slavery. A clean description of their logic had been annunciated long before by Charles I in 1642 in "His Majesties Answers to the XIX Propositions of both Houses of Parliament" (Weston 1965, pp. 263–265). The Glorious Revolution rebalanced interests within British society, granting more institutional power to the House of Commons and the commercial interests represented there.

During the eighteenth-century wars with France, the necessity for the Crown to raise large sums for military expenditures necessitated close association with the Commons. The close association reflected the need to create and manage a royal interest or party in the Commons. This was a corruption of the constitution in classical republican thinking because the alliance undermined the independence of Parliament. Of particular significance for economic historians was the clear identification of economic interests as the tools the Whig regime used to manipulate members of Parliament (Bailyn 1967, ch. 1). I have called this form of corruption "systematic corruption," the manipulation of economic privileges by a political group, in order to build or consolidate a political coalition (Wallis 2006).

Not everyone agreed exactly about how corruption manifested itself in the late eighteenth century. Many viewed the king's evil ministers as corrupting the legislature by building a network of "influence" and undermining constitutional agreements. Hume saw it the other way around. His essay on the independence of Parliament, which follows the famous passage that everyman must be considered a knave, argues:

> If, on the contrary, separate interests be not checked, and be not directed to the public, we ought to look for nothing other than faction, disorder and tyranny from such a government. In this opinion I am justified by experience, as well as by the authority of all philosophers and politicians, ancient as well as modern . . .
>
> But, in this opinion, experience shews they would have been mistaken. For this is actually the case with the BRITISH constitution. The share of power, allotted by our constitution to the House of Commons, is so great it absolutely commands all other parts of the government. The king's legislative power is plainly no proper check to it. For though the king has a negative in framing laws; yet this, in fact, is esteemed of so little moment, that whatever is voted by the two houses, is always sure to pass into a law, and the royal assent is little better than a form. The principle weight of the crown lies in the executive power. But besides that the executive power in every government is altogether subordinate to the legislative; besides this, I say, the exercise of this power requires an immense expence; and the commons have assumed to themselves the sole right of granting money. How easy, therefore, would it be for that house to wrest from the crown all those powers, one after the other, by making every grant conditional, and choosing their time so well, that their refusal of subsidies should only distress the government, without giving foreign powers any advantage over us? (Hume 1994, pp. 25–26)

Hume argues that the Commons suborned the independence of the king. Hume rescues balance in the mixed British government by appealing to the king's ability to manipulate the economic interests of members of Parliament:

> How, therefore shall we solve this paradox? [How is the Commons to be checked?] I answer, that the interest of the body is here restrained by that of the individuals, and that the house of commons stretches not its power, because such a usurpation would be contrary to the interests of the majority of its members. The crown has so many offices at its disposal, that, when assisted by the honest and disinterested part of the house, it will always command the resolutions of the whole; so far, at least, as to preserve the ancient constitution from danger. We may, therefore, give to this influence what name we please; we may call it by the invidious appellations of *corruption* and *dependence*; but some degree and some kind of it are inseparable from the very nature of the constitution, and necessary to the preservation of our mixed government. (Hume 1994, p. 26)

Hume turns the prevalent argument about the corrupt subordination of the Commons by the king on its head, arguing instead that it is only by the manipulation of the economic interests of individual members of Parliament that balance is maintained in the system of mixed government. Hume, however ingenious, nonetheless agrees about the basic nature of the constitutional agreement in Britain, a mixed government made up of distinct and balancing interests. Hamilton appeals to Hume's argument in his early essay, *The Farmer Refuted*.[2] Stourzh (1970, p. 78) suggests that "these reflections of Hume's illuminate in a flash the whole edifice of Hamilton's political science."

Rather than illuminating all of Hamilton's political science in a flash, I want to emphasize the shared commitment to the idea of balance in a system of mixed government that was widely held by both sides of what became the Hamilton/Jefferson divide in American politics as it had been on all sides of the debate about Whig policies in Britain. Theoretically, if mixed government defended liberties by balancing the power of the elements of government (the one, the few, and the many or the kings, lords, and Commons), then a threat to balance could come from the overweaning power of any of the elements. All the republican writers were concerned with the equality of the elements within the system, even as they understood that the elements themselves were made up of fundamentally different and unequal individuals. The king as an individual had to be more powerful than an aristocrat as an individual, but for balance to hold, the aristocracy as a whole had to equally balance the Crown. Mercantile and urban actors would be less powerful as individuals than the aristocrats, but as a whole equal to the power of the king or the aristocracy in order to maintain balance.

The phrase "equality between unequals" was not used in the eighteenth century. Yet, the notion of balance between organically constituted parts of society required a kind of equality of social, economic, and political power between groups. This balance went far deeper than formally institutionalized procedural checks. Charles I's answers to the question wrestled with equality between unequals in 1642: if the Commons were to acquire the power of preferment

since so new a power will undoubtedly intoxicate persons who were not born to it, and beget not only Divisions among them as equals, but in them contempt of Us as become and equal to them, and Insolence and Injustice towards Our people, as now so much their inferiors, which will be the more grievous unto them, as suffering from those who were so lately of a nearer degree to themselves, and being to have redress only from those that placed them, and fearing they may be inclined to preserve what they have made, both out of kindness and policy; since all great changes are extremely inconvenient, and almost infallibly beget yet greater changes, which beget yet greater Inconveniences." (quoted in Weston 1965, p. 264)

---

[2] Hamilton (1904, vol. 1, p. 73).

The balance between the parts of a mixed government, however perceived or constituted, was of necessity an equal balance, but it was a balance of groups with equal influence, not a balance between equal individuals.

Madison was explicit about the inequality in Federalist #10:

> The diversity in the faculties of men, from which the rights of property originate, is not less an insuperable obstacle to a uniformity of interests. The protection of these faculties is the first object of government. From the protection of different and unequal faculties of acquiring property, the possession of different degrees and kinds of property immediately results; and from the influence of these on the sentiments and views of the respective proprietors, ensues a division of the society into different interests and parties.

Inequality produces the different interests and parties that need to be in balance.

Madison clearly did not think of equality among men as a requirement for a republic. Again from Federalist #10: "Theoretic politicians, who have patronized this species of government, have erroneously supposed that by reducing mankind to a perfect equality in their political rights, they would, at the same time, be perfectly equalized and assimilated in their possessions, their opinions, and their passions." The species of government he refers to is democracy, and the theoretic politician is Montesquieu. This is part of Madison's argument for the extended republic against Montesquieu's conclusions that democratic republics must be small.

Montesquieu offers another level of the meaning of equality for the founders, which was a central concept for Montesquieu. The opening sentence of the 1757 edition of *The Spirit of the Laws* began:

> In order to understand the first four books of this work, one must note that what I call *virtue* is love of the homeland, that is, love of equality. It is not a moral virtue or a Christian virtue; it is a *political* virtue, and this is the spring that makes republican government move, as *honor* is the spring that makes monarchy move. (Montesquieu 1989, p. xli, italics in original)

Montesquieu distinguished four kinds of governments: despotisms, monarchies, aristocratic republics, and democratic republics.[3] Despotism was the rule of one over many without law, monarchy the rule of one under laws. Republics contained an element of representation. Aristocratic republics were ruled by representatives of elites, and democratic republics

---

[3] This is technically inaccurate since Montesquieu begins book 2 (1989, p. 10) with the statement that "[t]here are three kinds of government: REPUBLICAN, MONARCHICAL, AND DESPOTIC." Yet the differences between the two types of republics, aristocratic and democratic, are so large and meaningful that Montesquieu effectively has four types.

were ruled by representatives of the people. Each type of government had a characteristic animating principle. As Montesquieu says, the characteristic principle "is the spring that makes" society move.[4] Perhaps it is unwise to fit Montesquieu's argument into contemporary terms; something is surely lost by doing so. Nonetheless, Montesquieu's notion of characteristic political principle suggests that in each of the four types of government, the dynamics of how society is governed engenders in individuals a preference for certain types of behavior.[5] In a democratic republic, the principle political virtue is love of the homeland and equality (which are the same).[6] In an aristocratic republic, "*moderation* is the soul of these governments." Or "a certain moderation that renders the nobles at least equal among themselves, which brings about their preservation." In a monarchy, governed by laws, the political principle is honor, and in despotism, the principle is fear.

Montesquieu is famously complicated. Drawing out the distinction between the two republics and their characteristic principles, equality in a democratic republic and moderation in an aristocratic republic, matters because it is the logic of the aristocratic republic that motivates the founding generation, not the logic of the democratic republic. Equality was a political virtue for Montesquieu because it produced frugality. If everyone cared more for the republic than themselves, and loved equality above all, then the resources of the citizens would be available to the state.[7] Montesquieu (1989, p. 113) has democracies walking a very fine line when it comes to equality:

---

[4] Chapter 3 of Stourzh (1970) is titled "The Springs of Republican Government: Private Passions, Public Interest, and the Love of Fame" and concludes that "the love of glory emerges as a passion of prime significance in Hamilton's outlook" (p. 99).

[5] Montesquieu wanted to understand the dynamics of societies. He understood that in order for a specific political system to work, it would have to be consistent with the values that people held. A democratic republic required people to love equality; as a political system it would not work without such a virtue. But whether a society, or the political system, could create such values was an open question.

[6] "Virtue, in a republic, is a very simple thing: It is love of the republic; it is a feeling not a result of knowledge; the lowest man in the state, like the first, can have this feeling" (Montesquieu 1989, book 5, ch. 2, p, 42). "Love of the republic in a democracy is love of democracy; love of democracy is love of equality. Love of democracy is also love of frugality As each one should have the same happiness and the same advantages, each should taste the same pleasures and form the same expectations; this is something that can be anticipated only from the common frugality" (Book 5, ch. 3, p. 43).

[7] Machiavelli held similar views. In *Discourses on Livy*, Machiavelli equated the virtue of equality in the citizens with keeping "the state rich, and the people poor" (Stourzh 1970, p. 64).

The principle of democracy is corrupted not only when the spirit of equality is lost but also when the spirit of extreme equality is taken up and each one wants to be the equal of those chosen to command ... Therefore, democracy has to avoid two excesses: the spirit of inequality, which leads it to aristocracy or the government of one alone, and the spirit of extreme equality, which leads it to the despotism of one alone, as the despotism of one alone ends by conquest.

Montesquieu's claim is not that democracies are inherently virtuous in this way, but that in a democratic republic, the citizens must exhibit this virtue or their democracy will become corrupted. In fact, as Jacob Levy points out, "Montesquieu's insistence that republics were constituted by virtue was an *indictment* of them, since the obsession with monk-like virtue and self-abnegation was anachronistic in an age of commerce. And republics were far from being intrinsically free governments" (Levy 2014, p. 150). Montesquieu's democratic republic was not a blueprint for the new American republic. As Madison said in Federalist #10, the point of the constitution was to protect the differences in faculties among people, not to equalize them. Montesquieu saw the dangers of a democracy flowing from the ability of political actors to take advantage of the economic interests of the wider body of citizens. Unless the citizens are virtuous, desire a frugal equality, and shun the opportunity to use the government to improve their economic condition, democracy will easily be corrupted. Virtuous equality is a guard against systematic corruption.

You might think that, given the importance of equality in Montesquieu, he would argue for laws that treat everyone the same, that are impersonal. But he does not. The spirit of the laws must be consistent with the nature of the society, and only in a democratic republic would laws that treated everyone the same be consistent with society. In a democracy, therefore, Montesquieu says the laws would call for equal divisions of property. Montesquieu spent much more time discussing laws that are uniform, laws that are everywhere the same. And he is, in general, against those laws.

The reasons for opposing uniform laws relate to the instability of a system with uniform laws. Montesquieu believes that in a monarchy, as in an aristocratic republic, it is the presence of the *corps intermediare*, the privileged organizations of the nobility, the church, the towns, the guilds, and the courts that provides the defense against the power of the monarch and keeps government moderate. If the laws are everywhere the same, if they are uniform, then the privileges that sustain the *corps intermediare* vanish, and along with them the ability to check the monarch. It is necessary that the laws not treat everyone the same in order to maintain the balance of interests in a society that enables moderate government to be sustained. A similar notion of balance must remain in place in an aristocratic republic. It is the inequalities in the faculties of people that provide the differences in interest that enable a society to maintain a balance of interests.

Balance in a republic, therefore, is connected intimately with inequality: it is an equality of unequals. It is not an equality where everyone is treated the same. It is an equality where the unique privileges that powerful individuals and organizations possess enable the society to construct a balance of interests, capable of checking attempts by any one of the elements to tyrannize the remainder.

The raw normative power of the concept of equality plays such a central role in American history, and particularly in American economic history, that it can seem hard to doubt that a modern egalitarian concept of equality was not already an inherent part of American character and culture from long before the revolution. I have tried to show that the ideas of the founding generation about equality in a system of mixed and balanced government were explicitly about the equality of groups with different privileges. Their ideas could not project forward to a society with impersonal rules without undergoing a transformative change. To assume that a profound belief in equality as a virtue that the American society either possessed or engendered, and that such a belief not only created an American democratic republic but enabled it to succeed, is to make the mistake that Montesquieu cautions us against. The meaning of equality that came to dominate American political thinking and American political rhetoric in the 1830s and afterward, the notion that every free white male is equal and that the laws should apply equally to the governed and the governors, comes close to Montesquieu's notion of extreme equality. A virtuous belief in equality on the part of the population is too slender a reed for a society to base its freedom and liberty on. The equality inherent in balance, even if an equality of unequals, is far more durable and potentially important. As I will argue, the initial American republic(s) did not manage to attain the desired balance. Ultimately, encouraging and constructing a balance of unequals involved a much wider set of changes in the institutional structure of the economy and society than the founding generation perceived or conceived.

Banks

The founding generation thought, or hoped, that they had figured out the solution to the balance problem, but they had not. Consistent with their eighteenth-century republican heritage, they saw a distinct threat to balance coming from political manipulation of the economy. Very quickly after independence and the formation of state governments and the second national government, they were confronted with the necessity to deal with economic questions and found the old inherent tendency to use the economy to build political coalitions and political parties was still in operation. Contests for control over their new governments produced the same manipulation of economic privileges that Americans had revolted from Britain to escape. As states' governments formed, groups within the polity began to organize not just to contest elections, but to create economic privileges. Canal parties and bank parties were the two most prominent examples. As states wrestled with the dual problems of governing themselves and providing economic investments in the kind of public goods their citizens demanded (i.e., banks and canals, as Callender argued in 1902), they found themselves inextricably caught up in factional conflict.[8] Promoting banks and canals required states, by the very nature of the investments that they wanted to make, to make some groups better off than others.

Two of Richard Sylla's papers had a particular influence on my perception of how the interaction of political and economic development evolved: "American Banking and Growth in the Nineteenth Century: A Partial Review of the Terrain" in 1972, and "Early American Banking: The Significance of the Corporate Form" in 1985. The first is a review article of the reprint of Fritz Redlich's *Men and American Banking*, and indirectly of Schumpeter's *Business Cycles* and *The Theory of Economic Development*, in which Sylla questions the soundness tradition in economic and banking history. The soundness tradition emphasized the weaknesses of early American banking that echoes the concerns about corruption and banking so prevalent at the time; the appeal of the soundness tradition must therefore rest on its castigation of fraud and dishonesty in banking matters. But it appears to have over-magnified both the extent of these evils and their historical import to the point where it has stood in the way of reasoned economic analysis of banking history in a growth and development framework (Sylla 1972, p. 204). Sylla emphasized the importance of the early banking system for mobilizing and deepening capital in order to finance commerce, trade, and industrialization. This was a major accomplishment of the American economy before the Civil War that

---

[8] Goodrich (1960) and Larson (2001) echo and verify Callender's theme in more recent work.

deserves recognition as exceptional and unique in the historical record, not something to be degraded and despised.

The second paper by Sylla points to the critical connection between banking and the emergence of the corporate form in the United States, particularly the importance of free banking laws, or what are more widely known as general incorporation laws. The United States was the leader in opening access to the corporate form in the western world and so in human history. Sylla's subsequent work with Robert Wright has given quantitative significance to this conclusion.

Sylla's work articulates the successful institutional developments in the American economy that, in a way, are American inventions. These developments were not simply American; they became characteristic of modern development in any developed society over the next 200 years. The papers had a profound effect on me and continue to do so. My research is oriented toward understanding why the United States succeeded in creating a modern developed economy and polity, and largely within the framework of the "corporate form" paper.[9]

The economic history of banking did, in fact, move in the direction that Sylla predicted. Substantial research has shown that the banking system in the United States did pretty well. Rockoff (1974) shows that free banking and wildcat banks were not the disaster that the soundness tradition portrayed. Temin (1969) rescued the Bank of the United States and the state banking system from responsibility for the Panic of 1837 and the Crisis of 1839, with Rousseau (2002) dissenting on some margins. There were still problems. Unit banking created too many small banks, and the fractional reserve system was subject to periodic panics and almost certainly aggravated cyclical instability of the American economy. As Bordo, Redish, and Rockoff (1994, 1996, 2015) argue in a series of papers comparing the U.S. and Canadian banking systems, a banking network with a smaller number of larger banks might have been significantly more stable. But most of the recent work on banking fails to address the interactive role of politics in shaping the structure of the banking system in the United States.[10] Why did the shape of the banking system play a part in institutional solutions that made democracy work in America?

For the remainder of the chapter, I will take as given that the banking system in general promoted economic growth and ignore the Jacksonian

[9] For papers in American economic history that explore these questions, see Wallis (2005, 2006), and in the larger framework of modern development, see North, Wallis, and Weingast (2009) and Wallis (2011).
[10] An exception is Calomiris and Haber (2014).

claims that banking was, in and of itself, an unmitigated evil. I assume that most banks did not systematically defraud either the state governments or their customers, although there were undoubtedly banks that did. I first ask whether there was the appearance of systematic corruption in banking, of the use of bank chartering and fiscal policies to create coalitions that could dominate state or national politics. Then I ask whether there was substantial systematic corruption: was there fire as well as smoke? The answer to both questions is yes. I touch briefly on the well-known case of the First Bank of the United States and the banking system that developed under the Albany Regency in New York up to 1837. Less well known but equally important is the Federalist monopoly on banking in Massachusetts up to 1812. I close with Andrew Jackson and the Second Bank of the United States.

The political crisis that blossomed after Hamilton proposed the First Bank of the United States is well known. In the *Report on the Public Credit*, Hamilton suggested that "[i]f all the public creditors receive their dues from one source ... their interests will be the same. And having the same interests, they will unite in support of the fiscal arrangements of the government." As Banning (1978, p. 128) said of Hamilton's logic: "It is hard to imagine how by deliberate intent, Alexander Hamilton's economic program for the new republic could have been better calculated to exacerbate these [commonwealth] fears ... they inevitably brought to mind the entire system of eighteenth-century English governmental finance, with all the consequences that entailed for minds shaped by British opposition thought."

Was Hamilton attempting to systematically corrupt national politics? I suspect not. The long quote from Hume recounted earlier suggests a reasonable alternative view in which strengthening the executive in relation to the legislative branch could be seen as maintaining balance. In the 1790s, the national constitution and the state constitutions could be interpreted as giving undue weight to legislatures (Wood 1969; Kruman 1997). What is certain is that the establishment of the Bank of the United States was a tipping point in the political contest within the Washington administration that resulted in the formation of a competitive political party by Jefferson and Madison. By 1792, Madison saw his ideas about the extended Republic overturned. Not only did the Federalist party control all three branches of the national government, but a faction within the party had become ascendant.[11] The irony of forming a political party to oppose

---

[11] "The success of the Federalist Party in gaining control of all three branches of the national government called into question the fundamental premise of the Madisonian federalism of 1787–8: that durable factious majorities would be far less likely to coalesce at the national level of politics" (Ferejohn, Rakove, and Riley 2001, p. 3).

the actions of a political faction were not lost on Madison, who wrote a series of articles that appeared in the *National Gazette* defending the formation of the Democratic-Republicans.[12] Madison's logic parallels the depiction of republican thought from the previous section:

> In every political society, parties are unavoidable. A difference of interests, real or supposed, is the most natural and fruitful source of them. The great object should be to combat the evil: 1. By establishing a political equality among all; 2. By withholding unnecessary opportunities from a few to increase the inequality of property by an immoderate, and especially an unmerited, accumulation of riches; 3. By the silent operation of laws which, without violating the rights of property, reduce extreme wealth towards a state of mediocrity and raise extreme indigence towards a state of comfort; 4. By abstaining from measures which operate differently on different interests, and particularly such as favor one interest at the expense of another; 5. By making one party a check on the other so far as the existence of parties cannot be prevented nor their views accommodated. If this is not the language of reason, it is that of republicanism. (Madison, *National Gazette*, January 23, 1792, as reported in Banning 2014)

The problem of equality among unequals appears in the first days of the new republic. Would competition between political parties alone be the solution to maintaining balance?

Massachusetts was a leading state in the movement to charter banks and to expand the financial system following the Revolution. As Sylla (1985, p. 111) noted, Massachusetts started out limiting banks, partly to protect the state's financial investment in the first bank it chartered, but "[a]fter 1820, Massachusetts had essentially free banking in the general sense of that term, and the state remained a leader in terms of numbers of incorporated banks and capital invested in banking enterprises for several decades." Wallis, Sylla, and Legler (1994) explain the variation in the number of banks across states by the interaction of taxation and regulation. Massachusetts levied a tax on bank capital in 1812, which by the 1830s generated roughly half of

---

[12] "A final aspect of these essays is worth remark, since it represents a strain in Republican thought which we encounter again and again: it is the effort to reduce the issue between the two sides to a dispute over the merits of republican government. Today this seems a false question; the issues of funding, assumption, the bank, taxation, and foreign policy seem real and substantial enough without superimposing on them an artificial quarrel over a question of monarchy and hereditary power which all but the tiniest handful of Americans agreed. But the exaggerated passions of both sides can be understood if we remember that most politically conscious Americans were acutely aware of being involved in a political experiment in republicanism that was attended by difficulties of the most acute kind and that might face many hidden and unpredictable pitfalls. Both sides were nervous about the stability of republicanism in an extensive federal union pervaded by many differences of sensibility and interest" (Hofstadter 1969, pp. 84–85).

Massachusetts' state revenue (Sylla, Legler, and Wallis 1987). In contrast, Pennsylvania received a substantial amount of its revenue from selling bank charters and dividends on the bank stock it owned.[13] Pennsylvania had many fewer banks than Massachusetts because Pennsylvania's fiscal interests encouraged legislators to limit entry to make charters more valuable and dividends higher. Massachusetts also had more banks than New York, where a political faction manipulated the granting of bank charters for political purposes, as will be discussed.

We did not know where the tax on bank capital came from, however. The standard sources, Handlin and Handlin (1945, 1969) and Dodd (1954), noted when the tax came into force but not why. A graduate student of mine, Qian Lu, investigated how access to organizations opened in the United States, starting with banks in Massachusetts.[14] What Lu found was surprising. By 1810, Massachusetts had granted twenty-three charters to banks; all but three of the banks were dominated by Federalists. Democratic-Republicans complained that they could not get bank charters, and they continued to petition the legislature for charters, but none were forthcoming. In the legislative session of 1811–1812, for the first time in Massachusetts history, the Democratic-Republicans controlled both houses of the legislature and the governorship. In 1812, all of the bank charters of existing banks, with the one exception of the original Massachusetts Bank, were set to expire. The banks petitioned the legislature for charter renewals. The Democratic-Republicans refused to renew the charters any of the existing Federalist banks.

Instead the Democratic-Republicans chartered a new State Bank. The directors of the new State Bank were all Democratic-Republicans. The new bank was a reform bank. It was a very large bank: $3 million in capital, $1 million owned by the state. A key reform element was the imposing of a 1/2 percent tax on the capital of the State Bank, intended to generate a fiscal return to the taxpayer rather than lining the pockets of Federalist elites. In that, the capital tax was very successful. By the mid-1820s, the bank capital tax was producing more than 60 percent of state revenue. The second reform provision required all subsequent banks chartered in the state to include the tax on bank capital. This provision was honored when the Federalists regained control of the governorship and the assembly in the elections of 1812 and the existing banks were rechartered. All of the renewed charters contained the tax on bank capital.

---

[13] See Schwartz (1947) for a discussion of banking in Pennsylvania.
[14] See Lu (2014) and Lu and Wallis (2017) for an analysis of the Massachusetts data.

Lu was able to identify the names of all the bank presidents and directors of the Boston banks, as well as the names of the presidents and some directors of banks outside of Boston. He linked the names of the bank directors to the members of the state legislature. To our surprise, approximately three-quarters of all the bank presidents and directors we could identify before 1812 had at one time in the past, or would in the future, serve as a state legislator. The Federalist Party in Massachusetts was systematically corrupt. The bankers and state legislators were not just associated with one another in a political coalition, they were the same people.

As Sylla suggested, by the 1820s, Massachusetts had adopted an essentially free banking regime, without a free banking act that allowed anyone to get a bank charter through an administrative procedure (a general incorporation act for banking was passed in 1851, but few new banks were chartered under the act; they already had open entry). In a series of acts mirroring the provisions of the act creating the State Bank in 1812, the legislature standardized all banking charters and eventually required that any new charter that contained a provision not in an existing charter would automatically apply to all existing banks. In 1829 the state passed a general regulatory act requiring all bank charters to be the same.[15] Massachusetts had not only created open entry into banking, it had created impersonal rules for banking as well. Every bank in Massachusetts after 1829 would operate under the same set of rules.

Two aspects of the political debate in Massachusetts deserve emphasis. First, the struggle was not between an elite moneyed interest and the masses. The Democratic-Republicans not getting bank charters before 1811 were just as elite as the Federalists who got them. In addition to the State Bank, Massachusetts also chartered the Merchant's Bank of Salem in 1812. Joseph Story, who was named an Associate Justice of the U.S. Supreme Court in 1811, was a director of the Merchant's Bank. Story served as the Merchant's Bank's president from 1815 to 1835 (while also serving as Associate Justice). Benjamin Crowninshield, the first president, was a director of the Bank of the United States branch in Boston and

---

[15] New bank charters formally became standardized on February 29, 1829, with the passage of a general regulatory act which required that "from and after the passing of this Act, every Bank which shall receive a Charter, from or by the authority of this Commonwealth, and every Bank whose Capital shall be increased, or whose Charter shall be extended, shall be governed by the following rules, and subjected to all the duties, limitations, restrictions, liabilities and provisions, contained in this Act" (Massachusetts 1831, ch. XCVI, An Act to Regulate Banks and Banking, section 1, p. 145). That language appeared in bank charters as early as 1812 (Massachusetts 1812, ch. 26, "An Act to Incorporate the President, Directors, and Company of the Worcester Bank").

a director of the home bank in Philadelphia. Crowninshield stepped down in 1815 when he became Secretary of the Navy. These were politically powerful moneyed elites who, nonetheless, found themselves shut out of banking by the political dynamics of early nineteenth-century Massachusetts. The contests over banking were intra-elite conflicts at heart with a large dash of democratic rhetoric on the surface.

The second aspect is the very loose relationships between party identification and support for, or opposition to, banking. There were Federalist bankers and Democratic-Republican bankers. Both parties in Massachusetts were pro-banking, but the supporters of only one party were able to get charters. Although the Democratic-Republicans opposed the creation of a national bank, they were not, per se, against banking. Banking could easily become a partisan issue, both at the national and at the state level. Yet, the pro- and anti-banking positions were not consistently identified with one party or the other. Andrew Jackson was clearly anti-bank in 1832 and later, but there were plenty of Democrats in the House and Senate and throughout the country who supported banks. There were states dominated by Democrats with banking systems dominated by Democrats. Pro- and anti-bank forces in a given state were much less the creatures of party than they were created by internal division within commercial and political elites using state policies to favor one elite group or coalition over others. Intra-elite competition in the economic realm spilled over into the political realm, but it did not produce the kind of balanced outcomes envisioned by Madison.[16]

New York, right next door to Massachusetts, developed a bank party tied to the Democratic-Republicans and against the Federalists, shortly after the Federalist bankers dominated Massachusetts politics and banking. Howard Bodenhorn (2006) has recently retold the story of how the Albany Regency, a political machine organized by a group of New York politicians that included Martin Van Buren, used the chartering of banks to build a political organization that dominated New York politics for several decades. The Albany Regency was part of the Democratic-Republican coalition that became known as the "Bucktail" party (for wearing bucktails in their hats), and that became a key element in the

---

[16] The desire to identify pro- and anti-banking leanings with political parties has caused some distortions in the political history. For example, Sharp (1970) understands that important developments in banking occurred at the state level, but showing the link between the Democratic party and anti-bank sentiments is the goal of his book, *The Jacksonians versus the Banks*. This distorts the history by only focusing on divisions that are limited to partisan divisions, not coalitions within elites.

Democratic Party in the late 1820s. The story has been told before, particularly by Benson (1961), but not by a scholar who understands banking as well as Bodenhorn and is able to speak directly to the earlier generation of banking scholars who saw the New York Free Banking Act of 1838 as the result of egalitarian Jacksonian Democracy (Redlich 1968; Hammond 1957). The Regency took advantage of a provision in the 1821 New York constitution requiring a two-thirds majority in both houses to charter a bank. Only the Regency coalition was able, in some years, to get a two-thirds majority, and when they did, they gave bank charters only to their political allies. In 1829, under the guidance of the Regency, the legislature created the Safety Fund, under which banks paid premiums of 6 percent of their capital into an insurance fund. The number of banks increased after 1830, but as Bodenhorn shows, New York still remained woefully undeveloped financially compared to its financial rivals (Bodenhorn 2006, p. 239). As well, divisions within the Bucktail Democrats began to appear in the early 1830s.[17] In the wake of the Panic of 1837 and the election of a Whig legislature, a coalition of Whigs, Anti-Masons, and Locofoco's combined to pass the Free Banking Act of 1838.[18] Although party divisions played an important role, as well as the general movement toward more open and egalitarian policies, the move toward

---

[17] "Ultimately, free banking represented the confluence of Anti-Masonic populism, Democratic pragmatism, and pro-business American Whiggism" (Bodenhorn 2006, p. 232). "A proposed repeal of the Safety Fund system came from a Democratic splinter group known as the Loco-Focos (or, sometimes, the Equal Rights Party). These were mostly tradesmen and small entrepreneurs in New York City who believed that the current system threatened their economic well-being. They believed that economic independence was based on property ownership .... And more than anything else, equality of opportunity implied equality of access to bank credit. The elimination of chartered commercial banking and its replacement with private banking was the best means to achieve this end" (Bodenhorn 2006, p. 250).

[18] "But Anti-Masonry had little to do with radical agrarianism. Instead, it was the political manifestation of a growing discontent among western merchants about lack of access to banks and bank credit" (Bodenhorn 2006, p. 247). "Indeed, support for Anti-Masonry was stronger in townships with more improved acreage, higher population densities, and higher values per acre. Anti-Masonry leaders were mostly drawn from the middling to upper classes of western and southern New York regions where the transportation and financial revolutions had not yet fully arrived" (Bodenhorn 2006, p. 248). Anti-Masonry's appeal and, therefore, its political legitimacy, grew because reasonable men believed that Freemasonry disproportionately influenced the administration of justice (Vaughn 1983). Several sheriffs, prosecutors, judges, and other officials involved in the investigation and prosecution of the crime were Masons. Most discharged their duties fairly and impartially, but others manipulated the system to protect fellow Masons. Formisano and Kutolowski (1977, p. 153) conclude that a "widespread conviction that there had been a systematic corruption of justice ... was far from fantastic."

free banking was pushed by elite and middle-class interests who had been unable to crack open the Regency coalition. Bodenhorn reaches the conclusion that free banking and, later, general incorporation was but one consequence of the leveling impulse in New York. All of the histories that I know of reach a similar conclusion, that free banking was the result of the egalitarian leveling forces unleashed by Jacksonian democracy. The actual enactment of the act in New York, just as in Massachusetts, was not the result of a coalition of leveling interests, but a coalition of middle- and upper-class groups in a political system where the outcome of intra-elite competition led to some influential groups losing influence. Those groups had experienced "unequal treatment of equals."

In New York and Massachusetts, and ultimately most of the states, the solution was to tie the hands of the legislature and require them to offer the same corporate privileges in banking to any group that met minimum requirements through an administrative procedure: free banking. The institutional changes that produced free banking arose out of the failure of existing institutional arrangements to prevent the political manipulation of bank entry within the existing intra-elite competition.

Initially, most states were involved in promoting banking. Of the $115 million in bank capital in southern and western states in 1837, at least $60 million had been invested by state governments (Grinath, Wallis, and Sylla 1997). There were monopoly, or near monopoly, state banks in Indiana, Missouri, Illinois, Alabama, and Arkansas. Banks owned completely or largely by state governments dominated the banking systems in Kentucky, Florida, Mississippi, and Tennessee – these four states also chartered other banks in which the state did not invest. States throughout the west and south either prohibited entry altogether by creating one or more monopoly state banks, or created a few banks with enormous advantages over their competitors because of the scale of state investment and the state's financial patronage. Until the 1820s, bank entry was limited in most states outside of New England (Wallis, Sylla, and Legler 1994). In the 1830s and particularly in the 1840s, states began moving to free banking legislation, or more decisively, changing their constitutions to require legislatures to pass general incorporation acts for banks and other forms of business corporations (Wallis 2005).

This history took place at the state level. There is no national level parallel. The interaction of politics and economics that shaped the American banking system, and thus the American financial system, all took place at the state level. Most know the national story, however, and there Andrew Jackson dominates the stage. Jackson changed the American presidency by asserting his position as the only official elected by all of the people. He asserted that mandate to significantly increase executive power in relationship to legislative power. Jackson's veto of the bill rechartering the Second Bank of the United States played a pivotal role in the shift of power. Jackson's opposition to the Bank was not initially a party issue; it was a personal one.[19] When Jackson told Democrats in Congress to support his veto or suffer his wrath as party leader, his veto became a partisan and party issue in the presidential election of 1832. Pro-bank Democrats had no choice in 1832 but to support Jackson's veto if they wanted to remain Democrats, although throughout the country individual Democrats at the state level remained pro-banking and continued to play key roles in state promotion of banking.

Jackson devoted almost half of his farewell address on March 4, 1837, to the question of currency, banking, and corporations.[20] In light of the brief history presented here, Jackson's descriptions of the danger facing democracy echo the fears of faction and corruption of the founding generation, but an echo that comes back in a different key:

In reviewing the conflicts which have taken place between different interests in the United States and the policy pursued since the adoption of our present form of Government, we find nothing that has produced such deep-seated evil as the course of legislation in relation to the currency. (Richardson 1897, p. 1520)

It is one of the serious evils of our present system of banking that it enables one class of society – and that by no means a numerous one – by its control over the currency, to act injuriously upon the interests of all the others and to exercise more than its just proportion of influence in political affairs. (p. 1524)

The mischief springs from the power which the moneyed interest derives from a paper currency which they are able to control, from the multitude of corporations with exclusive privileges which they have succeeded in obtaining in the different States and which are employed altogether for their benefit; unless you become more watchful in your States and check this spirit of monopoly and thirst for exclusive privileges you will in the end find that the most important powers of Government have been given or bartered away, and control over your dearest interests has passed into the hands of these corporations.

The paper-money system and its natural associations – monopoly and exclusive privileges – have already struck their roots deep in the soil, and it will require all your efforts to check its further growth and eradicate the evil. The men who profit by the abuses and desire to perpetuate them will continue to besiege the halls of

---

[19] See Remini (1967).

[20] Richardson (1897), *The Messages and Papers of the Presidents (With Additions)*. The farewell address is on pages 1511–1527, and banking takes up from page 1520 to the end.

legislation in the General Government as well as in the States, and will seek by every artifice to mislead and deceive the public servants. (pp. 1525–1526)

You have no longer any cause to fear danger from abroad; your strength and power are well known throughout the civilized world, as well as the high and gallant bearing of your sons. It is from within among yourselves – from cupidity, from corruption, from disappointed ambition and inordinate thirst for power – that factions be formed and liberty endangered. It is against such designs, whatever disguise the actors may assume, that you have especially to guard yourselves. (pp. 1526–1527)

Jackson's message is not about the inevitability of different and unequal interests that must somehow be balanced; it is not about the operation of those forces within government that must be balanced; it is about the effects of the moneyed interests on the government, who will seek by every artifice to mislead and deceive the public servants. He draws on the terminology of the founders, but he speaks a different language. Madison relied on intra-elite conflicts to balance interests within the government and society. In Jackson's rhetoric, there is one homogenous elite group arrayed against the people. Jackson's message is about the necessity to abolish special and exclusive privilege or else Americans will find that "the most important powers of Government have been given or bartered away, and that control over [their] ... dearest interests will have passed into the hands of these corporations." Jackson was a democrat, not a republican. He was a modern, not a founder.

Sylla suggested in 1972 that the time was coming when we could begin to move past the castigation of fraud and dishonesty in banking matters, and begin to consider the role of banks in promoting growth and development. But getting past Jacksonian rhetoric is not enough; we have to change our substantive interpretation of American history. In none of the state histories discussed here did Jacksonian egalitarian democrats rise up and demand the end of banks and paper currency. In each state, disaffected middling and upper-class individuals were upset by the abuses of a class of people just like themselves. They were losing in the game of political competition and were unable to garner the benefits and privileges that their peers received because those privileges were instrumental to the maintenance of a political machine or coalition. They faced systematic corruption, the use of economic privileges to form and hold together a coalition on the basis of rents that required limited access, for some groups to be excluded.

Democracy made intra-elite competition more virulent and unpredictable than elite competition under the aristocratic patronage of the British

Whigs. Americans either needed to go backward to the older system, which few if any wanted to do, or they needed to fix the way democracy worked. Just how that was to be done lay in the seeds of the Massachusetts solution worked out after 1812.

Banks and Democracy

The rhetorical power and normative force of Jackson's appeal against privilege and in favor of equality has lost none of its force since the 1830s. It can very easily lead us to lay the rise of American democracy at the feet of Jacksonian populism, a triumph of the masses over the elites, and a great deal of American history suggests that equality triumphed because of its own virtue, virtues of American society, or virtues inherent in a democratic political system. This includes a good deal of economic history as well.

In 1811, Massachusetts was looking down the throat of a politically induced collapse of its financial system. The situation in Massachusetts was unique, as all such situations are. But the dynamics of intra-elite competition in Massachusetts were not unique; they played out repeatedly in other states: political elites manipulated economic privileges to secure political control. In every society, the configurations of political coalitions continuously adjust as circumstances change. The unfortunate comments of Alexander Hamilton in the Report on the Public Credit merely gave the appearance that he intended to exploit such manipulation. The reaction to Hamilton needs to be placed in a society that had developed a severe anxiety about the course of democracy throughout the eighteenth (and early nineteenth) century.

The nineteenth century is full of complaints about corruption. Unfortunately, economic historians have a particularly bad ear for such complaints: didn't people realize the Industrial Revolution was under way and growth was just around the corner? We know how the story ends; what were they worried about? In the end, equality triumphed over privilege. These economic historians fail to see about the complaints is what Bailyn (1967) saw about the ideological debates that led to the Revolution: people were not paranoid; they really believed that they were in danger of tyranny and slavery. The corruption they feared really existed and threatened their political arrangements. We have not extended the same courtesy to the early nineteenth century, in part because our histories focus almost exclusively on the national government. For reasons that the example of the two Banks of the United States make clear, it was difficult, almost impossible politically for the national government to pursue policies or projects that involved significant manipulation of or investment in the economy. The proponents of such investments were too liable to charges of corruption. In the end, when two geographic groups accused each other of systematically corrupting the process of national government, the grand evil conspiracies of both the North and the South, the Civil War resulted.

At the state level it was possible to work out arrangements between groups that facilitated state involvement in the economy. There were many dimensions to this involvement, but as Callender pointed out in 1902, by far the largest financial commitment was to investments in canals and banks. There is a parallel history of transportation infrastructure (Wallis 2005) that does not exactly trace out the history of banking. In few states was infrastructure as profitable to either state governments or private investors as banking. In no states did potential investors come to state governments, with money in hand. willing to pay the states for transportation charters, as they did for bank charters in the northeast. As the Massachusetts Federalists and the New York Albany Regency Bucktails knew, bank charters were a license to print money and a way to tie together commercial and economic interests in a network of credit relationships. Banks, particularly when only one bank served a community or a segment of the economy, were marvelous instruments for coordinating the political preferences of men. States did not resist the temptation to use banking to assemble and integrate a political coalition.

The movement in Massachusetts to an initially de facto open entry banking regime after 1813 was an attempt to delink politics and economics by eliminating legislative discretion and requiring legislatures to pass impersonal rules for banking. Gradually Massachusetts and other New England states moved toward general incorporation institutions for a wide range of economic and social organizations, and did so through legislation. States in the rest of the country moved toward similar economic institutions, often through constitutional changes (Wallis 2005). Creating economic institutions that allowed anyone to enter banking and to enjoy both the supports and restrictions of laws governing the operation of their banks and organizations was explicitly designed to achieve political ends, not economic ones. Free banking did not result from an inevitable unfolding of the founder's ideas; it was a hard-won solution to a set of serious problems that arise when a society decides to choose and regulate its governments through majoritarian democracy.

For the most part, neither political nor economic history has seen the problems that democracy poses for economic development. If an economic investment or rule benefits a minority of the population, it can be used to influence the interests of that group and coordinate the group within a political coalition. Voting exacerbates intra-elite competition; it does not reduce it. Americans came to understand this in the 1830s, and in the 1840s they moved to solve the problem by limiting the discretionary power of state legislatures to give economic privileges to some groups and not others. Under a general law, the rules governing entry into a line of economic, social, religious, or political activity were the same for everyone. It was open access.

The limits on the discretion of the legislatures had a direct and an indirect effect, both of them powerful. The direct effect changed the dynamics of the legislative process by reducing the ability of legislatures to create benefits for small groups that would ease the process of reaching legislative compromise. Second, and I suspect in the end more important, allowing open access to organizations changed the political dynamics in the larger society within which politics functions. Banks, businesses, canals, railroads, schools, churches, and towns were allowed to form in a sometimes chaotic mix of what earlier economic historians have called creative destruction and a release of energy. This new energy went into increased economic activity and growing income, but it also went into a more active, competitive, and broad-based political activity. Madison, channeling Montesquieu, wanted a balance of groups within society; he did not want equality. The checks on the discretionary power of government that Madison sought to establish through formal political mechanisms did not materialize.

By themselves, democracy and elections do not produce modern development. By itself, democracy encourages the formation of elite political coalitions that manipulate the economy, including limits on entry and access, as an integral way of maintaining political control and stability. Such systems are not stable over the long run because the factions among the elite that lose find it in their interest to change the rules (North, Wallis, and Weingast 2009). Modern development occurs when political institutions are paired with economic institutions in a way that leads to sustainable impersonal rules for the economy and society, rules that all of the influential groups have an incentive to support. Impersonal rules in banking, rules about entry and that govern the operation of banks were among the first impersonal rules for organizations in the United States, and thus in the world. A competitive open-access economy is necessary for a competitive open-access political system. Experience with banking taught the states a series of lessons that led to the institutions that made a developed society. Richard Sylla said more than he knew when he wrote "Early American Banking: The Significance of the Corporate Form." It was banks, and democracy.

References

Bailyn, Bernard. (1967). *The Ideological Origins of the American Revolution.* Cambridge, MA: Harvard University Press.

Banning, Lance. (1978). *The Jeffersonian Persuasion.* Ithaca, NY: Cornell University Press.

Banning, Lance. (2004). *Liberty and Order: The First American Party Struggle.* Indianapolis, IN: Liberty Fund.

Benson, Lee. (1961). *The Concept of Jacksonian Democracy: New York as a Test Case.* Princeton, NJ: Princeton University Press.

Bodenhorn, Howard. (2006). "Bank Chartering and Political Corruption in Antebellum New York Free Banking as Reform." In E. L. Glaeser and C. Goldin (eds.), *Corruption and Reform*, pp. 231–258. Chicago: University of Chicago Press.

Bordo, Michael D., Angela Redish, and Hugh Rockoff. (1994). "The U.S. Banking System from a Northern Exposure: Stability vs. Efficiency." *Journal of Economic History* 54(2):325–341.

Bordo, Michael D., Angela Redish, and Hugh Rockoff. (1996). "A Comparison of the Stability and Efficiency of the Canadian and American Banking Systems, 1870–1925." *Financial History Review* 3(1):29–48.

Bordo, Michael D., Angela Redish, and Hugh Rockoff. (2015). "Why Didn't Canada Have a Banking Crisis in 2008 (or in 1930, or 1907, or ...)?" *Economic History Review* 68(1):218–243.

Callender, Guy Stevens. (1902). "The Early Transportation and Banking Enterprises of the States in Relation to the Growth of Corporations." *Quarterly Journal of Economics* 17(1):111–162.

Calomiris, Charles W., and Stephen H. Haber. (2014). *Fragile by Design: The Political Origins of Banking Crises and Scarce Credit.* Princeton, NJ: Princeton University Press.

Dodd, Edwin M. (1954). *American Business Corporations until 1860; With Special Reference to Massachusetts.* Cambridge, MA: Harvard University Press.

Ferejohn, John, Jack N. Rakove, and Jonathan Riley. (2001). *Constitutional Culture and Democratic Rule.* New York: Cambridge University Press.

Formisano, Ronald P., and Kathleen Smith Kutolowski. (1977). "Antimasonry and Masonry: The Genius of Protest, 1826–1827." *American Quarterly* 29:139–165.

Goodrich, Carter. (1960). *Government Promotion of American Canals and Railroads.* New York: Columbia University Press.

Grinath, Arthur III, John Joseph Wallis, and Richard Sylla. (1997). "Debt, Default, and Revenue Structure: the American State Debt Crisis in the Early 1840s." Historical Working Paper No. 97, National Bureau of Economic Research.

Hamilton, Alexander. (1904). *The Works of Alexander Hamilton, Federal Edition.* New York: G. P. Putnam and Sons.

Hammond, Bray. (1957). *Banks and Politics in America: From the Revolution to the Civil War.* Princeton, NJ: Princeton University Press.

Handlin, Oscar, and Mary F. Handlin. (1945). "Origins of the American Business Corporation." *Journal of Economic History* 5(1):1–23.

Handlin, Oscar, and Mary F. Handlin. (1969). *Commonwealth: A Study of the Role of Government in the American Economy: Massachusetts, 1774–1861.* Cambridge, MA: Belknap Press.

Hofstadter, Richard. (1969). *The Idea of a Party System: The Rise of Legitimate Opposition in the United States, 1780–1840.* Berkeley: University of California Press.

Howe, Daniel W. (2007). *What Hath God Wrought: The Transformation of America, 1815–1848.* New York: Oxford University Press.

Hume, David. (1994). *Political Essays.* Edited by K. Haakonssen. New York: Cambridge University Press.

Kruman, Marc W. (1997) *Between Authority and Liberty: State Constitution Making in Revolutionary America.* Chapel Hill: University of North Carolina Press.

Larson, John L. (2001). *Internal Improvement: National Public Works and the Promise of Popular Government in the Early United States.* Chapel Hill: University of North Carolina Press.

Levy, Jacob T. (2014). *Rationalism, Pluralism, and Freedom.* New York: Oxford University Press.

Lu, Qian. (2014). "From Partisan Banking to Open Access: A Study on the Emergence of Free Banking in Early Nineteenth Century Massachusetts." Ph.D. Diss., University of Maryland.

Lu, Qian, and John Joseph Wallis. (2017). "Banks, Politics, and Political Parties: From Partisan Banking to Open Access in Early Massachusetts." In N. Lamoreaux and J. J. Wallis (eds.), *Organizations, Civil Society, and the Roots of Economic Development.* Chicago: University of Chicago Press.

Maier, Pauline. (1992). "The Debate over Incorporations: Massachusetts in the Early Republic." In C. Wright (ed), *Massachusetts and the New Nation.* Boston: Massachusetts Historical Society.

Maier, Pauline. (1993) "The Revolutionary Origins of the American Corporation." *William and Mary Quarterly* 50(1):51–84.

Massachusetts. (1812). *Laws of the Commonwealth of Massachusetts passed at the Several Sessions of the General Court Holden in Boston beginning May 31, 1809 and ending on the 29th of February, 1812.* Boston: Adams, Rhoades, and Co.

Massachusetts. (1831). *Laws of the Commonwealth of Massachusetts passed at the Several Sessions of the General Court, Beginning May, 1828 and Ending March, 1831.* Vol XI. Boston: Dutton and Wentworth.

Montesquieu, Charles de. (1989). *The Spirit of the Laws.* Translated and edited by A. M. Cohler, B. C. Miller, and H. S. Stone. New York: Cambridge University Press.

North, Douglass C., John Joseph Wallis, and Barry R. Weingast. (2009). *Violence and Social Order: A Conceptual Framework for Interpreting Recorded Human History.* New York: Cambridge University Press.

Pocock, J. G. A. (1975). *The Machiavellian Moment: Florentine Political Thought and the Atlantic Republican Tradition.* Princeton, NJ: Princeton University Press.

Pocock, J. G. A. (1985). *Virtue, Commerce and History: Essays on Political Thought and History Chiefly in the Eighteenth Century.* Cambridge: Cambridge University Press.

Redlich, Fritz (1968). *The Molding of American Banking: Men and Ideas.* New York: Johnson Reprint Company.

Remini, Robert V. (1967). *Andrew Jackson and the Bank War: A Study in the Growth of Presidential Power.* New York: W. W. Norton and Company.

Richardson, James D. (1897). *Messages and Papers of the Presidents.* Washington, DC: Bureau of National Literature.

Rockoff, Hugh. (1974). "The Free Banking Era: A Reexamination." *Journal of Money, Credit and Banking* 6(2):141–167.

Rossiter, Clinton. (1964). *Alexander Hamilton and the Constitution.* New York: Harcourt Trade Publishers.

Rousseau, Peter L. (2002). "Jacksonian Monetary Policy, Specie Flows, and the Panic of 1837." *Journal of Economic History* 62(2):457–488.

Schwartz, Anna J. (1947). "The Beginning of Competitive Banking in Philadelphia, 1782–1809." *Journal of Political Economy* 55(5):417–431.

Sharp, James Roger. (1970). *The Jacksonians against the Banks.* New York: Columbia University Press.

Skinner, Quentin, and Martin van Gelderen. (2002). *Republicanism: A Shared European Heritage*, Volume 1. Cambridge: Cambridge University Press.

Stourzh, Gerald. (1970). *Alexander Hamilton and the Idea of Republican Government.* Stanford, CA: Stanford University Press.

Sylla, Richard E. (1972). "American Banking and Growth in the Nineteenth Century: A Partial View of the Terrain." *Explorations in Economic History* 9(1):197–227.

Sylla, Richard E. (1985). "Early American Banking: The Significance of the Corporate Form." *Business and Economic History* 14(1):105–123.

Temin, Peter. (1969). *The Jacksonian Economy.* New York: W. W. Norton and Company.

Wallis, John Joseph. (2005). "Constitutions, Corporations, and Corruption: American States and Constitutional Change, 1842 to 1852." *Journal of Economic History* 65(1):211–256.

Wallis, John Joseph. (2006). "The Concept of Systematic Corruption in American Economic and Political History." In E. Glaeser and C. Goldin (eds.), *Corruption and Reform*, pp. 23–62. Chicago: University of Chicago Press.

Wallis, John Joseph. (2011). "Institutions, Organizations, Impersonality, and Interests: The Dynamics of Institutional Change." *Journal of Economic Behavior and Organization* 79(1–2):35–48.

Wallis, John Joseph, Richard Sylla, and John Legler (1994). "The Interaction of Taxation and Regulation in Nineteenth Century Banking." In C. Goldin and G. Libecap (eds.), *The Regulated Economy: A Historical Approach to Political Economy*, pp. 121–144. Chicago: University of Chicago Press.

Weston, Corinne Comstock. (1832). *English Constitutional Theory and the House of Lords.* New York: Columbia University Press.

Wilentz, Sean. (2005). *The Rise of American Democracy.* New York: Norton and Company.

Wood, Gordon S. (1969). *Creation of the American Republic.* Chapel Hill: University of North Carolina Press.

5

Financial Systems, Economic Growth, and Globalization in the Era of the Cold War

Niall Ferguson

Financial historians have long been interested in the relationship between financial innovation and economic growth (e.g., Rousseau and Sylla 2003). From the rise of the Dutch Republic to the golden age of the *pax americana*, banks, capital markets, and other institutions served to promote growth by reducing transaction costs and allocating capital more efficiently – taking it, in the words of the Third Lord Rothschild (1977, p. 17), "from Point A, where it is, to Point B, where it is needed." As such, financial innovation is also seen as a driver of globalization. There is, however, an equally important relationship between financial innovation and power. From the seventeenth century onward, superior Dutch, then English, then American financial institutions were among the most important advantages those countries enjoyed over rival empires, like those of Spain, France, Germany, Japan, and Russia. In this chapter, I seek to answer some questions about these relationships in the era of the cold war (1947–1991).

The four decades after World War II saw relatively high growth in the economies of the United States and its principal European and East Asian allies, as well as increasing international economic integration as a result of the dismantling of Depression and wartime tariff and nontariff barriers, and the increasing volume of international capital flows and, latterly, migration. However, financial historians generally discuss these developments with a minimum of references to the cold war context. Partly the omission is a matter of professional specialization: the "silo effect," as it has been called (Tett 2015). Financial historians know more about monetary systems than they know about weapons systems, so naturally they tend to write more about Bretton Woods than about the bomb. It is also the case that, by and large, the U.S. government institutionally separated economic policy and national security strategy. The defense budget was, of course,

Table 5.1 *Compound Annual Growth Rates of U.S. Real Per Capita Consumption, 1889–2008*

1889–1913	2.10
1914–1918	0.05
1919–1938	1.47
1939–1945	2.49
1947–1991	2.22
1992–2008	2.21
1889–2008	2.05

Source: Robert Shiller: www.econ.yale.edu/~shiller/data.htm.

a matter for the Treasury Department, but what the Pentagon did with the money was not. The Federal Reserve could not wholly ignore geopolitical factors, especially when they affected the U.S. balance of payments, but rarely were these the chairman's top priority. National security advisors were seldom selected on the basis of their economic expertise. Indeed, Henry Kissinger took delight in exaggerating his own ignorance of the dismal science. Often, the president alone seems to have determined the trade-off between guns and butter, with Truman choosing the former, Eisenhower the latter, and Kennedy and Johnson trying to have both. But the relationships between finance and foreign policy were a good deal more complex than the idea of a trade-off implies, as we shall see.

The cold war was, on the whole, a relatively prosperous time for Americans. Table 5.1 subdivides the period from 1889 until 2008 into six unequal sub-periods according to whether or not the world was at war or at peace. Although the forty-four years of the cold war could not quite match the high consumption growth of World War II, it was not far behind. For the median household, these were golden years, as the increased aggregate income of the post–cold war period was much less evenly distributed.

Yet there are two puzzles. First, the cold war was not cheap. Indeed, one influential study of the relationship between economics and grand strategy concluded, shortly before the end of the conflict, that high defense expenditures, and their mode of financing through increases in the federal debt, were having a deleterious effect on U.S. growth. It is interesting, after the passage of nearly three decades, to reflect on why that argument was wrong.

Second, and more important, the cold war was not without huge risks. Financial innovation and globalization were processes that got under way from the late 1960s under an appalling shadow: the possibility of a catastrophic third world war. Any attempt to understand the period from the late 1940s until the late 1980s needs to relate the financing of an unprecedented buildup in destructive capability with the potential for Armageddon that it implied. Why did that not exert a bigger drag on economic performance?

This chapter considers both these issues in turn and then concludes with a case study of a financier, Siegmund Warburg, whose contemporary writings on finance and geopolitics help us to understand why it was possible for financial innovation, globalization, and growth to go hand in hand with heavy defense burdens and an incalculable threat of Armageddon.

Economics of the Cold War

The cold war can be understood partly as a massive substitution of capital for labor in the realm of national defense. During the cold war period as a whole there was a steady fall in military participation ratios in many economically advanced countries. For the United States, the postwar military participation rate (military personnel as a percentage of population) peaked at 2.2 percent in 1952 and declined thereafter to less than 0.9 percent by the end of the 1980s. (The Vietnam peak in 1968 was 1.8 percent.)[1] At the same time, with the advent of nuclear weapons of ever-greater power and delivery systems of ever-greater sophistication, the superpowers' investments in hardware grew. In 1987, the British-born historian Paul Kennedy noted that:

Edwardian statesmen, appalled that a pre-1914 battleship cost £2.5 million, would be staggered that it now costs the British Admiralty £120 million and more for a replacement *frigate*! ... The new [American] B-1 bomber ... will cost over $200 billion for a mere one hundred planes ... Cynics [forecast] that the entire Pentagon budget may be swallowed up by *one* aircraft by the year 2020. (Kennedy 1989, pp. 442–443)

According to Kennedy, weapons prices in the 1980s were "rising 6 to 10 per cent faster than inflation, and ... every new weapon system is three to five times costlier than that which it is intended to replace" (p. 482). Despite a "near trebling of the American defense budget since the late 1970s," there had occurred by the late 1980s "a mere 5 per cent increase in the numerical size of the armed forces on active duty" (p. 521).

---

[1] Correlates of War Project, National Material Capabilities, version 4.0: www .correlatesofwar.org/data-sets/national-material-capabilities.

What did this capital-intensive arms buildup signify? There was, Kennedy argued, "a very significant correlation *over the longer term* between productive and revenue-raising capacities on the one hand and military strength on the other" (Kennedy 1987, p. xvi). To be sure, Kennedy warned against "the trap of crude economic determinism" and acknowledged the importance of "geography, military organisation, national morale, the alliance system . . . individual folly . . . and extremely high battlefield competence" (p. xxiv). But he nevertheless insisted on "a very strong correlation between the eventual outcome of the *major coalition wars* for European or global mastery, and the amount of productive resources mobilized by each side . . . victory has repeatedly gone to the side with the more flourishing productive base" (pp. xxiii–xxiv):

The fact remains that all of the major shifts in the world's *military-power* balance have followed alterations in the *productive* balances; and further, that the rising and falling of the various empires and states in the international system has [sic] been confirmed by the outcomes of the major Great Power wars, where victory has always gone to the side with the greatest material resources. (p. 439)

Thus, the rise of Habsburg Spain, the Dutch Republic, the British Empire, Russia and, finally, the United States had its roots in the realm of economic history, as did the failure of Germany and Japan to achieve the global power to which they aspired in the 1930s and 1940s.

By the same token, the *decline* of great powers could also be understood in economic terms:

Wealth is usually needed to underpin military power, and military power is usually needed to acquire and protect wealth. If, however, too large a proportion of the state's resources is diverted from wealth creation and allocated instead to military purposes, then that is likely to lead to a weakening of national power over the longer term. In the same way, if a state overextends itself strategically . . . it runs the risk that the potential benefits from external expansion may be outweighed by the great expense of it all. Great powers in relative decline instinctively respond by spending more on "security," and thereby divert potential resources from "investment" and compound their long-term dilemma." (Kennedy 1987, p. xvi)

The key point was that if a great power became strategically overextended, the costs of defending its empire would leave less room for "productive investment," leading to a "slowing down" of economic output which could only have "dire implications for [a state's] long-term capacity to maintain both its citizens' consumption demands and its international position" (pp. 539):

There looms today a tension between a nation's . . . search for strategic security . . . and . . . its search for economic security, which depends upon growth (which in turn flows from new methods of production and wealth creation), upon increased output, and upon flourishing internal and external demand – all of which may be damaged by excessive spending upon armaments. ... A top-heavy military establishment may slow down the rate of economic growth and lead to a decline in the nation's share of world manufacturing output, and therefore wealth, and therefore *power*. (pp. 444–445)

Though derived from the experience of all the major Western empires since sixteenth-century Spain, Kennedy's general proposition was carefully framed with an eye to the present. The United States, he claimed, already ran "the risk ... of what might roughly be called 'imperial overstretch'" (Kennedy 1987 p. 515). It spent too much on military research and development compared with Germany and Japan, which were able to concentrate on more productive civilian investment in innovation. The implication was clear: Germany and Japan, relatively unburdened by military commitments, would sooner or later outstrip the United States economically; after which a shift in the balance of economic power would be more or less inevitable. "In the largest sense of all," Kennedy concluded, "the only answer to the question increasingly debated by the public of whether the United States can preserve its existing position is 'no'" (p. 533).

Kennedy's argument plainly owed a substantial debt to the British experience of imperial "overstretch" and economic decline from the late nineteenth century onward. His words of warning were therefore a conscious echo of those Victorian and Edwardian critics of British imperialism who insisted that the cost of maintaining naval bases, colonial armies, and subsidized governments across a vast proportion of the globe was higher than any economic benefits could justify. Yet the parallel with the "weary titan" was not the only one Kennedy drew. At one point, reflecting on the Reagan administration's fiscal policy, he cited pre-revolutionary France as "the only other example which comes to mind of a Great Power so increasing its indebtedness in *peacetime*" (Kennedy 1987, p. 527).

The Rise and Fall of the Great Powers was enormously influential at the time of its publication. A more or less instantaneous best seller, the book spawned countless op-ed articles on the theme of America's incipient decline. "In the long run, then, the United States must decline, Professor Kennedy concludes," was how the *New York Times* reviewer summed up the book's final chapter.[2] "This nation's military spending is outstripping its economic strength, which could lead to a decline in American power," was another summary. "Great powers in decline almost always hasten their demise by shifting expenditure from ... the creation of wealth ... to

---

[2] Christophe Lehmann-Haupt, "Books of the Times," *New York Times*, Jan. 7, 1988.

military expenditure," wrote Kennedy's fellow Oxonian Michael Howard, approvingly. "Spain, the Netherlands, France and Britain did exactly that. Now it is the turn of the . . . United States."[3] Commentators lost no time in applying the point to current U.S. policy.[4] Attacked by (among others) Zbigniew Brzezinski, Samuel Huntington, and Joseph Nye,[5] Kennedy struck back: "On a relatively weakened industrial base, with a yawning Federal deficit and with the educational system producing fewer and fewer engineers, then allocating 10 per cent or even 6 per cent of GNP to defense might need to be called into question."[6] The federal deficit, he contended, was "awful." Kennedy lamented the fact that the U.S. education system was producing "fewer and fewer engineers and more and more . . . stock jobbers."[7]

But just how relevant were Kennedy's historical examples to the United States of the 1980s? In a footnote, he provided a more precise definition of what he meant by "excessive" military spending. "The historical record," he wrote, "suggests that if a particular nation is allocating *over the long term* more than 10 per cent (and in some cases – when it is structurally weak – more than 5 per cent) of GNP to armaments, that is likely to limit is growth rate" (Kennedy 1987 p. 609 n. 18). Although it is true that the U.S. defense budget as a share of gross domestic product rose above 10 percent during the Korean War, its trend was steadily downward after 1953, with only a one-year surge above 9 percent in 1968, the high point of the U.S. commitment in Vietnam. The increases in defense spending under Ronald Reagan in the mid-1980s took the defense budget no higher than 6.2 percent of GDP in 1986. Clearly, the cold war average of 7.3 percent is much higher than the 3–4 percent we have since grown accustomed to, but it would only have been a problem for the United States, under Kennedy's definition of "overstretch," if the United States had been "structurally weak" at that time. It was not.

The real point of Kennedy's argument about excessive military expenditure was, of course, that it applied to the Soviet Union, not the United States. Estimates of defense spending as a proportion of GNP for the Soviet Union in the mid-1980s were as high as 16 percent. This is just another way

---

[3] Michael Howard, "Imperial Cycles: Bucks, Bullets and Bust," *New York Times*, Jan. 10, 1988.

[4] Leonard Silk, "The Geopolitics of the Budget," *New York Times*, Jan. 27, 1988. See also Peter Schmeisser, "Is America in Decline?" *New York Times Magazine*, Apr. 17, 1988.

[5] See, e.g., Joseph Nye, "America's Decline: A Myth," *New York Times*, Apr. 10, 1988.

[6] Nicholas Wade, "The Ascent of Books on Decline of U.S.," *New York Times*, Apr. 10, 1988.

[7] Paul Kennedy, "A Guide to Misinterpreters," *New York Times*, Apr. 17, 1988.

of saying that Moscow was funding roughly the same size of military establishment with an economy less than 40 percent of the size. From 1950 until around 1974, the Soviet Union was probably achieving real growth rates comparable with those of the United States. But from the mid-1970s, Soviet growth lagged behind; indeed total factor productivity declined. To put it simply, between 1980 and 1989, the United States was able to increase defense spending in real terms by around 50 percent, but per capita consumption in the same period rose by more than 20 percent. The equivalent figures for the USSR were 15 percent for real defense spending and barely 5 percent for per capita consumption (which was in any case less than a quarter of the U.S. level) (Bergson 1997). Partly this was because in the Soviet system there could be no spin-offs from military research and development as there was no technology transfer to the private sector; indeed, there was hardly any private sector at all. When Mikhail Gorbachev gambled on economic "restructuring" in the hope of closing the economic and technological gap between East and West, he unwittingly caused the output of the planned economy to collapse, and the political "transparency" he introduced at the same time merely revealed that the system had lost popular legitimacy.

True, the Strategic Defense Initiative does not seem to have played as big a part in the Soviet collapse as Reagan himself was led to believe (FitzGerald 2000). Nevertheless, it can be argued that the increase in American defense expenditures helped win the cold war by tipping an already rotten rival over the edge into dissolution. If that is correct, then Reagan's policy paid a tremendous dividend, although to call it a "peace dividend" would be a misnomer, for it was the hawks not the doves who earned it. A simple calculation suffices to illustrate the point. Between 1981 and 1989, under Presidents Reagan and Bush, the annual American defense budget (adjusted for inflation) averaged $378 billion–$100 billion a year higher than under President Carter. It was this increase that aroused so much anxiety among the prophets of national decline. In the 1990s, however, real spending on defense fell back to just $270 billion (the 1998 figure), largely as a result of the collapse of the Soviet Union and the Warsaw Pact. If, as seems likely, the Reagan push to win the arms race contributed significantly to the Soviet regime's external and internal crisis, then the long-run cost of Reagan's policy was much lower than was claimed in the 1980s. In fact, by now it has more than paid for itself.

Contrary to Kennedy, then, high levels of military expenditure are not economically damaging per se. Under the right circumstances, rising public expenditure on military technology can co-exist with rising consumption. Yet there was also a financial explanation for the divergence of the two systems, very different from the convergence predicted by so many contemporary commentators. An equally important advantage enjoyed by the United States was the ability to *finance* increased arms spending by selling bonds to private and foreign investors through the uniquely deep and wide American capital markets. The big nominal rise in the federal debt under Reagan may have worried the sage of New Haven, but as a way of paying for a temporary increase in military spending – which the Reagan defense hike was – borrowing made good economic sense. Focused as he was on the strategic importance of manufacturing, Kennedy wholly overlooked the ease with which the United States financed its increased debt burden.

At the end of World War II, the federal debt in public hands had amounted to nearly 110 percent of GNP. However, that figure fell steeply in the postwar years, thanks to a combination of growth and inflation, to a low point of just 24 percent of GNP in 1974. Set in this perspective, the subsequent increase of the debt under Ronald Reagan was modest. The federal debt was just 45 percent of GDP when the Soviet Union collapsed. Moreover, despite the high real interest rates of the early Reagan years, the cost of debt service was modest. Net interest payments as a component of federal outlays went from less than 1.5 percent of GDP in the early 1970s to just 3.3 percent in 1991. By contrast, after the suspension of domestic bond sales in 1957, the Soviets relied on much more distortionary forms of finance to cover their rising defense budget (such as credits to state enterprises and forced loans from ordinary savers), which almost certainly played a part in the economy's declining productiveness. When Moscow belatedly turned to the international capital markets under Gorbachev, it had to pay a substantial risk premium. A good parallel can be drawn here with Britain's victory over ancien régime France in the eighteenth century. In each case, the state with the more developed bond market had the deeper pockets and hence could sustain a comparably large military effort at a much lower economic cost (Schultz and Weingast 1996). Kennedy's parallel between the United States and pre-revolutionary France was wrong. The correct analogy was between the Soviet Union and the ancien régime.

Political and Financial Risk

Reagan thus used leverage smartly. The additional investment in programs such as "Star Wars", financed by easily affordable increases in the federal debt, helped win the cold war. There is only one flaw with this story: the escalation of the arms race might conceivably have triggered the one kind of conflict that the United States could have lost – a hot war. History cannot ignore the things that did not happen; if people expected them to happen, then the non-events also played a role. On September 26, 1983, world war three nearly happened when the Soviet's early warning center at Serpukhov-15 appeared to detect an American missile attack. Had it not been for the good sense of the deputy chief for combat algorithms, Stanislav Petrov, who correctly judged that it was a false alarm, historians – had any survived – might have judged the Reagan administration's hawk-ish foreign policy a catastrophe (Morris 2014, pp. 3–4). Certainly, the likelihood of an American first strike seemed high enough to the Soviet leader Yuri Andropov for him to arm Soviet aircraft in East Germany with nuclear weapons in November 1983. At that time, the two superpowers had between them nearly 60,000 nuclear warheads, many of them with blasts equal to seven hundred Hiroshimas or more – enough to kill every-one and level every building within three miles and inflict second-degree burns and radiation poisoning on those within an eleven-mile radius. Although strategic theorists, including Henry Kissinger, had written about the possibility of a limited nuclear war, few people believed a catastrophic escalation could be avoided once the first missile had been launched.

As the cold war recedes from memory into history, the most important thing to remember about it is that it *was* a war. It was not just a hot peace. The second most important thing to remember is that it was never the war that its many prophets foresaw from the moment the phrase "cold war" was first coined. Most of those who predicted a U.S.–Soviet conflict in the later 1940s assumed that it would at some point manifest itself as a full-scale third world war. But that was precisely the war that did not happen. Instead, the cold war was fought as a series of localized conflicts almost everywhere *except* Europe, with Asia as the main war zone. American and Soviet forces never directly fought one another, but at least one of the sides in every war fought between 1950 and 1990 was – or was believed to be – a superpower proxy.

With the benefit of hindsight, we can say that the cold war evolved into a "self-regulating system . . . which nobody designed or even thought could last for very long, which was based not upon the dictates of morality and justice but rather upon an arbitrary and strikingly artificial division of the world into spheres of influence, and which incorporated within it some of the most bitter and persistent antagonisms short of war in modern history" but which nevertheless "survived twice as long as the far more carefully designed World War I settlement." (Gaddis 1993, p. 1 f.) After the fact, we can speculate why that was: the inherent simplicity of a bipolar system, the essential separation of the superpowers from each other, the domestic constraints on both of them, the coexistence of "paranoia and prudence" that was at the heart of mutual deterrence, the modicum of transparency made possible by reconnaissance (not to mention rampant espionage), the rejection by each side of the goal of unconditional surrender by the other, the evolution of a variety of conflict-minimizing "rules of the game." Because the world avoided nuclear Armageddon, historians are tempted to conclude that the "balance of terror" worked as a system of mutual deterrence. (For a compelling critique of this view, see Gavin 2012, p. 60 f.)

At the time, however, almost no one expected such a benign outcome, and most informed observers saw the superpower rivalry as highly unstable. President Dwight Eisenhower was very clear what the consequences of all-out war would be: "[L]et me tell you that if war comes, it will be horrible," he told the South Korean President Syngman Rhee in 1954. "Atomic war will destroy civilization. . . . There will be millions of people dead. . . . [T]he results are too horrible to contemplate. I can't even imagine them." A top-secret assessment a year and a half later persuaded him that in the wake of a full-blown war "something on the order of 65 percent of the [U.S.] population would require some kind of medical care, and in most instances, no opportunity whatsoever to get it. . . . It would literally be a business of digging ourselves out of the ashes, starting again" (Gaddis 1982, pp. 173–174).

Humanity came perilously close to suffering this fate on more than one occasion during the cold war. The "doomsday clock," adjusted twice a year by the Science and Security Board of the *Bulletin of the Atomic Scientists* (BAS), implied that the risk of "technology-induced catastrophe" reached its peak in the years 1953–1959, when the clock showed two minutes before midnight. Perhaps reflecting their political biases, the scientists turned the clock back to 11:48 during the presidency of John F. Kennedy. In reality, it was probably in the autumn of 1962 that the knell of a nuclear "midnight for . . . civilization" came closest to sounding.[8] President Kennedy himself put the odds of disaster – meaning a thermonuclear war that could have claimed the lives of 100 million Americans, more than 100 million Russians, and comparable millions of Europeans – at "between one out

---

[8] "1953: It Is 2 Minutes to Midnight," available at http://thebulletin.org/clock/1953.

of three and even" (Allison 2012, p. 256). Arthur Schlesinger, Jr. (1999, p. 7) later called it simply "the most dangerous moment in human history."

What made the cold war so dangerous was the pace of technological innovation. In a matter of years, the superpowers went from atomic to thermonuclear bombs; from strategic bombers to intercontinental ballistic missiles; from submarine launched missiles to MIRVs (multiple independently targetable reentry vehicles). It was almost impossible for strategic theory to keep up with the destructive capability that the scientists were generating. We forget how frequently the United States changed its doctrine: from George Kennan's essentially diplomatic and conventional "containment," to the full spectrum dominance of Paul Nitze's NSC-68, to Eisenhower's "new look" strategy of "massive retaliation," to the "flexible response" of John F. Kennedy's best and brightest, to "mutually assured destruction" even before the Soviet warhead stockpile overtook the American. Most military people assumed that world war three would be fought with Europe as the battleground and both nuclear and conventional forces in the field. In 1979, a retired British general named Sir John Hackett published *The Third World War: August 1985*, which soberly imagined a full-scale conflict beginning in Yugoslavia and leading to a Soviet onslaught on Western Europe. Though their vast invasion force was held up at Krefeld, the Soviets would still be able to obliterate Birmingham before (following the reciprocal destruction of Minsk) the Politburo was overthrown by Ukrainian nationalists (Hackett 1979).

Hackett's ending was wishful thinking. The Soviets might conceivably have won a hot war had one broken out in the 1970s or 1980s. In 1992, after a 22 percent reduction in the number of superpower warheads and not including nonstrategic nuclear warheads, the total yield of the Soviet strategic nuclear arsenal was still more than 4 million kilotons, compared with a figure of just over 1 million for the United States (Fieldhouse 1992). In its war with Nazi Germany, the Soviet regime had already proved its ability to withstand millions of civilian as well as military casualties; and in the event of a hot war, it would have been much less susceptible than its American opponent to popular pressure for peace. Mass civilian death would have been a new experience for Americans, but not for Russians. The total number of U.S. servicemen who died in the Vietnam War was 57,939; that alone was enough to trigger widespread civil disobedience in the form of draft card burning. If, on the other hand, the United States had responded to Soviet nuclear strikes with defiance rather than defeatism, there might have been no winner in the war. Given that the bomb dropped on Hiroshima in 1945 killed around 100,000 people instantly and a further 100,000 subsequently through radiation sickness, the superpowers in 1992 had the notional capacity to destroy (with their strategic forces alone) 387,302 Hiroshimas. To put it another way, given that the Hiroshima bomb destroyed around 4.7 square miles, the superpowers had the capability to lay waste to 1.8 million square miles, an area rather larger than the state of India. It is scant consolation to reflect that this amounts to just 3 percent of the planet's land surface, since the lethal radiation after such a conflagration would have spread much further as fallout. Given that the population of the world in 1992 was approximately 5 billion, their vast nuclear arsenals gave the superpowers the notional ability to destroy the entire human race fifteen times over.

The paradox that a golden age of economic growth was taking place on the threshold of Armageddon must be central to any understanding of the cold war. Understandably enough, people feared world war three. Asked during the fifties and sixties whether they thought there would be a world war in the next five years, between 40 and 65 percent of Americans who had an opinion answered "yes." By the 1980s that percentage had risen to 76. Asked if, in the event of a world war, the hydrogen bomb would be used against the United States, between 60 and 75 percent of Americans again said "yes." Growing up in Britain in the 1970s and 1980s, I shared this fear. In 1978, when I was fourteen, the British punk band The Jam released "A-Bomb in Wardour Street," the chilling lyrics of which still linger in my memory ("Where the streets are paved with blood / With cataclysmic overtones . . .") Four years later Raymond Briggs published his quintessentially English *When the Wind Blows*, a bleakly funny cartoon strip about an elderly couple trying to cope in the aftermath of a Soviet nuclear strike on the basis of the 1980 government instruction manual entitled *Protect and Survive*.

But what was the economic significance of such fearful expectations? According to a series of papers by Joel Slemrod (Slemrod 1986, 1990; Russett and Slemrod 1993), there had to be some, because the expectation of premature death must have had an impact on household behavior. "[T]he threat of nuclear catastrophe," Slemrod (1986, p. 416) argued, "has influenced the growth path of the economy and will continue to affect the willingness of individuals to postpone consumption for the sake of capital accumulation." A society faced with the changing probability of a cataclysmic war would, he argued, logically vary the amount it saved for the future. According to his estimates, which used the BAS doomsday clock as a proxy for the perceived risk of an all-out war:

[a] change in the perceived threat of nuclear war from its lowest post-war level to its highest level is accompanied by a decline in the annual savings ratio of at least 1.7 percentage points ... the increase in international tensions since 1979 may have caused the rate of saving to be more than one percentage point lower than it would otherwise have been ....

The perceived threat of nuclear war should theoretically affect the level of the stock market and other asset prices, the term structure of interest rates, the rate of investment in human capital, the mix of investment between long- and short-lived assets, among other phenomena." (pp. 416–417)

Slemrod (1990) advanced the same hypothesis on the basis of Gallup opinion poll data for twenty OECD (Organisation for Economic Co-operation and Development) countries in the years 1981–1984. He found that "a 10 percent increase in the fraction of the population that believe[d] a world war [was] likely [was] associated with a decline of 4.1 percentage points in the net private saving rate" (p. 647). Here the data and the intuition went hand in hand. Americans feared war more than most OECD citizens – 49 percent of the respondents indicated at least a 50–50 chance of a world war occurring within ten years – and their savings rate was among the lowest. Japan, where only 15 percent of those interviewed admitted to a high fear of world war, had one of the highest savings rates. Pursuing his hypothesis through the easing of superpower tensions in the later 1980s, Slemrod argued that "the level of fear about the likelihood of nuclear war was significantly [negatively] related to .... the probability of being a saver rather than a dissaver" (Russett and Slemrod 1993, p. 1032). This seemed a plausible story. It also lent some credibility to the remarkably widespread view that the U.S. economy was performing badly in the 1980s.

Another relationship that attracted the attention of economists at this time was the one between geopolitical risk and interest rates. Building on Slemrod's work, Hendershott and Peek (1991, 1992) sought to explain movements in real rates in the early 1980s partly in geopolitical terms. They dismissed fiscal policy as a factor and downplayed monetary policy, arguing instead for the importance of "the erosion of the second OPEC shock" and "a nuclear-fear-induced decline in the propensity to save" in the rise in real rates between 1978–1980 and 1981–1984.

Twenty-five years after the fall of the Berlin wall, there is now a rather serious problem with these arguments. Slemrod's explicit prediction was that in a post–cold war world, with the risk of nuclear war suddenly reduced, private saving would recover, especially in the United States. It did nothing of the kind. Even as the doomsday clock was wound back to 17 minutes to midnight in the wake of the Soviet collapse, the personal savings rate continued to slump, from 9.4 percent of disposable income in 1983 – when the world teetered on the brink of disaster – to 2.5 percent in 2005. Only by invoking the increased dangers of nuclear terrorism and climate change (as the keepers of the doomsday clock have done) could one hope to salvage his hypothesis. Yet it would be a brave economist who argued that the dangers of climate change – slow acting, its worst consequences in the distant future – could somehow be equated with the dangers of nuclear war, which would have incinerated a large proportion of humanity in a matter of days, if not hours.

A different approach has been to examine the impact of changes in political risk to asset prices. In a pioneering study, Cutler, Poterba, and Summers (1989) explored the role of political news in stock price movements. Looking at data for monthly stock returns between 1926 and 1985 and annual data starting in 1871, they were skeptical that major news – including news of diplomatic crises presaging war – had a statistically significant impact on the U.S. stock market. Indeed, they showed that some of the major geopolitical crises of the cold war had only minimal effects on investor sentiment. The only real major market move associated with a cold war event was on June 26, 1950, when the S&P index dropped 5.4 percent in response to the outbreak of the Korean War. The announcement that the Soviets were stationing nuclear missiles on Cuba, by contrast, led to just a 2.7 percent market drop. The Gulf of Tonkin incident, which furnished Lyndon Johnson's pretext for escalating the U.S. military involvement in Vietnam, was marked by 1.3 percent market decline. By contrast, the huge market moves of October 1987 had no obvious geopolitical cause. Of the top fifty daily market moves, only four were cold war related.

In a previous study, I carried out a similar exercise for movements in bond yields during the cold war using high frequency data to identify large short-run moves in risk premia. The five biggest percentage rises in the yield on U.S. long-term bonds all occurred between 1979 and 1984. It is at least arguable that the bond market was simply following the Federal Reserve's increases in short-term interest rates. That was certainly the case in October 1979, when Paul Volcker introduced his new policy of controlling non-borrowed reserves and raised interest rates to 12 percent. In the same month, the long-bond yield rose 9 percent or 76 basis points. However, yields rose twice as much (18 percent or 152 basis points) in February 1980. Was this another response to monetary tightening? Or was it a reaction to the superpower tension sparked by the Soviet invasion of Afghanistan? This had begun on Christmas day the previous year and was denounced by President Carter on January 8, 1980, as the biggest threat to world peace since World War II. On January 23, a day after martial law had been proclaimed in Kabul, Carter went further, warning the Russians against any interference in the Persian Gulf, where the United States was grappling with the unforeseen regional crisis caused by the Iranian Revolution. A similar coincidence between politics and the bond market occurred in January 1982. On December 19, 1981, President Reagan imposed economic sanctions on the Soviet Union in retaliation for the introduction of martial law in Poland. Bond yields rose by 10 percent (85 basis points) that day. There were somewhat smaller though still substantial rises in yields – both of the order of 8.7 percent – in August 1981 and May 1984. On August 9, 1981, Reagan announced his decision to proceed with the manufacture of the neutron bomb; ten days later, U.S. planes shot down two Libyan fighters off the Libyan coast. On May 24, 1984, Iranian planes attacked oil tankers off the coast of Saudi Arabia, prompting the United States to send Stinger anti-aircraft missiles to the Saudis (Ferguson 2001).

Yet it must remain an exercise of dubious historical value to try to match market movements and news stories. Missing is any kind of credible rationale for shifts in and out of any asset class in response to the changing probabilities of a war that had the potential to eradicate civilization. Prior to the invention of nuclear weapons, it certainly made sense for investors to attach probabilities to the risk of world war. Before 1914 they did a rather bad job of foreseeing the dire consequences of what at first seemed like just another Balkan assassination (Ferguson 2006). Before 1939, by contrast, investors saw clearly that the policy of appeasement was not going to avert war, but merely postponed it (Ferguson 2008). There were meaningful decisions about asset allocation to be made in both cases. Gold was worth owning in case a liquidity crisis struck the banking system. Armaments stocks made more sense than those of companies geared toward Anglo-German trade. British government bonds looked preferable to those of continental countries. But during the cold war such calculations made much less sense. What kind of portfolio could possibly be constructed that would preserve financial capital in the event of a Dr. Strangelove scenario? In practice, it made much more sense to consign the possibility of a third world war to the realm of incalculable uncertainty – beyond, as it were, the tails of the distribution – and to focus instead on protecting wealth against imaginable and therefore calculable risks.

Here we begin to see the limits of statistics to the historian. Ultimately, the "risk" of a nuclear war was not, for practical purposes, a risk that could be managed financially. Those who were interested in this kind of risk went and studied game theory with John von Neumann, John Nash, or Thomas Schelling. Those who wished to study risk that could be managed financially studied portfolio theory with Harry Markowitz, William Sharpe, and Merton Miller. The two intellectual tracks led in quite different directions. Nuclear strategy throughout the cold war remained the prisoner of the prisoner's dilemma: it was always just a two-player game, and there was always the nightmare that the two players would not arrive at the Nash equilibrium. Financial risk management in the era of the cold war, by contrast, grew ever more sophisticated. Traditional financial concepts such as leverage, futures, insurance, and reinsurance were reinforced by diversification, hedging, options, and swaps. Investors learned to think of their balance sheet as something that could be managed in an increasingly rigorous fashion. It is striking that no parallel developments occurred in the realm of superpower relations. Even as the technology of nuclear warfare grew more sophisticated, the conceptual framework of geopolitical risk managed remained embedded in the nineteenth century, a reality exemplified by the fact that its most skilled practitioner was an authority on Metternich and Bismarck.

Cold War Financier: Siegmund Warburg

If we cannot infer the financial significance of the cold war from statistics, where else might we look? The best answer is in the archives of cold war financiers. Siegmund Warburg was certainly the most successful merchant banker in London after World War II; indeed the rise of S. G. Warburg & Co. more or less exactly coincides with the cold war. What role did the superpower rivalry play in his life and thought?

Unlike many people in Britain and the United States – and Warburg was transatlantic to a fault – Warburg had no illusions about the consequences for those on the wrong side of the coming "Chinese Wall" across Europe, a phrase he used as early as 1944.[9] The more aggressive Soviet policy became – particularly at the time of the Berlin blockade – the more vehement Warburg became in his denunciations of Stalin's "totalitarian" and "bellicose" regime.[10] He was hypersensitive to anything that could

---

[9] Siegmund G. Warburg Papers (SGW), London School of Economics, SGW VME/CL/ CZ../2. SGW to Otto Benzinger, Aug. 15, 1944. See also VME/CL/CZ../2, Security and a Future Order for Europe, n.d. 1945.

[10] SGW VME/CL/CZ../2, SGW to Otto Kaulla, Sept. 25, 1948.

remotely be construed as "appeasement" of Moscow.[11] He consistently refused to have any dealings whatever with communist governments.[12] Warburg was also quick to see that the Soviet Union would succeed in overcoming its disadvantage in the nuclear arms race: "If the Russians really have the atomic bomb on any worthwhile scale," Warburg wrote to his friend William Schubart in October 1949, "then I am quite sure they will be able to carry it as far as the United States."[13]

Yet Warburg was intuitively right about the magnitude of the risk of nuclear war, just as he was quick to grasp the stabilizing implications of deterrence.[14] Even at the height of the Korean War, when General Douglas MacArthur's combination of extreme belligerence and political ambition suggested to him a disquieting parallel with Erich von Ludendorff, who had led Germany to disaster in World War I, Warburg still understood that a full-scale "hot" war between the superpowers was less likely than "a continuation of the cold World War [sic] accompanied by a few isolated hot wars as in Korea and Indo-China":

I even visualize the possibility that in due course we may start to consider the cold war as a sort of normal habit for the next one or two decades and we may then gradually settle down to it in a less nervous tension than prevailed hitherto.[15]

Indeed, as early as 1951, Warburg ventured to look ahead to a time of what would later be called "détente" and even "convergence" between the superpowers:

If one is prepared to indulge in particularly optimistic anticipations, one might even visualise that after ten years or so of further cold wars, East and West may get used to a co-existence in a spirit which will be a strange mixture of mutual suspicion and mutual tolerance. It is an old experience of psychology that, although there is, abstractly speaking, a conflict between suspicion and tolerance, in reality a good dose of suspicion mixed with a good dose of tolerance results in quite a sound spiritual catalyst in settling relations between contrary mental attitudes; this applies alike to individuals and nations. Thus, after a long interval, East and West may slowly adopt a more peaceful attitude towards one another and at the same time the East may tend to develop in a less totalitarian and less centralized direction, whilst the West may become organised on a wider regional basis and on a more socialist pattern.[16]

[11] SGW Box 62, SGW Report, Jan. 15, 1949; DME/AA../CNZZ/5. SGW to Ziegler, Oct. 9, 1949.
[12] See, e.g., SGW Box 63, SGW Note, May 21, 1951.
[13] SGW VME/CL/CZ../2, SGW to Schubart, Oct. 10, 1949.
[14] SGW DME/AA../CNZZ/5, SGW to Liddell Hart, Mar. 3, 1955.
[15] SGW VME/CL/CZ../2, SGW to Randall, Dec. 29, 1950.
[16] SGW VME/CL/CZ../2, SGW to Lamm, Jan. 13, 1951.

What produced this somewhat uncharacteristic optimism was Warburg's gradual realization that Western leaders were not about to repeat the mistakes of the appeasement era. "Compared with the autumn of 1938 or the spring of 1940," he told one correspondent, "the Western World is today, although still in great danger, much more awake than was the case at that time. By the way, a slight strengthening of my optimism results from the fact that almost all those who pooh-poohed my convinced forebodings of World War II during the years 1933–1939 are the ones who now accept the third World War as just around the corner. The Neville Chamberlains who believed in 1938 and even in 1939 in 'Peace in our time' are now the gloomy [ones] prophesying imminent disasters."[17]

One important institution that helped to stabilize the cold war was the North Atlantic Treaty Organization (NATO), which rapidly established itself as a credible guarantor of the security of Western Europe (and, as it seemed, the division of Germany). Warburg was a fully fledged Atlanticist. As early as May 1950, he had become convinced that the security of the West depended on "a real defense and currency union between North America and Western Europe."[18] He even proposed the formation of a bipartisan association – "Friends of the Atlantic Union" – which was intended to rally "Industry, City and Trade Unions" behind the emerging Western alliance.[19] Interestingly, Warburg described this venture as "immensely more important than the various associations which try to further the purposes of the United Nations, of Federal Union and of European Union."[20] As he explained to his New York friend Paul Mazur – who feared that "Russia would profit from . . . isolated hot wars" and that "the only possibility of beating Soviet Russia [lay] in a Third World War" – Warburg was confident that "a well-concerted policy of the Western Powers and their friends [would] weaken Russia continuously without leading to a Third World War."[21]

At the same time, Warburg appreciated that the Soviet Union was an antagonist different in character from Nazi Germany. "In the case of Nazi Germany," he observed in a letter to the military historian Basil Liddell Hart, "there was never any readiness for co-existence, only passion for world domination. In Soviet Russia, however, the situation is different from what it was in Nazi Germany":

---

[17] SGW VME/CL/CZ../2, SGW to Lamm, Jan. 13, 1951.
[18] SGW VME/CL/CZ../2, SGW to van Biema, May 8, 1950.
[19] SGW Box 64, SGW Note, Jan. 9, 1951; Box 63, SGW Note, Jun. 9, 1951; SGW Note, Aug. 1, 1951.
[20] SGW DME/AA../CNZZ/5, Warburg to Shinwell, May 25, 1951; Jun. 4, 1951.
[21] SGW VME/CL/CZ../2, SGW to Mazur, Mar. 20, 1951.

There are despots in the Kremlin as ruthless as were the Hitlerites, but besides these despots there are some very shrewd and constructive thinkers who are trying to get the upper hand of the tyrants. Nobody can foresee, of course, how this fight between the reasonable and unreasonable elements in the Kremlin will be resolved but there is at least a chance that the East-West conflict may end in ... coexistence. The only ways to achieve this are, first, by continuously building up the strength of the Western allies, second, raising the standard of living in the East (particularly in South-East Asia), and third, by a relaxation of tension.[22]

Warburg was also quick to grasp how easily the apparently monolithic communist bloc might fracture. If Yugoslavia could break with Stalin, what was to stop China one day from breaking with his successors? (This important point was first suggested to Warburg as early as 1954 by the ambitious Labor Party frontbencher and later prime minister Harold Wilson.)[23] Warburg came to see Eisenhower's Secretary of State, John Foster Dulles, as partly responsible for throwing "the Chinese and the Russians into one another's arms" with his tactic of brinkmanship.[24]

In Warburg's eyes, then, the cold war was fundamentally a contest between two somewhat similar military-industrial – and bureaucratic – complexes. In 1955 he was intrigued to hear Harold E. Talbott, the then U.S. secretary for the air force, "talk about the American Air Force as against the Russian Air Force ... like the managing director of one industrial company talking about another industrial company."[25] The danger was not that one side or the other would strike with the malice of the 1930s dictators. It was that they would make the sort of "very serious mistake" that Warburg expected Khrushchev sooner or later to make. "The fact that the collective dictatorship of the important post-Stalin period has now given way to individual dictatorship will have, I think, the consequence that Khrushchev, like Hitler and Mussolini before him, will over-play his cards," Warburg predicted in April 1958. "I think it will be the old story of a dictator who is not being properly informed by his underlings because they do not want to tell him unpleasant news and who, due to being supplied with insufficient intelligence service, will draw wrong conclusions."[26] He deplored Khrushchev's "disgusting and bullying" behavior in 1960 – epitomized by his intemperate denunciation of the "American imperialists" at the United Nations on October 12 – and

---

[22] SGW DME/AA../CNZZ/5, SGW to Liddell Hart, Aug. 3, 1954.

[23] SGW Box 63, SGW Report, Sept. 1, 1954.

[24] SGW DME/AA ... /CNZZ/5/, SGW to Spiegelberg, Jun. 7, 1960.

[25] SGW Box 64, SGW Report, May 28, 1955.

[26] SGW Box 1, SGW to Miss Ovington, Apr. 7, 1958.

correctly foresaw a crisis over Berlin.[27] Confrontations such as the construction of the Berlin wall (1961), the Cuban Missile Crisis (1962), and the escalation of American involvement in Vietnam thereafter gradually revived Warburg's earlier fear of "a drift towards an atomic war." But it was still an accidental war that he feared: "No-one really wants it, but no-one among the real powers . . . is prepared to take resolute steps to protect humanity from committing suicide."[28] Incompetence generally struck Warburg as a bigger threat than belligerence.[29]

Yet there was incompetence on the Western side, too. "Present developments in our Western business world," he confessed to Ernst Spiegelberg in March 1959,

give me very often the feeling as if the leaders and major or minor operators of the so-called capitalist community, are participating in a cruise on a super Cunard luxury boat which may go on for two, three or four years but which will end in the super Cunard boat hitting an iceberg. In the meantime practically all the passengers of the cruise enjoy to the full their cocktail parties, dinner parties and dancing parties and completely eliminate from their minds that there is bound to be a very unpleasant awakening from the orgies. While the aimless cruise is going on the East is making continuous progress in the Cold War.[30]

Warburg harbored early doubts about the viability of the Bretton Woods monetary system, doubts that merely increased in the early 1960s as American investors hurried to snap up European assets, conjuring up the troubling prospect of a dollar devaluation as capital left the United States.[31] As early as 1961 he was looking ahead – ten years ahead, as it proved – to a world of managed but flexible exchange rates, unfettered by the dollar's "ridiculous tie to those various lumps of gold stored at Fort Knox."[32] To be sure, he never lost his faith in the transatlantic strategic ties embodied by NATO, pouring scorn on those who pinned more faith on either the United Nations ("United Hypocrites") or a militarily autonomous Europe (which Warburg dismissed as a Gaullist chimera).[33] Yet Warburg's ultimate assumption was that "a Continental Federation and

---

[27] SGW DME/AA . . . /CNZZ/5/, SGW to Spiegelberg, May 23, 1960.

[28] SGW DME/AA . . . /CNZZ/5/, SGW to Fromm, Oct. 31, 1966.

[29] See his illuminating letter to Edmund Stinnes, drawing a parallel with the outbreak of the First World War: SGW DME/AA../CNZZ/5, SGW to Stinnes, Jun. 4, 1967.

[30] SGW Box 2, SGW to Spiegelberg, Mar. 12, 1959.

[31] SGW DME/AA . . . /CNZZ/5/, SGW to Spiegelberg, Aug. 30, 1960; SGW to Schiff, Nov. 1, 1960.

[32] SGW Box 8, SGW to Mazur, Jul. 21, 1962.

[33] SGW DME/AA../CNZZ/5, SGW to L. V. Randall, Jun. 20, 1967; SGW box 20, SGW to Dilworth, Nov. 24, 1967.

North Atlantic Union" – both of which institutions he favored – would be the ideal combination.[34] He remained passionately committed to "the strengthening of co-operation between Britain and North America and between Britain and the European Continent," in the belief that "if we are not to lose the cold war, these two key aspects of the Atlantic Community seem to me to require the utmost effort."[35]

As we have seen, like a number of other Western intellectuals (notably the Harvard economist John Kenneth Galbraith and Dutch Nobel Prize winner Jan Tinbergen), Warburg toyed with the idea that the United States and the Soviet Union were converging. "What we are experiencing today," he wrote in April 1967, "is a strong evolution – on the one hand in Soviet Russia and on the other hand in the old Capitalist countries of the West – in opposite directions" toward the same destination:

namely in Soviet Russia from Socialism to a mercantilist system and in the old Capitalist countries of the West from Capitalism to a mercantilist system. I use the term mercantilist deliberately in the sense of ... the eighteenth century. It is interesting that the new mercantilism which is in the process of formation is similar in both cases ... namely containing a mixture between three elements: first, overall government planning, secondly, partial government ownership of the means of production and thirdly, partial private ownership of the means of production.[36]

But such musings suffered a blow when the Soviets sent their tanks into Prague the following year, whereupon Warburg promptly reverted to his earlier view that the USSR was "a ruthless regime which acts counter to any respect for personal values in general and privacy in particular."[37] As late as 1975, he could envisage "the Southern flank of Europe from Portugal to Spain in the West to Greece and Turkey in the East" as "almost an invitation for interference from Russia."[38] Nixon's Vietnam policy was, in Warburg's view, "the opposition [sic] of the appeasement policies which were practiced in the thirties and which led to Hitler's war and to Hitler's atrocities."[39]

I know few things are nowadays as fashionable among international intellectuals as attacks on Nixon and on his policy in Vietnam. However, as we know from historical experience – even going back as far as the period of Athens at the end of the Peloponnesian war – there are certain continuously recurring types of

---

[34] SGW DME/AA../CNZZ/5/, SGW to Coudenhove-Kalergi, Nov. 12, 1951.
[35] SGW Box 64, SGW to "members of S. G. Warburg & Company Limited", Dec. 31, 1959.
[36] SGW Box 18, SGW to Louis Warren, Apr. 22, 1967.
[37] SGW Box 32, SGW to Rubinski, Oct. 13, 1972.
[38] SGW Box 35, SGW to Birrenbach, Oct. 17, 1975.
[39] SGW Box 31, SGW to Dreifuss, Jan. 2, 1973.

intellectuals who detest straightforward realism and common sense but who love to indulge in . . . wishful non-thinking.

Such views, needless to say, accorded well with those of another Jewish refugee from Nazi Germany whose career in the United States had been even more brilliant than Warburg's in the United Kingdom. So highly did Warburg esteem Henry Kissinger that, even before the latter stepped down as Secretary of State, he was being considered as possible future director of S. G. Warburg & Co. Indeed, Kissinger struck Warburg as nothing less than "the greatest hope of our Western world of to-day."[40]

Warburg liked Kissinger more than he liked the policy of détente, it is true. Toward the end of his life, Warburg approved of Reagan's tougher stance toward the Soviet Union, writing in January 1981 that he found it:

very reassuring that throughout the new Washington establishment the old liberal misconceptions and Vietnam guilt complexes have at least disappeared and the Americans seem to be on the point not only of regaining their self-confidence but of being filled with a new wish to give a lead to the world and to turn over a fresh leaf in their domestic policy.[41]

Warburg, the veteran cold warrior, was sincerely "relieved" to see an American president "resolutely confronting the Russians."[42] Yet, in the final analysis, it is not clear how important "confronting the Russians" really was to Warburg; or, rather, it is clear that any confrontation was always supposed to stop well short of war.

Writing in 1949, Warburg – who had witnessed the Blitz from the roof of his City of London office – had foreseen how military technology was fast annihilating distance and unprecedented ways:

No geographical distance is today any protection. The only relatively safe places today are probably [those] . . . which are comparatively remote from centres of population and of industry. Talking on this subject I am reminded of the story of the refugee from Central Europe who came to England in 1938 or so, and worried as to the next place to which he should move on, and could not make up his mind. He was asked "Where do you really want to go?" and he answered "Far, far away." He was again asked "Far away from where?" He answered "Far away from everywhere."

But this was not the fearful cast of mind Warburg favored:

A point of view such as this is today more widespread than at any previous time. It is a sign of the both futile and hysterical attitude which is the accompaniment of

---

[40] SGW VME/CL/CZ../2, SGW to Goldmann, May 17, 1979.
[41] SGW Box 43, SGW to Sir Edwin Leather, Jan. 15, 1981.
[42] SGW Box 43, SGW to Shirasu, Aug. 5, 1981.

the moral, social and economic disintegration which started in our world with the First World War and which has made steady progress almost ever since in spite of short interruptions by brighter spells.

How then should civilized people conduct themselves in such a disintegrating world? Warburg's answer was revealing:

In the face of this disintegration most of those who are not prepared to be subdued by hysterical complexes can either act in accordance with Voltaire's prescription "Il faut cultiver le [*sc.* notre] jardin" or lead an active life in accordance with the "as if" philosophy, namely act and behave as if there were no disintegration around us.[43]

There is an important sense in which Warburg's generation did indeed have to live the rest of their lives "as if" the world were neither so dangerous (nor so decadent) as they knew it to be.

Conclusion

The cold war is a much harder event to understand than World Wars I and II. With the benefit of hindsight, and by looking only at the experience of Western Europe and North America, it is possible to speak of a "long peace." But for large parts of the world, the years between 1947 and 1991 were anything but peaceful. Even for those far from the war zones, the burdens of defense and of waging proxy wars were substantial. And for most of the cold war there was a real if incalculable risk that the arms race would lead to a nuclear third world war.

It was therefore not wholly absurd to expect greater economic benefits from the cold war's end: a fiscal peace dividend from lower defense spending and a macroeconomic advantage (of some unspecified kind) in the form of higher household savings. Yet the growth of consumption turned out to be fractionally slower in the post–cold war era, even excluding the financial crisis that began in 2008, and in the United States the household savings rate sank still lower. We can now see why this was. In practice, the costs of the cold war – to the United States, though not the Soviet Union – had been less than appeared at the time, while the threat of Armageddon could never really be "priced in." Even a sophisticated investor could not easily sell a call option on Judgment Day. So one carried on, paying attention to the ups and downs of superpower relations without necessarily letting them influence one's everyday business activity.

---

[43] SGW VME/CL/CZ../2, SGW to Schubart, Oct. 10, 1949.

This was precisely Siegmund Warburg's point when he talked about "lead[ing] an active life in accordance with the 'as if' philosophy, namely [to] act and behave as if there were no disintegration around us."[44] Most people did just that in the cold war, and the results – in terms of financial innovation, growth, and globalization – were not such a bad advertisement for insouciance as a coping strategy.

References

Allison, Graham. (2012). "The Cuban Missile Crisis." In S. Smith, A. Hadfield, and T. Dunne (eds.), *Foreign Policy: Theories, Actors, Cases*, 2nd Edition. Oxford: Oxford University Press.

Bergson, Abram. (1997). "How Big Was the Soviet GDP?" *Comparative Economic Studies* 39(1):1–14.

Cutler, David M., James M. Poterba, and Lawrence H. Summers. (1989). "What Moves Stock Prices?" *Journal of Portfolio Management* 15(3):4–12.

Ferguson, Niall. (2001). *The Cash Nexus: Money and Power in the Modern World, 1700–2000*. New York: Basic Books.

Ferguson, Niall. (2006). "Political Risk and the International Bond Market between the 1848 Revolution and the Outbreak of the First World War." *Economic History Review* 59(1):70–112.

Ferguson, Niall. (2008). "Earning from History: Financial Markets and the Approach of World Wars." *Brookings Papers in Economic Activity* 39(1):431–477.

Fieldhouse, Richard. (1992). "Nuclear Weapons Developments and Unilateral Reduction Initiatives." *SIPRI Yearbook: World Armaments and Disarmament*, pp. 74–119.

FitzGerald, Frances. (2000). *Way Out There in the Blue: Reagan, Star Wars and the End of the Cold War*. New York: Simon & Schuster.

Gaddis, John L. (1982). *Strategies of Containment: A Critical Appraisal of Postwar American National Security Policy*. New York: Oxford University Press.

Gaddis, John L. (1993). "The Long Peace: Elements of Stability in the Postwar International System." In S. M. Lynn-Jones and S. E. Miller (eds.), *The Cold War and After: Prospects for Peace*. Cambridge, MA: MIT Press.

Gavin, Francis J. (2012). *Nuclear Statecraft: History and Strategy in America's Atomic Age*. Ithaca, NY, and London: Cornell University Press.

Hackett, General Sir John. (1979). *The Third World War: August 1985*. New York: Macmillan.

Hendershott, Patric H., and Joe Peek. (1991). "Interest Rates in the Reagan Years." In A. P. Sahn and R. L. Tracy (eds.), *The Economic Legacy of the Reagan Years: Euphoria or Chaos?* Westport, CT, and London: Greenwood, Praeger.

Hendershott, Patric H., and Joe Peek. (1992). "Treasury Bill Rates in the 1970s and 1980s." *Journal of Money, Credit and Banking* 24(2):195–214.

---

[44] SGW VME/CL/CZ../2, SGW to Schubart, Oct. 10, 1949.

Kennedy, Paul. (1989). *The Rise and Fall of the Great Powers: Economic Change and Military Conflict from 1500 to 2000.* New York: Random House.

Morris, Ian. (2014). *War! What Is It Good For? Conflict and the Progress of Civilization from Primate to Robots.* New York: Farrer, Straus and Ginoux.

Rothschild, Lord [Victor]. (1977). *Meditations of a Broomstick.* London: privately published.

Rousseau, Peter L., and Richard Sylla. (2003). "Financial Systems, Economic Growth, and Globalization." In M. D. Bordo, A. M. Taylor, and J. G. Williamson (eds.), *Globalization in Historical Perspective*, pp. 373–416. Chicago: University of Chicago Press.

Russett, Bruce, and Joel Slemrod. (1993). "Diminished Expectations of Nuclear War and Increased Personal Savings: Evidence from Individual Survey Data." *American Economic Review* 83(4, September):1022–1033.

Schlesinger, Arthur M., Jr. (1999). "Foreword" to Robert F. Kennedy, *Thirteen Days: A Memoir of the Cuban Missile Crisis.* New York: W. W. Norton.

Schultz, Kenneth A., and Barry R. Weingast. 1996. "The Democratic Advantage: The Institutional Sources of State Power in International Competition." *Hoover Institution on War, Revolution and Peace Essays in Public Policy* 67:30–40.

Slemrod, Joel. (1986). "Saving and the Fear of Nuclear War." *Journal of Conflict Resolution* 30(3):403–419.

Slemrod, Joel. (1990). "Fear of Nuclear War and Intercountry Differences in the Rate of Saving." *Economic Inquiry* 28(4):647–657.

Tett, Gillian. (2015). *The Silo Effect: The Peril of Expertise and the Promise of Breaking Down Barriers.* New York: Simon & Schuster.

6

Reputation, Regulation, and the Collapse of International Capital Markets, 1920–1935

Marc Flandreau

This chapter discusses one aspect of the interwar crisis: the collapse of the international capital market. In 1931, this market was hit by a wave of foreign government debt defaults. By the middle of the 1930s, 40 percent of Europe's and 82 percent of Latin America's external debt was in arrears. The center of the cyclone was New York, where most issues now in default had taken place during the 1920s (Foreign Bondholders Protective Council 1934; Madden, Nadler, and Sauvain 1937; Lewis 1938; Mintz 1951). The episode left deep scars in the international financial system. The global capital market became notoriously narrower and remained effectively durably closed to foreign borrowers (Eichengreen 1989). Public capital (the Marshall Plan) replaced private lending after World War II, and new institutions such as the International Monetary Fund (IMF) were created in order to deal with downsized international financial relations (Van Dormael 1978). Reflecting this, statistical measures of the evolution of current account openness – an indicator of the accessibility of capital markets – nosedived during the 1930s and did not recover until the 1970s (Obstfeld and Taylor 1998; Flandreau and Rivière 1999; Bordo and Flandreau 2003). "Globalization" had ended in the interwar period and would only "resume" in the 1970s.

An early draft of this chapter was written while the author was visiting Princeton University in the fall of 2011. The draft subsequently evolved to its present form. It was discussed in research seminars at New York University, Princeton University, Rutgers University, and Oxford University where it benefited from comments and criticism before it was presented at the Conference in Honor of Richard Sylla, Stern School of Business, New York University March 27–28, 2015. The author is very grateful to his discussant Mary Rodgers for her remarks and suggestions. Feedback from Olivier Accominotti, Carolyn Biltoft, Charles Calomiris, Barry Eichengreen, Rui Pedro Esteves, Price Fishback, Norbert Gaillard, Harold James, Larry Neal, Peter L. Rousseau, Richard Sylla, Paul Wachtel and Eugene White was most valuable, yet the author remains solely responsible for any errors or omissions. Generous funding from the EU Macrohist Grant is gratefully acknowledged.

Previous economic historians have generally discussed the interwar debt crisis using the language of macroeconomics, prescribing in retrospect those remedies with which intelligent policy makers might have mitigated the dislocation of the international financial system. In their accounts, the crisis was initiated by adverse shocks made worse by the failure of self-regulating markets, and then morphed into a full-scale disaster owing to misguided policies, such as adherence to the gold standard. The actions of contemporary policy makers are read as the negative of the collapse: had policy makers made the right policy choices, the crisis would never have been so bad. This view is widely shared among scholars of different political hues (Temin 1991, 2010; Eichengreen 1992, 2015a; James 1996, 2002, 2009).

As a result of the existing consensus among economic and financial historians, this reading of the interwar period has played a crucial role in legitimizing among economists, policy makers, and public opinion the response to the subprime crisis. The evolution of the international financial architecture of national and international capital markets is usually seen as endogenous to the demand shocks. The same applies to changes in the regulatory setup. Financial regulation, it is said, resulted from macroeconomic failures. For instance, Harold James portrays the New Deal's Glass-Steagall Act as a necessary response to the U.S. banking crisis of 1931–1933 (James 2009, p. 41; DeLong and Ramirez 2001). In contrast, this chapter articulates a supply-side or structural story of the interwar foreign debt crisis. This perspective is new.

The main contribution of this chapter is to suggest an alternative perspective that reverses the usual direction of causality. Rather than seeing the New Deal financial acts as part of the policies motivated by the financial turmoil of the early 1930s – a "response" to a "shock" – it argues that the acts were part of the crisis itself. Specifically, it will be argued that causality did run from New Deal regulations to the closure of the foreign debt market. New quantitative and qualitative evidence is marshalled to support this argument. This novel perspective on the 1930s, while at odds with the axioms of macroeconomic history, shares connections with business history, most prominently with the work of Vincent P. Carosso, who argued that New Deal regulations hampered the business of underwriting and suggested that the financial acts of the 1930s were part of a crusade waged against investment banks by the Roosevelt administration (Carosso 1970a, 1970b).[1] This chapter also has kinship

---

[1] See also Chernow (1990); DeLong and Ramirez (1995); Stratton (2015).

with analyses that have focused on the political economy of the New Deal financial acts, their links with ongoing disputes within the financial system, and regulatory capture (Stigler 1964, 1971; Tabarrok 1998; Mahoney 2001). However, Carosso only focused on corporate securities. Moreover, he did not elaborate on the relevance of the microeconomic disruptions caused by the New Deal financial acts for macroeconomic outcomes. This is also the case with Stigler, Tabarrok, and Mahoney. By contrast, the following discussion focuses on the foreign debt markets and is explicitly concerned with articulating the microeconomics of those markets with aggregate trends.

The microeconomic history offered in this chapter rests, first, on a methodological innovation. It is argued that the logic of the interwar debt crisis – instead of being captured through such concepts as debt, GDP, and the current account – is best observed from the vantage point of the industrial organization of capital markets in the 1920s. In particular, building on previous research by myself and collaborators, this chapter shows how, until the crisis, certification of foreign government debt was delegated to a handful of prestigious underwriting banks. In practice there was a tight correlation between the prestige of any underwriting bank and the probability that the debts it underwrote would deliver their promise. This is what made the system comprehensible to outsiders. Keeping it this way provided substantial rents to the more prestigious houses. Therefore, they had incentives to go to almost any length to protect what was effectively a grading system. This emphasis, backed with data, enables me to debunk the widespread myth that bankers had failed. At the time, all underwriters were vilified under the rubric "international bankers," an amorphous term that has been used in subsequent research (Lewis 1938; Mintz 1951; Eichengreen 1989). However, as will be shown, what really mattered were the hierarchies of prestige within this group – a group that was anything but amorphous.

Second, this vantage point enables me to introduce a new element into the history of the interwar debt crisis which I document with the help of new data and insight, backed by evidence from Thomas W. Lamont's paper at the Baker Library in Harvard. The chapter suggests that the ownership of the grading or prestige system was a prize worth fighting for, as the efforts the New Dealers made to take it away from the prestigious banks suggest. For so doing, reformers had to question the performance of the existing arrangement and thus argued, opportunistically but incorrectly, that international bankers had failed. As we shall see, conflating all kinds of bankers and behaviors enabled critics of the existing order to introduce reforms whose ultimate effect was precisely to annihilate the bankers' ability to deliver according to previous expectations. In other words, at the heart of the New Deal financial acts and of the international financial dislocations of the 1930s was a ferocious and destructive political fight over control and ownership of existing procedures of certification. The author is not aware of any previous history that has made foreign government debt quality certification and its ownership a relevant historical concept – and yet it was.

Third, this chapter ties into broader evidence on the evolution of the international financial system. While it is generally accepted that the inter-war debt crisis was a turning point in the history of global capitalism, it is also emphasized that financial globalization eventually resumed so that once again *plus ça change plus c'est la même chose* (Reinhart and Rogoff, 2009). However, while macroeconomic measures of financial globalization rose again after 1970, the microeconomics of financial globalization – the way the business of originating and distributing foreign government debt is orga-nized – were profoundly transformed and no longer the same. The modern international bond market differs from predecessors in several fundamental respects. Sovereign defaults used to concentrate on securities originated by less prestigious intermediaries, but they are now evenly distributed among super-competitive international banks. Until the interwar era, conservative, prestigious banks exhibited a high degree of care for their customers, but they do not pay attention today. In the modern world, the certifying and gate keeping has been markedly relaxed. Flandreau, Flores, Gaillard, and Nieto-Para (2010) argue that rating agencies now play the role of assessing foreign debt while international financial institutions take care of the troubleshoot-ing when problems arise. This chapter suggests that the foundations of this modern setup were laid out during the interwar period.

Fourth, in my narrative, the New Deal financial legislation can be seen as having brought about, in the international finance arena, a transition from personal to impersonal exchange akin to processes already documented by historians of national financial systems. For instance, there is an obvious analogy between Naomi Lamoreaux's analysis of the role of kinship in New England banking (Lamoreaux 1986) and the private bankers–based system of personalized screening of government credit discussed here. In both cases, personalized links substituted for incomplete information and acted as crutches for the market mechanism. By underscoring the disruptions this system experienced in the 1930s, this chapter claims that such transi-tions from personal to impersonal exchange need not be smooth. In other words, there may be significant adjustment costs of moving from a regime with tightly held information to an arms-length and competitive one. The interwar foreign debt crisis illustrates this point.

Last, the analytical elements in this chapter explain why the histories of geopolitics and histories of global finance have had so much in common, as has often been remarked (Kindleberger 1988), because ownership of the scale against which the reputations of governments are weighed is a tremendous international prize. By bringing in new and so far unacknowledged actors of international finance – prestige, certification, and their ownership and benefits – this chapter makes this point clear.

The result may provide new ways of thinking about international financial crises, present and past. The importance of the certification system and the value of its ownership are at the heart of the current European debt crisis. The concern shown by authorities – the European Central Bank (ECB), Germany – to make sure Greek debt would eventually be delivered after several restructurings, may be interpreted within the framework of this chapter. On the one hand, a Greek default would void the reassurances given during the 2000s by the ECB and Germany that the euro was a serious thing and default was not really an option. Default would cast doubt on the credibility of European policy makers. On the other hand, forcing the Greeks to repay rescues earlier pledges and covers the back of the same policy makers. It may be that Greece is really "bailing out" Germany. Observers fixated on the disruptions the policy might create, just as observers obsessed with the "errors" of the interwar blame the politicians and talk of political stupidity or incompetence.[2] But as this chapter will show, for the stupid, stupidity has its perks.

The balance of the chapter is organized as follows. The first section covers the political economy of prestige, and the next section describes the fight between New Dealers and the prestigious houses, in particular the House of Morgan. The following section articulates the likely effects of the New Deal financial acts for the political economy of prestige and is followed by the observed results. The final section discusses implications for borrowers and for policy makers. It shows that key features of the modern system were introduced by the New Deal financial acts. The chapter's conclusion emphasizes the importance of brands, the ownership of quality signals, and more generally the "immaterial" foundations of the material economy. This approach can be conceived as an economic alternative to ill-defined references to "mentalities" of which cultural historians are fond and which some economic historians have espoused (Eichengreen and Temin 2000; Temin 2010).

---

[2] See Eichengreen (2015b) for a recent illustration.

The Political Economy of Prestige

The Argument: Reliable Bankers

The foreign debt market played a special role in the rhetoric of the 1930s according to which Wall Street had failed Main Street. In the language of the time, people spoke of how the "international bankers" had failed "Tom, Dick and Harry." Although the foreign debt market represented only a fraction of the asset classes that experienced considerable stress at the time, it was a significant one, both directly, because it controlled the export of capital, and indirectly, because it was used as a lesson for the capital market at large. Several reasons explain this focus on the foreign debt market. It was in this market that the first wave of bond defaults took place at a fairly early stage of the Great Depression, as early as January 1931 and accelerating in the fall of that year. The first congressional hearings – the U.S. Senate Committee on Finance Hearings on the Sale of Foreign Bonds hearings organized by the end of 1931 – focused on foreign government debt. When newspapers and politicians looked for an example in order to denounce what came to be known as "banksterism," they turned to issues by Bolivia and the Dominican Republic. And when they looked for an example to motivate the Glass-Steagall Act, which contemplated the separation of commercial and investment banking, they turned to the failures of Charles E. Mitchell, chairman of the National City Bank, a leading commercial bank whose security affiliate (the National City Company) had been responsible for bringing to the market a number of sovereign and sub-sovereign deals that went bad. Some subsequent business historians, having examined the matter more closely, came to doubt the charges, however. Benston (1990) reviews allegations of bankers' misconduct that attracted public scrutiny during either the Senate Committee on Finance Hearings on the Sale of Foreign Bonds (1931–1932) or the subsequent hearings of the U.S. Senate Committee on Banking and Currency (started January 1933) and finds evidence of widespread accusations that are limited and unpersuasive. Huertas and Silverman (1986) take a look at the quality of the portfolio underwritten by the National City Company and find no compelling evidence of wrongdoing.[3]

---

[3] Early attempts to debunk some of the financial myths on which the reforms of the New Deal fed include Moore (1934) and Edwards (1942). See Kroszner and Rajan (1994) for a modern treatment; these authors, however, focus on the classic argument that the security affiliates of commercial banks underperformed. This perspective is different from the one adopted in this chapter.

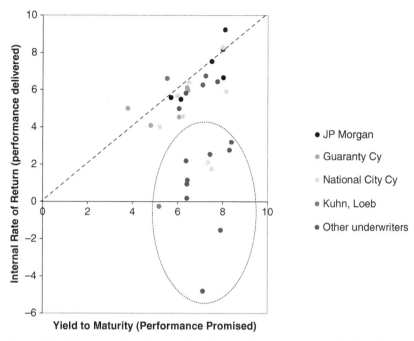

Figure 6.1 Delivering value: deals, underwriters, and performance in the New York
market.
Source: Author, from Flandreau, Gaillard and Panizza (2010) and Eichengreen and Werley (1988).

A natural starting point, therefore, is to provide more systematic
empirical evidence on the performance of banking houses in the foreign
debt market. To that end, Figure 6.1 plots the actual (realized) returns of
a given bond (measured by tracking later coupon payments, conversions,
or reimbursement) against its promised return (measured as the initial
yield to maturity, an indicator of the initial payment promise). If, for a
given security, the realization matched the promise, the bond is located
on the diagonal 45 degree line. If all or most of the deals originated by a
given underwriter are found along the diagonal 45 degree line, then all or
most of that underwriter's deals may be said to have performed and the
said underwriter is reliable. By contrast, less reliable bankers have realized returns that fall short of promised yields and show up below the
45 degree line. For data, the chart relies on a selection of thirty-nine
sovereign bonds issued in New York during the 1920s, which for simplicity can be treated as a "sample." It comes from Eichengreen and Werley
(1988) who compute realized performance for a number of New York

issues.[4] This selection was matched against the population of foreign issues in New York in Flandreau, Gaillard, and Panizza (2010), enabling the author to identify the yield at issue and the underwriter. In the figure, each underwriter is identified by circles of different shades. To ensure legibility and drive the point home, the figure simply distinguishes the four main sovereign debt underwriters by market share (JP Morgan, National City Company, Kuhn and Loeb, and Guaranty Trust) from the collection of smaller underwriters, called "others."[5]

The novel result is the marked difference that existed between the reliability of leading underwriters and the rest. All but three of the twenty-two deals made by the four more important houses are found at or near the reliability line. Not a single Morgan or Morgan-controlled Guaranty Trust deal is found away from it. Perhaps consistently with contemporary criticism, two of the three problem deals were with the National City Company. However, for this sample at least, this represented only a fraction of the securities the National City Company had underwritten. By contrast, nine of the seventeen deals (about half) from the other houses are found in the disappointment area. This indicates that behavioral hazard was not uniformly spread, but tended to concentrate on smaller underwriters. This result appears to have been known to insiders. On March 27, 1933, Morgan's partner Thomas W. Lamont sent Franklin Roosevelt a memorandum stating that "because of the natural publicity given to witness-stand disclosures, particularly in the case of National City Bank officials, the country seems to have gained the impression that questionable practices prevail in the New York banks and that these banks are largely responsible for the country's banking difficulties. This is clearly not the case."[6]

The logic whereby banks might have behaved responsibly can be interpreted in the language of modern theories of signaling and of the role of

---

[4] Eichengreen and Werley (1988) provide returns on forty-three "sovereign" bonds (as well as seventy-three sub-sovereigns, not considered here). Matching this against the list in Flandreau, Gaillard, and Panizza (2010) gives thirty-nine deals. The four "missing" deals are three Canadian deals (which underwriters did not consider as "foreign" and were excluded from the Flandreau, Gaillard, Panizza dataset) and one French deal (French National Mail Steamship, which could not be ascribed to an underwriter). The sample in Eichengreen and Werley (1988) is different from the one mentioned in Eichengreen and Portes (1989a, p. 14), which had "over 200 dollar bonds." Data for this larger sample is no longer available. The author thanks Barry Eichengreen for discussing this with him.

[5] Flandreau, Gaillard, and Panizza (2010) identify forty-four different names. Only a fraction of them shows up in Eichengreen and Werley (1988).

[6] TWL 127–31. Memorandum to FDR, March 27, 1933.

reputation in disciplining intermediaries. These arguments suggest that an intermediary with a large market share will worry about losing market power and will consistently be led to adopt a prudent behavior. Spence (1973) provides the foundations of signaling theory. Shapiro (1983) explains investments in quality by showing that reputation is a source of rents. Diamond (1989) emphasizes the role of repeat play in bringing about a kind of weeding out of less serious intermediaries. A relevant application of this insight to economic history is Gorton (1996), who suggests that intermediaries' reputation formation deters wrongful behavior. All of these arguments converge to emphasize the importance of prestige as an immaterial yet valuable asset. A large literature concerned with underwriters' reputation has explored the theoretical and empirical association between prestige (which is tied to either market share or capital) and the performance of public offerings. Chemmanur and Fulghieri (1994) are credited with the first relevant model in which financial intermediaries' reputation for veracity mitigates the moral hazard problem in information production. Carter, Dark, and Singh (1998) show that, over the long run, issues managed by prestigious houses outperform those managed by ordinary ones.

Table 6.1 provides a test of these arguments in the context of the interwar foreign debt crisis. Unlike in Figure 6.1, which documents a sample, Table 6.1 compares the performance of sovereign debt deals per underwriter for the entire population. Performance is proxied by the average default rate. In line with theories of signaling, we identify the

Table 6.1 *Market Shares, Default Rates, and the Capital of New York Underwriters*

	Market Share *	Performance: (Own Default Rate)/(Others' Default Rate) **	Capital Stock 1927–1929 (Millions USD)
J. P. Morgan	31%	0.26	94.0
City Company	13%	0.74	22.5
Kuhn and Loeb	6%	0.57	21.5
Guaranty Company	6%	0.54	10.0 †
Others (average)	1%	1	n.a.

Source: Author's computation from database in Flandreau, Gaillard and Panizza (2010). For capital stock, see note to Figure 6.2.

* As a percentage of the amount of capital raised, 1920–1929.

** Based on number of defaults occurring before the end of World War II. Excluding post-1934 defaults substantially

† Estimate based on data for 1933.

underwriter's market share and capital as relevant variables influencing the banks' behavior. Specifically, these theories predict a negative connection between performance measured as the firm's default rate compared to that of the population, excluding the four leading underwriters and market share or capital. The J. P. Morgan line in Table 6.1 reads as follows: Morgan originated the largest share (31 percent) of the amount of capital raised in New York for foreign loans, the incidence of default among its securities was the lowest (a quarter, or 0.26 of the population's average) and its capital stock before the crisis was the largest ($94 million). As seen from the other cells, Table 6.1 supports the idea of a negative association between market share and capital on the one hand and the incidence of sovereign default on the other (note again the somewhat "too" high default rate of the National City Company). At broad brush, the evidence lends support to the views of Jacob H. Schiff, former principal of Kuhn and Loeb, that "our only attractiveness is our good name and our reputation for sound advice and integrity. If that is gone, our business is gone, however attractive our show window might be" (Birmingham 1967, p. 181).

This striking result has been either ignored or downplayed in the literature, especially the economic literature. Mintz (1951) is the only author to have discussed whether reputational concerns could have mattered, reporting some data consistent with our findings, but she remained skeptical of the possibility. Eichengreen has energetically criticized the reputation argument, suggesting that in the context of New York in the 1920s, when the market for sovereign debt was new, the forces of reputation would have been counterbalanced by a "lemons" problem:

> While [the logic of the reputation argument] is impeccable, it may apply imperfectly to the 1920s by virtue of the fact that many institutional participants in the international bond market were recent entrants . . . If, in the long run, track record in comparison with incumbents will drive unsuccessful entrants out of the market, there is no reason to suppose that these forces had much effects between 1921 and 1929. (1989, pp. 122–123)

But the evidence in Figure 6.1 and Table 6.1 does suggest otherwise.

The London Precedent

One way to understand better how the forces of reputation operated in the New York market for foreign debt in the 1920s is to put them in perspective. New York followed on the steps of the experience of London, whose techniques it adopted. Flandreau and Flores (2009, 2012a) discuss the set of techniques used by the London sovereign debt market in the nineteenth century. They construct foreign debt "league tables" and find that the nineteenth century had two leaders: by decreasing order of prestige, Rothschilds and Barings. These two had the largest market share in London during all sub-periods and had the lowest market share in defaulted securities. Rothschilds, in particular, was famous for "specializing" in reliable securities. As early as the 1820s, in the midst of a fierce foreign debt crisis, Rothschild's entire portfolio of originated loans (which included countries as diverse as Prussia, Brazil, Russia, and the Kingdom of Naples) thoroughly held its ground. The habit of making good loans persisted during the entire nineteenth century (Flandreau, Flores, Gaillard, and Nieto-Para 2010).

When booms took place, the London market witnessed the entry of new underwriters – "wildcats" – who came in for a quick buck and then walked away after the crash. As a result, reliability charts similar to Figure 6.1 can be drawn for nineteenth-century London. Flandreau and Flores (2012a, p. 364) provide such a picture for deals originated between 1845 and 1875. The graph shows Rothschild's deals on the reliability line, a few Baring deals off it, and other underwriters' deals failing to deliver (which made sense, since the high yields at issue precisely reflected the rational expectation that many of them would fail). Thus, since the underlying economics were understood by the market, deals originated by less prestigious banks initially sold at significantly lower prices than those originated by prestigious banks, creating incentives for borrowers to try and persuade the prestigious banks to take care of their loans (Suzuki 1994). Flandreau and Flores (2012b) estimate the spread to have been as large as 150–300 basis points. Foreign debt booms may have weakened discipline owing to investors' exuberance, but they did not topple it altogether. This was observed even in the early stages of the market (Flandreau and Flores 2009).

When defaults in the portfolio of prestigious underwriters took place, the bankers worked to make sure investors would nonetheless get compensated. A case in point was the Baring crisis, whereby Argentina's default was followed by the collapse of the House of Barings (through its exposure to a public utility). Investors in Argentine securities (a substantial fraction of which had been originated by Barings) were still compensated. Another interesting case was the Brazilian Funding Loan of 1898. Years of poor macroeconomic management had put Brazil on the verge of default. A default would have reflected poorly on Rothschild's track record because for years they had distributed the debts of this country. Instead, Rothschild's managed to implement a debt restructuring that protected the ex post performance for investors. This ensured that their brand would be perceived as reliable. The point is that prestigious bankers had something to give away, enabling them to monitor borrowers. In sum, good borrowers were not so much "discovered" by prestigious banks as they were "produced" (Flandreau and Flores 2012a), or to use the expression that interwar American investment bankers would prefer, "constructed." An important consequence was the inherent tendency of the system to persist. Once prestigious brands came to own the ability to signal new loans, they also secured the good will of the borrowers who could share the gains of discipline by showing good behavior and the trust of investors who did not run away at the first sign of trouble, thus enabling the bankers to do their job.

Transition

Emphasis on persistence suggests that shifts in leadership were difficult to obtain. Before World War I, London-based institutions had indeed managed to protect the incumbency of the city. Why was New York able to challenge London successfully? Carosso and Sylla (1991) discuss the beginning of foreign debt underwriting in New York before World War I and show it had been originally contained to issues relevant to the U.S. "backyard" (Asia, Central America). For outsiders willing to dig an inroad in the prestige system, the dilemma can be summarized as follows: one's concern with prestige limits risk taking, but without risk taking, how can one ever topple the incumbent? Early accounts explaining the transformation that occurred afterward point to the rise of the United States as a creditor country (Dickens 1933; Lewis 1938; Stallings 1987). However, the availability of resources is not the same as the ownership of an information asymmetries–reducing technology: an intermediary is not the same thing as an investor. It is the ownership of the signaling technology, not the ownership of capital, that determines where the market is located.

What was needed to shift the equilibrium was a shock that would prevent the former system from operating. World War I provided the occasion. As a result of the drain that the war created on

Britain's balance of payments, foreign issues were suspended. Then, once peace was restored, foreign issues were subjected to the tight supervision of the Bank of England (Moggridge 1972). So it is not that Britain had less capital; rather, its intermediation role was hampered. Atkin (1977, p. 28) describes the succession of bans imposed on foreign loans. Until 1925 foreign (and often colonial) loans were banned or subject to clearance by the Bank of England. The ban was resumed in 1929. Foreign borrowers found the London market sealed when they needed it. Rather than fighting the new trends, European banks offered support to their clients by redirecting them to the New York houses. The situation opened an opportunity for New York bankers.

Previous authors have emphasized the role of the House of Morgan in "Americanizing" London financial techniques (Parrini 1969). Indeed a critical cog in achieving the transition from London to New York certification was the link that existed between J. P. Morgan in New York and J. S. Morgan in London. It enabled Morgans (and their allies) to grow inside the existing framework.[7] One reason why Morgans were natural candidates for providing certification services to an expanding New York capital market was that they had already pioneered in railway and other corporate underwriting activities the signaling techniques on which the management of sovereign debt would rest. According to DeLong (1991), the men that the House of Morgan put on the boards of railway and other companies served to resolve the information asymmetries that plagued the operation of the New York capital market in the age of the "robber barons."[8] The monopoly power of Morgans and Money Trust was a source of valuable signaling. In other words, Morgans and Money Trust banks provided a prestige technology. Given this, it is not surprising that before World War I, the handful of foreign government debt deals that New York managed to win in cooperation with other financial centers were precisely secured by

---

[7] This was not unlike what had happened a century earlier when London had succeeded Amsterdam as the main market for foreign government debt. After the introduction of the Continental System by Napoleon in 1806, the House of Hope, a former leader in the Amsterdam market for foreign debt merged with Barings. This paved the road for the rise of Barings as a leader in foreign underwriting (Buist 1974).

[8] For a dissenting view, see Leslie Hannah (2007). For a recent empirical study, see Frydman and Hilt (2014).

Morgans and their Money Trust allies (Dickens 1933; Carosso and Sylla 1991).

Notwithstanding the financial economics rationale for the Money Trust suggested by DeLong, it remains that the political acceptability of the arrangement was considerably weaker in the United States than it had proved to be in the United Kingdom. Because the arrangement, known to the public as the "Money Trust," conferred considerable market power to the Morgans and their allies, the Morgans came under intense public scrutiny. One result was the Pujo Committee in 1912–1913, which enabled lead attorney Samuel Untermeyer to investigate the noncompetitive practices of bankers. Influential critics such as Louis Brandeis criticized the inherent conflicts of interest of financial intermediaries and found that Morgan's monopoly power was a source of abuse (Brandeis 1914). The Money Trust was, Brandeis argued, servant of two masters: the investors and the borrowers. It could not be honest vis-à-vis both. This was something that was to play a critical role in the upheaval of the 1930s.

London as Counterfactual

According to Karl Polanyi, in the 1920s, "J. P. Morgan had replaced N. M. Rothschild as the demiurge of a rejuvenated nineteenth century" (Polanyi 1944). And indeed, the parallel between the arguments heard in two public hearings that followed waves of sovereign defaults the British Select Committee on Loans to Foreign States (1875) and those proffered before the American Senate Committee on Finance Hearings on the Sale of Foreign Government Bonds (1931–1932) is striking. Just as Nathaniel de Rothschild had boasted that he was dealing 'with good loans only' (Select Committee on Loans to Foreign States, minutes of evidence, p. 270), representatives of the leading New York houses emphasized their prudence and concerns with the interests of the investor. For instance, asked whether they had engaged in "strong-arm salesmanship" (forcing securities on ignorant buyers), Otto Kahn from Kuhn and Loeb declared,

[S]uch practices as what you might term 'strong-arm methods' of selling, making raids on rather unwilling buyers, exercising undue persuasiveness, tempting buyers by excessive facilities, inducements or exactions, in short, high-powered methods of salesmanship are against the dignity and the ethics of banking. They are not within the permissible functions of a bank or banker." (U.S. Congress, Senate Committee on Finance 1931–1932, p. 394)

In fact, Kahn argued, "the banker is called upon to exercise a greater degree of care than pretty nearly anyone else who is dealing with the public, because he is dealing with a commodity as to which he is considered to be an expert adviser and as to which many people rely on his integrity" (U.S. Congress, Senate Committee on Finance 1931–1932, p. 353).

Refusal to act as intermediary for loans that were considered dubious was a matter of pride at Morgans just as it had been at Rothschilds, and Thomas W. Lamont insisted that they would "never issue a bond unless [they did] believe it to be good" (Adamson 2006, p. 204).

Another parallel between London merchant bankers of the nineteenth century and New York investment bankers of the twentieth century is the function they fulfilled in their respective geopolitical contexts. Corti (1928) and Polanyi (1944) provide evidence that the House of Rothschild was "in the employ" of the Holy Alliance and became an instrument to protect peace and the interests of the alliance. Flandreau and Flores (2012b) explain why this might have been so: the success of Rothschild loans to members of the alliance (Prussia, Russia, and Austria) was dependent on the continuation of peace. Rothschilds used its certification role to design contracts that would favor peace. An illustration was the crisis triggered by Belgium's independence from the Netherlands in 1830 when a clause conditioning the disbursement of funds upon political moderation was included in the contract.[9] In other words, high finance was politically supported by government as an instrument for shaping geopolitics.

A similar situation was observed regarding the rise of New York bankers as vehicles of global certification when the State Department, at the end of World War I, decided to delegate the monitoring of foreign financial policy to international bankers. In 1921, an agreement was adopted between bankers and President Harding. Bankers would manage the export of capital but would check with the State Department whether individual loans were in conflict with policy agenda. Foreign lending was being embedded in the broader template of the U.S. administration.[10] The

---

[9] In a similar spirit, Oosterlinck, Ureche-Langau, and Vaslin (2014) describe how the Duke of Wellington used Barings in the early nineteenth century as an instrument to bring pressure to bear on the French.

[10] Contemporary observers and participants have abundantly discussed the resulting cooperation between international bankers and the U.S. administration (Lamont 1920; Dulles 1926; Edwards 1928). It is now a standard subject in the academic literature (Lewis 1938;

result was that banking elites came to identify themselves with subsequent Republican presidencies and their policies. They became the advisors and architects of Polanyi's "rejuvenated nineteenth century." Like their British predecessors, they ardently promoted free trade, which would ensure the repayment of the loans.[11] And also like their British predecessors, they thought of themselves as "peacekeepers."[12]

However, this identification between prestigious bankers and the U.S. policies of the 1920s became the bankers' principal liability after 1929 and even more so after 1931, when the crisis spread and previous attitudes were questioned. It became a bone of contention during the Senate committee hearings of 1931–1932. It was alleged that the tacit support of the administration had created a moral hazard problem by persuading the investing public that the U.S. government stood behind foreign loans (bankers insisted before the Senate committee that this was not the case). Thus the committee hearings rekindled the embers of the Money Trust investigations, which were anything but extinguished. In 1924, the publication of two articles by Samuel Guy Inman in *The Atlantic Monthly* denounced U.S. foreign loans and the dollar policy as imperialism, sparking an important controversy. The matter was then buried in the so-called Ladd Senate hearings of 1925 (Rosenberg 2003). But by the time the presidential campaign for the election of November 1932 had begun, the infamous "international bankers" were a natural political prey. Franklin Roosevelt was quick to seize the opportunity, and in his August 20, 1932, speech in Columbus, Ohio, he announced sweeping financial reforms: greater disclosure and liability in the underwriting of securities, the separation of commercial and investment banking, the rigid supervision of banks, and so on. Regarding the "international bankers," he promised the American public "that it will no longer be possible for international bankers or others to sell foreign securities to the investing public of America

---

Parrini 1969; Abrahams 1976; Stallings 1987). A recent, thorough discussion is Adamson (2002, pp. 483–487).

[11] As Thomas W. Lamont explained to Charles E. Hughes, "[I]t must be obvious that if the country is really to act the part of a creditor nation it must be prepared to handle the situation broadly and without restrictive and crippling measures." TWL, 94–18, "Foreign Credit," letter to Hon. Charles E. Hughes, March 31, 1922.

[12] For instance, when he discussed the quality of bonds underwritten by Kuhn and Loeb, Otto Kahn emphasized that they declined military loans (U.S. Congress, Senate Committee on Finance, 1931–1932, p. 357).

on the implied understanding that these securities have been passed on or approved by the State Department or any other agency of the Federal Government."[13]

The link between the earlier teachings of Louis Brandeis and FDR's financial endeavors during the 1930s is both evident and essential. By the time the New Deal was launched, Louis Brandeis was a deeply revered figure and an influential judge on the Supreme Court. Through his protégé, Harvard Law School professor Felix Frankfurter, Brandeis had managed to create a generation of young lawyers who were committed to his ideas. As an illustration of this legacy, we have FDR's repeated, almost obsessive, use of the phrase "other people's money" in many campaign speeches, a phrase which he took from the title of Brandeis' 1914 book. We also have the wording of the new president's inaugural address on the "money changers," whom FDR wanted swept "out of the temple," again connecting with Brandeis' characteristic rhetoric. Moreover, we have the fact that Felix Frankfurter's students – men such as Benjamin V. Cohen, Thomas V. Corcoran and his Harvard Law School colleague James M. Landis, as well as lawyers who had been directly inspired by Louis Brandeis, such as William O. Douglas – soon became involved in the financial reforms brought about by the New Deal and articulated a new catechism of regulation. Or again, the New Deal relied on Guy Inman, the leader of the campaign against American imperialism in the 1920s, as the living "symbol of a change toward a 'good neighbor policy.'" In 1933, Inman would accompany Secretary of State Cordell Hull to the Seventh Pan-American Conference and remained an active advisor to both Hull and Roosevelt.[14]

This turn of events was unlike anything that had taken place in Britain. In fact, the dislocation of the previously near perfect parallel between London in the nineteenth century and New York in the 1920s provides a methodological inspiration. Knowledge of the London market and the way it responded to financial turmoil and handled debt crises provides a means for constructing a counter-factual that sheds light on the dynamics of the evolutions experienced by the New York market for foreign debt during the 1930s.

---

[13] At American Presidency Project, www.presidency.ucsb.edu/index.php.
[14] Rosenberg (2003, p. 137).

The Politics of Brands

Roosevelt's Ohio speech lashed out at international bankers but craftily avoided alienating the House of Morgan and the banking elite, describing investment banking as a "legitimate business." The Morgan partners may have believed that FDR had to concede reforms in order to attract the median voter, but when they approached the new president with free advice, they soon realized that FDR planned substantial changes and reducing their power was part of that plan. The signs of times were abundant. Chernow (1990, p. 355) writes that when Senator Carter Glass was approached about taking the Treasury job in the Roosevelt administration, he suggested he would want to hire two Morgan men (Leffingwell and Parker Gilbert); however, Roosevelt "cringed": "We simply can't tie up with 23 [23 Wall Street was the home of Morgans]," he said.

The Hearst press emphasized the exclusion of Morgans from decision-making centers and interpreted it as a loss of prestige. *New York American*'s financial editor, Julius Berens, argued that the shift had begun during the compulsory "Bank Holiday" in early March 1933: "Morgan partners have been noticeably absent from the innermost circles of the new Administration. Invariably, during the last Administration, the Morgan firm was called in instantly whenever a financial crisis developed." And to be fully sure, he added, "[Morgan]'s decline in prestige was emphasized by the fact that none of the emergency meetings which preceded the Bank Holiday were held in Morgan offices." This underscores the extent to which prestige did not solely rest on the track record, but also on government support, whether tacit or explicit.[15]

Because this was a conflict about the "democracy and finance nexus" as identified by New Dealer and Securities and Exchange Commission chairman William O. Douglas in a famous pamphlet (Douglas 1940), it mobilized the tools of democracy. The press, and press reports of the latest developments in the capital markets, played a critical role in building the case against the "international bankers." In the final run-up to the election of FDR, the Hearst press (which until 1934 supported Roosevelt) stepped up pressure and published accusations against international bankers who, "as you all know from exposure and experience, are centered on foreign loans and big commissions, rather than on the essential interests of the American people." The claims were then backed by more or less vague and vaguely stated "facts," which were vaguely amended when Lamont

---

[15] *New York American*, March 10, 1933.

confronted Hearst with threats of legal action.[16] Father Coughlin, whom Lamont assumed to have been "somewhat sponsored" by "Old Henry Morgenthau" (Roosevelt's Treasury Secretary), preached for the benefit of millions of midwestern radio listeners that "until a few years ago, the banker was as respected as a clergyman .... Today [... those in] the international group – the gold group – are not only in disrepute. Their presence amongst respectable Americans is becoming obnoxious. Their bankcraft at New York is more pernicious than was witchcraft at Salem."[17] And then of course there was the Senate Committee on Banking and Currency, which under Ferdinand Pecora went on to "expose" Wall Street malpractice. These "Pecora hearings" claimed several symbolic prizes. In addition to the shaming and resignation of Charles E. Mitchell, president of National City Company, which per se "proved" the wrong-doings, Pecora managed to produce Morgan balance sheets under threat of subpoena, thus violating the privacy of the most secret private bank. This, plus the interruption of a midget who jumped on Jack Morgan's lap during the hearings, were public statements that "prestige" was not above the "American People," a notion captured in the title of Pecora's *Wall Street under Oath: The Story of Our Modern Money Changers* (Pecora 1936).

These events were significant because they made a decisive contribution to a process of wilting, which ended up undermining the reputation of the elite banker. As suggested, political destruction of prestige came from a number of avenues, and Lamont's papers bear witness to the bank's losing efforts to deal with the loss of reputation. One way to fully capture the significance of this process is to contrast it with what happened in Britain under similar circumstances. As indicated, parliamentary commissions comparable to the Senate committee hearings of 1931–1932 had taken place in Victorian Britain. The 1875 House of Commons Committee on Loans to Foreign States provides proof. Its concerns had been very similar to those of the Senate Committee Hearings on the Sale of Foreign Bonds: the high fees, the dishonest promotion of Latin American loans, and the manipulation of market prices. The key difference, however, was that the British debate, virulent as it was and despite the intervention of some radical politicians, had been mostly conducted by the elite, principally within elite media (such as *The Economist* and *The Times*), and for the benefit of the elite, and it accepted the notion that the uninformed outsider

---

[16] TWL papers, 98–2. Statement by Randolph Hearst during a broadcast of the National Broadcast Company Network, December 2, 1933.
[17] TWL Papers, 84–16. Letter by TWL, December 28, 1933; Rev. Chas. E. Coughlin, transcript of broadcast, November 19, 1933, 4 p.m. eastern standard time.

who had bought bonds "out of greed" deserved no compassion. In such a context, the hearings resulted not in complaints about bankers' malpractice but in the condemnation of some specific "wildcat" bankers and the admonishment of the middle class investor for the hubris it had displayed in investing its money in a Paraguay loan at 10 percent when British government bonds yielded 3 percent. Not so, perhaps, in a country where democracy was deeply entrenched (Calomiris and Haber 2014).

To summarize, the very fact that banks' floatation and distribution of foreign government securities could be questioned was per se a judgment – very much like the production of Morgan's balance sheet. This interpretation is consistent with Carosso (1970b), who argues that one of the goals of the New Deal acts was "harassing [bankers] out of business."[18] However, the present analysis adds the following: since the business of underwriting foreign sovereign debt rested on prestige, public harassment itself was a form of undermining. How could bankers bring to the market funding loans and implement stabilization programs in the same successful way as their London predecessors had, at the very same time when they were named and shamed on Main Street?

The Rock and the Hard Place

I now turn to the consequences that the New Deal had for the underwriting of foreign government debt. Financial legislation that was adopted after the election of FDR followed a multi-pronged regulatory program that had two main, complementary dimensions. It sought to reorganize security underwriting by increasing "transparency" (the preferred word was "publicity"), and it sought to police the distribution of securities (Carosso 1970a, 1970b). In a long list of changes, three acts, debated from the spring of 1933 onward should specifically command our attention. They were the Banking Act (more popularly known as the Glass-Steagall Act), which divorced commercial and investment banking; the Amended Securities Act, which increased underwriter's liability; and the Securities Exchange Act, which created high standards of disclosure and forced banks to reveal information surrounding security issues. This section discusses their effects, focusing on how the acts interfered with the economic logic of foreign debt certification as it has been described earlier in this chapter.[19]

---

[18] Carosso (1970b), p. 439.

[19] These acts were followed by a long series of other pieces of meaningful legislation, not discussed here for the sake of simplicity; For a list of major New Deal security laws, see Carosso (1970b, p. 433, n. 22).

Glass-Steagall and the Crowding Out of Prestige

Glass-Steagall is well known for having achieved the separation of investment and commercial banking. This is usually understood as meaning the exclusion of security affiliates from the market for securities, a change that did not mean any business difficulty for investment banks such as J. P. Morgan or Kuhn and Loeb. Commercial banks were those facing the dilemma: a spin-off of their security affiliate would create a bank operating under the same "name," but the main bank would no longer have control over it. Moreover, a change of name would destroy reputational capital. The case of National City Bank offers valuable evidence. According to Cleveland and Huertas (1985, pp. 197–198), National City Bank's new chairman, James H. Perkins (who had succeeded Charles E. Mitchell), worried that selling off City Bank's security affiliate, the National City Company, would amount to selling the affiliate's "goodwill," which was embedded in National City Bank's name, but now borne out by an entity the National City Bank would no longer control. On the other hand Glass-Steagall forbade control of the separated affiliate. Should the spin-off misbehave after the split, this might impact National City Bank's own reputation. But, if the name was removed – that is, once stripped of prestige – then the security affiliate was not worth much. Thus, the immediate effect of the divorce of investment and commercial banking was to crowd out the capital of the more reliable security affiliates.

This was good news for the investment banks, who would see their potential market share increase and whose leaders would not only retain their operation, but expand and match the increase in required personnel by their capital outlays to compensate for security affiliates' withdrawal. Such was the working hypothesis leading investment banks took as a starting point of their lobbying effort during the discussion of Glass-Steagall (Carosso 1970b). As such, Glass-Steagall was good for them. An illustrative statement is found in the March 1933 Lamont memorandum to FDR already quoted. There, Thomas W. Lamont argues that

the corollary to the suggestion that commercial banks should dispense with their affiliates and withdraw from the capital issues must be that private bankers, issuing houses and dealers should be encouraged and facilitated to resume their former place in the national economy to the end that the machinery for handling capital issues shall be recreated and so recovery from depression facilitated.[20]

---

[20] TWL 127–31, March 27, 1933, p. 9. Likewise, a handwritten note (March 1933, probably by Lamont) in TWL Papers, 80–13, states: "If it is determined to take the banks out of the investment securities business then it must be the policy of the Government to strengthen

But the New Deal had something in store for investment banks, too. Following the Bank Holiday, the initial spirit of an amicable divorce was replaced by something much more hostile. Public attention was focused on the problem of bank runs, to which their closure by FDR had been an emergency response. The press was full of calls to ring-fence the balance sheet of commercial banks. The industry, represented by Chase's Winthrop W. Aldrich, retaliated by arguing that if commercial banks were to be parked into the dull business of deposit taking, at least they should be rewarded by some kind of monopoly. And if commercial banks would not be underwriting, Aldrich suggested, then unregulated investment banks should not get into deposit taking. He succeeded in having this provision drafted into the final Glass-Steagall bill, which was signed into law in June 1933. Evidence from a letter by Carter Glass to Leffingwell suggests that the provision, drafted by Aldrich, was foisted on Senator Glass by Roosevelt.[21]

In other words, the new turn the Glass-Steagall bill was taking was a direct challenge to the more prestigious investment banks. This was understood to be the case by contemporary observers: the press took notice of this and immediately interpreted it as a challenge to Morgans.[22] The problem can be understood in light of standard arguments about the role of deposits in relationship banking, which emphasize that bankers learn about their customers by studying the evolution of deposits (Black 1975; Fama 1985). Now, if unsupervised investment banks were authorized to keep those deposits, while the security affiliates were shut down, this would be to the advantage of J. P. Morgan and Kuhn and Loeb. The transfer would also increase the flow of valuable current account information and would boost the investment banks' ability to monitor customers. Not so if investment banks were prevented from taking deposits. The challenge had special significance for the foreign debt market. In the past, leading

the investment bankers rather than hamper them since the flow of capital must be resumed." With similar logic, Carosso (1970a) argues that J. P. Morgan initially sought to exploit the new regulation as a way to get rid of competitors, which was reflected in the initial blueprint of Glass-Steagall, and had been the main focus of Senator Glass.

[21] Chernow (1990, p. 375, and footnote 87).

[22] TWL 80–13. *New York American*, March 10, 1933, "Rockefeller Seen Challenging Supremacy of Morgan – Program Interpreted as Rockefeller Challenge to Morgans." Article by Julius Berens: "There was no alternative for Wall Street than to interpret the Aldrich declarations as a direct challenge by the John D. Rockefeller faction to the private banking houses headed by J.P. Morgan & C°, and comprising the whole gamut of publicly unregulated creators and vendors of securities who also, under present practices, are recipient of enormous deposits." *New York Times*, March 10, 1933, "Aldrich Proposals Stir Private Banks."

investment banks such as J. P. Morgan along with leading commercial banks such as the National City Bank had been among the principal New York recipients of foreign government deposits (Eichengreen and Flandreau 2009). The reform thus threatened the ability of Morgans to receive the deposits of the governments it lent to, while National City Bank could take such deposit but would not lend.

Thus, the addition to Glass-Steagall of provisions preventing investment banks from deposit taking deeply modified the way they were conducting sovereign debt business. On the one hand, accepting supervision would force disclosure and would thus deprive prestigious banks of the ability to draw on their own buffer of prestige during crises. On the other hand, giving away deposits would both weaken their balance sheet and their ability to stand on the edge of valuable information flows. Fundamentally, the shedding of deposits weakened the relation between prestigious banks and their sovereign customers.[23] It raised questions about the viability of older ways and was likely to lead investment banks to reconsider their options. This was indeed Morgan's view: in a brief to *New York Times* financial editor Alexander Dana Noyes, Lamont emphasized that if put into effect, the divorce of investment and commercial banking as envisioned would "make it impossible for commercial banks to handle securities ... [A]t the same time [it would deprive] the private banks of the means of serving the public in this way ... If put into effect, they would result in tearing down all existing methods of handling securities, without substituting any adequate mechanism in their place."[24]

Liability and Transparency

The second group of significant transformations arising from New Deal financial acts resulted from the Securities Act of 1933 and the Securities Exchange Act of 1934, which amended the former. The Securities Act was concerned with primary markets while the Securities Exchange Act dealt with secondary trading. Both had in sight so-called bankers' malpractices that had emerged from congressional hearings and public debates, in particular price rigging and fictitious purchases that were said to happen during new issues. The reforms sought to raise standards of transparency

---

[23] For instance, Berlin and Mester (1999) argue that a relationship with depositors provides a co-insurance mechanism. That is, depositors receive support which protects the bank's balance sheet against withdrawals.

[24] Thomas W. Lamont, "Memorandum for A.D.N.," TWL papers 80–113.

and information dissemination at the same time they created civil liability for the underwriters.

Carosso (1970b) has contrasted the Banking Act, which would have changed the industry's landscape, and the Securities Act, which would have "merely" modified underwriters' practices without altering, over the long run, "investment bankers' primary role of channeling savings into long-term investment" (Carosso 1970b). Indeed, the New Deal's transformations did not succeed in driving investment banking out of its former niches, since a bank called J. P. Morgan-Chase was still recently the leader in foreign government debt underwriting (Flandreau, Flores, Gaillard, and Nieto-Para 2010). But this view downplays the fact that the change in practices the new rules encouraged brought about a microeconomic and informational revolution.

With the new disclosure requirements resulting from the Securities Act, all issuers were bound to reveal more. This weakened the informational advantage of prestigious houses. Moreover, the new disclosure standards were completed by a number of provisions such as the institution of a mandatory "cooling off" period of twenty days between registration with the Stock Exchange and the time when an offering could be sold to dealers and the public. The goal was to permit brokers and investors to "study" the new issue and form an "independent" opinion, there again limiting the information wedge between prestigious and less prestigious banks. This was furthered by a provision of the subsequent Securities Exchange Act that enforced transparency regarding price support operations. Explicitly intended to prevent fictitious deals that were said to deceive uninformed traders, they also increased the operational risk of prestigious houses whose public offerings, which typically involved such interventions, when needed, were now conducted in the open and thus made the prestigious investment houses more vulnerable to adverse speculation. According to Carosso (1970b, p. 433), the acts had the end result of making "[responsible investment houses] even more cautious."

Second, a critical change (brought about by the Securities Act, and partly weakened, under intense lobbying by the industry in the Securities Exchange Act) was the creation of civil liability for the underwriters. Civil liability had been repeatedly considered in the London market.[25]

---

[25] Following the American states debt debacle in the early 1840s, the *London Times* had vented investors' anger and talked about the need to replace the "moral liability" of merchant banks with "legal liability" (Hidy 1949, p. 309).

However, it was felt that this would weaken market discipline: bad loans had to be costly for investors, or else investors would never learn the lesson. Adopting civil liability as was done in the 1930s thus changed the whole microeconomics of sovereign underwriting. The inherently limited enforceability of sovereign debt contracts required that high-quality certification capital be pledged and rewarded. Holding them accountable for mishaps was a potent deterrent. The natural outcome was to make prestige "more cautious." In and by itself, the measure encouraged more prestigious investment banks to just walk out of the market, leading to a collapse of foreign debt.

The Crowding Out of Prestigious Capital and the Rise of Modern Underwriting

The previous two sections detailed a number of predictions regarding the effects of New Deal financial acts. In broad terms, two types of responses might have been expected. One would have been an outright reduction of high-quality (prestigious) capital. Another would have been the continuation of underwriting but in a much more reduced capacity as a simple "prime broker" in charge of building the order book and then walking away once the deal is completed. What this section suggests is that the two responses were observed over different time horizons. Perhaps because of their association with political hostility, the New Deal financial acts were disruptive over the short run. Over the long run they implied a reconstruction of the business of underwriting along new lines of business, characterized by reduced incentives to screen deals and support those who failed.

The Flight of High-Quality Capital

As stated previously, New Deal regulations put the various firms in a quandary. Certification capital was crowded out by regulation and regulatory risk. J. P. Morgan eventually decided to give up investment banking and focus on its relationship with its clientele of prime corporate depositors. A consonant avatar (Morgan Stanley and Co.) returned in late 1934 but with drastically reduced capital. The National City Bank shut down its security affiliate as did the Guaranty Trust. Only Kuhn and Loeb remained in the trade. One way to capture this evolution is to construct a series for the "reputable capital." The prediction is that one ought to observe a dramatic absolute decline in available prestigious capital (see Carosso

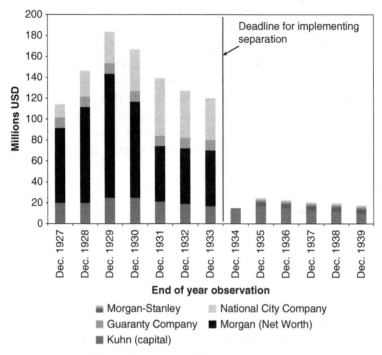

Figure 6.2 Available certification capital from four most prestigious underwriters (millions USD)

Source: Author. Bankers' Almanac, various issues (National City Company), Lehman Brothers Archive Baker Library (Kuhn and Loeb), Committee on Banking and Currency (1934) (Morgan), ProQuest's online balance sheets of the Guaranty Trust Company (Guaranty Company); Chernow (1990) (Morgan-Stanley, Created 1935).

1970b, p. 432). Figure 6.2 shows the total capital stock of the top four foreign government debt certifiers, which controlled close to 60 percent of the market before the New Deal acts. This line is the relevant measure because, while a number of investment banks entered the underwriting game using skilled staff from divested structures such as the National City Corporation, they lacked a name and a record (Stratton 2015). Note that because the capital of investment banks collateralized both corporate and investment banks, the data shown in Figure 6.2 must be taken as an upper bound. Since corporate but not sovereign debt was revived after 1935, the inference for sovereign debt is even more powerful than the chart suggests.

Figure 6.2 delivers a powerful message. The impact of the New Deal financial acts on the supply of certification capital was drastic: huge quantities of high-quality capital evaporated. Since at the same time,

London was still struggling with controls over foreign debt issues, New York international finance one-way street had come to a dead end. Note that this was happening in the midst of a violent sovereign debt crisis, precisely when supporting capital ought to have been expanded. This is prima facie evidence of the pro-cyclical effects of the New Deal on sovereign debt markets.

The Rise of Modern Foreign Securities Underwriting

I now argue that the new rules on security underwriting caused a radical change in the way senior investment banks conducted business. It led them to shed their former status as conscience of the market and adopt the more modest role it plays today of a broker matching sovereign borrowers and the institutional investors. However, establishing this proposition is not straightforward. With the retreat of high-quality capital from underwriting, the short-run effect of the change in rules was the effective closure of the New York market to foreign government issues, meaning that one cannot "observe" the effects of New Deal changes in the immediate or even medium run. One must therefore rely on a heuristic way to establish the conjecture. First, we observe what happened in the corporate securities market at the time of the financial acts. Next we describe the long-run transformation that has taken place in sovereign debt. The parallel between the two evolutions provides prima facie evidence that the New Deal financial acts played a critical role in the transformation.

Unlike the foreign debt market, corporate issues were not completely destroyed by the New Deal financial acts, probably because (as emphasized by theoreticians) the marketing and management of corporate securities does not face as enormous information asymmetries and enforcement problems as sovereign debt, and also because (as stated earlier) the New Dealers' hostility toward investment banks was absolute when it came to foreign debt. But since New Deal regulations applied across the board, their effect on corporate debt underwriting is a guide to their potential effect on sovereign debt, thus offering a kind of counterpart experiment.

Business historians' description of the responses investment bankers adopted in the market for corporate securities provides insight consistent with my prediction. Investment bankers reacted to New Deal financial acts by reducing the scope of their underwriting services, now merely working to match supply and demand. Equipped with lawyers who included covenants that limited their legal liability, they now retreated from firm commitment and started adding clauses that parked losses in subsequent price fluctuations with the issuers. Lawyer expenses became a non-negligible part of the fees they charged, while fees were gradually reduced in relation to the lesser services provided to borrowers. In turn, investment banks sought to compensate the smaller revenues by increasing the number of deals they participated in, and this raised the competitive outlook. Prime brokerage firms such as Lehman Brothers, which had previously developed niche markets, availed themselves of this new opportunity and developed the profitable business of assisting corporations intent on direct sale by helping them plan their offerings to meet market conditions, as well as compiling the necessary data for submissions to institutional buyers (Carosso 1970b, p. 437).

All these are characteristics also observable in the long-run evolution of the market for sovereign debt as described by Flandreau, Flores, Gaillard, and Nieto-Parra (2010). They emphasize that, unlike until the 1920s when sovereign underwriting rested on a formal commitment by the underwriter or underwriting syndicate to purchase part or all of the security issue and then take care of disposing of it through subscriptions and sales in the open market, modern sovereign debt underwriting involves a much less comprehensive role of the so-called underwriter who really acts as a broker, contributing to make the market and assisting in the issue, but without having as much skin in the game as it used to. This is reflected, for instance, by the fact that, while so-called firm commitment was the rule in the old system, so-called best efforts prevail today instead. It is also reflected by the fact that the modern system, which began to emerge in the interwar, was characterized by much greater competition. Herfindahl-Hirschman indicators of foreign debt market concentration suggest that the market moved from being very concentrated in the 1920s to being nonconcentrated today.

Some important aspects of the modern informational setup of foreign debt markets can also be traced to the transformations brought about by the New Deal financial acts. For instance the "red herring" a pre-prospectus circulated in advance, before which serves today as a focal point for the release of information illustrates the importance of the New Deal financial acts in changing the rules of the game in foreign debt market. Its institutionalization resulted from the New Dealers' view that it was important to create a "study time" when investors are supposed to avail themselves of the merit of a given issue. A consequence of this was the central role rating agencies came to play in the foreign debt market. Modern rating agencies produce their enlightened opinion on the theory that any proposition stands on its own merits, rather than on the merit of those who propose it.

This section is too brief and opens more issues than it can deal with – in particular, one would want to know more about the subsequent regulatory and market dynamics between the years of the New Deal and the modern era. Although there is a need for much more research on the subject, the most likely conjecture remains that New Deal financial acts deeply modified the ways in which the business of sovereign underwriting had been conducted. The change was not merely the escape of prestigious capital from the sovereign debt market that was observed in the short run. And if over the long run, investment banks remained the chief intermediaries of that market (later joined again by commercial banks when Glass-Steagall was eventually repealed), they did it in completely different ways than they had before – now fearful of liability, limited, noncommittal – reflecting the deep changes the New Deal had introduced.

Borrowers' Responses and the Crowding in of Public Capital

The previous three sections have articulated and tested predictions on the effects of New Deal financial acts for certification of foreign government debt. This final section resumes the historical narrative. Building on the previous insights, it organizes the narrative so as to underscore the manner in which the prestige system would have responded if unhampered, using the British record as a counterfactual. This enables us to underscore differential dynamics. The new system did not emerge immediately from the destruction of the old. Rather, a process of *tâtonnement* occurred, which ultimately involved institutional innovations.

Dismantled Loyalties

Early accounts of the interwar debt crisis have emphasized the gradual "deterioration" in the quality of foreign loans originated during the 1920s (Lewis 1938, Mintz 1951). Such a process was also typical of previous experiences. Flandreau and Flores (2012a,

p. 368) describe the evolution of the market share of prestige during nineteenth-century sovereign debt boom-and-bust cycles in Britain. They find that as the boom expanded, new intermediaries ("wild-cats") entered the market. Logically, incumbent prestigious banks remained cautious, avoiding the compromising of their brand in a battle against the ordinary. Taken together, these evolutions resulted in a decline in the market share of prestige. At the peak of the boom, a lull followed, which preceded the market crash. Following the crash, new loans were radically restricted and defaults began spreading. As this happened, prestigious banks regained their relative market share because defaults concentrated on new intermediaries. But more More capitalized prestigious banks could help their sovereign customers to maintain or regain market access. In the new, difficult context, "old wisdoms" were relearned and the prestigious banks' ability to address information asymmetries was prized again by investors.

Until 1931, the New York sovereign debt interwar boom-and-bust cycle did exhibit these traditional characteristics. Morgans started the market for foreign government loans in the early 1920s, and until 1925 their supremacy, along with that of other first order houses, was complete. When the boom spread to central Europe and Latin American countries beyond Argentina, Morgans and the other prestigious banks remained circumspect. They tried to organize the banks into a top-of-the-shelf underwriters' cartel – the South American Group – in order to "filter" these countries' loans and embed foreign lending into fiscal workouts that would construct the credit of the borrower. They gave up when they found that as soon as governments agreed to something with the group, they tried to secure a better deal with a lower-ranked bank and consistently eschewed the more painful adjustments. According to Thomas W. Lamont:

They would say – Yes, Yes – to everything, but the moment that somebody came along and offered them a loan for spending money at a rate that seemed to them 1/8 to 1% more favorable than what they could get from the Group, they would jump overboard and abandon all our carefully laid plans for establishing their credit and building it up step by step over a series of years ... We became so hopeless that we disbanded the Group.[26]

---

[26] TWL Papers, 102–20. On J. P. Morgan's a strong anti-Latin American loans bias, see Adamson (2006).

Kuhn and Loeb partner Otto Kahn explained later that in order to avoid succumbing to such competitive pressures "from the bottom," the bank had decided to ignore them altogether: "It is a strict tradition of my house not to compete either in South America or elsewhere."[27] Forecasting how it would all end, prestigious banks watched the boom stoically and lost market share as the boom developed (Mintz 1951; Adamson 2002, p. 483). At the peak of the boom in 1927, prestigious bankers publicly complained about "rash or excessive lending" (Winkler 1933; Adamson 2005, p. 598). They managed to enroll the Secretary of Commerce Herbert Hoover to endorse their concern to limit foreign loans.[28]

The reward was about to come after 1931, when self-restraint began to pay off in the shape of lower default rates than the underlings, something about which Morgan and Kuhn and Loeb partners boasted before the Senate Hearings on the Sale of Foreign Bonds or Securities in the United States (U.S. Congress 1932). It was now time for "house-cleaning." If previous London experiences are used as yardstick, there should have been much activity in advising client countries through the mire or in inspiring restructurings or debt renegotiations. Although this was not the type of business that brought immediate rewards in terms of fees, it nonetheless provided visibility and the opportunity for an edifying display of the moral authority of the banker.[29] Morgans and their allies already owned a stake in the shape of embryonic organizations created to deal with foreign default, although the "tranquil" 1920s (as far as sovereign debt crises are concerned) ensured that until 1931 the activity of such groups was limited. Nonetheless, in 1918, a Foreign Securities Committee (FSC) had been created within the Investment Bankers' Association in response to investors' inquiries about Russia.[30] The committee was initially chaired by Thomas W. Lamont and

---

[27] U.S. Congress, Senate Committee on Finance, 1931–1932, p. 343.

[28] "Hoover and Lamont would Limit Loans," *New York Times*, May 3, 1927.

[29] According to a memorandum written in October 29, 1928 (TWL 100–108): "We have not now to deal with any great loans in default; what we have now to do is to study developments in those countries to which we have made loans with a view of seeing that the debtor country takes no action impairing the security or rights of holders of its bonds in this country."

[30] See TWL papers, 100–108. This occurred when Hayden, president of the Investment Banking Association, inquired with Morgan's about the opportunity of setting up a body comparable to the Corporation of Foreign Bonders (CFB) formed in 1868 by British bondholders. Hayden's approach to Morgan's underscores the perception of its authority as a certification body.

subsequently by Charles Sabin, president of the Guaranty Trust.[31] The ad hoc country committees that were set up to deal with occasional defaults such as the International Committee of Bankers on Mexico, emanated from the FSC (Adamson 2006).

But this imaginary history of the way the House of Morgan and its allies would have "normally" found themselves dealing with the post-1931 debt crises is one that never occurred. Rather than being able to exploit the crisis as their "I told you so" against the lower banks, Morgan's found its ability to act hampered by political hostility. The Roosevelt campaign's attacks against "international bankers," which amalgamated under the same criticism of all bankers – small and large, prudent and reckless, investment bank and security affiliate of commercial banks – prevented Morgans from behaving in the usual ways of their London predecessors. Instead of being on the front line, negotiating with foreign governments, the House of Morgan's foreign debt desk was put on holiday (Adamson 2002, p. 487). One year after the Roosevelt election, Thomas W. Lamont complained that he found things "terribly dead down here."[32]

The old regime had rested on prestige being an asset. Its existence and ownership provided discipline to borrowers who were to be helped and rewarded, if they behaved as instructed. It provided discipline to underwriters who had to be careful lest they lose that prestige. At the other end of the rope, the exit of prestigious capital from the foreign debt market was bound to dismantle loyalties. For instance, the new chairman of National City Bank, James H. Perkins, worried that the liquidation of the National City Company would cause disruption because its balance sheet had been used to support the price of issues that had not gone well. Glass-Steagall forced Perkins to "get rid of the thing." But doing so triggered further declines in the securities the National City Bank had sponsored. Perkins wished he could "keep the organization together because it will be necessary for the men to handle a number of bond issues which have gone bad[,] to service those issues and give the best results possible to the owners of the bonds" – an impossible task under the New Deal (Cleveland and Huertas 1985, p. 197).

Thus, Glass-Steagall signaled to borrowers that any current efforts to adjust would not be paid back since any relationship with

---

[31] TWL papers, 100–107, 108.
[32] TWL papers, 105–107, letter to W. Lippmann, January 30, 1934.

prestigious banks was about to come to an abrupt end with the disappearance of the bank itself. Thus, the New Deal changed the time horizon of bilateral bargaining between banks and sovereigns. Borrowers did not need to be very sophisticated to understand this. It was evident when there was nobody left to call, as in the case of the National City Company and J. P. Morgan. In other cases, calls may have been returned, but it is doubtful that bankers could be encouraging (Kuhn and Loeb). But if the New Deal was destroying relationship banking as an encouragement to pay back the debts, we should expect defaults of high-quality debtors to have increased after Glass-Steagall. Figure 6.3 shows the number of monthly defaults and identifies those defaults on securities underwritten by the four prestigious banks. The chart also displays a Glass-Steagall time frame that ranges between the Bank Holiday in March 1933 when the main provisions of the Glass-Steagall "Revolution" emerged and were widely discussed, and June 1933 when the act was formally ratified by FDR. As can be seen, the opening Glass-Steagall window was followed by a major wave of defaults. In particular, for those two prestigious houses that did walk out of the market as a result of the act, the number of post–Glass-Steagall defaults (excluding those after the outbreak of World War II, when enemies of the United States defaulted) surpassed pre–Glass-Steagall defaults. There were fourteen National City Company defaults *after* Glass-Steagall and only seven before. The only two prewar Morgan defaults that occurred were post–Glass-Steagall events. This is consistent with the notion that borrowers gave up hope.

Of course, Figure 6.3 does not control for other factors that may have lowered borrowers' incentives to repay independently from the strategic behavior considered here.[33] But it remains that, given the evidence, Figure 6.3 is consistent with the notion that the Glass-Steagall Act stifled the ability of prestigious underwriters to provide borrowers with the rewards and penalties that had been a critical aspect of the operation of foreign bond markets under the old regime. Granted this, the foundations of a snowballing mechanism were laid out. Further defaults weakened the bankers' case and fortified their opponent's narrative. At the end of the day, the bankers' failure story was born.

---

[33] Post–Glass-Steagall defaults include German defaults, which may have been favored by Hitler's takeover in January 1933.

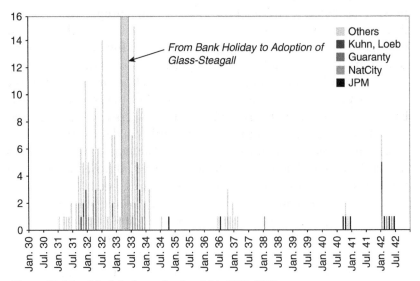

Figure 6.3 Monthly defaults on foreign debts 1930–1942.
Source: Author, from data in Flandreau, Gaillard and Panizza (2010).

Filling the Void

New Deal financial regulations crowded out old ways, but crowded in new ones, too. The bashing of bankers, the refusal to let them act, and the choice to refrain from at least compelling them to "take their responsibilities" created a political void. At the same time, the very process through which this was happening did point to where authority now lay. If the political system denounced bankers as inept, then the political system had to take charge.[34] The bondholding public understood it and naturally redirected inquiries toward the State Department, where the staff were reported to be crumbling under the volume of mail.[35] In March 1933, immediately after FDR's inauguration, Herbert Feis began working on the blueprint for a foreign bondholders' protection organization, which would substitute for institutions such as the Foreign Securities Committee that were backed by the bankers. Feis was an economist with the State

---

[34] An aggravating factor was the recurrent accusation that foreign loans had received the blessing of the State Department (see Adamson 2002 for a discussion). However, a similar claim had been made against British policy makers in the 1820s who were accused of tacitly encouraging Latin American loans because they reduced the Spanish hold in the region (Jenks 1927).

[35] Eichengreen and Portes (1989b, p. 216); Adamson (2002, p. 487).

Department and the author of a celebrated book published in 1931 under the auspices of the Council for Foreign Affairs. It reviewed and criticized British and continental lending practices in the nineteenth century, characterizing them as the product of European imperialism (Feis, 1931). Adamson (2002, p. 487) describes Feis as the "chief architect" of the resulting Foreign Bondholders Protective Council (FBPC). It was included in the Securities Act of 1933, which stated that a corporation would be created "for the purpose of protecting, conserving and advancing the interests of the holders of foreign securities in default". The formal creation of the FBPC was announced by Roosevelt in October 1933. As emphasized by Winkler (1933, p. 174) the Securities Act of 1933 excluded from the board of directors anyone "who within the five years preceding has had any interest, direct or indirect, in any corporation, company, partnership, bank or association which has sold, or offered for sale any foreign securities." Next, the Johnson Act of 1934 forbade the selling of any new loan or financial product from a government in arrears with U. S. investors. Conditionality was being nationalized.

This different diagnosis of the emergence of the FBPC may help clarify existing debates. Previous authors have speculated on the reasons for the mixed public–private nature of the newly created foreign bondholders organization (Eichengreen and Portes 1989a, 1989b). In fact, those reputational problems that previously confronted bankers now confronted the Roosevelt administration. Roosevelt, while relishing the opportunity to praise some countries for their creditworthiness (as he famously did for Finland, which he dubbed "a country that pays its debts" [Arola 2006, p. 189]), understood the dangers of reputational liability. This may explain his preference for chartering a semi-independent, private body, in charge of representing the bondholders – one that was distinct from the government so as to deflect public criticism. Likewise, previous writers have suggested that the FBPC encountered difficulties in reaching satisfactory settlements (Eichengreen and Portes 1986, 1989a, 1989b). The evidence in this chapter may give some clues as to why this was the case. The new administration could not be overly committed to making the FBPC a success. After all, a good performance by the FBPC would have restored the honor of international bankers, showing the deals to have been successful; showing failure was essential to reach the goal that the New Deal financial acts were aiming at. Consistent with this interpretation, Adamson emphasizes that the

"Roosevelt administration's support for the FBPC was half-hearted at best" and that Roosevelt considered "the billions of dollars [of foreign government loans] 'gone for good'" (Adamson 2002, p. 492).

What the narrative in this chapter underscores is that, while the resulting "banker-free" FBPC lacked conflicts of interest, it also lacked (for the same reason) critical incentivizing tools such as the "carrot" of market access. But such had never been its role. The FBPC had been created to serve as a P.O. box for letters lamenting the losses of foreign debt. After this had been played out long enough, the Roosevelt administration and especially the State Department started to take a more assertive role. They began replacing the FBPC by more direct, "imperial" policies, using such things as trade policy as an instrument of coercion and matching the demands of policy credibility with adequate policy weapons (Adamson 2002).[36] The result was a greater use of political conditionality when it could be successfully implemented, a process that effectively transformed the U.S. administration into a powerful financial agent. Later on, and again for political reasons, these mechanisms would be multilateralized with the help the Bretton Woods Treaty, whose article IV permitted monitoring and supervision through multilateral agencies. This led to the creation of the International Monetary Fund and the International Bank for Reconstruction and Development (later the World Bank), which came to embed the new system of reputation production. While this evolution is consistent with the New Dealers' eagerness to support the "use [of] public capital to promote overseas stabilization and development" (Adamson 2002, pp. 487–488), this chapter suggests that it also constituted an inescapable response and solution to the destruction of the earlier order.

The end result of this history is familiar to the reader. After the long sleep of the "first Bretton Woods" era of capital controls, global finance was reinvented during the late 1980s and 1990s under new rules of the game. In today's regime, investment banks do the selling, rating agencies do the assessing, and the IMF does the troubleshooting. This chapter has suggested that the deep foundations of this system were laid out during the 1930s. They were really associated with the political efforts of the Roosevelt administration to reclaim foreign financial policies from the hands of the investment bankers – a process which,

---

[36] See also www.sechistorical.org/museum/galleries/imp/imp02a.php, which provides relevant Securities Exchange Commission's Historical Society's material.

this chapter has suggested, had the not unintended effect of deepening the interwar debt crisis.

Conclusion

The interwar collapse of the international capital market is usually considered to have been a major disruption. It was also a period, to paraphrase Charles Dickens' famous opening words in *A Tale of Two Cities*, that was so far like the present period, that the best authorities (Dickens writes "noisiest") insist on "its being received, for good or for evil, in the superlative degree of comparison only": the "Great Transformation" according to Polanyi (1944), the "End of Globalization" according to James (2002), or the "Great Reversal" according to Rajan and Zingales (2003). The present narrative, differs from existing accounts because it seeks to integrate new elements. The story this chapter has told is a story of brands and reputations being significant factors in the history of global capitalism. From there may perhaps result the elements of a new way of writing global economic history, one detached from the physical markets in a way and yet tied to them in another. Narrating the history of the global system of rating as this chapter has tried here in a limited way may provide a novel perspective on the evolution of the material economy, one that would give its full role to its immaterial underpinnings – a material story of the immaterial, so to speak.

At its bottom, the story of the interwar foreign debt collapse is the story of a failed transplant. And the failure, as the chapter argued, occurred not for economic reasons but for political ones. Perhaps it had been ill advised from the beginning to seek to adapt or "Americanize" business manners that had grown up and developed in Britain. As Walter Lippmann's syndicated column of May 31, 1933, declared under the title "The Morgan Inquiry": "The only check upon [Morgans] has been the conscience of the firm and its banking tradition. Now the possession of such a great power by private individuals who are not publicly accountable is in principle irreconcilable with any sound conception of a democratic state."[37] The democratic state required at least the appearance of free entry. By contrast, the existing order rested on rents accruing" before to a

---

[37] "Material and Drafts about Two Articles by Lippmann about Activities of JP Morgan," TWL, 105–107.

financial oligarchy; this set up was perhaps unavoidably bound to succumb to the blows of its critics. But if this is true, then the conclusion is that the political origins of the interwar debt crisis cannot be overemphasized. These were not incompetent policy makers, but extremely shrewd ones. They understood the functioning of the system, which they set to destroy, successfully. Granted this, we can measure the enormous effects that the domestic politics of the country responsible for providing international reputations has on the global financial system. Polanyi's Great Transformation would bear witness to this, and my alternative tale points to a quite different direction than the conventional lamentations on the gold standard "mentality" and the stupidity of policy makers (Eichengreen and Temin 2000; Temin 2010).

At one level, therefore, the story narrated here is that of a crucial moment in the evolution (progress?) of international finance from a regime with tightly held information (Rothschild, Morgan) to an arms-length and competitive one. Considering it that way brings a last question, which was raised by the editors and with which this paper does conclude. Did the adjustment costs brought about by the transition necessarily entail the destructions that occurred? The obvious answer is: in theory, no. It is, of course, possible to draw, from an armchair, the path of a smoother transition to the new regime from the old, and indeed, economic journals are full of such speculations in other contexts. However, things may have been slightly more complicated in practice. As we indicated, the New Dealers needed the default of many foreign debt securities in order to bolster their claim that reform was needed. As the ever-unfolding crisis in Europe reminds us again, the problem may not be that there are good or bad policies, but that for better or worse, politicians are elected and macroeconomic policies are only a portion of what the world is about. Is it cynical to observe that catastrophes have their beneficiaries?

References

Archive

Thomas W. Lamont's Papers (TWL), Baker Library, Harvard University.

Reports of Parliamentary Commissions

Great Britain, House of Commons. 1875. Report from the Select Committee on Loans to Foreign States; together with the proceedings of the committee, minutes of evidence, appendix, and index. London: Her Majesty's Stationary Office.

U.S. Congress. Senate. 1925 and 1927. Arrangements engaging the responsibility of the Government in financial arrangements between its citizens and foreign Governments. Hearings before the subcommittee of the U.S. Senate Committee on Foreign Relations, Hearings relative to.

U.S. Congress. Senate. 1931–1932. Sale of Foreign Bonds or Securities in the United States. Hearings before the Committee on Finance. Washington, DC: Government Printing Office.

U.S. Congress. Senate. 1932–1934. Stock Exchange Practices. Hearings before the Committee on Banking and Currency, Washington, DC: Government Printing Office.

References

Abrahams, Paul Philip. (1976). *The Foreign Expansion of American Finance and Its Relationship to the Foreign Economic Policies of the United States 1907–1921*. New York: Arno Press.

Adamson, Michael R. (2002) "The Failure of the Foreign Bondholders Protective Council Experiment, 1934–1940," *Business History Review* 76(3):479–514.

Adamson, Michael R. (2005). "'Must We Overlook All Impairment of Our Interests?' Debating the Foreign Aid Role of the Export-Import Bank, 1934–41." *Diplomatic History* 29(4): 589–623.

Adamson, Michael R. (2006). "Debating Sovereign Bankruptcy: Post-Revolutionary Mexico, 1919–1931." *Financial History Review* 13(2):197–215.

Arola, Mika. (2006). *Foreign Capital and Finland, Central Government's First Period of Reliance on International Financial Markets, 1862–1938*. Unpublished Ph.D. Diss., University of Helsinki.

Atkin, John Michael. (1977). *British Overseas Investment, 1918–1931*. New York: Arno Press.

Benston, George J. (1990). *The Separation of Commercial and Investment Banking: The Glass-Steagall Act Revisited and Reconsidered*. New York: Oxford University Press.

Berlin, Mitchell, and Loretta J. Mester. (1999). "Deposits and Relationship Lending." *Review of Financial Studies* 12(3):579–607.

Birmingham, Stephen. (1967). *Our Crowd: The Great Jewish Families of New York*. New York: Harper and Row.

Black, Fischer. (1975). "Bank Funds Management in an Efficient Market." *Journal of Financial Economics* 2(4):323–339.

Bordo, Michael D., and Marc Flandreau. (2003). "Core, Periphery, Exchange Rate Regimes, and Globalization." In M. D. Bordo, A. M. Taylor, and J. G. Williamson (eds.), *Globalization in Historical Perspective*, pp. 417–472. Chicago: University of Chicago Press.

Brandeis, Louis D. (1914). *Other People's Money and How Bankers Use It*. New York: Frederick A. Stokes Co.

Buist, M. G. (1974). *At Spes non fracta: Hope & Co, 1770–1815, Merchant Bankers and Diplomats at Work*. Rotterdam: Bank Mees & Hope N.V.

Calomiris Charles W., and Stephen H. Haber. (2014). *Fragile by Design: The Political Origins of Banking Crises and Scarce Credit*. Princeton, NJ: Princeton University Press.

Carosso, Vincent P. (1970a). *Investment Banking in America, a History*. Cambridge, MA: Harvard University Press.

Carosso, Vincent P. (1970b). "Washington and Wall Street: The New Deal and Investment Bankers, 1933–1940." *Business History Review* 44(4):425–445.

Carosso, Vincent, and Richard Sylla. (1991). "US Banks in International Finance." In R. Cameron and V. I. Bovykin (eds.), *International Banking 1870–1914*. Oxford: Oxford University Press.

Carter, R. B., F. H. Dark, and A. K. Singh. (1998). "Underwriter Reputation, Initial Returns, and the Long-Run Performance of IPO." *Journal of Finance* 53(1):285–311.

Chemmamur, T. J. (1993). "The Pricing of Initial Public Offerings: A Dynamic Model with Information Production." *Journal of Finance* 48(1):285–304.

Chernow, Ron. (1990). *The House of Morgan: An American Banking Dynasty and the Rise of Modern Finance*. New York: Grove Press.

Cleveland, Harold van B., and Thomas F. Huertas. (1985). *Citibank, 1812–1970*. Cambridge, MA: Harvard University Press.

Corti, Egan Caesar. (1928). *The Rise of the House of Rothschild*. New York: Cosmopolitan Book Corp.

DeLong, Bradford J. (1991). "Did J. P. Morgan's Men Add Value? An Economist's Perspective on Financial Capitalism." In Peter Temin (ed.), *Inside the Business Enterprise: Historical Perspectives on the Use of Information*, pp. 205–236. Chicago: University of Chicago Press.

DeLong, Bradford J., and Carlos Ramirez. (1995). "Banker Influence and Business Economic Performance: Assessing the Impact of Depression-Era, Financial Market Reforms." In Michael Bordo and Richard Sylla (eds.), *Anglo-American Financial Systems, Institutions and Markets in the Twentieth Century*, pp. 161–178. New York: Irwin Press.

DeLong, Bradford J., and Carlos Ramirez. (2001). "Understanding America's Hesitant Steps toward Financial Capitalism: Politics, the Depression, and the Separation of Commercial and Investment Banking." *Public Choice* 106(1/2):93–116.

Diamond, D. W. (1989). "Reputation Acquisition in Debt Markets." *Journal of Political Economy* 97(4):828–862.

Dickens, Paul D. (1933). The Transition Period in American International Financing: 1897 to 1914. Unpublished Diss., George Washington University.

Douglas, William O. (1940). *Democracy and Finance*. New Haven, CT: Yale University Press.

Dulles, John F. (1926). "Our Foreign Loan Policy." *Foreign Affairs* 5(1):33–48.

Edwards, George W. (1928). "Government Control of Foreign Investments." *American Economic Review* 18(4):684–701.

Edwards, George W. (1942). "The Myth of the Security Affiliate." *Journal of the American Statistical Association* 37(218):225–232.

Eichengreen, Barry. (1989). "The U.S. Capital Market and Foreign Lending, 1920–1955." In Jeffrey Sachs (ed.), *Developing Country Debt and the World Economy*, pp. 237–248. Cambridge, MA: National Bureau of Economic Research.

Eichengreen, Barry. (1992). *Golden Fetters: The Gold Standard and the Great Depression*. Oxford: Oxford University Press.

Eichengreen, Barry. (2015a). *Hall of Mirrors. The Great Depression, the Great Recession, and the Uses – and Misuses – of History*. Oxford: Oxford University Press.

Eichengreen, Barry. (2015b). "Saving Greece, Saving Europe." *Project Syndicate* July 13, 2015. Retrieved from www.project-syndicate.org.

Eichengreen, Barry, and Marc Flandreau. (2009). "The Rise and Fall of the Dollar, or When Did the Dollar Overtake Sterling as the Leading Reserve Currency?" *European Review of Economic History* 13(3):377–411.

Eichengreen, Barry, and Richard Portes. (1986). "Debt and Default in the 1930s. Causes and Consequences." *European Economic Review* 30(3):599–640.

Eichengreen, Barry, and Richard Portes. (1989a). "After the Deluge: Default, Renegotiation and Readjustment in the Interwar Years." In Barry Eichengreen and Peter Lindert (eds.), *The International Debt Crisis in Historical Perspective*, pp. 12–47. Cambridge, MA: MIT Press.

Eichengreen, Barry, and Richard Portes. (1989b). "Settling Defaults in the Era of Bond Finance." *The World Bank Economic Review* 3(2):211–239.

Eichengreen, Barry, and Peter Temin. (2000). "The Gold Standard and the Great Depression." *Contemporary European History* 9(2):183–207.

Eichengreen, Barry, and Carolyn Werley. (1988). "How the Bondholders Fared: Realized Rates of Return on Foreign Dollar Bonds Floated in the 1920s." *Working Paper No.8869*, University of California, Berkeley.

Fama, E. (1985). "What's Different about Banks?" *Journal of Monetary Economics* 15(1):29–39.

Feis, Herbert. (1931). *Europe, The World's Banker: 1870–1914*. New Haven, CT: Council of Foreign Relations.

Flandreau, Marc, and Juan Flores. (2009). "Bonds and Brands: Foundations of Sovereign Debt Markets 1820–1830." *The Journal of Economic History* 69(3):646–684.

Flandreau, Marc, and Juan Flores. (2012a). "Bondholders vs. Bond-Sellers? Investment Banks and Conditionality Lending in the London Market for Foreign Government Debt, 1815–1913." *European Review of Economic History* 16(4):356–383.

Flandreau, Marc, and Juan Flores. (2012b). "The Peaceful Conspiracy: Bond Markets and International Relations during the Pax Britannica." *International Organization* 66(2):211–241.

Flandreau, Marc, Juan Flores, Norbert Gaillard, and Sebastian Nieto-Parra. (2010). "The End of Gatekeeping: Underwriters and the Quality of Sovereign Bond Markets, 1815–2007." In Lucrezia Reichlin and Kenneth West (eds.), *NBER International Seminar on Macroeconomics 2009*, vol. 6, pp. 53–91. Chicago: The University of Chicago Press and NBER.

Flandreau, Marc, Norbert Gaillard, and Ugo Panizza. (2010). "Conflicts of Interest, Reputation and the Interwar Debt Crisis: Banksters or Bad Luck?" Working Paper, HEID.

Flandreau, Marc, and Chantal Rivière. (1999). "La Grande Re-Transformation"? Contrôle de capitaux et integration financière international 1880–1996." *Economie Internationale* 78(2):11–58.

Foreign Bondholders Protective Council. (1934). *Annual Report*. New York: Foreign Bondholders Protective Council, Inc.

Frydman, Carola, and Eric Hilt. (2014). "Investment Banks as Corporate Monitors in the Early 20th Century United States." Working Paper No. 20544, National Bureau of Economic Research.

Gorton, Gary. (1996). "Reputation Formation in Early Banknotes Markets." *Journal of Political Economy* 104(2):346–397.

Hannah, Leslie. (2007). "What Did Morgan's Men Really Do?" Mimeo: University of Tokyo.

Hidy, R. W. (1949). *The House of Baring in American Trade and Finance: English Merchant Bankers at Work, 1763–1861*. Cambridge: Cambridge University Press.

Higgs, Robert. (1987). *Crisis and Leviathan: Critical Episodes in the Growth of American Government*. Oxford: Oxford University Press.

Huertas, Thomas F., and Joan L. Silverman. (1986). "Charles E. Mitchell: Scapegoat of the Crash?" *Business History Review* 60(1):81–103.

James, Harold. (1996). *International Monetary Cooperation since Bretton Woods*. New York: Oxford University Press.

James, Harold. (2002). *The End of Globalization, Lessons from the Great Depression*. Cambridge, MA: Harvard University Press.

James, Harold. (2009). *The Creation and Destruction of Value: The Globalization Cycle*. Cambridge, MA: Harvard University Press.

Jenks, L. H. (1927). *The Migration of British Capital to 1875*. London: Thomas Nelson.

Kindleberger, Charles P. (1988). *The International Economic Order: Essays On Financial Crisis And International Public Goods*. Brighton: Wheatsheaf.

Kroszner, Randall S., and Raghuram G. Rajan. (1994). "Is the Glass-Steagall Act Justified? A Study of the U.S. Experience with Universal Banking before 1933." *American Economic Review* 84(4):810–832.

Lamont, Thomas W. (1920). "Foreign Government Bonds." *The Annals of the American Academy of Political and Social Science* 88:121–129.

Lamoreaux, Naomi R. (1986). *Banks, Personal Connections and Economic Development in Industrial New England*. Cambridge: Cambridge University Press.

Lewis, Cleona. (1938). *America's Stake in International Investments*. Washington, DC: Brookings Institution.

Madden, John T., Marcus Nadler, and Harry C. Sauvain. (1937). *America's Experience as a Creditor Nation*. New York: Prentice-Hall.

Mahoney, Paul G. (2001). "The Political Economy of the Securities Act of 1933." *Journal of Legal Studies* 30(1):1–31.

Meyer, Charles H. (1934). *The Securities Exchange Act of 1934, Analyzed and Explained*. New York: F. E. Fitch.

Mintz, Ilse. (1951). *Deterioration in the Quality of Foreign Bonds Issued in the United States, 1920–1930*. New York: National Bureau of Economic Research.

Moggridge, Donald E. (1972). *British Monetary Policy, 1924–1931: The Norman Conquest of $4.86*. Cambridge: Cambridge University Press.

Moore, Terris. (1934). "Security Affiliate versus Private Investment Banker – a Study in Security Originations." *Harvard Business Review* 12(4):478–484.

Obstfeld, Maurice, and Alan Taylor. (1998). "The Great Depression as a Watershed: International Capital Mobility over the Long Run." In Michael D. Bordo, Claudia Goldin, and Eugene White (eds), *The Defining Moment: The Great Depression and the American Economy in the Twentieth Century*, pp. 353–402. Chicago: University of Chicago Press.

Oosterlinck, Kim, Loredana Ureche-Langau, and Jacques-Marie Vaslin. (2014). "Baring, Wellington and the Resurrection of French Public Finances following Waterloo." *The Journal of Economic History* 74(4):1072–1102.

Parrini, Carl. (1969). *Heir to Empire: U.S. Financial Diplomacy, 1916–1923*. Pittsburgh: University of Pittsburgh Press.

Pecora, Ferdinand. (1936). *Wall Street under Oath. A Story of Our Modern money-Changers*. New York: Simon and Schuster.

Polanyi, Karl. (1944). *The Great Transformation*. Toronto: Rinehart.

Rajan, Raghuram, and Luigi Zingales. (2003). "The Great Reversals: The Politics of Financial Development in the Twentieth Century." *Journal of Financial Economics* 69(1):5–50.

Roosevelt, Franklin D. (1938). "Campaign Address at Columbus, Ohio, August 20, 1932." In *The Public Papers and Addresses of Franklin D. Roosevelt*, vol. 1, 1928–32, p. 624. New York: Random House.

Rosenberg, Emily. (2003). *Financial Missionaries to the World: The Politics and Culture of Dollar Diplomacy 1900–1930*. Durham, NC: Duke University Press.

Securities Exchange Commission's Historical Society. "The Imperial SEC? – Foreign Policy and the Internationalization of the Securities Markets, 1934–1990." Retrieved from www.sechistorical.org/museum/galleries/imp/imp02a.php.

Shapiro, Carl. (1983). "Premiums for High Quality Products as Returns to Reputations." *Quarterly Journal of Economics* 98(4):659–679.

Spence, Michael A. (1973). "Job Market Signaling." *Quarterly Journal of Economics* 87(3):355–374.

Stallings, Barbara. (1987). *Banker to the Third World*. Berkeley: University of California Press.

Stigler, George J. (1964). "Public Regulation of the Securities Markets." *Journal of Business* 37(2):117–142.

Stigler, George J. (1971). "The Theory of Economic Regulation." *Bell Journal of Economics* 2(1):3–21.

Stratton, Trevin. (2013). "The Banking Act of 1933: Informing a Macroprudential Approach to Financial Regulation, Unpublished Diss., Graduate Institute of International Studies and Development."

Suzuki, Toshio. (1994). *Japanese Government Loan Issues on the London Capital Market 1870–1913*. London: Athlone Press.

Tabarrok, Alexander. (1998). "The Separation of Commercial and Investment Banking: The Morgans versus the Rockefellers." *Quarterly Journal of Austrian Economics* 1(1):1–18.

Temin, Peter. (1991). *Lessons from the Great Depression*. Cambridge, MA: MIT Press.

Temin, Peter. (2010). "The Great Recession and the Great Depression." *Daedalus* 139(4):115–124.

Van Dormael, Armand. (1978). *Bretton Woods: Birth of a Monetary System*. London: Macmillan.

Winkler, Max. (1933). *Foreign Bonds: An Autopsy*. Philadelphia: Roland Swain.

Ziegler, P. (1988). *The Sixth Great Power: Barings, 1762–1929*. London: Collins.

7

Protecting Financial Stability in the Aftermath of World War I: The Federal Reserve Bank of Atlanta's Dissenting Policy

Eugene N. White

When inflation picked up speed after World War I, central banks responded by quickly raising interest rates, leading to the severe recession of 1920–1921. The Federal Reserve Bank of Atlanta (FRBA) could not offset the national deflationary policy, but it carried out an important lender-of-last-resort (LOLR) function, as described by recent theoretical advances (Freixas and Parigi 2014). There would have been no need for the Atlanta Fed's intervention, if the interbank market for funds had worked perfectly to enable banks in all the Federal Reserve districts to manage their differing demands for liquidity, attributable to the regionally uneven recessionary shock (Allen and Gale 2000; Freixas, Parigi, and Rochet 2000).[1] The intense shock to Atlanta's Sixth District, arising from its dependence on cotton and agricultural commodities, imposed a sharper contraction and a higher demand for liquidity from its banks. As the commodity-collateralized assets on their balance sheets were opaque to other banks, especially those outside of the region, troubled banks found it difficult to access the interbank market for liquidity because of the information asymmetry. Finding themselves illiquid, Sixth District banks

The author would like to thank the participants at conferences and seminars at the Banque de France, the Federal Reserve Bank of Atlanta, and New York University, especially Michael D. Bordo, Gary Richardson, Peter Rousseau, William Roberds, Hugh Rockoff, Paul Wachtel, and David C. Wheelock. This chapter would not have been possible to write without the Federal Reserve Bank of Atlanta's gracious opening of its archives to scholars. Financial support from the National Science Foundation under Grant No. 1127094, Rutgers University's ARESTY program and Rutgers' Research Council grants is gratefully acknowledged.

[1] Allen and Gale (2000) and Freixas, Parigi, and Rochet (2000) have modeled multi-region economies with systemic risk where the interbank market provides liquidity-short regions with funds from excess-liquidity regions. A shortage of aggregate liquidity can transmit a shock from one region to another, forcing unexpected liquidation of long-term contracts and potentially creating a general crisis.

refused to renew loans, forcing producers and factors to dump their commodity stocks on the market. This situation presented the possibility of a "fire sale," where cotton and cotton bills might sell below their fundamental prices, leading to a cascade of bank failures and a panic (Shleifer and Vishy 1992; Caballero and Simsek 2009; Diamond and Rajan 2009).[2] To prevent a fire sale, the FRBA, informed by bank examinations and by its discounting history with each bank, used its discretion to provide liquidity and assist with capital injections.

To carry out this policy, the FRBA needed to borrow gold reserves from Federal Reserve banks that had surplus reserves. By borrowing heavily from other Reserve banks, the FRBA acted where the interbank market did not, to reallocate liquidity, even as the money stock contracted.[3] If the commodity shock had been permanent, sweeping bank liquidations would have eventually been required; but the recovery of cotton prices proved it to be a temporary shock, where the FRBA-enabled reallocation of liquidity was consequently temporary. The Atlanta Fed was not worried about moral hazard because it believed that the brutal recession was an extraordinary, not-to-be repeated event that was understood by its member banks.[4] Although the Federal Reserve Board opposed the Atlanta Fed's efforts, it later relented and publicly admitted that the FRBA had acted appropriately as a LOLR. Its success may have emboldened the FRBA to be more expansionary than other Federal Reserve banks during the 1929 Florida panic and Great Depression without incurring the wrath of the Federal Reserve Board, which in 1920–1921 had pressed the Atlanta Fed to adhere more closely to the deflationary policy specified by the Board.

This episode shines a light on the pre-Depression history of the Federal Reserve, which has been generally treated as a period when the Fed did not act as a LOLR. The Federal Reserve Act of 1913 did not contain any instructions on how the new central bank should act as a LOLR. Some of the founding fathers of the Fed, such as H. Parker Willis and Carter Glass,

---

[2] See Shleifer and Vishny (2011) for a survey of the literature on fire sales.

[3] The similarities between the gold settlement fund's facilitation of inter-Reserve bank borrowing and the recent Eurozone crisis where semi-autonomous financial systems are linked together by a common currency and face profound imbalances are examined in Eichengreen et al. (2014).

[4] Hautcoeur, Riva, and White (2014) and Mishkin and White (2014) have found that even during the classical gold standard era and in the early twentieth century, central banks exercised discretion to intervene when faced with the collapse of what would be termed today SIFIs (systemically important financial institutions) while injecting liquidity into the financial system as a whole. When successful, these interventions were accompanied by strong actions to limit moral hazard.

believed that if the Fed put the real bills doctrine into effect, there would be no panics in the future. Others such as Paul Warburg saw that there was a clear need for the new central bank to be prepared to act in accordance with Bagehot's (1873) dictates.[5] Bordo and Wheelock (2013) argue that the Federal Reserve Act impeded the Fed's ability to act as a LOLR by limiting its lending capacity, creating a decentralized governance structure, and restricting its membership. These constraints on the LOLR function appear to have been confirmed by historical accounts of the Fed that, for the most part, center on decision making by the Federal Reserve Board. Its first real LOLR challenge is typically seen as occurring during the four banking panics of 1930–1933 (Friedman and Schwartz 1963). However, before the New Deal reform of the Fed, much of policy was conducted by the twelve, semi-autonomous Reserve banks, each of whom had individual responsibility for maintaining gold reserves above the minimum reserve ratios, supervising member banks, and setting discount rates with the approval of the Federal Reserve Board. Consequently, there was a diversity of LOLR experience, and a full history requires an inclusion of the Federal Reserve banks' actions as lenders of last resort. Differences in policies during the Great Depression between Federal Reserve banks have enabled Richardson and Troost (2009) to examine a quasi-experiment that revealed the effectiveness of an easier liquidity policy, comparing the FRBA and the Federal Reserve Bank of St. Louis. In the last local crisis before the Depression, Carlson, Mitchener, and Richardson (2011) find that the Atlanta Fed's "bold, transparent, and targeted liquidity support" altered depositor expectations and halted a panic in Florida in 1929, limiting the number of bank failures.

This study is informed primarily by the minutes of the FRBA's board of directors and its executive committee, preserved in the archives of the Atlanta Fed. These are vital records for understanding how policy was conducted in the Federal Reserve System before the New Deal concentrated more authority in the board of governors (Meltzer 2003). The FRBA's board and the executive committee formulated and were deeply involved in the implementation and execution of policy; their minutes thus constitute a detailed record of the Reserve bank's management. Unfortunately, while the activities of all the regional Feds merit inclusion in a study of this period, this chapter is limited to the Atlanta Fed

---

[5] Surveying the Bank of England's responses to financial crises, Bagehot (1873) recommended that a central bank should lend freely at a high rate against good collateral to supply liquidity.

because the archives of the other Reserve banks are not yet fully opened. Drawing on the largely unexplored archival resources of the FRBA and focusing on the severe recession of 1920–1921, I find that from its inception, the FRBA staked out its own LOLR policy, taking actions not countenanced by the Federal Reserve Act. Under the leadership of Governor Maximlian B. Wellborn, the Atlanta Fed implemented central banking innovations that helped to buffer the Sixth District from the recession in spite of the board of governors' efforts to impose a strict contractionary policy across the system.[6]

In the first section of this chapter, the recessionary shock of 1920–1921 is described. Next, the conduct of policy by the Federal Reserve Board is examined, followed by how policy developed at the Federal Reserve Bank of Atlanta from 1914 to 1920. The difficult years of 1920–1921 and the previously unstudied acrimonious debate between the Board and the Atlanta Fed are detailed in the penultimate section. The final section concludes with how the Board came to terms with the dissenting policy of the Atlanta Fed.

An Unparalleled Series of Shocks, 1918–1921

Key dimensions of the shocks delivered to the American financial system by the termination of World War I can be seen in Figure 7.1, which displays the rate of inflation on the right-hand vertical axis and the percentage of national and state bank failures on the left-hand axis from 1866 to 1929.[7] After the Civil War (1861–1864), the United States experienced a mild secular deflation until the 1890s, when gold discoveries resulted in a mild secular inflation, with prices fluctuating around these trends (Friedman and Schwartz 1963). Over the short-run of a few years, under the gold standard regime, there was typically no persistent inflation or deflation. In contrast to Europe, the United States had no central bank in this era to smooth adjustment to shocks or to manage financial crises, as the Second Bank of the United States had lost its charter in 1836. The only federal banking or monetary agency was the Office of the Comptroller of the Currency (OCC), created by the National Bank Act of 1864, which also established a national and uniformly regulated banking system with what

---

[6] Wellborn was an Alabama banker involved in real estate and railroads and was chairman of the First National Bank of Anniston. The title of "governor" for the chief executive of Federal Reserve Banks was changed to "president" in 1936.

[7] There is no equivalent series for state-chartered bank failures for this whole period (White 2013).

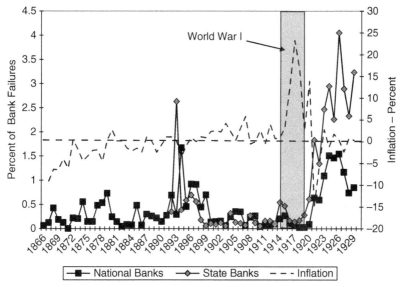

Figure 7.1 Inflation and bank failures, 1866–1929.
Note: The right-hand vertical axis records the percentage of national banks and the percentage of state banks that failed. The horizontal dashed line represents an inflation rate of zero. The shaded area indicates the period of World War I.
Source: White (2013).

were then considered strict rules. Until the revival of state-chartered banking in the 1890s, federally chartered national banks were the dominant financial institution. Supervised by the OCC, national banks had relatively low failure rates, as seen in Figure 7.1, although there were some spikes in the bad years of the 1890s. When banks were examined by the OCC, their assets were marked to market and promptly closed when found to be insolvent. State banks were more weakly regulated and tended to be smaller and more rural, with higher failures rates, but their failures followed the same pattern as national banks (White 2013).

The OCC had no means to assist troubled banks and did not attempt to do so; its head office was provided with a limited budget by Congress that paid for little more than salaries, whereas the OCC's examiners were compensated by fees from the examined national banks. Regulations, notably double liability, created incentives that, coupled with supervision, left very small aggregate losses in the period 1865–1913 from national bank failures, approximately $44 million (or $1 billion in 2013 dollars) and less than 1 percent of GDP for any year (White 2013). In the absence of a central bank, the only assistance available to troubled banks came from the privately organized clearing houses, located in major cities, whose member banks might act collectively to provide temporary funds if they believed a bank to be inherently insolvent and a threat to financial stability (Friedman and Schwartz 1963; Moen and Tallman 1992).

Inflation during World War I and the postwar boom, where the price level nearly doubled, was followed by the sharp deflation of 1920–1922, when prices fell 22 percent. This experience was largely unanticipated. Although there had been a major inflation during the Civil War, the postwar deflation that enabled the country to return to the gold standard was gradual, lasting from 1865 to 1879. Financial institutions were not subjected to a giant shock, as occurred after World War I, and there was no upsurge in bank failures. For the fifty-year period preceding 1914, there were only 501 national bank insolvencies. In contrast, bank failures rose to new heights in the 1920s, with 766 national bank and 4,645 state bank failures. Losses to national bank depositors during the 1920s were higher than for the whole of the period 1865–1913, totaling $565 million or nearly 1 percent of 1925 GDP (Calomiris and White 1994). Figure 7.1 displays the national picture, but bank failures were concentrated in agricultural regions where commodity prices plummeted suddenly. During the war, there had been a major expansion of agricultural production, fulfilling the demands for war commodities, such as cotton, and replacing European production of foodstuffs, such as wheat. Acreage had expanded and farmers had taken out mortgages and loans for inputs to expand output. When prices fell, farmers and their suppliers failed to make payments on their loans. Nonperforming assets for rural banks increased quickly, threatening local financial systems.

The Sixth Federal Reserve District was dominated by cotton production. The movement of cotton prices is depicted in Figure 7.2. After fluctuating for decades between 5 cents and 15 cents a pound, the price of cotton soared to more than 30 cents in 1917. In the brief, immediate postwar recession, the price in New York hovered around 33–35 cents a pound in August–September 1918, falling to 28–29 cents in March–April 1919, a modest drop. This national recession was quickly reversed by a vigorous expansion characterized by inventory accumulation and commodity speculation. The boom was reflected in the price of cotton that moved to a monthly peak of 42 cents a pound in April 1920. Because the general price level, measured by the Consumer Price Index, had only increased 109 percent from 1913 to 1920 (Measuring Worth 2014), the real price of cotton had effectively doubled. Yet, by 1921, cotton prices plunged below 12 cents – a 70 percent drop – while the price level declined only 16 percent,

Figure 7.2 Monthly wholesale New York cotton prices.
Source: NBER (2008).

implying a huge fall in real terms and a big swing in the terms of trade
between the agricultural and manufacturing sectors. Although the
American economy as a whole may have bounced back fairly quickly in
1921–1922, the cotton economy did not. Prices did not exceed 23 cents
a pound until late 1922, and they did not recover to the 33–35 cents range
of 1918 until the end of 1923.

To make matters worse, the cotton crop reached a historic high in 1921.
The Atlanta Fed estimated that there were inventories of 4 million bales of
low-grade cotton. Not only did the price of cotton fall, but so did the prices
of rice, sugar, peanuts, naval stores, and livestock. Merchants and general
stores that had made collateralized loans for supplies could not collect,
leaving them unable to repay wholesalers, jobbers, and manufacturers for
goods they had bought on credit (Federal Reserve Bank of Atlanta, *Annual
Report* 1920). The precipitous decline in the price of cotton wreaked havoc
on banks' balance sheets in the Atlanta district. Many loans were collateralized by cotton or assets tied to cotton production. If borrowers were
unable to repay a loan, sale of the collateral could cause large losses on
banks' capital accounts. Worse yet, any generalized effort to realize collateral could produce a fire sale, harming banks further. This assessment

matches Shleifer and Vishny's (2010) summary of the threat that fire sales pose to financial stability, where a shock to the value of bank assets or their common underlying collateral can produce a cascade of declining asset prices, shrinking bank net worth, falling financial intermediation, and failing businesses.

The position of banks in the Sixth District was thus acute. Compounding the problem was that while all national banks had been required to become members of their respective Federal Reserve banks, it was optional for state-chartered banks. In spite of considerable efforts by the Atlanta Fed and the other Federal Reserve banks, few became member banks. If they were not member banks, they could not borrow from the Atlanta Fed's discount window. However, they could borrow from member banks; typically small-town rural banks borrowed from their larger city banks that were members. This extensive interbank borrowing linked the fate of all banks. The whole system, even those institutions not directly lending to cotton producers and the cotton industry, were thus endangered by the collapse of the price of cotton.

Policy Making at the Center: The View from the Federal Reserve Board

The asymmetric character of the shocks that hit the American economy after World War I produced a struggle between the regional Reserve banks and over how much policy decision making should be centralized at the Federal Reserve Board in Washington, DC. Those shocks were aggravated by the postwar efforts of the Fed to regain independence from the Treasury, leading it to commit "several mistakes, some avoidable, some unavoidable in the circumstances" (Meltzer 2003, p. 90).

Immediately after the cessation of hostilities in 1918, economic activity in the United States slowed, as orders for munitions were terminated and there was considerable uncertainly in the general economic outlook. Friedman and Schwartz (1963) characterized the contraction from August 1918 to March 1919 as sharp but brief and followed by an intense boom that peaked in January 1920. Contributing to this expansion was the low interest rate policy of the Fed, still obliged to assist the Treasury with bond sales. The rate for discounts and advances on eligible paper at the Federal Reserve Bank of New York had been set at 4 percent in April 1918, well below market rates. This New York rate remained at that level until November 1919, and none of the other eleven Reserve banks posted a rate of more than 4½ percent. At these attractive rates, member banks discounted heavily, contributing to a monetary expansion and inflation. Measured by the GDP deflator, inflation rose from 4.3 percent in the first quarter of 1919 to 15.8 percent during the last two quarters of the year (Meltzer 2003). Real rates were negligible if not negative.

This expansionary policy was driven, in part, by the U.S. Treasury's pressure to prevent a decline in the price of government bonds because of the feared consequences for commercial banks that had amassed huge holdings of war bonds and the final Victory bond issue (Friedman and Schwartz 1963). It was, however, an unsustainable policy, given the Federal Reserve System's gold reserve requirements. The gold reserve ratio for the whole system that had been as high as 50.6 percent in June 1919, quickly fell to 42.7 percent in January 1920, just above the 40 percent minimum. After a long battle within the Federal Reserve Board, the New York Fed was permitted to raise its rates to 4¾ percent in December 1919 and most banks followed suit.[8] To strengthen this modest increase in discount rates, Congress passed the Phelan Act of 1920 granting the Fed the power to impose progressively higher discount rates on member banks that were heavy borrowers. When no agreement could be reached on how to implement this power, the Fed conceded it to the individual Federal Reserve banks (Meltzer 2003, p. 105). As the commodity boom progressed, member banks in agricultural districts were undeterred by discount rates of 5 or 6 percent, as they often lent above 10 percent. The Atlanta, Dallas, Kansas City, and St. Louis Reserve banks then took the lead and implemented progressive rates to deter these borrowers. Yet, this uneven policy did not deter member bank borrowing. Belatedly, in late January 1920, the Fed permitted a number of Reserve banks to jack up their discount rates to 6 percent, which became uniform across all banks the following month.

As the business cycle had just turned downward in January 1920, this action was probably excessive, and Friedman and Schwartz comment, "The rise in the discount rates in January was not only too late but also probably too much" (1963, p. 231), turning a mild recession into a dramatic one. Yet, this interest rate hike seemed to have little immediate effect, as member banks did not cut back, and their borrowings at the Fed

---

[8] When the Federal Reserve banks of New York and Boston voted to further increase their discount rates, the move was rejected by the Board. When the head of the New York Fed, Benjamin Strong, insisted that the banks had the right to regulate their discount rates, the Secretary of the Treasury, Carter Glass, threatened to remove him from office and obtained an opinion from the attorney general that gave the Board veto power over discount rate changes voted by the district banks. This significant victory ensured that only modest deviations in discount rates would be tolerated by the Board (Meltzer 2003).

were higher than their reserve balances. Consequently, the New York Fed raised its rediscount rate to 7 percent on June 1, 1920, quickly followed by Boston, Chicago, and Minneapolis, and lastly by Atlanta on November 1, 1920, with the remaining Federal Reserve banks keeping their basic rate at 6 percent.

Through the summer and into the fall of 1920, the Fed came under political pressure to reduce discount rates, and in autumn, the Board was urged to rescind a ruling made the year before that sharply limited the discounting of notes of cotton factors. By the end of 1920, Congress increased pressure on the Fed to cut rates, with a bill being introduced in the Senate to cap discount rates at 5 percent; Senator Robert L. Owen, former chairman of the Senate Banking Committee, wrote two letters to the Board protesting the "Board's alleged policy of indiscriminate deflation and the refusal of credit to legitimate industries" (Harding 1925, p. 197). Governor of the Federal Reserve Board[9] William P. G. Harding's answer to these challenges was to argue that the authority and initiative for discount rate changes lay with the Federal Reserve banks, never mentioning the pressure that he and other officials placed on Atlanta for failing to conform to what they viewed as systemwide policy.

Responding to the increased discount rates in the second half of 1920, member banks reduced their borrowings from the Federal Reserve banks, which meant, in turn, that the banks refused to renew loans to their customers. Friedman and Schwartz (1963) point out that it was easier to liquidate loans in the east than in agricultural regions where customers found it increasingly difficult to repay their loans. Many farmers did not survive the drop in agricultural prices, and many rural banks went under. From 63 in 1919, bank insolvencies climbed to 155 in 1920 and 506 in 1921. Unemployment jumped from 4 percent in 1920 to 12 percent in 1921, and industrial and agricultural production fell 23 and 14 percent, respectively, with wholesale prices tumbling 37 percent (Meltzer 2003). But there was not an immediate cut in the Fed's interest rates. Concerned about their ability to exercise control, many Fed officials were opposed to lowering discount rates, as market rates remained higher (Meltzer 2003).

Benjamin Strong, governor of the New York Federal Reserve Bank, was adamantly opposed to any decrease because the discount rates were not yet serving as "penalty rates." He wanted to see member borrowing from the Reserve banks drastically reduced because it had fallen only 4 percent, and

---

[9] The title of "governor" of the Federal Reserve Board was changed to "chairman" of the Board of Governors of the Federal Reserve System in 1936.

he believed that a 20 percent decline was needed. Like many Fed officials, he thought that a larger deflation was necessary to stabilize the economy and that any reduction in discount rates would ignite inflation. In his view, the Fed had to follow "Bagehot's gold rule" (quoted in Chandler 1958, pp. 173–174) and lend only at above-market rates. Popular opposition to this policy, especially in agricultural states, stirred up criticism in Congress. In response, Congress revived the War Loan Corporation in January 1921 to finance agricultural and other exports, considered setting limits on discount rates, and opened a Joint Commission of Agricultural Inquiry to investigate the Fed's role in agriculture's economic distress (Meltzer 2003).

Pressure mounted on the Fed to cut rates, but even when the Secretary of the Treasury, Andrew Mellon, met with the Board in April 1921 and recommended a reduction to 6 percent, he was met with opposition. As late as the Governors' Conference of April 12, 1921, only the governors of the Boston and Atlanta Federal Reserve banks favored a decrease to 6 percent, which was conceded to them three days later. Finally, the discount rate was lowered in New York to 6½ percent in May 1921 (Friedman and Schwartz 1963). Rate cuts for all banks began in July, which was the month that the recession reached its nadir (Board of Governors 1943; NBER [www .nber.org] Business Cycle Dates). In following months, industrial production recovered quickly, although agricultural output remained sluggish, so that real GDP did begin to grow until the second quarter of 1922. Deflation and high interest rates prompted large gold inflows, and by October 1921, the New York Fed's gold reserve ratio reached 82 percent, leading to a new round of interest rate cuts, with the New York rate returning to 4 percent on June 23, 1922. Policy was thus restrictive in the recovery with high real rates in a deflationary environment, yielding declining systemwide discounts and advances until September 1922.

Policy Making at the Regional Level

As organizations, owned by their member banks who provided capital by stock subscriptions and governed by member-elected boards of directors, the Federal Reserve banks were not government agencies, even though they had been created by an act of Congress. In conception, they owed much to the numerous private city clearinghouses that assisted with the clearing and collection of checks, and which in times of crisis, had given assistance to members in need of liquidity, sometimes even rescuing members who were near collapse. The clearinghouses' usefulness was recognized when the government sponsored similar organizations that could provide temporary liquidity under the Aldrich–Vreeland Act of 1908, passed after the Panic of 1907. Thus, twelve Federal Reserve banks were similar in conception to the clearinghouses and Aldrich–Vreeland associations, assisting their members with the clearing and collection of checks, providing short-term loans, and exercising some supervision.

In terms of lending authority, the Federal Reserve Act of 1913 carefully specified the powers of the Federal Reserve banks (Section 14, Federal Reserve Act 1915). They were permitted to "discount notes, drafts, and bills of exchange arising out of actual commercial transactions" "for agricultural, industrial or commercial purposes," but they were forbidden to discount such instruments for carrying "stocks, bonds or other investment securities" except U.S. government securities. The maturity of discounts was limited to 90 days, except for those for agriculture or livestock, or bills of exchange for imports and exports where a maturity of six months was allowed. The Federal Reserve banks were also permitted to discount acceptances for imports and exports with maturities up to three months (Section 13, Federal Reserve Act 1915). In addition to these discounts, the Federal Reserve banks could engage in open-market operations, directly purchasing or selling any of the listed financial instruments.

Each Federal Reserve Bank had limited monetary authority, being able to change its discount rates, subject to approval of the Federal Reserve Board. Although the Board exercised this authority, it did not impose uniform rates; there was divergence of up to 1 percent among banks in the system's first decade (Board of Governors 1943, table 115). In addition, Reserve banks had some discretion over the quality, though not the type, of collateral that could be discounted. Each bank was also required to maintain in gold and lawful money a reserve of 35 percent against its deposits and a reserve of 40 percent against its Federal Reserve notes in circulation. Gold could be held in each bank's vaults or by certificates for gold at the Treasury. The reserve ratios thus had the potential to constrain the expansionary activities of individual Reserve banks. If either ratio fell below the required minimum, a Federal Reserve bank would be forced to reduce its lending. However, a deficit Reserve bank could request that a surplus Reserve bank rediscount bills that it had discounted for member banks in exchange for gold. The rediscounting Reserve bank then wired the "Gold Settlement Fund" in Washington, DC, which transferred gold certificates between the accounts of the two banks, after which their reserve ratios were adjusted, raising the ratio for the borrowing bank and lowering it for the lending bank (Eichengreen et al. 2014). If Reserve banks were unwilling to provide assistance, the Federal Reserve Act empowered the Board to compel assistance at a rate that it fixed.

Unlike the financially constrained OCC, the Federal Reserve banks had substantial financial resources that had been accumulated during World War I, when they were induced to buy bonds for their own account and to lend to the public to purchase the bonds to assist the massive financing needs of the federal government. As their balance sheets swelled, so did Federal Reserve banks' earnings. In 1916, the earnings of the FRBA were a mere $141,774, but by 1918, they stood at $1,758,000 (Gamble 1989). While they paid dividends to their member banks from this income, the Federal Reserve banks increased their surplus and their capacity to aid troubled member banks.

Officially, direct intervention in the affairs of a member bank was not countenanced by the Federal Reserve Act, and Federal Reserve banks were limited to the acquisition of information. Under the 1913 act, the Comptroller of the Currency continued to conduct twice yearly examinations of national banks, and the state banking authorities examined state-chartered banks; but the Federal Reserve banks were given authority to conduct special examinations of both national and state member banks within their districts "to inform the Federal Reserve bank of the condition of its member banks and of the lines of credit which are being extended by them" (Section 21, Federal Reserve Act 1915).

While this legal framework would seem to have kept interactions of the Federal Reserve banks with their member banks at arms' length, some Federal Reserve banks took a much broader view of their role from the very beginning. A history of the Atlanta Fed (Gamble 1989) described the intentions of the new Federal Reserve Bank of Atlanta. To smooth the seasonal cycle of agriculture, the FRBA projected that it would rediscount bills of its member banks, enabling them to provide more credit to their farmer customers during the peak season of planting and at times when crop prices were low so that they would not have to dump their crops. In addition, the Atlanta Fed believed that it could strengthen the cotton economy by lessening its dependence on New York banks.

As early as 1915, the minutes of the board of directors of the Federal Reserve Bank of Atlanta record interventions that moved well beyond the role specified in the Federal Reserve Act for a Federal Reserve bank. Concerned about the weak condition of the Third National Bank of Fitzgerald, Georgia, the board expressed a "willingness to help if it can be done with safety," as assistance "would not only probably save this institution but would redound to the best interests of the Federal Reserve

System" (FRBA, board of directors minutes, May 14, 1915). A Federal Reserve Bank director and the head of the Credit Bureau visited the bank with authorization to discount up to $15,000 of the bank's paper and to obtain the assistance of neighboring banks in providing another $15,000 and hopefully $20,000 in discounts. As part of this operation, the Third National Bank had to consent to the placement in the bank of an individual chosen by the Atlanta directors who would represent the interests of the Federal Reserve Bank (FRBA, board of directors minutes, May 14, 1915). Ultimately, the bank had to be rescued. The minutes of July 8, 1915, reported that the bank's capital had been wiped out by bad debts and loans, and that the Federal Reserve Bank assisted with a new subscription of capital stock for a reorganized bank. Subscribers to the new capital stock agreed to pay part in cash and part in notes, of which $50,000 to $55,000 could be discounted immediately at the Federal Reserve Bank.

Discounting gave the Atlanta Fed a window into some potentially troubled banks that seemed to be using credit from the Fed to stay afloat. In early 1915, the executive committee of the board of directors rejected $28,000 of the $71,400 notes that Heard National Bank of Jacksonville, Florida, had presented for discount, and again three months later it rejected $54,000 of the $113,796 notes presented (FRBA, executive committee minutes, January 15 and March 23, 1915). Finally in November it refused a request for $25,000, stating that the committee felt "that sufficient accommodations had already been granted to said bank" (FRBA, executive committee minutes, November 26, 1915). In 1916, the FRBA's governor, Wellborn was called to Washington, DC, for a meeting with Board Governor Harding and Comptroller John Skelton Williams about the Heard National Bank. The OCC's chief district examiner had found that Heard had sustained loan losses of $700,000 to $800,000, dwarfing its reported losses of $250,000. At the behest of the OCC and with the apparent blessing of the Federal Reserve Board, the FRBA's cashier, J. P. Pike, was made vice president of the bank with effective control wrested from the president, who remained as a figure head. The FRBA also agree to discount up to $500,000 for the Heard bank, which the Atlanta Fed's board of directors approved (FRBA board of directors minutes, August 10, 1916). But, even this remedial action did not save the Heard National Bank, which failed and left the FRBA with a substantial loss (FRBA board of directors minutes, April 25, 1917).

Yet, while the Third National and the Heard National received special assistance, other banks such as the Island City National Bank of Key West, Florida, apparently did not. The board was primarily concerned that Island

City's notes discounted at the Fed were past due. The Island City bank received a special inspection by cashier J. B. Pike, but was then liquidated under the authority of the OCC (FRBA board of directors minutes, September 15 and October 15, 1915). Such an intimate involvement in the management of banks was not contemplated by the Federal Reserve Act, although clearinghouses had sometimes provided similar assistance (Friedman and Schwartz 1963). In discussions of these banks in the FRBA's directors' minutes, there is no reference to any threat to financial stability or any statement of a rule for intervention, making it appear that these were discretionary actions that today would be deemed likely to induce moral hazard. However, as they only involved a few banks and were not part of a systemic problem, they attracted little notice. This state of affairs changed abruptly when the recession of 1920–1921 hit, and many more banks in the district were threatened by failure. As the problem was district-wide, the FRBA's efforts to save failing banks drew upon the resources of other Federal Reserve banks and created a furor within the system.

Protecting District Financial Stability: The Atlanta Fed and the Recession of 1920–1921

The greater severity of the recession of 1920–1921 in the Sixth District and the predisposition of the Atlanta Fed to assist struggling banks set up a confrontation with the Federal Reserve Board, which was convinced that a large deflation was necessary to reduce the price level and ensure the "liquidation" of loans by Federal Reserve banks to their member banks. What is surprising is how little of the conflict over policy was seen outside of the Fed. In the Atlanta Fed's annual reports, there was no evidence of the pressure that the Board had put on the FRBA to contract its balance sheet. The 1920 report blandly stated, "Probably never in the history of this country has its financial structure been so severely tried as during 1920, certainly the Federal Reserve System has received a most severe test, and successfully performed the functions for which it was inaugurated" (FRBA, *Annual Report* 1920, p. 7). Similarly, the Federal Reserve Board's annual report for 1922 records the extraordinary interregional bank transfers but gives little hint at the struggle between the Federal Reserve banks in heavily agricultural regions and the rest of the system.

The most detailed public account is found in the memoir of Harding, former governor of the Federal Reserve Board (1925), which provides a neutral description of the 1920–1921 deflation with no hint of the internal conflicts with the Fed. Harding wrote:

Because of the low reserve percentage of the banks and of the constant tendency of balances to shift from one Federal Reserve District to another, it had become necessary in 1919 to resort to large and frequent rediscount transactions between the Federal Reserve Banks themselves. Such transactions increased both in frequency and in volume during the year 1920 and continued in a smaller degree for several months in 1921. (Harding 1925, p. 182)

After listing the lending and borrowing Reserve banks, Harding then commented:

The banks, however showed such a spirit of cooperation that no compulsion was ever necessary, although there were times when at least one of the banks (Cleveland) was rediscounting larger amounts for other Federal Reserve Banks than it was for its own member banks. No application of a Federal Reserve Bank for rediscount accommodation was ever declined. (Harding 1925, p. 183)

Defending the Fed from a charge "in the halls of Congress and elsewhere of the 'murderous deflation' alleged to have taken place during the year 1920," (Harding 1925, p. 183), Harding presented a table to show that there was "no contraction of credit or currency during that year," by which he meant no decline in bills discounted or notes in circulation for the year 1920 for the whole system. But, while bills discounted increased from $2.1 million to $2.7 million, bills purchased fell from $561,313 to $255,702. Of course, this narrow frame covers only part of the recession that the NBER dates from January 1920 to July 1921 (NBER [www.nber .org], Business Cycle Dates). Between end-of-year 1919 and 1920, there was a 21 percent increase in bills discounted, but this was followed by a drop of 57 percent the next year, most of this coming from agricultural districts (Board of Governors 1943, table 87).

Even recent researchers treat the operation of the Federal Reserve System in this period as cooperative and almost seamless. To offer historical perspective on the debate over TARGET2 imbalances between the national central banks of the euro, Eichengreen, Mehl, Chitu, and Richardson (2014) examined the period 1913–1960 and claim that mutual assistance between Reserve banks was common, stating:

Fortunes could change quickly with earlier emergency recipients of gold turning into providers. Imbalances did not grow endlessly but narrowed once shock subsided. Mutual assistance did not excite experts or the American public, nor in most cases did they trigger insurmountable tensions between regions. (Eichengreen et al. 2014, p. 5)

Citing the 1920 annual report of the Federal Reserve Board, they view this cooperation as arising out of wartime patriotism: "there has . . . been such a spontaneous spirit of cooperation between the Federal Reserve Banks that all transactions suggested by the Federal Reserve Board have been made voluntarily." Although this selfless accommodation by Federal Reserve banks may have been typical during World War I or post–World War II, it did not characterize some earlier years. In particular, the recession of 1920–1921 weighed unevenly among regions, and inter–Federal Reserve district assistance was vigorously contested.

The dimensions of the regional stress experienced by the Federal Reserve banks during the recession of 1920–1921 are mapped out in Figure 7.3 from the January 1922 *Federal Reserve Bulletin*, which displays the rediscounts from surplus Reserve banks to deficit Reserve banks that effected transfers of gold certificates through the Gold Settlement Fund and enabled the latter to maintain their legal minimum gold reserve requirements. The uneven regional effects of the recession are clear as inter-district accommodation rose during the contraction, peaking at $280 million in October 1920. This sum was considerable as it was larger than the total assets of many Federal Reserve banks; the Atlanta Fed, for example, had total assets of $275 million at the end of December 1920.

In the early months of the recession, from January through March 1920, most demand for accommodation came from the New York and Philadelphia Federal Reserve banks, with several other Reserve banks supplying gold certificates. This pattern may be explained by the international gold losses, primarily in New York, which gave rise to the New York Fed's urgent demands for a rise in discount rates that moved from 4¾ percent to 6 percent on January 23, 1920. But, for the remainder of the year, after the first quarter, there was a clear regional division between agricultural and nonagricultural Federal Reserve districts. From March through December 1920, the Federal Reserve banks of Richmond, Atlanta, Chicago, St. Louis, Minneapolis, Kansas City, and Dallas continuously required accommodation from Philadelphia, Cleveland, and San Francisco. The New York Fed provided surplus gold reserves from April through July but then required modest assistance for the rest of the year (*Federal Reserve Bulletin* January 1922, p. 29). By far, the largest supplier of reserves to deficit districts was the Federal Reserve Bank of Cleveland. For example, at the end of October 1920, total accommodation reached $260 million, of which Cleveland supplied $139 million, followed by Boston giving $84 million and Philadelphia $21 million. The Atlanta Fed was one of many borrowers; its peak borrowing was $45 million in September, which was also the month that borrowing by the Dallas Fed hit a high of $37 million. In October, the Kansas City Fed reached

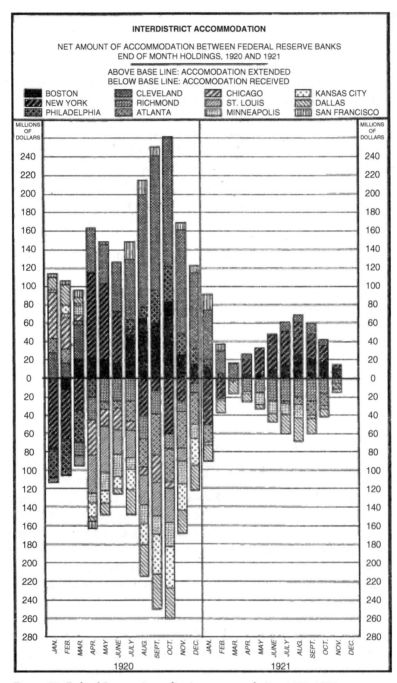

Figure 7.3 Federal Reserve inter-district accommodation, 1920–1921.
Source: Board of Governors of the Federal Reserve System, *Federal Reserve Bulletin* (January 1922), p. 28.

$45 million, St. Louis $37 million, and Minneapolis $26 million – with the New York Fed also drawing $61 million from other districts.

Yet, from the archival records available, it appears that Atlanta received the harshest criticism from the Federal Reserve Board, responding to complaints by the Cleveland Fed. In terms of reserve ratios for its Federal Reserve notes, the Atlanta Fed was not the worst offender. In the difficult month of September 1920, the FRBA had a reserve ratio of 40.5 percent. But when borrowed reserves were subtracted, the "adjusted" reserve ratio would have been 17 percent. For all other months, its adjusted reserve ratio was above 20 percent. Other Federal Reserve banks fell below this 20 percent mark more frequently; St. Louis, Minneapolis, and Kansas City were below it for two months in 1920. The Dallas bank was probably the weakest, with its adjusted reserve ratio falling below 20 percent for the last six months of 1920, then hitting just 10 percent in September 1920.

What may have made Atlanta the center of attention was its willingness to increase bills purchased and discounted from member banks, significantly expanding its balance sheet in the difficult months of 1920. Table 7.1 presents some monthly data for the FRBA, drawn from a variety of sources, primarily the daily balance sheets preserved in the Reserve banks' library. Unfortunately, these balance sheets for the critical year of 1920 are missing, but some of the monthly data can be reconstructed from other sources. During 1919, when the postwar boom rapidly picked up steam, bills discounted and purchased by the FRBA increased from $86 million to $110 million, with the reserve ratio generally remaining well above the 40 percent minimum. Its overall balance sheet grew from under $200 million to $280 million. The value of bills discounted and the official and adjusted reserve ratios are shown in Figure 7.4, with the recession of 1920–1921 shaded in grey.

Heading into the recession in 1920, the Atlanta Fed did not "liquidate" member bank borrowings but expanded them, peaking at $145 million in November 1920, as seen in Table 7.1 and Figure 7.4. As members drew on these loans, the Federal Reserve bank's reserves dropped and the reserve ratio would have fallen below the legal minimum if the bank had not received accommodation for other Federal Reserve banks. By 1921, the Atlanta Fed was shrinking its balance sheet and liquidating member bank borrowing, but it could not halt the drain in reserves. With the economy still in the downward phase of the recession until July 1921, it again required accommodation from other Federal Reserve banks between August and November 1921.

Unfortunately, only the minutes of the Federal Reserve Bank of Atlanta's board of directors and its executive committee were available,

Table 7.1 *Balance Sheet, Reserves, and Borrowings of the Atlanta Fed*

Month	Total Assets ($M)	Bills Discounted and Purchased	Reserve Ratio	Adjusted Reserve Ratio	Total Discounts for Other FRBs ($M)	Total Discounts from Other FRBs ($M)
January 1919		86	45.7%			3.1
February 1919	197	83	47.9%			
March 1919	206	89	45.7%			
April 1919	201	89	45.4%			
May 1919	209	89	46.9%			
June 1919	203	93	43.7%			
July 1919	215	85	49.9%			
August 1919	209	102	40.1%			
September 1919	224	104	41.4%			12.3
October 1919	256	119	40.7%			5.5
November 1919	264	115	46.0%			
December 1919	280	110	52.8%	56.7%	5.1	5
January 1920		106	48.5%	56.0%	15	
February 1920		110	44.2%	52.2%	16.2	
March 1920		116	48.3%	50.0%	3.4	
April 1920		112	41.4%	41.4%		
May 1920		123	40.4%	36.2%		8.5
June 1920		120	40.6%	36.1%		7.9
July 1920		119	40.8%	29.3%		21.6
August 1920		120	40.4%	23.5%		31.9
September 1920		122	40.5%	17.0%		45.5
October 1920		127	40.5%	24.2%		36.1
November 1920		145	40.1%	21.2%		40.2
December 1920	275	139	40.7%	24.8%		33.7
January 1921	261	135	42.2%	28.7%		31.9
February 1921	259	129	42.7%	42.7%		
March 1921	252	123	42.0%	42.0%		
April 1921	244	116	46.0%	46.0%		
May 1921	245	110	46.4%	46.4%		
June 1921	232	101	44.4%	44.4%		
July 1921	220	106	41.6%	39.5%		13.5
August 1921	206	100	40.8%	35.6%		8.9
September 1921	222	108	40.4%	29.4%		16.8
October 1921	211	104	40.3%	32.3%		14.1
November 1921	205	97	40.5%	35.9%		7.4
December 1921	215	95	42.6%	42.6%		

Sources: Federal Reserve Bank of Atlanta, *Annual Reports* (1919, 1920, 1921); Board of Governors Minutes (1919–1921), daily balance sheets. Board of Governors *Federal Reserve Bulletin* (January 1922).

Note: The adjusted reserve ratio subtracts reserves borrowed from other Federal Reserve banks.

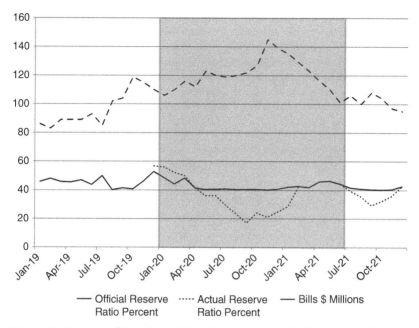

Figure 7.4 Response of the Atlanta Fed to the cotton crash bills discounted and Reserve ratios, 1919–1921.
Note: The shaded area represents the recession of 1920–1921.
Source: See Table 7.1

and the discussions and correspondence of the officers and members of the boards of the remaining eleven Reserve banks were not consulted. The Atlanta minutes reveal that cooperation between Reserve banks was often grudging and hesitant. While, in the words of Governor Wellborn, the Federal Reserve bank was "caring for the demands of member banks," trying to stave off a banking collapse, it was subjected to considerable pressure to rapidly "liquidate" its discounts and advances to member banks. Grateful member banks were buffered. J. R. Morgan, the cashier (chief financial officer) of the Bank of Union Springs Alabama, described the Atlanta Fed's actions from a cotton bank's point of view:

All we country bankers could do was endorse notes and send them to the Federal Reserve. Governor Wellborn met every legitimate demand . . . .. For its duration it was the worst we ever had, though it only lasted six to eight months. Governor Wellborn broke it by throwing the whole resources of the Federal Reserve behind the banks of the south. (quoted in Garrett n.d., ch. 9)

As the depth of the recession became apparent in the summer of 1920, Wellborn reported to the Atlanta Fed's board of directors:

Your Executive Committee feels that in order to effectually cooperate with the Federal Reserve Board in their earnest efforts towards deflation and control of credits, that it is necessary and essential that we rely not only on repeated admonitions to member banks, but that we continue to exercise that discretion permissible under the law as to the desirability of certain paper, and especially the frequency and volume of discount transactions of certain members banks with the Federal Reserve Bank. (FRBA board of directors minutes, August 6, 1920)

The leaders of the Atlanta Fed viewed themselves as tough, but they were uncomfortable with carrying through a "liquidation" of loans as encouraged by Washington, D.C. In the FRBA board's July meeting, it was noted that some banks were angry because they had been forced to pay off their loans from the FRBA, even though they were offered the chance to keep the loans by posting more collateral. Wellborn described one group of loans that the Reserve bank wanted off of its books.

A statement of borrowing by textile people, especially hosiery mills, in the Chattanooga district, shows that we have a total of $927,000, and while the aggregate amount involved is not very excessive, still it is quite large for one community. The mills claim that jobbers are holding off, consequently very few sales are being made. We feel that it would probably be best that we begin to insist on a gradual liquidation of this class of paper. (FRBA board of directors minutes, August 6, 1920)

Still, Wellborn felt that too much pressure was being placed by Washington on the Atlanta Fed. In particular he voiced the board of directors' frustration that other districts had a 5 percent discount rate approved by the Federal Reserve Board, while the Atlanta Fed had a 6 percent rate. He commented, "[I]t seems to me that our rate should be on a level with theirs and a reduction made for the same reason that theirs was made – that is, to stimulate and encourage a revival of businesses" (FRBA Board of Directors minutes, October 8, 1920).

While the Federal Reserve Board may have tolerated accommodation for troubled banks in the first years of the Fed, by the end of 1920, the Federal Reserve Board and several Reserve banks believed that the Atlanta Fed ought to be reined in. On December 3, 1920, Harding wrote a letter to Wellborn about the Federal Reserve Board's alarm at the FRBA's interbank borrowing, singling out the fact that it had borrowed $35 million from the Federal Reserve Bank of Cleveland, while the FRBA had only $11 million capital and surplus. Minimizing the problems of banks in the South, Harding sternly told Atlanta that:

The Board is of the opinion that your present experience should convince you that your lending policy has been rather too lenient and that in some cases credit was granted in such large amount to banks when no emergency existed as to impair your ability to make loans out of your own resources when a real emergency did arise.[10]

Noting that to continue lending to Atlanta, Cleveland might have to borrow from other banks, he appeared to threaten Atlanta: "Here again I may say that I do not believe the Board would permit such transactions to take place but would be more inclined to allow the reserve of the Atlanta Bank show a depreciation." What this meant was unclear, especially as par clearance was mandated by the Federal Reserve Act, but it was a chastisement in the ordinarily courtly language of the Fed. Coming from Harding, these words must have been especially dismaying for Wellborn, as Harding, a fellow Alabama banker, had been instrumental in persuading him to head the Atlanta Fed in 1914 (Garrett n.d., ch. 3, pp. 39–40).

On December 9, 1920, Wellborn wrote back to Harding with a spirited defense of the Atlanta Fed's actions in the face of "the increased restlessness of the Cleveland bank," arguing that the regional economies were too tightly integrated to allow a disaster to occur in one and not expect severe repercussions throughout the whole. Wellborn emphasized the magnitude of the shock from the drop in cotton prices, stating that "[n]o section of our country could stand the full unmitigated shock of such a disaster without ruin." Then, he made his appeal:

I submit, if this bank had failed to stand as a buffer between the business of this section and disaster, it would not only have failed in its duty, but it would have permitted a situation to develop which would have seriously affected all other sections of the country and every other reserve bank. To carry the load under these emergency conditions of course mean borrowing and rediscount . . . . This bank does not consider that its efforts along these lines have been directed at the stimulation of an artificial price. We have not undertaken to draw upon the reserves or the resources of other sections, to hold our crops for artificial or inflated prices . . . . In such a situation the Atlanta bank does not stand as a private business venture, asking for credit for itself alone, or for the purpose of making profits. The bank stands as a public institution, designed within limited and legitimate lines to prevent disaster . . . . The commerce of all the states are too closely knit together to permit the confining of the results of financial upheaval to any one particular state or group of states. The Cleveland District itself, counts this section one of its principal markets. The Sixth District is filled with farm implements, trucks, automobiles and other manufactured products emanating from the Cleveland District. The commercial banks of the Sixth District have financed the local dealers [of] many of these commodities, that such local dealers

---

[10] These letters are recorded in the FRBA board of directors minutes for the December 10, 1920, meeting.

might pay cash to the manufacturers in the Cleveland District. To shut off completely, or hamper the buying power of this and other agricultural districts, would bring about a situation which would be felt from the Pacific to the Atlantic. (FRBA, board of directors minutes, December 9, 1920)

Wellborn then criticized the Cleveland bank for taking a parochial position and the rest of the Federal Reserve System for its short memory:

In the present crisis it seems to me it is not a time for individual reserve banks, which are rediscounting for other reserve banks, to attempt to impose upon the borrowing bank, onerous conditions. If the Cleveland bank is "restless" on account of the credit which it has in the past, and must almost of necessity in the future, on account of its high reserve position, extend to Atlanta, the Cleveland bank simply takes a rather narrow and personal view of the situation . . . . May I not be permitted to call your attention to the fact that last winter and spring when your Board called upon the Atlanta bank to rediscount for New York, Boston and Philadelphia we did not raise any objection . . . . [W]e did not think it proper to ask any questions because we recognized that your body was the sole judge of the expediency and that you had the full authority to compel interbank rediscounting. (FRBA board of directors minutes, December 9, 1920)

As for the vague threat that Harding had made in his letter of December 3, Wellborn pointed out the potentially calamitous consequences of exposing to the public the awkward position of the Atlanta Fed or allowing a "depreciation."

With regard to your statement that your Board has "an inclination to allow the Atlanta bank show a depreciation." I do not question that your Board has a legal right to do this, but it is a responsibility that rests upon your Board, and in these perilous times I hardly think your Board would care to assume such a fearful risk. The mere publication of our actual reserve position might possibly have the effect of causing the failure of numerous banks, not only in this District, but in others as well, and bring on a panic of great magnitude. (FRBA board of directors minutes, December 9, 1920)

When Harding responded on December 15, 1920, his letter was more focused on when the Atlanta Fed would begin to reduce its rediscounts. He began by commenting: "In your letter you do not express any opinion as to when your bank will be able to pay off its rediscounts without falling below its legal minimum reserve, and on the other hand, you assume that it will be necessary for other Federal Reserve banks to extend your bank accommodation for an indefinite period." Moderating his tone, Harding stated that the "Board at no time suggested drastic and immediate liquidation but has repeatedly reiterated its preference for orderly processes." Still Harding let Wellborn and the Atlanta board know that the

Federal Reserve Board thought that the Atlanta Fed had taken on excessive risks:

The Board has never advised farmers to produce a larger crop of cotton and does not, therefore, coincide with your view that the Federal Reserve Bank should carry loans indefinitely for member banks until cotton reaches a price that is satisfactory to the producers. As a matter of fact your reports indicate that you are not carrying an excessive amount of cotton for member banks and our statements show that you are well margined on what you are carrying. An analysis of the list of your large borrowing banks, which you sent in your letter of December 10th shows that seven banks in your district, located in commercial and industrial centers, are borrowing $71,803,469, and that you are lending to each of four banks an amount in excess of the total capital and surplus of your own bank. Since the loans to these banks constitute a large proportion of your total loans, the Board is forced to the conclusion that your credit situation is not caused entirely by agricultural conditions. (FRBA, board of directors minutes, December 15, 1920)

While accepting that the FRBA would not be able to quickly reduce its interbank loans, Harding told the Atlanta officials that they should write directly to borrowing banks to reduce their lines of credit and that the Atlanta Fed should provide an additional 15 percent margin of collateral for the Cleveland loans in the form of commercial paper.

Wellborn replied on December 23, 1920, that it was impossible to forecast when liquidation of its loans would take place as only three-quarters of the new cotton crop had been sold. As for the banks that Harding identified as untroubled by cotton loans, Wellborn pointed out that the large borrowings of the city banks were a result of the fact that they had provided accommodation to their country correspondent banks – often state banks who were not members of the Fed – for production and marketing of the cotton crop. Not all banks had joined the Fed and thereby gained direct access to the discount window. Only 85 of the 1,609 state banks in the Sixth District were member banks; credit to them was being intermediated by the city banks. Hence, low cotton prices threatened all banks. In Wellborn's opinion, the Atlanta Fed had a broad responsibility for the whole of the financial system in the Sixth District, not to just the member banks, because of the highly interconnected nature of the banking system (FRBA board of directors minutes, December 23, 1920).

Finally, winding up this exchange, Wellborn condemned any effort to rapidly reduced credit that might risk a fire sale and banking crisis. The Atlanta Fed only gave borrowers modest extensions after the "bulk of farmers' notes fell due, and our policy is merely to give them reasonable time to find a market in these disturbed times, in order to keep them from 'dumping' their products on the market at one time" (FRBA, board of directors minutes, December 23, 1920). As to whether the Atlanta Bank was acting correctly, Wellborn quoted an April 10, 1920 speech of Dr. Miller of the Federal Reserve Board:

Credit control to my mind, therefore, at this juncture does not mean *contraction*. It means preventing a further expansion, *except* as that further expansion can be definitely validated by the necessities of industries that are contributing to the sum-total of goods in the country ... I think that forced contraction or liquidation might be one of the most disastrous of things. (FRBA, board of directors minutes, December 23, 1920)

While Wellborn offered a spirited defense of the Atlanta Fed's actions, the bank did begin a liquidation of member bank borrowings and shrank its balance sheets as viewed in Table 7.1 and Figure 7.4. At the first meeting of 1921, Wellborn told his board that "[q]uite a large number of our member banks have rediscounted more than two or three times their capital and surplus. Write to them that they must reduce their borrowings" (FRBA board of directors minutes, January 14, 1921). By the March meeting, he reported that (adjusted) reserves had risen from 37.6 percent on February 8 to 44 percent on March 8; this rise was brought about largely by liquidation of $9.9 million of member bank borrowings by the Atlanta Fed's branch in New Orleans (FRBA board of directors minutes, March 11, 1921).

Nevertheless, the Atlanta bank remained very active, hoping to avoid large bank failures. In the board's March 11, 1921, meeting, Wellborn described how the FRBA had helped to manage the absorption of the weak Citizens and Southern Bank of Savannah by the Hibernia Bank, which assumed all of its liabilities and assets. The absorption was handled "by the tact and good management of Mr. Campbell," the deputy governor of the Atlanta Fed (FRBA board of directors minutes, March 11, 1921), but it needed assistance. In addition to obtaining $2 million via bills payable to other banks, Hibernia obtained more than half a million in discounts from the FRBA.

The pressure brought to bear on the Atlanta Fed to shrink its lending had political repercussions. In July 1921, Congress launched the Joint Commission of Agricultural Inquiry to investigate the causes of agriculture's distress. The Federal Reserve Board was grilled and appears, as a result, to have changed its attitude. On July 20, the Board held a conference with the Reserve bank presidents in the cotton growing districts – Richmond, Atlanta, St. Louis, Kansas City, and Dallas. At the end of the meeting, an announcement was issued that the Federal Reserve banks,

in addition to credits already extended, are able and stand ready to extend further credit for the purpose of harvesting and marketing the coming crop, in whatever amount may legitimately be required, either directly to their member banks or, under a ruling now issued by the Federal Reserve Board, indirectly to nonmember banks acting through the agency and with the endorsement of a member bank." (Joint Commission 1921, vol. 2, pp. 346–347)

The new release emphasized the "urgency of rendering all proper assistance to" cotton dealers and producers "during such abnormal times." Ironically, this new policy was announced just as cotton prices were recovering, as illustrated in Figure 7.2. Rural banks in cotton and other agricultural regions remained weak and experienced high but declining rates of failure; and the urgency of action faded.

In the second half of 1921, the FRBA continued to provide new forms of assistance to its many troubled member banks. To help weak banks generally, Wellborn proposed to the Atlanta board a plan to execute repurchase agreements for U.S. government war bonds with members banks because their holdings were disproportionately large relative to their capital and surplus. As interest rates had risen, bond prices had fallen and member banks might incur losses that would impair their surplus or even capital, when examiners marked their portfolios to market. In addition, holdings of these bonds lowered earnings because the coupon rates were lower than the discount rate. In order to "minimize such losses to the member banks and enable them, in a measure, to amortize the carrying value down to the market value the Officers of the Federal Reserve Banks .... hereby authorize, acting under Sect. 14 of the Federal Reserve Act" to execute renewable sixty-day repurchase agreements for bonds that are in excess of a member bank's capital and surplus. Every thirty days, banks would pay the Federal Reserve Bank one-tenth of 1 percent of the aggregate principal amount of the bonds until payments equaled the loss represented by the market price (FRBA board of directors minutes, August 12, 1921).

Some banks still suffering from the after effects of the recession received special attention. The FRBA sought to ensure that they would be healthy enough to resume normal operations. One example of this activity occurred in December 1921. In consultation with Chief National Bank Examiner John W. Pole and Atlanta Fed's Assistant Cashier J. B. Tutwiler, Wellborn decided to help First National Bank of Colquitt, whose capital stock was wiped out. The bank examiner was of the opinion that maintaining the bank would have a favorable influence on the general market for the financial instruments it bought and discounted. He believed that it was unlikely that the Colquitt bank would realize as much as 20 cents on the dollar for its underlying collateral if it were closed, but more it if continued as an ongoing bank. In response, the Atlanta Fed released the Colquitt bank from repayment of $30,000 of bills receivable that the FRBA had discounted and purchased $84,000 of doubtful assets from the bank for the sum of $30,000 that it was releasing (FRBA board of directors minutes, December 7, 1921).

In the last meeting of the board of directors of the Atlanta Fed for 1921, Wellborn summarized his vision of the task of the Reserve bank:

The daily problem which our Executive Committee must meet, is that of properly taking care of those of our member banks which are in straitened condition. Many of those banks have been very heavy borrowers through the year; and, while this season of the year would naturally demand that there be curtailment, deposit declines are in larger volume than in collections . . .. The reports of examination of such banks are watched very closely, and the paper they offer for rediscount is scrutinized to the last degree. (FRBA, board of directors minutes, December 7, 1921)

Wellborn had not retreated from the position that he had set forth in his exchange of letters with Harding a year before, stating, "I feel that it is the duty of our Committee to sustain and back up to the furthest point possible, our member banks, by accepting their paper for rediscount where it is reasonable to do so." He posed the regional central bank's dilemma thusly:

On the one hand, we are confronted with the danger of extending so much aid to a member bank that, if it failed we should incur a very considerable loss . . .. On the other hand, if we go to a great length and save a member bank so that it can, in time, work out of its difficulties, I feel that we would be accomplishing what was intended in the establishment of the Federal Reserve System. It is our fundamental duty to take care of extremes and emergencies and while the responsibilities are exceedingly heavy, still I believe that we should show the proper nerve and fortitude, and go as far as is possible in saving any member bank which is in difficulty. (FRBA board of directors minutes, December 7, 1921)

Afterwards

Some officials who had opposed Wellborn's strategy later conceded that he had acted wisely. D. W. Crissinger, who had been the Comptroller of the Currency and became Chairman of the Federal Reserve Board in 1923, commented: "We were inclined at first to disagree with Governor M.B.

Wellborn of the Atlanta bank, in some of the policies which he pursued, but ... he was right and we – the members of the federal reserve board – were wrong" (quoted in Gamble, 1989, "The Bank Meets Its First Crisis"). Certainly Wellborn's Sixth District constituency and many influential southern congressmen were satisfied with his stewardship of the Atlanta Fed. When Congress held hearings into allegations that the Federal Reserve had aided speculators in the cotton crash, Wellborn was lauded by senators from the Cotton South (Gamble 1989).

In modern debates over whether a central bank should do more than flood the market with liquidity during a crisis, Wellborn and the Atlanta Fed stand in the corner of the interventionists. Their concern focused on the threat that a sharp drop in liquidity would force a crisis-inducing fire sale of bank assets. They believed that the Reserve bank should intermediate reserves from other districts, supplying liquidity directly to its member banks and indirectly to the nonmember banks. Thus, financial stability would be preserved in the absence of a responsive interbank market for funds. Nowhere in the minutes of the board of directors of the Sixth District Reserve bank is there a discussion of the problem of moral hazard that modern noninterventionists have emphasized. Wellborn saw the collapse of the post–World War I boom as an exceptional event that would not be repeated, a fact that he believed the district's banking community understood well. His member banks had not acted recklessly but patriotically by expanding credit during and after the Great War; some may have offered excessive credits during the boom, but he regarded this behavior as a minor factor. Consequently, the Atlanta Fed should have accommodated its member banks during the harsh recession and readied them to resume normal operations in the 1920s. Of course, what he did not anticipate was that a second and even greater shock would occur a decade later.

References

Allen, Franklin, Elena Carletti, and Douglas Gale. (2009). "Interbank Market Liquidity and Central Bank Intervention." *Journal of Monetary Economics* 56(5):639–652.

Bagehot, Walter. (1873). *Lombard Street: A Description of the Money Market.* London: Henry S. King and Co.

Board of Governors of the Federal Reserve System. (1922, January). *Federal Reserve Bulletin.*

Board of Governors of the Federal Reserve System. (1943). *Banking and Monetary Statistics, 1914–1941.* Washington, DC.

Bordo, Michael D., and David C. Wheelock. (2013). "The Promise and Performance of the Federal Reserve as a Lender of Last Resort, 1914–1933." In M. D. Bordo and

W. Roberds (eds.), *A Return to Jekyll Island: The Origins, History and Future of the Federal Reserve*, pp. 59–98. Cambridge: Cambridge University Press.

Caballero, Ricardo J., and Alp Simsek. (2013). "Fire Sales in a Model of Complexity." *Journal of Finance* 68(6):2549–2587.

Calomiris, Charles A., and Eugene N. White. (1994). "The Origins of Federal Deposit Insurance." In C. Goldin and G. D. Libecap (eds.), *The Regulated Economy: A Historical Approach to Political Economy*, pp. 145–88. Chicago: University of Chicago Press.

Carlson, Mark, Kris James Mitchener, and Gary Richardson. (2011). "Arresting Banking Panics: Fed Liquidity Provision and the Forgotten Panic of 1929." *Journal of Political Economy* 119(5):889–924.

Chandler, Lester V. (1958). *Benjamin Strong, Central Banker*. Washington, DC: Brookings Institution.

Diamond, Douglas W., and Raghuram G. Rajan (2011). "Fear of Fire Sales, Illiquidity Seeking and Credit Freezes." *Quarterly Journal of Economics* 126(2):557–591.

Eichengreen, Barry, Arnaud J. Mehl, Livia Chitu, and Gary Richardson. (2014). "Mutual Assistance between Federal Reserve Banks, 1913–1960." Working Paper No. 20267, National Bureau of Economic Research.

Federal Reserve Act (1915). "An Act To provide for the establishment of Federal reserve banks, to furnish an elastic currency, to afford means of rediscounting commercial paper, to establish a more effective supervision of banking in the United States, and for other purposes," (December 23, 1913), *The Statues at Large of the United States*, vol. XXXVIII. Washington, DC.

Federal Reserve Bank of Atlanta. (1919, 1920, 1921). *Annual Report*. Atlanta.

Federal Reserve Bank of Atlanta. Office of the Secretary, Board of Directors, minutes.

Federal Reserve Bank of Atlanta. Office of the Secretary, Executive Committee of the Board of Directors, minutes.

Federal Reserve Bank of Atlanta. Library, daily consolidated balance sheets.

Federal Reserve Board. (1919, 1920, 1921, 1922). *Annual Report*. Washington, DC.

Freixas, Xavier, and Bruno M. Parigi (2014). "Lender of Last Resort and Bank Closure Policy." In A. N. Berger, P. Molyneux, and J. O. S. Wilson (eds.), *The Oxford Handbook of Banking*, 2nd edition, pp. 475–504. Oxford: Oxford University Press.

Freixas, Xavier, Bruno M. Parigi, and Jean-Charles Rochet. (2000). "Systemic Risk, Interbank Relations and Liquidity Provision by the Central Bank." *Journal of Money, Credit and Banking* 32(2):611–638.

Friedman, Milton, and Anna J. Schwartz. (1963). *A Monetary History of the United States 1867–1960*. Princeton, NJ: Princeton University Press.

Gamble, Richard H. (1989). *A History of the Federal Reserve Bank of Atlanta, 1914–1989*. Atlanta, GA: Federal Reserve Bank of Atlanta. Retrieved from www.frb atlanta.org/about/publications/atlanta-fed-history/first-75-years/the-bank-meets-its-first-crisis.aspx.

Garrett, Franklin. (n.d.). "History of the Federal Reserve Bank of Atlanta." Archives of the Federal Reserve Bank of Atlanta, unpublished.

Harding, W. P. G. (1925). *The Formative Period of the Federal Reserve System*. London: Constable and Company Ltd.

Hautcoeur, Pierre-Cyrille, Angelo Riva, and Eugene N. White. (2014). "Floating a 'Lifeboat': The Banque de France and the Crisis of 1889." *Journal of Monetary Economics* 65(July):104–119.

Joint Commission of Agricultural Inquiry. (1921). *Hearings Before the Joint Commission of Agricultural Inquiry*, Sixty-Seventh Congress, First Session, 3 vols. (July, August, and November). Washington, DC: Government Printing Office.

Measuring Worth, Consumer Price Index. (2014). Retrieved from www .measuringworth.com/uscpi/.

Meltzer, Allan H. (2003). *A History of the Federal Reserve, Vol. I, 1913–1955*. Chicago: University of Chicago Press.

Mishkin, Frederic S., and Eugene N. White. (2014). "Unprecedented Actions: The Federal Reserve's Response to the Global Financial Crisis in Historical Perspective." Working Paper No. 20737, National Bureau of Economic Research.

Moen, Jon, and Ellis W. Tallman. (1992). "The Bank Panic of 1907: The Role of the Trust Companies." *Journal of Economic History* 52(3): 611–630.

National Bureau of Economic Research. (n.d.). U.S. Business Cycle Expansions and Contractions. Retrieved from http://nber.org/cycles/cyclesmain.html.

National Bureau of Economic Research. (2008). Macro History IV. Prices. New York Wholesale Price of Cotton, 1870–1945. Retrieved from www.nber.org/databases/ macrohistory/contents/chapter04.html.

Richardson, Gary, and William Troost. (2009). "Monetary Intervention Mitigated Banking Panics during the Great Depression: Quasi-Experimental Evidence from a Federal Reserve District Border, 1929–1933." *Journal of Political Economy* 117(6):1031–1073.

Shleifer, Andrei, and Robert W. Vishny. (2010). "Asset Fire Sales and Credit Easing." *American Economic Review* 100(2):46–50.

Shleifer, Andrei, and Robert W. Vishny. (2011). "Fire Sales in Finance and Macroeconomics." *Journal of Economic Perspectives* 25(1):29–48.

White, Eugene N. (2013). "To Establish a More Effective Supervision of Banking: How the Birth of the Fed Altered Bank Supervision." In M. D. Bordo and W. Roberds, *The Origins, History and Future of the Federal Reserve: A Return to Jekyll Island*, pp. 7–54. Cambridge: Cambridge University Press.

8

Rediscovering Macro-Prudential Regulation: The National Banking Era from the Perspective of 2015

Charles W. Calomiris and Mark Carlson

Someone familiar with the complexities of U.S. banking regulations as of 2015 might wonder what could possibly be learned from the national bank regulatory system of the late nineteenth century. After all, this was an era that saw repeated banking panics. Many thousands of inefficient, geographically isolated, undiversified, and uncoordinated "unit" banks (both those chartered by the states and those chartered under the national banking system) blanketed the financial landscape of America. That structure not only fomented instability in rural areas and nationwide suspensions of convertibility, but perennially deprived the manufacturing sector of access to credit or access to a national network for placing stock offerings, like the one operating in Germany at the time (Calomiris 2000). The regulatory system governing national banks was rudimentary by current standards. There was no minimum equity ratio requirement on banks, no Federal Reserve System and hence no Fed credit provision or regulatory oversight of banks or bank holding companies by the Fed, and no deposit insurance. Government lending sources established in the twentieth century to subsidize leveraging investments in agricultural or residential real estate – such as the Federal Land Banks, Federal Home Loan Banks, Fannie Mae, Freddie Mac, the Federal Housing Administration, the Farm Credit System – were also absent. National banks at this time had little involvement in asset management or securities underwriting, and they were forbidden from offering guarantees (such as bankers' acceptances or bills of exchange). How could such a simple and primitive setting provide useful lessons for today?

We thank Peter Rousseau, Richard Sylla, Paul Wachtel, David Weiman, and other conference participants for helpful comments on a prior draft. The opinions expressed are those of the authors and should not be attributed to the Bank for International Settlements or the Board of Governors of the Federal Reserve System.

We can think of many answers to that question, and three strike us as particularly obvious. First, precisely because the national banking era (1863–1913) was one without a lender of last resort (LOLR) or deposit insurance, or the micro-prudential bank capital ratios, it offers a unique opportunity to see how unprotected banks operate in an environment of raw market discipline. Calomiris and Carlson (2016a) show how endogenous choices by banks about ownership structure, corporate governance procedures, cash holdings, and leverage were all part of that market discipline equilibrium.

Second, despite all of its costs, the unit banking network structure of the past offers a uniquely valuable laboratory for examining the operation of interbank payment and credit networks. The geographical isolation of unit banks made it possible to observe spatial networks of bank operations, which can provide unique insights about the nature of interbank relationship formation. For example, Calomiris and Carlson (2016a) show that banks with different business models connected with the interbank network differently. Additionally, Calomiris and Carlson (2016b) and Mitchener and Richardson (2015) show that interbank networks played important roles in concentrating liquidity risk at nodes within the reserve pyramid, which contributed to bank distress during both the national banking era and the Great Depression.[1]

Third – and the subject of this paper – the national banking era provides unique evidence about the contributions provided by regulatory and supervisory activities in a disciplined banking environment (i.e., one in which banks did not enjoy either access to the Fed discount window or the protection of deposit insurance). These insights are particularly useful today as an input to the debates over macro-prudential regulation and supervision and the means of enhancing market discipline (to avoid moral hazard and taxpayer-funded bailouts of banks).[2] We will show that, from

---

[1] Regulatory requirements incentivized banks to hold at least some of their reserves as deposits at banks in financial centers. Banks in much of the country could count balances in specified "reserve cities" – generally larger cities such as Boston, Kansas City, and San Francisco – or "central reserve cities" – New York and later Chicago and St. Louis – as part of their reserve. Banks in reserve cities could count balances at banks in central reserve cities as part of their legal reserve. These rules thus gave rise to a pyramid structure of reserves.

[2] Micro- and macro-prudential regulation use common tools (capital requirements, cash reserve or liquid asset requirements, risk weighting of assets, provisioning rules, etc.) but have different goals. Micro-prudential regulation focuses on the safety and soundness of individual banks. Macro-prudential regulation focuses on stabilizing the banking system as a whole, for example, by seeking to limit systemic contagion by requiring money center banks to maintain higher cash reserves than peripheral banks, by requiring larger banks to

a micro-prudential perspective, supervision and regulation played an important complementary role to market discipline during the national banking era, and this complementarity was very much the self-conscious intent of *regulators and bankers.*

Furthermore, regulation and supervision were not only focused on the stability of individual banks; indeed, the prudential rules that were enacted and enforced only make sense from the standpoint of systemic goals for banking stability. Thus, the national banking era provides an important precedent regarding the perceived benefits of taking a macro-prudential view of the proper role of bank regulation and supervision.

The four most important aspects of national banking era prudential regulation were: (1) the structure of bank reserve requirements, (2) the prohibition on national bank lending against real estate, (3) the examination and auditing of national banks by examiners, and (4) mandatory disclosures (the publication of the banks' accounts in local newspapers several times a year and in the Comptroller of the Currency's published annual volume reporting the condition for all national banks). These regulations, examinations, and disclosures ensured the credibility and transparency of the financial reporting by national banks about variables of central interest to market participants. After reviewing the regulatory arrangements of the national banking era, describing their impact, and arguing for their largely macro-prudential intent, we consider the lessons of the national banking era for current macro-prudential regulation in light of the 2008 crisis.

The National Banking Era: Stable or Unstable?

Between the Civil War and World War I, the U.S. banking system was developing rapidly along with the rest of the economy. It was a turbulent time for the banking system; there were severe strains in the financial sector in 1884, 1890, and 1896 (reflected in different degrees of collective action by the New York banks' clearinghouse to respond to those strains) and severe banking panics that resulted in the suspension of convertibility of deposits in New York in 1873, 1893, and 1907. The Panic of 1893 was a particularly severe episode, during which many national and state-chartered banks failed, as shown in Figure 8.1 (see also Calomiris and Gorton 1991; Carlson 2005).

maintain higher capital ratios, or by leaning against episodes of very rapid lending growth
by increasing minimum capital ratio requirements.

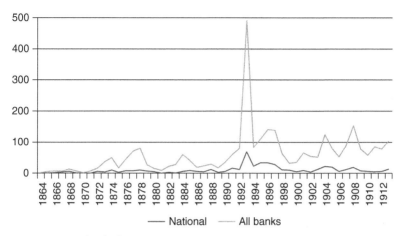

Figure 8.1 U.S. bank closures, 1864–1913.

What is the record of the severity of systemic banking system performance during the national banking era? As many researchers have pointed out, the U.S. unit banking system was uniquely panic prone during the period 1873–1907 – a time when virtually no other countries suffered panics comparable to those in the United States. Nevertheless, despite the numerous disruptive panics, none of them was a severe nationwide insolvency crisis. The worst of the national banking era crises – in 1893 – saw aggregate negative net worth of failed banks of roughly 0.1 percent of GDP, in contrast to the 1920s, the Great Depression, the S&L crisis, and the subprime crisis, all of which saw negative net worth of failed or intervened banks relative to GDP more than an order of magnitude larger than that.

It is also worth noting that banks in the national banking era had to contend with an economic environment that contained significant exogenous risks that banks do not face today. The seasonal agricultural cycle had significant effects on loan demand, which strained U.S. banks during the spring and fall (Hanes and Rhode 2013), creating seasonal swings in deposit default risk and bank liquidity risk. U.S. national banks operated under a global gold standard and were exposed to risks associated with global deflationary shocks (such as during the early 1890s), although there were no protracted periods of significant monetary shocks comparable to 1929–1933.

The lack of both a lender of last resort and any government guarantee of creditors likely affected the relative stability of national banks, too. Judging from studies of the effects of the founding of the Fed (Miron 1986; Mankiw and Miron 1987; Bernstein, Hughson, and Weidenmier 2010; Hanes and Rhode 2013; Calomiris, Jaremski, Park, and Richardson 2015), the creation of the Fed smoothed the severe seasonal fluctuations in loan demand and made banks more stable in the years immediately after its founding. In contrast, without government guarantees, creditors were more likely to monitor and limit the amount of risk taking by the banks.[3] Thus, the absence of explicit deposit insurance promoted creditor discipline of the national banks and contributed to their stability. State-chartered experiments with deposit insurance in the first three decades of the twentieth century all ended badly, and the ones that imposed mandatory, long-lived deposit insurance on state-chartered banks resulted in a dramatic boom and bust in lending, which lead to widespread bank insolvency (Calomiris 1989, 1990, 1992). More recent experience has confirmed that government guarantees, through implicit guarantees of the largest banks (often referred to as "Too Big to Fail" – or TBTF) or explicit deposit insurance, if unchecked can result in increased risk taking – an effect that has been blamed as one of the primary sources of systemic risk during the recent spate of global banking and financial crises (Demirguc-Kunt and Detragiache 2002; Demirguc-Kunt, Kane, and Laeven 2008; Laeven and Valencia 2013; Afonso, Santos, and Traina 2014; Anginer, Demirguc-Kunt, and Zhu 2014; International Monetary Fund 2014).

The main systemic deficiency of the national banking era, in contrast to the U.S. system since the 1980s, was the structural flaw of unit banking. Unit banking made individual banks undiversified, inefficient, and excessively subject to liquidity risks related to the interbank network.

The fact that the banking crises of the national banking era were not very severe – despite a unit banking structure, the lack of a lender of last resort, the presence of severe seasonal loan demand shocks of a predominantly agricultural economy, and the deflationary risks of the global gold standard – suggests that there were other aspects of the national banking era that helped to stabilize banks. In our view, the combination of market discipline and the presence of a very effective regulatory and supervisory regime, especially for national banks, were key positives during that time.

---

[3] The generally small size of the banks in this period meant that the failure of any particular institution would not pose a systemic threat, and there was no expectation that the government would intervene to rescue a failing bank.

National bank regulation and supervision combined a few important prudential rules governing lending and cash holdings with an effective, credible examination, disclosure, and discipline process. Even though the various prudential rules were not always strictly enforced, supervision and regulation empowered market discipline in preventing individual bank abuses while also limiting the systemic consequences of market discipline by imposing various regulations that helped to stabilize the system. In particular, with respect to regulation, we emphasize the key roles of sensible systemic regulation of cash reserves – which differentiated across different bank locations – along with limits on the real estate lending exposure of banks. Effective and credible examination and disclosure of information about banks entailed periodic visits by examiners, the collection of information about a variety of relevant characteristics, the reporting of basic balance sheet information, and the potential disciplinary actions against banks whose practices were found wanting.

In what follows, we discuss the regulations and examination process of national banks in detail, relying on public sources, as well as on private information contained in national bank examination reports. We discuss why and how these had important consequences for individual and systemic banking system stability. Potential implications of this history of regulatory success for policy reforms are many, given how far the U.S. today is from a system based primarily on market discipline, de facto limitations on the ability of banks to become TBTF, limited real estate risk exposure, high cash requirements, and clear and credible disclosure of banks' circumstances. Potential reforms include limiting banking system exposures to real estate assets, enhancing market discipline, raising bank cash requirements, and improving the credibility and transparency of bank accounting. Indeed, efforts to include a number of these items in the modern regulatory framework have been initiated in recent years.

In the remainder of this chapter, we review the experience during the national banking era, and particularly, the main tools of successful macro-prudential regulation during that period: the bank examination and disclosure process, the regulatory limits on banks' real estate lending, and the regulation of reserve holdings. We begin with a review of the purpose and structure of national bank regulations and examinations, discuss the examination process in detail, and review evidence that examination contributed to banking stability. Finally, we return to a broader discussion of the lessons of prudential regulation during the national banking era for today.

The Process and Intent of Regulating and Examining National Banks

The reports filed by the national bank examiners are a unique and rich source of information about the condition of national banks.[4] They show that examiners were careful and insightful in their examinations of banks, and that the examination process was intended to play a crucial role in ensuring that highly relevant information about national banks was available to the public, specifically to empower market discipline by bank creditors, especially depositors and other bankers.

The deposits of national banks in pre-approved reserve agents (other banks) were verified by examiners, and the quantity of bank capital (which could be reduced by loan losses) was also verified by a diligent process through which loan losses were estimated. The law prohibited real estate lending and limited large exposures.[5] Examiners investigated these issues closely as well as tracked loans to bank insiders.

It was not uncommon for banks to have some loans that violated regulatory limits. Such violations were recorded in the examination reports in specifically designated sections. Examiners had discretion about whether these violations were significant enough to warrant disciplinary action or whether ongoing monitoring was sufficient. Such decisions involved a general assessment of the condition of the bank. Moreover, the Comptroller's office in Washington, DC, could review the reports and make its own recommendations.

In addition, the Office of the Comptroller of the Currency (OCC) published an annual volume collecting each national banks accounts, and required national banks to report their accounts publicly in a local newspaper. Furthermore, banks had to send newspaper clippings of their (roughly quarterly) published accounts to the OCC to verify compliance with that requirement.

The examiners also determined whether corporate governance and risk management standards, and overall bank operations, were structured appropriately. The OCC had enforcement tools to discipline bankers that violated those standards.

---

[4] The original bank examiners' reports, as well as various other materials related to the national banks and the examination process, for the first half-century or so of the existence of the Examining Division of the Office of the Comptroller of the Currency are available in the National Archives.

[5] Loans were limited to a proportion of paid in capital.

For all these reasons, despite the fact that examination reports them-selves were not released to the public, depositors and other creditors could infer much positive information about the accuracy of bank accounts and the propriety of a bank's practices just from the fact that a national bank – subject to this examination discipline – remained open for business.[6] The empowerment of market discipline through the creation of credible information was an intentional outcome that drove the examination process.

In the 1890 Report of the Comptroller of the Currency, the comptroller called for increasing the frequency of the published compilation of all banks' balance sheets to a semi-annual frequency (p. 57). In that discus-sion, the comptroller explains that the publication of each bank's balance sheet in the annual volumes, and the more frequent newspaper publica-tions (five times a year), had the intention of "enabl[ing] its creditors to judge, in some degree, as to the wisdom of its management and the amount and character of its assets" (p. 57). He went on to explain the rationale for increasing the frequency of the nationwide publication and pointed out that the banks themselves shared the same goal of improving creditor information so as to boost creditor confidence in properly managed banks. The specifics of his wording are quite revealing:

Once in each year these reports are printed and form a second volume accompanying the report proper of the Comptroller of the Currency. While those living in the immediate vicinity of a particular bank may, through the publication in the local newspapers, have access to the five reports made in each year, non-residents are practically excluded from this source of information and can only avail themselves of the yearly reports issued from this Bureau.

Each association has correspondents in one or more of the reserve cities, and of necessity the relation of debtor and creditor is at once established and uninter-ruptedly maintained between banks thus related. Usually the city bank is the debtor, but frequently this condition is reversed. It is therefore clear that each bank is interested in ascertaining as often as practicable the condition of its correspondents .... Twelve months seems a long time to wait, in this progressive age, for information so important. Nor is this semiannual publication desired by

---

[6] This information flow is somewhat similar to current practices. Examination reports remain confidential. While not published in newspapers, call reports are available online through the Federal Financial Institutions Examination Council (FFIEC). Reports of enforcement actions are also available on regulators' websites (and cover a considerably larger set of enforcement actions than the dramatic action of revoking a charter). Additionally, most banks now provide quarterly and annual reports to investors that provide a considerable amount of information about the health of the institutions; although these are not part of the supervisory process, institutions must provide faithful representations of their situation in these disclosures.

the national banks alone. Every person having to employ an association located elsewhere than in his immediate vicinity is interested in having this information published more frequently . . . .

The semiannual publication was asked for by the American Bankers Association, which met at Kansas City, Mo., in September, 1889, and the resolutions adopted by it were forwarded to the Secretary of the Treasury and the Comptroller of the Currency.... (Report of the Comptroller of the Currency 1890, p. 57)

According to this report, banks favored increasing the frequency of the publication of the results of their examinations because they believed that they would benefit from the improved creditor confidence that would result, especially the confidence from other banks.

In September 1908, then Comptroller Lawrence Murray wrote to the presidents of all the national banks asking each of them to complete a survey designed to elicit their views on how to improve the examination process. Here, again, the comptroller placed a great deal of confidence in the bankers' opinions because he believed that the incentives of the bankers as a group were aligned with those of the examiners and the comptroller – namely, to create timely and reliable information that would maintain market confidence in the bank.

The responses to this survey were summarized in the 1908 Report of the Comptroller. Of the 3,596 national banks that responded, 1,846 expressed the opinion that the existing system and methods were satisfactory. Of those who found the existing regime unsatisfactory and who expressed an opinion about the changes that were needed, the suggested changes reported by the comptroller (who admittedly might not be entirely disinterested) pointed to preferences for additional monitoring rather than less. The most common suggestion, by 684 banks, was that "more time should be devoted to examinations than at present," 45 recommended "more frequent examinations," 460 urged "more careful inspection of loans and discounts," 24 suggested that closer attention should be given items in transit and accounts current," 61 urged "greater attention to loans to officers, directors, and stockholders, and 184 called for "verification of individual ledger balances." Additionally, "a number" of bankers called for the OCC to play a new role to track the "character and financial standing" of large borrowers involved in the bills market. Here, the bankers seem to be calling for the OCC to create a credit registry akin to Dun & Bradstreet to track large borrowers' balance sheets to avoid the over-extension of credit by banks in particular locations that are unable to observe all of the borrowers' dealings. Consistent with many bankers' desire for examinations to become more careful and lengthy, many bankers also supported changing the compensation structure of examiners to move to a salary-based system rather than paying a fee per examination.

Despite the intention of bolstering creditor discipline, national banking era regulation also was motivated by concerns about the potential systemic consequences of widespread deposit withdrawals. The Federal Reserve Board made an internal study of the pre-Fed examination process, which was contained in an internal unpublished study by Crays (1941). This discussion shows that regulators were concerned about possibly adverse systemic consequences of market discipline, especially as it pertained to interbank deposits. Protecting the payment system, not just the solvency of individual banks, required a focus on deposit withdrawal risk. In particular, following the Panic of 1873, more attention was paid to the health of banks as "their failure meant not only a loss of wealth to individual depositors but, in the aggregate, widespread suspension of the means of payment in the hands of the public, the effects of which were felt in the commerce and trade of the country" (p. 5). Supervision during this period was intended to "preserve intact the check and deposit system" and to avoid "any suspension of the accepted means of payment" (p. 5).

Concern about systemic risks is apparent in various aspects of the regulations governing national banks. For instance, the variations in the cash reserve requirements for national banks reflected (broadly) the centrality of the banks to the financial system and were thus specifically designed to bolster systemic stability: country banks could hold the least amount of reserves in cash, reserve city banks had to hold a higher proportion in cash, and central reserve city banks in New York and Chicago had to maintain the highest proportion. It was well understood that disruptions in the provision of liquidity to other banks by the reserve center banks had systemic implications and externalities that the higher requirements were intended to address (Carlson 2015).

Another example for how systemic concerns were reflected in regulations is the prohibition on real estate lending, which reflected the view (embodied in the so-called real bills doctrine) that real estate loans were inappropriate for commercial banks. Real estate booms and busts tend to occur in waves and be associated with the business cycle, and the underlying assets are very hard to liquidate in response to depositor withdrawals during recessions.[7]

---

[7] Concerns about the dangers of lending to speculators in real estate have been discussed by banking commentators at least as far back as Tucker (1839), and this idea would have been

The Content of Examination Reports: Analysis of a Sample of National Banks

The examiner reports contain a significant amount of qualitative and quantitative information not available elsewhere, which indicates a level of detail and care that is impressive. Examiners probed deeply the corporate governance process, asset composition, and liabilities structure of national banks, and looked at the loan book very carefully, with a particular focus on large loans, loans to insiders, and loans related to real estate, which were analyzed in detail. (Although banks could not originate mortgages, they were able to take real estate as collateral subsequently to secure previously existing loans; it was these activities that were monitored. We discuss this later in the chapter.) The reports were standardized, which ensured that all topics considered to be important by OCC headquarters were covered. The level of detail provided in the reports makes possible a rich understanding of the condition of the banking system at this time, and provides a wealth of information about the process of banking supervision.

Our analysis of the examiner reports focuses on a sample of 206 banks located in thirty-seven cities during the early 1890s. We chose to focus on this particular time period because of the interesting events in the banking system that were occurring, and also because the examination reports became more detailed around this time. The sample is not random or representative of all national banks in the United States.[8] It consists of all the national banks in thirty-seven significant cities located in the middle, south, and west of the country, including many so-called reserve cities, as defined under the laws governing national banks. For the sake of comparability, we exclude the very largest cities in these regions (Chicago, St. Louis, and San Francisco) because of the special attributes of banks in those cities (their large size, importance, and nodal status in the interbank deposit market), and the large number of banks located in each (the coding of each observation in our sample requires significant effort, and we sought to include a complete list of national banks in each subject city). The banks in our sample tend to be involved in interbank markets and payment

---

familiar to regulators in the national banking era. A number of modern authors have pointed to property prices as an indicator of building financial imbalances that could potentially result in a crisis (Borio 2012; Drehman, Borio, and Tsatsaronis 2012; Jorda, Schularick, and Taylor 2015).

[8] It is worth noting, however, that the New York banks described in Bodenhorn and White (2014) appear fairly similar to those we examine, which suggests that they were reasonably representative.

systems at the regional level. Thus the banks in the sample are all in roughly the same peer group; they are of roughly the same size and most seem to be engaged in the interbank market as both holders of deposits of smaller banks and providers of deposits to banks in the central reserve cities. Our sample affords a detailed study of the mid-tier of the national banks operating during the early 1890s.

The thirty-seven cities we cover in our sample are located in twenty-one states. The cities are often large cities, although we also include a few cities of more modest size. A list of the cities we use and their population from the 1890 census is shown in Table 8.1. The largest city is Cincinnati, OH, which is also one of the most eastern cities; the smallest city is Albuquerque, NM.

We divide the territory of our coverage into four regions: the Ohio River Valley/South (consisting of OH, IN, KY, TN, LA, and AL), the Plains (consisting of IA, MN, MO, NE, and ND), the Mountains/Southwest (consisting of CO, MT, NM, TX, UT, and WY), and the Pacific (consisting of CA, OR, and WA).[9] We investigate how banking practices and behaviors differed across these regions.

Our sample of 206 banks consists of all the national banks in each of our thirty-seven cities that existed in late 1892 and that had an examination report filed prior to May 1, 1893 (which we take as the start of the Panic of 1893).[10] The distribution of these banks across cities is also shown in Table 8.1. Cincinnati has the most banks at thirteen, followed by Denver and Kansas City, MO, at eleven. The largest bank in the sample is also located in Cincinnati, although St. Paul, MN, has the largest average size of banks. The smallest bank is located in Rochester, MN.

To establish our snapshot of the banking industry, we look at the banking examination report most closely preceding May 1, 1893. Typically these examinations were conducted in late 1892 or early 1893. We also determined when the prior exam took place. We look at this pre-panic period for two reasons. First, in 1891, the comptroller expanded the report from three pages to seven pages, so looking at the examination reports during this period provides considerably more information than was

---

[9] We looked at whether our southern cities differed from cities in the Ohio River Valley, and found they looked fairly similar. This finding may reflect the fact that New Orleans, which had a long history as a banking center, represents a sizable part of the sample.

[10] In particular, we select banks that filed a call report in September 1892; while we do not use the call report much here, we do so extensively in related work. We exclude one bank from Kansas City, which was chartered in mid-1892, has an exam report in September and early November, and liquidates in mid-November. Given the short life span of the bank, it has an unusual balance sheet and exam profile.

Table 8.1 *Cities and Banks Used in the Sample*

State	City	Population 1890	Number of Banks	Avg. Assets	Min. Assets	Max. Assets
Alabama	Birmingham	26,178	4	962	342	1,617
	Mobile	31,076	2	968	369	1,568
California	Los Angeles	50,395	4	1,320	578	2,264
	San Diego	16,307	2	964	786	1,143
Colorado	Denver	106,713	11	2,768	993	5,695
	Pueblo	24,558	6	1,016	229	3,055
Indiana	Indianapolis	105,436	5	2,513	1,840	4,076
Iowa	Des Moines	50,093	4	1,145	906	1,282
	Dubuque	30,311	3	1,138	407	1,558
Kentucky	Lexington	35,698	7	681	295	1,353
	Louisville	161,129	10	1,824	1,018	3,726
Louisiana	New Orleans	242,039	10	2,719	962	5,976
Minnesota	Minneapolis	164,738	7	2,725	510	6,100
	Rochester	5,321	3	415	164	651
	St. Paul	133,156	5	4,581	1,516	6,768
	Stillwater	11,260	2	1,285	1,195	1,376
Missouri	Kansas City	132,710	10	3,072	401	7,734
	St. Joseph	52,324	4	2,242	1,880	2,438
Montana	Helena	13,834	6	1,845	327	4,388
Nebraska	Lincoln	55,164	5	1,050	516	2,525
	Omaha	140,452	9	2,633	646	6,669
New Mexico	Albuquerque	3,785	2	878	536	1,220
North Dakota	Fargo	5,664	4	673	389	1,257
Ohio	Cincinnati	290,908	13	4,060	1,312	8,308
Oregon	Portland	46,385	8	1,424	355	4,558
Tennessee	Knoxville	22,535	6	735	244	1,377
	Memphis	64,495	4	1,515	1,246	1,727
	Nashville	76,168	4	2,765	2,366	3,247
Texas	Dallas	38,067	9	987	288	2,001
	El Paso	15,678	3	554	451	625
	San Antonio	37,673	5	744	232	1,781
Utah	Salt Lake City	44,843	6	1,134	551	2,293
Washington	Spokane	19,922	7	677	423	1,019
	Tacoma	36,006	8	775	269	1,329
Wisconsin	Milwaukee	204,408	3	3,510	2,596	4,716
	Racine	21,014	3	1,102	756	1,468
Wyoming	Cheyenne	11,690	2	849	720	978
All			**206**	**1,862**	**164**	**8,308**

Note: Assets here are based on 1892 Call Report to avoid seasonality concerns; data are thousands of $. Population data for El Paso is for the county as the city population is not available for 1890.

available prior to 1891 (although in both periods, supplemental pages were sometimes included if the examiner felt a particular need to comment at length about some aspect of the bank). Second, we would like to gain a better understanding of banking practices in normal times to provide a benchmark for understanding how the banking system might be affected during the panics.

Examinations typically took about two days, but they could take a bit longer for banks farther west, larger banks, or banks in reserve cities. Banks were typically examined every nine or ten months. Whether all the banks in the town were examined at about the same time depended on the number of banks. In towns with fewer banks, they were all examined in short order. If there were many banks, the examiners would look at several of them, leave for a month or so, and then return to examine the rest. This approach likely reflected a balancing of the benefits of surprise examination and the desire to economize on time and transportation costs.

The material in the examination report covered both the operations of the bank and its balance sheet. It provides information on the ownership, the corporate governance practices, and the management of the bank. Many, but not all, banks were owned substantially by insiders, with the largest shareholder often being the bank president, although sometimes a board member who was not part of the management team was the largest shareholder.

Corporate boards of directors employed several means of regulating and monitoring the behavior of officers, including instituting an independent discount committee to examine loans, appointing more independent directors to the board, or requiring various bank officers to post surety bonds. Such practices tended to be more prevalent in the more eastern and southern locations within our sample. These findings suggest an evolution in the purpose and obligations of the boards of directors of banks relative to their purpose in the antebellum period in the east (Lamoreaux 1994; Hilt 2008; Bodenhorn 2013). As we will discuss in more detail, we find that the use of formal governance substitutes for close bank ownership; in banks where the top three officers (president, vice president, and cashier) own large shares of the bank's stock, there is less of a tendency to employ formal corporate governance practices (see also Calomiris and Carlson 2016a).

There is considerable detail about the loan book in the examiner reports. Most loans were made "on time" rather than "on demand" and, while generally not secured by collateral (owing to the prohibition on real estate lending), loans often had a second signatory to ensure payment of the loan. We find that some banks, particularly those farther west, had a considerable portion of their loans in real estate mortgages despite the strict legal prohibition on national banks' originating *any* such loans. Such prohibitions appear to have been evaded by incorporating real estate as secondary collateral after the origination of the loan. On average, real estate loans constituted 3.6 percent of all loans, but the median percentile was much lower (1.1 percent), and the 75th percentile was only 1.2 percent; clearly only a small proportion of national banks made a significant proportion of their loans in real estate (the maximum exposure was 11.2 percent). Examiners monitored loans related to real estate especially closely, tracking their total amount and commenting on their performance.

The information about liabilities includes the amounts of each type of liability as well as information about the rates of interest paid. Consistent with other studies of regional differences in interest rates (Davis 1965; Sylla 1969; Smiley 1975; James 1976), rates paid on time deposits for the banks in our sample tended to be higher farther west. We also learn from the examiner reports about the use of collateralized certificates of deposit as a form of interbank borrowing. This form of borrowing, which examiners viewed as similar to bills payable or rediscounts, has not been noted much previously. We observe that the use of all types of interbank borrowing tended to increase in October and diminish in February, a phenomenon that represents another facet of the seasonality in interest rates and flows of money to and from New York City during this period that has been noted by others (Kemmerer 1911; James 1978; Miron 1986).

The examination reports also provide information about the quality of managers, about dividend payments and about examiners' opinions regarding likely losses on different assets. Banks generally paid dividends twice a year. Banks farther west were somewhat more likely to have not paid dividends recently – either because they were new or because they had higher expected losses – but those banks tended to pay higher dividends per share when dividends were paid. Expected losses primarily reflected probable loan losses rather than write-downs of any other type of asset. Additionally, some banks listed as assets a large amount of furnishings, and the examiners noted when such extravagance was likely to make a material contribution to total loss. As Calomiris and Carlson (2016a) note, this tended to occur in situations where both the stock ownership of the bank was diffuse and there was a relative absence of formal corporate governance discipline.

We organize our detailed discussion of the examination report by following the structure of the reports themselves. The next section provides information about the nature of the examinations, such as their length of time and the frequency with which they were conducted. In the following sections we describe examination report information relating to ownership and corporate governance and provide information about balance sheets. The examination reports also contained a recapitulation section, which is described next.

Timing and Frequency of the Examiner Reports

All of our sample cities contain at least two national banks, and some cities have as many as thirteen. In cities with a relatively small number of national banks, the examiner would typically examine all the banks in one visit. In towns with a larger number of national banks, the examiner would often look at some banks, leave for a time, then return to review the rest during a second visit. For example, in Omaha, four banks were examined in November of 1892 and the remaining five banks were examined in March of 1893. Typically when the examinations for national banks in a particular location were separated, the break would last about a month, but gaps of three or more months were not uncommon. Although the timing of returns to a city probably were not quite "random" dates for starting the exam, the breaks between the examinations of different subsets of banks within a city likely alleviated some of the window dressing in anticipation of an exam (whereby banks would alter their financial condition once the examiner first appeared in town).

The typical examination in our sample lasted one or two days (with two days being slightly more common than one day – see Table 8.2). Having the exam take more than four days was uncommon and occurred for less than 10 percent of the sample.[11] Larger banks tended to have longer exams; the typical exam length was roughly one day longer for banks with assets at or above the median of the sample than for banks with assets less than the median in the sample.

In the early 1890s, the comptroller's office switched from requiring annual to requiring bi-annual examinations.[12] For our sample, the preceding examination had, on average, occurred about ten months earlier.

---

[11] In at least one of these cases, the examiner reported being called away in the middle of the exam to assist with matters at another institution. While some examiners appeared to work on weekends, others did not, which might have contributed to lengthening the observed duration of their exams.

[12] See Robertson (1968) for a discussion of the history of the national banking system and the role of the bank examination process in that context. White (1983) discusses the regulatory environment for both national and state-chartered banks and in particular describes how regulations for state banks varied from state to state.

Table 8.2 *Regional Variation in Examinations*

		Exam Length (Days)		Time Since Prior Exam (Days)		
	Banks	Mean	Median	Bottom Quartile	Median	Top Quartile
Overall	206	2.9	2	207	287	373
By size						
Larger banks	103	3.3	3	202	270	371
Smaller banks	103	2.6	2	208	314	376
By reserve city status						
Country bank	130	2.8	2	212	319	380
Reserve city bank	76	3.0	3	198	245	314
By region						
Ohio River Valley/South (OH, IA, KY, TN, LA, AL)	71	2.1	2	209	264	303
Plains (IA, MN, MO, NE, ND)	56	2.8	2	184	314	373
Mountain/Southwest (CO, MT, NM, TX, UT, WY)	50	3.8	4	197	316	382
Pacific (CA,OR, WA)	29	3.6	3	328	382	409

However, it was not uncommon for the previous exam to have occurred a little more than one year earlier (the upper quartile for the number of days between exams is 373 days). The frequency of examinations appears to have varied regionally. For banks along the Pacific coast, the median time between exams was just over one year, whereas for banks in the Ohio River Valley/South, the median time between exams was just under nine months.

The examination reports used here include the work of twenty different examiners. Examiners could cover a wide area; for instance, we observe one examiner covering Alabama, Louisiana, and parts of Tennessee.

Ownership Structure, Management, and Corporate Governance

One page of the examination report was devoted to the governance and management of the bank. Examiners were asked to list each member of the board of directors, the number of shares of stock in the bank each director held, their city of residence, the amounts they owed to the bank (or the debts of others that they had endorsed), and the other occupation they might have. The examiner was then asked to comment on the oversight exercised by the board: the frequency with which they met, the operations of the independent committees to monitor the bank, and whether the board had been elected in a proper fashion. Examiners were also asked to provide information on the officers of the bank: the president, vice president, cashier (in today's parlance, the chief operating officer of the bank), assistant cashier, teller, and bookkeeper. The information here included their indebtedness, salaries, surety bonds, if any, as well as general comments on their quality including "whether the officers are capable, prudent, and of good reputation or not, and whether in your opinion, their management is efficient and successful, or otherwise."

Ownership Structure

We classify shareholders into three groups. Our first group consists of management of the bank, particularly the president, vice president(s), and cashier. The second group of shareholders consists of independent directors, defined as members of the board of directors that were not officers of the bank. (The president of the bank was always on the board, and it was not uncommon for at least one other officer to be as well.) The third group consists of the other outside shareholders – non-officers and non-board members.

The distribution of ownership ranged considerably. As shown in Figure 8.2, in some banks, the majority of shares were owned by the management while at other banks managers owned almost no bank shares. In our sample of banks, the median ownership share by management was 17 percent, but exceeded 37 percent for one-fourth of the banks in the sample.[13] Management ownership tended to be somewhat higher in the Mountain/Southwest and Pacific parts of the country. Ownership by outside directors tended to be a bit more modest with the median proportion being 12 percent. Outsiders held the remainder. The single largest observed shareholder tended to be the president, which was the case at 60 percent of the banks. However, at about 30 percent of the banks, an outside director was the largest observed shareholder, and at about 10 percent of banks, the cashier was the largest shareholder.

---

[13] Thus is appears that, in general, ownership was less concentrated than it had been for banks operating in New York early in the nineteenth century as reported by Hilt (2008).

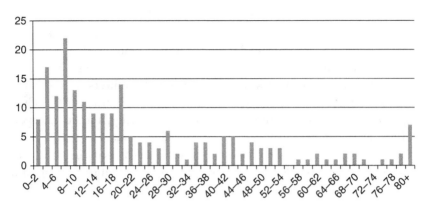

Figure 8.2.A Distribution of ownership by management.

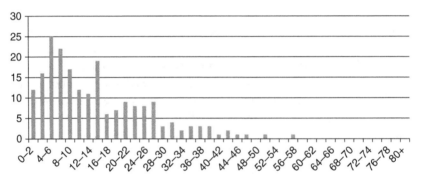

Figure 8.2.B Distribution of ownership by independent directors.

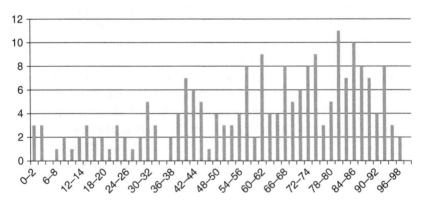

Figure 8.2.C Distribution of ownership by outsiders.

The Board of Directors

Boards of directors clearly were regarded as important in exercising oversight of the bank. The number of directors varied greatly. In our sample, banks had an average of nine directors, although some institutions had as many as twenty-three or as few as four (Table 8.3).[14] Boards tended to be bigger at larger banks and at banks located more to the east.

The majority of the board usually consisted of independent directors (although every bank was required to have at least one independent director). The average portion of the board that consisted of independent directors was a bit more than two-thirds. Independent directors, in theory, acted as the voices of outside shareholders and served on the board to protect the interests of outside stockholders.[15] Independent directors also traditionally helped attract business to the bank and could provide independent analysis of the creditworthiness of potential borrowers.[16] The occupations of the independent directors in our sample are consistent with these responsibilities.

The most common occupation for the independent directors, as indicated in Table 8.4, was that of "capitalist." Presumably such individuals, especially if they were shareholders themselves, would, at least in part, be willing and able to promote actions that would enhance the value of bank shares. Independent directors, of course, such as managers, could face conflicts of interest. In particular, they might themselves be bank borrowers and thus could conceivably collude with management to receive favorable terms on loans at the expense of shareholders. Indeed, as we will discuss, we find that when boards are dominated by outside directors, outside directors receive more loans from the bank.

Merchants, particularly wholesale merchants, were also a very common occupational category of members on bank boards. Such individuals were also potential customers of the bank and would likely have been particularly aware of shifting business conditions. Thus, they could have fulfilled

---

[14] The average number is quite similar, although the standard deviation considerably larger, to that found by Bodenhorn (2013) for the number of directors on bank boards in mid-nineteenth-century Massachusetts.

[15] In his handbook providing suggestions to national bank shareholders, Coffin (1891) argues that the directors of the national bank are intended to be the representatives of the shareholders and that shareholders ought to elect individuals whose "integrity, ability and judgment" will best represent their interests.

[16] For instance, the examiner reported that for one bank, "The directors have been selected from the heavy business men of the place, partly for the prestige their names give the bank and partly to obtain their patronage." From the examination report of the Helena National Bank dated January 4, 1893.

Table 8.3 *Governance Indicators, Averages*

	Board Size	Indep. Directors as a Share of Board	Share of Loans to Indep. Directors	Share of Banks w/ Active Discount Committee	Salary of President	Share of Banks w/Cashier Bonded
Overall	9.1	69.5	5.4	59.7	$4,400	57
By size						
Larger banks	10.4	73.1	4.5	65.4	$5,900	56
Smaller banks	7.9	65.7	6.3	53.9	$2,500	59
By reserve city status						
Country bank	8.9	67.3	6.0	49.6	$3,300	52
Reserve city bank	9.6	73.2	4.6	78.9	$6,100	67
By region						
Ohio River Valley/South (OH, IA, KY, TN, LA, AL)	9.6	74.8	5.4	84.5	$4,800	70
Plains (IA, MN, MO, NE, ND)	10.0	70.3	4.6	62.5	$4,600	71
Mountain/Southwest (CO, MT, NM, TX, UT, WY)	8.6	65.0	6.5	30.0	$4,200	34
Pacific (CA, OR, WA)	7.2	62.6	5.0	44.8	$3,200	38

Note: Shares are in percent

Table 8.4 *Occupations of Independent Shareholders*

	Share of Total (#)
Capitalist	22.8
Merchant (wholesale)*	13.2
Merchant*	8.4
Lawyer	7.1
Mining or commodities	4.0
Banker (at other bank)	3.7
Real estate	3.5
Manufacturer	3.1
Other finance	2.1
Railroad	1.5
Farmer or rancher	1.3
Other	29.3

* These should be thought of as lower bounds on the share of individuals engaged in these professions. Many individuals are listed according to the particular product they sold.

the goals of attracting business and of advising management about business conditions and the relative merits of different credits.

Lawyers and attorneys were somewhat common as board members, constituting about 7 percent of independent directors. There were some recognizable regional patterns to the occupation of board members, with lumbermen being more common in Minnesota and distillers were listed only in and around Kentucky. One bank in Los Angeles listed both the governor of the state and a minister among the members of its board. A few notable individuals appear on the boards occasionally; for instance, Messrs. Proctor and Gamble, president and vice president of a corporation of the same name, appear on the board of the Citizens National Bank of Cincinnati, OH.[17]

By chance, we observe a handful of instances where officers/directors appear at multiple banks. For instance, the president of the Manufacturer's National Bank in Racine, WI, is also president of the First National Bank in Fargo, ND. The president of the First National Bank of Albuquerque, NM, is also president of the First National Bank of El Paso, TX. In these cases, it is

[17] Another notable name, Henry Weinhard, brewer, appears on the board of the Commercial National Bank of Portland, OR. No doubt Mr. Weinhard was an expert on the importance of liquid assets.

Table 8.5 *Independent Director Control and Borrowing, Shares in Percent*

	Share of Loans That Were Made to Independent Directors at Banks with Below Average (Median) Control by Independent Directors	Share of Loans That Were Made to Independent Directors at Banks with Above Average (Median) Control by Independent Directors
Control measured by size of bank board of directors	4.5	7.7
Control measured by proportion of board consisting of independent directors	4.4	6.6
Control measure by stock ownership of independent directors	5.2	5.7

the cashier who runs the second bank with the president stopping by only a few times a year. We also observe that the president of the Lumberman's National Bank of Stillwater, MN, also sits on the board of the Second National Bank of St. Paul, MN. The examiner's report for Rochester National indicates that the largest stockholder is the estate of the former president (deceased) who apparently owned a few other banks as well.

Frequently at least some directors borrowed from the bank. On average, about 5 percent of the loans of the bank were to members of the board, although this share reached as high as 27 percent. On average, banks with a higher than median number of directors, a larger than median proportion of independent directors, or a larger than median ownership share by independent directors tended also to show a higher proportion of loans to independent directors (Table 8.5). There was little regional variation in such lending.[18] The principle systematic source of variation in loans to directors reflected differences in corporate governance practices. When banks employed formal corporate governance more – more frequent board

---

[18] Insider lending has received considerable attention in studies of early banking in the United States. For instance, Lamoreaux (1994) argues that antebellum banks in New England were in large part loan clubs where a considerable portion of the banks' lending was to the members of the board of directors. Lamoreaux argues that such lending declined as a share of lending over the nineteenth century and finds that by the 1890s only about 9 percent of loans were to members of the board, a number similar to what we find here (especially if we include the bank officers that also served on the board).

Table 8.6 *Board of Directors Meeting Frequency*

	Share of Sample (%)
Weekly	14
Twice monthly	10
Monthly	35
Quarterly	14
Semi-annual	8
Regular	4
Irregular	8
Other	7

meetings, more independent directors, and the creation of a formal loan review committee in which an independent director participated – directors tended to have a larger share of the total amount of total insider lending; when such practices were absent, directors had a smaller share and managers had a larger share. In other words, control rights tended to be accompanied by a greater proportion of insider loans (Calomiris and Carlson 2016a).

Most commonly, board meetings were held monthly, but weekly or quarterly meetings were not unusual (Table 8.6). At a considerable number of banks, the meeting frequency was reported as "irregular," much to the disapproval of the examiner. Frequent meetings were more common in the Ohio River Valley/South region where nearly one-third of the banks had weekly board meetings. Meetings were less frequent farther west, with quarterly meetings being the second most common frequency in the Plains and Mountain/Southwest regions. While nearly half of the banks in the Pacific had monthly meetings, the second most common frequency was "irregular" at 17 percent.

Independent discount committees that reviewed the new loans being extended were an important part of corporate governance. Such committees were present at about 60 percent of the banks. At the remaining institutions, the examiner indicated that the discount committees were inactive and that management was left to the officers. There is clear regional variation in the use of such committees. An overwhelming majority of banks in the Ohio River Valley/South had them, but only a minority of the banks in the Mountain/Southwest did. Reserve city banks were also more likely than other banks to have independent committees.

Examiners were also asked to make notes about the annual meetings. In nearly all cases, annual meetings and the election of directors was described as regular. The number of shares being represented, either in person or by proxy, was listed.

Management

The three primary officers were the president, vice president(s), and cashier. There were a number of instances in which there were multiple assistant cashiers, tellers, and bookkeepers, especially in the larger banks; in small banks some of these latter positions were vacant.

The examination reports provide useful information on compensation. Presidents had the highest average salaries at \$4,416. The average salaries for the cashiers at \$3,416 slightly exceeded those of the vice presidents at \$3,113. Salaries of the presidents, vice presidents, and cashiers topped out at \$50,000, \$9,000, and \$20,000, respectively. On occasion it was noted that one or more of the top three officers did not received any fixed salary. Not surprisingly, salaries were much higher at larger banks, at reserve city banks, and in more eastern parts of the country.

Requiring officers to post surety bonds was a fairly common practice. These bonds could be seized by the bank shareholders (or bank receiver) in the event that the officer posting the bond committed some offence, such as fraud or absconding with funds. Bonds could be personal (backed by assets held in escrow) or provided through a surety company.[19] Given that the cashiers were typically responsible for overseeing the books, and given that they therefore enjoyed ample opportunity to commit fraud or hide funds, it is not surprising that the cashiers were the class of officers that posted bonds most frequently (60 percent). The presidents and vice presidents posted bonds somewhat less frequently (35 percent and 15 percent of the time, respectively).[20] The bonds were typically about five to ten times the salary of the individual in question. In addition to checking whether the bonds were posted, the examiners also verified that the bonds were being held by someone other than the individual posting the bond.

Mirroring the phrasing of the question on the examination form that the examiners were asked to address, officers were typically described as "capable, prudent, and of good reputation." It seems that so long as the

---

[19] For more information about surety bonds, especially those provided by surety companies, see Lunt (1922).

[20] It was uncommon for the president or vice president to be bonded if the cashier was not, but it did happen in a few instances.

bank was profitable, the management was described as efficient and successful. In only 13 percent of cases did the examiners indicate concerns about the officers. When concerns arose, examiners would point to inexperience, excessive salaries, having outside interests that took too much of their attention, or a lack of prudent management. (Frequently there were other problems at these banks as well, with troubled loans and expected losses on assets tending to be higher on average.) In one case the examiner flagged the personal reputation of the management in matters other than banking, stating that "officers appear capable and rather prudent. President and cashier have the reputation of being fond of 'women and wine.' Other officers of good reputation."[21]

The Balance Sheet

Here we review the information contained in the bank balance sheet that was included in the examination reports.

Loans

Loans accounted for about 60 percent of assets, on average. Commensurately, a considerable portion of the examination report was devoted to discussing the loan book. Examiners were first asked to provide a numerical overview of the loan book and then to provide more descriptive information.

The numerical information took the form of a table that reported the dollar volumes of loans by type and then by quality. Loan type was based on whether the loans were "on demand" and could be called at any time by the bank, "on time" with a fixed maturity date, and whether the loans were secured, either by collateral or by other individuals who might act as guarantors. These exclusive categories were (with each average share in brackets):

A: on demand, paper with one or more individual or firm names [7.2%]
B: on demand, secured by stocks, bonds, and other personal securities [5.3%]
C: on time, paper with two or more individual or firm names [38.5%]
D: on time, single-name paper (one person or firm) without other security [22.8%]

---

[21] Examiner report of the City National Bank of Dallas, TX, dated February 23, 1893.

E: on time, secured by stocks bonds and other personal securities [21.1%]

F: on time, on mortgages or other real estate security [3.6%]

For the quality assessments, examiners were asked to determine whether the loans were past due according to statutory criteria and whether loans were overdue for other reasons. These two categories appeared on the table as items:

G: bad debts, as defined in section 5204, Revised Statutes [1.9%]

H: other suspended or overdue paper [7.1%]

Examiners were also asked to note loans to directors. The numbers here should (and did) match those reported in the discussion of the management and were reported as item:

I: Liabilities of directors (individual and firm) as payers [8.3%]

Items G, H, and I were subsets of items A–F.

As is clear from the preceding numbers, most of the loans made during this period were time loans that were not formally secured by collateral. However, these loans often had a second signatory to whom the bank could turn in case the primary borrower was unable to pay. Demand loans, where the bank could demand repayment at any time, were generally not a large part of the loan portfolio but were somewhat more common in the Ohio River Valley/South and the Pacific parts of the country (Table 8.7).[22] Some contemporaries indicated that these loans may have served as a secondary liquidity reserve because banks could call these loans in as needed (Moulton 1918). However, at some banks, demand loans might be less liquid because they consisted partly of loans that had previously matured but whose borrowers were having difficulty repaying; restructuring the loans into demand loans was a way of allowing the loan to stay current while still allowing the bank to exert discipline on the borrower. Although National Banks were prohibited from originating mortgage loans, mortgages and real estate loans appear to have been a non-negligible part of the banks' loan portfolios; we discuss these further.[23]

---

[22] See also James (1978, especially pp. 54–71) for a discussion of different types of loans.

[23] While examiners regularly reported the interest rates paid on several types of liabilities, they only infrequently provided details on the interest rates charged on loans. The few reported rates for time loans were around 10 percent. Interest rates on overdrafts were apparently quite a bit higher with rate of 12 or 24 percent reported. The rates we find on loans are generally consistent with other reports for the time such as James (1978) and White (2001).

Table 8.7 *Loan Book Shares in Percent*

	Demand Loans as Share of Total Loans	Share of Banks with Excessive Loans	Troubled Loans as Share of Total Loans	Share of Banks Habitually Allowing Overdrafts	Share of Banks with Mortgage Loans	Real Estate Loans as Share of Total Loans
Overall	12.7	55	9.1	47	70	3.6
By size						
Larger banks	14.5	55	6.5	45	46	2.3
Smaller banks	10.5	56	11.8	47	46	4.9
By reserve city status						
Country bank	11.6	64	11.5	54	70	4.6
Reserve city bank	14.6	41	5.1	29	70	1.9
By region						
Ohio River Valley/South (OH, IA, KY, TN, LA, AL)	15.0	37	5.4	39	62	1.9
Plains (IA, MN, MO, NE, ND)	9.2	50	6.7	24	70	2.2
Mountain/Southwest (CO, MT, NM, TX, UT, WY)	8.2	78	14.1	84	80	5.4
Pacific (CA, OR, WA)	21.6	72	14.7	43	72	7.3

During the national banking era, banks were not supposed to make loans to any single counterparty for more than 10 percent of the banks' paid-in capital. This rule apparently was not strictly enforced: a bit more than half of the banks in our sample had at least one "excessive" loan. Examiners for the most part chided the banks for having such loans, but unless such loans were substantial in number, the examiners did not often demand that these "excessive" loan amounts be reduced. One reason the examiners were lenient was an unlevel playing field; examiners sometimes noted that the state-chartered banks with whom the national banks were competing did not face such loan limits so that the national banks needed to be able to extend such loans in order to remain competitive. Evidence of some discretionary forbearance in enforcing some rules raises the question of whether regulation and supervision were actually effective. We consider this question in detail later in the chapter, where we argue that supervision was somewhat flexible but did not tolerate repeated or egregious violations.

As part of the more descriptive information included in the report, examiners were asked to comment on the overall quality of the loan portfolio as well as whether it was "well distributed." (The precise meaning of "well distributed" is not clear, but it typically appears to be interpreted by the examiners as asking whether the loans were distributed across a larger number of smaller borrowers.) Examiners were generally favorably impressed with loan quality. They characterized the quality of loans as something other than good – such as poor or fair – for just twenty-eight banks (although for fourteen banks an overall characterization could not be determined from the examiner's comments). So long as the bank did not have too many excessive loans, its loans were described as well distributed.

Troubled loans typically constituted about 10 percent of loans. The loan portfolios of banks in the Mountain/Southwest and Pacific regions tended to have a greater proportion of troubled loans than banks in other regions. Examiners also were asked to provide descriptive comments on suspended or overdue paper; the comments that were provided varied substantially across examiners, and we found it difficult to devise a way to usefully capture the information that was provided.[24]

---

[24] Though sometimes these notes produced some colorful comments such as from the examiner report of the First National Bank El Paso, TX, dated June 20, 1892, that "suspended debts $1500 due since May 1891, maker in jail for murder forcing collection from surety."

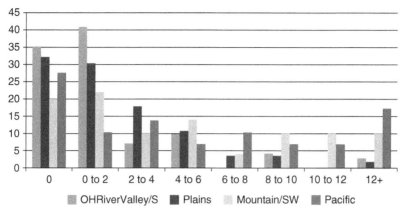

Figure 8.3 Distribution of real estate loans as a share of all loans.

Nearly 70 percent of the banks in the sample had at least some loans secured by mortgages or real estate. As noted before, although banks were prohibited from originating such loans, banks were allowed to take real estate as (additional) collateral for loans already extended (Coffin 1896, Paine 1914). Of banks that held mortgages, the average number was five such loans, although one bank held forty-seven. The average share of loans that consisted of real estate loans was 3.6 percent, but the proportion reached as high as 50 percent. The proportion of the loan portfolio that consisted of mortgages was lowest in the Ohio River Valley/South (at about 2 percent of loans) and highest in the Pacific (at 7 percent). The distributions of real estate loans by region are shown in Figure 8.3.

The final part of the loan book that was discussed was the use of over-drafts. Most examiners commented on whether the overdrafts were granted "habitually" to the bank's customers (a practice that was frowned upon) and whether the overdrafts were secured. The practice of allowing habitual overdrafts was much more common in the Mountain/Southwest region than in other parts of the country. As with "excessive" loans, examiner commentary suggests that national banks adopted overdraft lending in large part because of unlevel playing field concerns; one examiner reported that the overdrafts were "[h]abitually granted according to Western custom and in competition with state banks."[25] Bank officials sometimes worried that they would lose customers if they did not grant overdrafts:

---

[25] From the examiner report of the Commercial National Bank of Salt Lake City, UT, dated August 3, 1892.

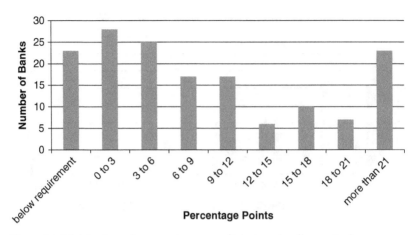

Figure 8.4 Distribution of reserves in excess of what was legally required.

[Overdrafts] Not secured, habitually granted, all temporary but allowed by the president [out of] fear of losing a customer. Some of the parties are chronic in overdrawing and always in red, that being their favorite color. The only recompense the officers have is to collect from the 24% interest while balance is running. Book keeper said not a bad account among them.[26]

Overdrafts were generally reported to be unsecured.

Reserves

Examiners were asked to provide information on bank's reserves and how recent levels – both its current level and average over the past thirty days – compared with the required reserve holdings. (The reserve ratio was defined as cash and balances at reserve banks relative to individual deposits plus net interbank deposits, with some adjustments allowed for national bank notes and items due from clearinghouses. For banks located in reserve cities, the reserve requirement was 25 percent, and for other banks the reserve requirement was 15 percent.) The reserve ratio exceeded the legal requirement most of the time, but was deficient at the time of the exam for about 18 percent of the banks in our sample. Figure 8.4 shows a histogram of the amount by which the average thirty-day reserve ratio reported by the examiners exceeded the legal requirement (the thirty-day average ratio was provided for 156 of our 207 banks); we focus on the

[26] From the examiner report of the Albuquerque National Bank of Albuquerque, NM, dated July 4, 1892.

excess reserve as banks in different cities were subject to different requirements.[27] For the median bank in our sample where the reserve ratio was reported, the reserve held by the bank exceeded the legal requirement by 6.25 percentage points. For about 10 percent of banks the reserve ratio exceeded the required ratio by at least 25 percentage points. Clearly, for many banks, their holdings of reserves were dictated by business considerations (e.g., for controlling risk or signaling the quality of their risk management to their depositors) rather than by regulatory requirements. In general, banks in reserve cities tended to hold smaller buffers than banks in country towns.

The thirty-seven cities in our sample include many of the larger ones in the western and southern parts of the United States.[28] A number of them were designated as "reserve cities" for purposes of regulatory cash reserve requirements. Deposits held at banks in reserve cities could count as part of a "country" bank's legal reserve, and these deposits often served as part of the regional payment system (see James 1978 for further detail). Some of the other cities, even though they were not technically reserve cities, were important enough regionally that other banks held deposits there. Thus, many of the banks in our sample played important roles as intermediaries in interbank markets. Nevertheless, our sample includes a number of banks from smaller cities as well.

Cash reserve requirements specified a certain level of cash and deposits in reserve city banks relative to deposits and net due to banks. The macro-prudential purpose of these reserve requirements is clear from their regional structure: all banks had to maintain reserves above 25 percent of deposits, but the required composition of reserves depended on the location of the national bank. Banks outside major cities need to hold a 15 percent reserve, three-fifths of which could be held as deposits at banks in larger "reserve" cities or, "central reserve" cities – New York, Chicago, or St. Louis. Banks in reserve cities needed to hold a 25 percent

---

[27] Actually, the thirty-day ratio is not reported for that many banks. In a few cases, the examiner reported instead the ratio for that day and stated it was pretty close to the average. When the thirty-day average is missing but an examination day number is reported, we use the one day number.

[28] The cities again are Birmingham, AL; Mobile, AL; San Diego, CA; Los Angeles, CA; Denver, CO; Pueblo, CO; Indianapolis, IN; Des Moines, IA; Dubuque, IA; Lexington, KY; Louisville, KY; New Orleans, LA; Minneapolis, MN; Rochester, MN; St. Paul, MN; Stillwater; MN; Kansas City, MO; St. Joseph, MO; Helena, MT; Lincoln, NE; Omaha, NE; Albuquerque, NM; Fargo, ND; Cincinnati, OH; Portland, OR; Knoxville, TN; Memphis, TN; Nashville, TN; Dallas, TX; El Paso, TX; San Antonio, TX; Salt Lake City, UT; Spokane, WA; Tacoma, WA; Milwaukee; WI; Racine, WI; and Cheyenne, WY.

reserve, half of which could consist of deposits in a central reserve city. Deposits in New York, and to a lesser extent in other central reserve cities, played a key role in the settling of interregional payments. Given their position at the top of the interbank pyramid of deposits, banks in central reserve cities had to maintain their reserves in cash. This system of requirements ensured that the central nodes of liquidity in the system were relatively insulated from potential disruptions in the interbank network (e.g., suspensions of convertibility) because their reserves were held in the form of cash within their own vaults.

Other Assets

Examiners listed the stocks, securities, and other claims held by the banks. Claims could include judgments against other parties arising from court decisions. Examiners were asked to list the book value and the current market value. Generally items were held at roughly their market value, although for about 17 percent of banks in the sample, the examiner noted that the bank held too many securities that were booked at values in excess of market values or were of questionable value.

Examiners were also asked to provide information on deposits due from reserve agents, banks, and bankers as well as to comment on cash items. With respect to deposits due from other banks, examiners often simply noted that they were seeking verification on items due from other institutions; comments, where provided, might note the number of banks that owed funds to the bank being examined. Occasionally, copies of the form letters sent to correspondents to verify funds were included with the report. Cash items included checks due on local banks, any disputed items (sometimes forged items), and occasionally expense items; the latter two items were required to be written off by the bank. Often the examiner would simply describe cash items as "regular."

The condition of the banking house was also covered in the exam. Most buildings were described as "suitable and convenient" with a vault and safe that were "good and secure." In a few cases, the examiner indicated that the bank had an overly expensive banking house (possibly a management perquisite taken at the expense of shareholders). In one case the examiner expressed concern: "While vault and safe are secure, I am compelled to say their banking room is in bad shape as it has been allowed to go so long without repair that the walls are dirty and dingy and in many places the plastering has fallen off and it needs fixing up badly."[29] Examiners also indicated whether the furniture and fixtures were worth book value or whether their values needed to be written down.

In a few cases, an examiner would note that the bank shared offices with another financial institution, typically a state-chartered savings bank, which would have overlapping management. The examiners often expressed concerns about this arrangement. In a few exceptional cases, it appears that there was incomplete separation of the two financial institutions.

> The business of the People's Savings Bank of Denver, which is under the same management, is conducted in the same room as the banking office and the counter and vaults are used in common. The business of the savings bank appears to be about as active as that of the national bank. If for any cause a run should be made on the savings bank, no doubt the national bank would be affected thereby as the business of the two institutions appear to be as closely connected.[30]

The last asset item that was discussed was the banks' holdings of "Other Real Estate and Mortgages Owned." Typically these were properties acquired when a loan went bad. Among banks that owned such real estate, the average number of properties held was four, and the value of the loans associated with these properties represented, on average, about 3.5 percent of loans. Typically the value of real estate owned exceeded the indebtedness of the borrowers that had pledged the real estate as collateral.

Capital Account and Earnings

As part of their discussion of the capital account of the bank, examiners were asked to verify that the ledgers containing the identity of stockholders were correct and that surrendered stock certificates were properly canceled. Under national bank law (prior to 1935), stockholders suffered the risk of double liability: stockholders could be assessed to cover capital impairments or shortfalls to liability holders in the event of a receivership in an amount equal to their interest in the bank's paid-in capital. As noted by Bolles (1890), the bank ledgers were the source for the identities of the shareholders. The examiners found that the ledgers were generally kept correctly, and in only two instances were stock certificates reported as signed in blank (which enabled the stock to be more easily sold but made it

---

[29] Examiner report of the National Bank of Commerce of Omaha, NE, dated March 21, 1893

[30] From the examiner report of the People's National Bank of Denver dated April 18, 1893. As described by Carlson (2005), runs on the savings banks did indeed have negative effects on the associated banks during the crisis of 1893.

more difficult to determine the identity of the holder). Examiners also reported on whether the bank held its own stock as collateral for loans or otherwise; about 13 percent of banks were reported to do so.

Double liability meant that stockholders could be assessed for an additional amount equal to the paid-in capital of the bank if the bank were placed into receivership. Consequently, the actual amount of equity that acted as a buffer against loss, from the standpoint of bank depositors, was more than the amount of paid in capital and accumulated retained earnings. This is probably best understood as a means of allowing bank stockholders to avoid having to liquidate assets deployed elsewhere when investing in banks.

It is important to note that double liability of stockholders was not a capital adequacy micro-prudential regulation because there was no minimum capital ratio relative to assets or debt. In other words, banks were free to maintain as low a proportion of equity-to-assets as they liked. Minimum capital requirements did exist, but those simply limited the minimum size of the bank's equity base, not the size of equity relative to assets or relative to total bank risk. This difference in treatment of the regulation of equity and cash is interesting and points clearly to the macro-prudential motivation of national bank regulations. Market discipline was relied upon to ensure individual bank safety and soundness, and capital ratios were not regulated. In contrast, given the externalities of liquidity that arose from interbank transactions, minimum amounts of reserves were required in proportion to deposits, and the structure of those requirements (cash vs. deposits in other banks) varied according to the location of the national bank.

The examination reports also contained information on when the most recent dividend had been paid, whether profits were carried through to surplus, and whether profits were used to charge off losses or to write down the value of securities or the banking house. Examiners could also note whether they thought there was a reason that the bank should not pay a dividend during the upcoming period. Nearly 70 percent of banks had paid a dividend within the six months prior to the exam (Table 8.8). Those dividends were, on average, about $5 per share. Dividends were somewhat less likely to have been paid recently in the Mountain/Southwest and Pacific parts of the country, but when they were paid, they tended to be a bit higher in terms of dollars per share. About three-fourths of banks had recently used profits to write off at least some losses. Examiners generally did not see much reason for banks to refrain from paying dividends. They provided a reason for not doing so at about 16 percent of the banks in our

Table 8.8 *Dividends and Writedowns*

	Share of Banks That Paid Dividends in Past 6 Months (%)	Dividends per Share (Dollars)	Share of Banks That Wrote off Losses in Past 6 Months (%)
Overall	69	$4.90	53
By size			
Larger banks	80	$4.00	66
Smaller banks	58	$6.00	41
By reserve city status			
Country bank	67	$5.50	51
Reserve city bank	72	$3.80	57
By region			
Ohio River Valley/South (OH, IA, KY, TN, LA, AL)	80	$4.10	63
Plains (IA, MN, MO, NE, ND)	70	$3.70	52
Mountain/Southwest (CO, MT, NM, TX, UT, WY)	66	$6.00	54
Pacific (CA, OR, WA)	45	$9.10	31

sample, most commonly noting that the bank was fairly new and needed to build up its surplus, that the banks needed to deal with accumulated bad assets, or that it should restore the surplus after having used it to write down bad assets.

Liabilities

Much of the remainder of the report concerned the structure of liabilities. Examiners first commented on money that the bank owed to other banks and whether this took the form of "open accounts" (most common) or certificates of deposit (less common). The examiners' reports indicate that most banks that took deposits from other banks and paid interest did so at a rate of 2 percent at this time. James (1978) notes that New York banks also paid a rate of 2 percent on correspondent balances; it is interesting that this rate appears to have been fairly common across the country and did not vary regionally, unlike some other rates. Examiners then reported on deposits more generally. Some detailed information on the constituent parts of individual deposits was included in the examination report. As shown in Table 8.9, the bulk of deposits were checking accounts (74 percent), followed by demand certificates (14 percent), and time

Table 8.9 *Liabilities (Shares and Ratios in Percent)*

	Ratio of Checking to Individual Deposits	Ratio of Time and Demand Certificates to Individual Deposits	Rate on CDs to Individuals (%)	Share of Banks Borrowing via CDs	Share of Banks Borrowing from Banks in Any Form
Overall	74	24	4.0	15	34
By size					
Larger banks	77	22	3.5	10	24
Smaller banks	72	27	4.4	20	44
By reserve city status					
Country bank	71	27	4.4	16	34
Reserve city bank	77	20	3.3	14	33
By region					
Ohio River Valley/South (OH, IA, KY, TN, LA, AL)	86	13	3.0	4	33
Plains (IA, MN, MO, NE, ND)	63	35	4.0	12	32
Mountain/Southwest (CO, MT, NM, TX, UT, WY)	73	25	4.5	21	28
Pacific (CA, OR, WA)	67	30	5.3	34	48

certificates (11 percent). Time and demand certificates of deposit were not much used in the Ohio River Valley/South, but they accounted for 25–35 percent of individual deposits in other parts of the country.

The examination reports also provide some information on the cost of different types of funds. Interest was almost never paid on checking accounts. Public funds were an important source of funding for banks, and these accounts did bear interest. Some public accounts were very large, and the examiners would comment if the bank appeared overly dependent on them.

Examiners reviewed the certificates of deposit (CDs) and checked whether the certificate books were properly kept. The rate of interest on CDs was also often recorded. The average rate paid on CDs in late 1892 and early 1893 was about 4 percent, although it reached as high as 7 percent. Some examiners reported that the banks offered CDs of several maturities and that they paid a lower rate for CDs with a shorter maturity (typically around 3 months) and a higher rate for CDs with longer maturities (around 6 months). There was also some regional variation: rates were lowest in the Ohio River Valley/South with particularly low rates being paid by banks in Cincinnati (at 1 percent) and Indianapolis (at 2¾ percent). Rates moved up progressively with distance west, with banks on the Pacific, particularly Oregon and Washington, paying the most (in excess of 5 percent). These regional patterns are consistent with previous work on interregional interest rate variation (Davis 1965; Sylla 1969; Smiley 1975; James 1976). That the regions with the highest level of interest rates are also those where troubled loans were a greater share of the portfolio and where dividend payments were more infrequent, is also consistent with the idea in Odell (1989) that some of the differences in interest rates may reflect differences in risk.

Borrowing from other banks received special attention and was viewed as a possible signal of bank weakness (the inability to access normal retail funding sources). Such borrowing tended to carry higher interest rates and involved collateral and was generally viewed negatively by examiners. Whereas borrowing in the form of bills discounted or rediscounted has been discussed in other academic work and appears on the call reports, the examiner reports indicate that banks also borrowed from each other via CDs. These CDs were collateralized (unlike CDs issued to individuals), apparently carried higher rates of interest, and were viewed by examiners as similar to other forms of borrowings from banks. Fifteen percent of banks borrowed from other banks using CDs while about one-third of banks were reported to have borrowed money from other banks in any

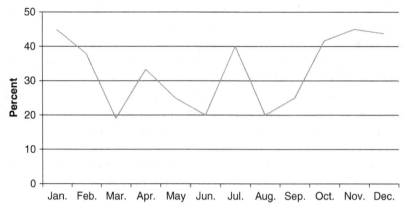

Figure 8.5 Share of banks using borrowed funds by month of examination report.

form (bills discounted, rediscounts, or CDs issued for the purpose of borrowing money). Lockhart (1921) claims that there was some stigma associated with borrowing from other banks and that banks would sometimes borrow using CDs because such borrowing was not grouped with other interbank borrowing on the call report and thus enabled banks to disguise the full extent of their interbank borrowing.[31] Consistent with Lockhart's claim, some examiners noted that this form of borrowing was reported with individual deposits by the bank.

As shown in Figure 8.5, there appears to have been a strong seasonality in the use of interbank borrowing. The fraction of banks using borrowed money is elevated from October to February and is fairly modest for much of the rest of the year (there is a spike in July, although we have somewhat fewer observations in this month). The seasonal needs for rediscounts and other borrowing were noted by the examiners.[32] For instance, in November of 1892, the examiner looked at the First National Bank of Minneapolis and had this to say:

The business of the bank is very large. I consider its condition good and prosperous although while I think it has too much borrowed money, one can hardly see how it can be avoided. It takes a great deal of money to handle the wheat, lumber, and flour at this point. The regular customers of the bank are largely of this class and they expect their full lines or nearly so of discounts at this season of the year and the management feels as though they must accommodate when possible. Toward

[31] Lockhart (1921) also notes that the national banking act restricted bank indebtedness, other than through notes and deposits, to be no more than paid-in capital, which created an additional incentive for banks to not reveal the extent of their interbank indebtedness.

[32] The seasonality is consistent with reports elsewhere, such as James (1978).

Spring the reserve is usually the condition and the money comes back. I suggested to the cashier that perhaps it would be better to carry certificates of deposit that were issued for the purpose of borrowing money as bills payable.[33]

The rates paid on money borrowed from other banks were typically around 6 percent, although they reached as high as 10 percent for some banks while a few banks were able to borrow in this way for as little as 4 percent. Among banks that borrowed, most amounts were fairly modest, with the average amount being about 6 percent of assets. However, a few banks were heavy borrowers, with borrowings by one bank amounting to almost 20 percent of assets. Examiners reported that such borrowing had been explicitly approved by the board of directors in nearly two-thirds of the cases where examiners commented on this topic. Banks often obtained funds through rediscounts or through borrowing on CDs from banks in New York City, another indication of the importance of institutions in New York for providing liquidity to the banking system at this time. Borrowing was also done, but to a lesser degree, from banks in the other central and the regional reserve cities (Chicago, St. Louis, and San Francisco) and occasionally from other local banks or from country banks located in a distant part of the country.

Recapitulation

The final portion of the examination report was a recapitulation. Part of the recapitulation consisted of a table providing the examiner's estimate of losses and necessary write-downs on loans, securities, and other assets. These losses were compared to surplus and undivided profits, after accounting for other expenses, to determine if the bank's capital was impaired. The recapitulation also included a narrative description of the condition of the bank that included any recommendations about regulatory measures that should be taken in the event the bank was having difficulties. These steps could include the suspension of dividends, or in extreme cases, write-downs of capital and assessments of stockholders.

Most banks were successful, with expenses running lower than undivided profits for all but a handful of banks. Losses for our sample of banks, shown in Table 8.10, also tended to be small and were less than 15 percent of surplus and undivided profits for three-fourths of the banks. In 13 cases the examiner indicated that the capital of the bank was impaired.

---

[33] Examiner report of the First National Bank of Minneapolis, MN, dated November 14, 1892.

Table 8.10 *Losses and Recapitulation (Percent)*

	Ratio of Losses to Surplus and Profits (Median)	Ratio of Loan Losses to Total Losses (Median)	Estimated Loss Rate on Loans (Median)	Share of Exams Where Mgmt. Criticized	Share of Exams Where Assets Criticized
Overall	4.0	90	10	9	17
By size					
Larger banks	2.4	100	18	5	10
Smaller banks	6.2	84	7	13	24
By reserve city status					
Country bank	4.6	85	10	9	19
Reserve city bank	2.7	94	13	8	12
By region					
Ohio River Valley/South (OH, IA, KY, TN, LA, AL)	2.0	100	10	4	8
Plains (IA, MN, MO, NE, ND)	4.2	87	18	9	18
Mountain/Southwest (CO, MT, NM, TX, UT, WY)	7.3	84	3	8	27
Pacific (CA, OR, WA)	5.7	81	14	21	17

Losses were reported for several categories of assets including "bad loans," other loans, securities, banking house, furniture and fixtures, and other real estate and mortgages. Most losses were related to loans, although examiners did recommend writing down the value of the banking house or "fixtures and furniture" in several cases. As examiners reported both the book value and losses expected for the various asset categories, it is possible to gauge the anticipated loss rates. The median loss rate on loans across the banks in our sample (in cases where losses were expected to occur) was about 10 percent of the book value of the loans.

Examiners could note in the recapitulation whether banks faced sufficient troubles that they should be disciplined in some way. If there were only a few troubled assets, the examiner would often recommend that those specific assets be charged off; bank officials were generally willing to comply with these recommendations. In cases where problems were more substantial, one of the most typical sanctions was to recommend the suspension of dividend payments.[34] As noted earlier, examiners recommended this for a modest portion of the banks in our sample. In some cases, the bank officers indicated that they would voluntarily suspend dividend payments to either charge off bad assets or rebuild their surplus; in these cases, the examiner would often not comment on whether he would also recommend the stopping of dividend payments. The examiner sometimes expressed the opinion that the management ought to be replaced, but also made clear that it was the responsibility of the board of directors to determine whether any change would be made.

There were thirteen banks for which the examiner considered problem assets to be so substantial that the capital of the bank was impaired. In several of these cases, the examiner noted that the management had recently been replaced and expressed the opinion that the new management would likely help put the bank on better footing. There were three cases, however, where the examiner made exceptional recommendations. One examiner recommended that the bank charge off bad loans against surplus and capital and then permanently reduce capital (by returning some funds to shareholders); reductions in capital would reduce the maximum loan size that the bank could make and presumably result in a smaller bank.[35] In a second case the examiner recommended an assessment against capital. In the third case, the examiner recommended the appointment of a receiver.

---

[34] One could think of such action as an early form of prompt corrective action.

[35] See Paine (1914, especially pp. 80–82) for a discussion of assessments against deficiencies.

The general condition of the bank is bad and its business is not prosperous. It is impossible for me to make an intelligent estimate of the losses that the bank will probably meet on its assets. So much of its funds are tied up in real estate that has no market value now but some of these properties may and probably shall at some time become very valuable. The amounts I have put down as probably losses is surely low enough and it would not astonish me it fully one-half of the capital of the bank is finally lost ... Its capital is badly impaired and it would, I think, be better for the reputation of the [national banking] system if the bank were placed in the hand of a receiver but it would cause great loss to the shareholders and make much trouble here if the receiver tried to realize on the real estate paper. It is shameful and wicked that so much money should be fooled away in so short a time and prove the folly of having real estate speculators as manager of banking institutions.[36]

In the narrative descriptions, banks that were doing well often were characterized favorably in the recapitulation using statements similar to "bank is in a sound and healthy condition and its business is prosperous."[37] Banks that were not doing as well were characterized less charitably. "This bank's wretched condition appears to have been caused by inefficient management particularly in granting large lines of credit without adequate security."[38] One simple way of summarizing some of the information in the descriptive section is to note whether the examiner criticized the management, the asset quality, or both. Out of the 205 banks where comments were made (no comments were provided for one bank), management problems were cited nineteen times and asset quality issues thirty-five times. As might be expected, problems with management, and especially with asset quality, were more likely when estimated losses were higher.

In addition to the quality of the bank's management and assets, some descriptions contained other useful information. For example, some comments discuss the competitive environment:

General condition of the bank is good but the competition of the old established institutions prevent it from making much money. The banks here are all fighting for business and too many concessions are made to borrowers. Overdrafts are seldom refused and paper is allowed to run as long as the borrower wants it without renewal. It is the custom of the place and all the banks follow it.[39]

---

[36] Examiner report of the Washington National Bank of Tacoma, WA, dated December 28, 1892.

[37] This one from the examiner report of the United States National Bank of Portland, OR, dated April 11, 1893.

[38] Examiner report of the Bankers and Merchants National Bank of Dallas, TX, dated November 8, 1892.

[39] Examiner report of the American National Bank of Helena, MT, dated January 6, 1893.

Other comments provide information about local economic conditions.

> Bad paper in the bank is largely a relic of the past – the boom of the city and [subsequent] harder time especially among real estate men from whom the greater part of these losses come. The management is exerting itself in every way by suit and otherwise to force collections and reduce this amount of past due paper. General business is very large and active and its earnings capacity good as will be seen from the statement of profit since July 1, 1892.[40]
>
> [The] bank is gradually coming into good condition and its business is improving. While property is still greatly depreciated there seems to be a marked improvement in affairs in and about San Diego within the last nine or ten months. Business generally has considerably improved, the back country is filling up with settlers, a large amount of land has been planted to citrus and deciduous fruit trees and a large area will come into bearing with the year. The hotels are filled to overflowing with Eastern tourists, many of them investing. Indebtedness is being gradually liquidated and much property is getting into hand of strong holders.[41]

These sorts of comments provide useful characterizations of the banking environment, but are not easily categorized or quantified.

How Do We Know That Regulation and Examination Mattered?

Our summary of the process of examination and the content of examination reports shows that the process was taken seriously both by examiners and bankers, and that the content of examination reports was quite rich. Furthermore, bankers expressed their beliefs that examinations were useful, and many supported reforms to lengthen and deepen the existing process. Nevertheless, as we discuss earlier in this chapter, we also find that examiners occasionally did not strictly enforce all the rules, allowing, for example, modest violations of loan-to-one-borrower limits and temporary shortfalls in cash reserve ratios. Our reading of the record contained in the examination reports is that examiners took a broad view of compliance. If a bank was well managed and prudent, a small or temporary technical violation was noted but did not result in a disciplinary action. Examiners tracked compliance over time, giving banks the opportunity to correct significant violations so long as they did so speedily and in good faith. Additionally, there are at least three sets of reasons to believe that the regulation and supervision of banks was effective and contributed to the health and systemic resilience of the banking system.

---

[40] Examiner report of the National German American Bank of St. Paul, MN, dated November 28, 1892.

[41] Examiner report for the Consolidated National Bank of San Diego, CA, dated February 27, 1893.

First, examiners and their boss, the Comptroller, did not lack the power to enforce their will if bankers ignored their concerns over capital, earnings, loan performance, governance, funding structure, or other aspects that received attention in examination reports. Among the tools at the comptroller's disposal was the authority to order the reduction or elimination of bank payments of dividends, and in extreme circumstances, to revoke a bank's charter. That power also meant that the comptroller and his examiners could exercise soft power by expressing their concerns to bank managers and directors – for example, calling for changes in practices or staff. They did so frequently in correspondence that has been preserved alongside the examination reports, and the responses to those expressed concerns show that regulators and examiners were taken quite seriously by bankers. In the cases we tracked of violations or problems detected by examiners (in particular, shortfalls in reserves relative to required reserves), we find that violations did not typically persist. Furthermore, a key factor contributing to the power of examiners and the Comptroller was the support of bankers for an effective and credible regulatory and supervisory process. Bankers realized that depositor confidence in healthy banks was enhanced by effective and credible regulation and supervision, and therefore, they had a strong incentive to provide political support for the OCC's powers.

Second, the subject matter that examination reports focused on was highly pertinent to bank health and stability, judging from an empirical analysis of the consequences of bank behavior for their ability to attract deposits and their risk of failure (Calomiris and Carlson 2016a). With respect to corporate governance, deposit market discipline clearly rewarded banks that employed the formal corporate governance tools tracked by examiners with higher leverage and tolerance for taking on risk, especially if bank managers did not own sufficiently high stakes in their banks to otherwise gain depositor confidence. Real estate loans and non-depository funding sources (interbank bills that examiners frowned upon or regarded as a sign of trouble) were in fact associated with greater risk of suspension during the Panic of 1893. Maintaining adequate capital and cash were also key to retaining depositor confidence, in the 1890s, and subsequently (Calomiris and Mason 2003; Calomiris and Wilson 2004; Calomiris and Carlson 2016a).

Third, Calomiris and Carlson (2016c) analyze examiners' estimates of loan losses – an outcome of the examination that had clear consequences for banks' write-downs of loans and computation of capital – and find that these estimates effectively incorporated highly relevant hard and soft information about loan quality. Our modeling of the predictive content of examiners' loss estimates shows that they incorporated not only public and private quantitative information about risk, but also included judgments by examiners that proved to have predictive value during the Panic of 1893.

Conclusion

The examination reports discussed here provide considerable insight into the banking system of the early 1890s and the regulatory and supervisory practices of the Office of the Comptroller of the Currency. They also help illuminate the management and governance of the banks, the characteristics of their loan portfolios, and the nature of their liabilities.

As highlighted in this chapter, there tended to be substantial heterogeneity in bank structure and decisions, often reflecting regional differences in the banking environment. For example, although, on average, banks with low managerial ownership and greater formal corporate governance structures tended to undertake greater risk (Calomiris and Carlson 2016a), in the Ohio River Valley/South we find that greater use of formal governance tools and less ownership by management are associated with less risk taking and fewer problem assets. Perhaps as a consequence, these banks paid less to borrow funds. Moving west across the country, where there may have been less frequent scrutiny by examiners, there were more violations of the banking rules, less formal oversight by boards and greater ownership by management, more risk taking, more problem assets, and greater returns to shareholders (when dividends were paid). The commentary from the examination reports suggests that some of the banking practices observed in the western parts of the country reflected greater competition from nearby state-chartered banks that were subject to less stringent rules than the national banks.

Differences in individual bank risk choices were tolerated under the national banking system. Indeed, there were no minimum requirements for capital relative to assets. Furthermore, banks had wide latitude in their corporate governance choices and ownership structures.

The focus of national bank prudential regulation was macro-prudential, as evidenced by the emphasis on the adequacy of cash relative to debt, with special attention to the externalities created in the interbank market (hence the higher proportions of required cash to interbank deposits for banks in reserve cities or central reserve cities).

The main function of examiners was to ensure the accuracy of bank accounts, which promoted the confidence of depositors in the entire system. Examiners not only verified the accuracy of reported capital through their close examination of the loan book, they also verified that cash deposits were actually made in each of the bank's listed reserve agents. And they made sure that national banks met their obligations for publicizing their accounts in local newspapers.

Finally, in keeping with traditional banking philosophy of the time, and with its macro-prudential intent, national bank regulation sharply limited exposure to real estate lending. The fortunes of real estate, as economists have long noted, are closely linked to the business cycle, which makes real estate lending a key source of nondiversifiable risk in bank portfolios. Moreover, especially during adverse times, real estate assets are highly illiquid, making bank recoveries against real estate loans that default slow and uncertain. The pro-cyclicality of bank lending produced by loan-supply effects of bank losses has been an important feature of the financial accelerator (Bernanke and Gertler 1989; Calomiris and Mason 2003). Although examiners permitted national banks to skirt the absolute prohibition on real estate lending, they kept a close eye on real estate exposures and were highly critical of excessive real estate lending.

In the national banking era, both the public and the national banks themselves relied upon effective supervision and regulation, and sought to strengthen it, to ensure that depositors were willing to invest in banks. This stands in contrast to more recent experiences worldwide under deposit insurance, where banks have often lobbied for, and succeeded in obtaining, supervisory and regulatory forbearance (Brown and Dinc 2005, 2011). Furthermore, while the national banking era has often been thought of as unstable given the sensational banking panics that periodically struck the system, failures of national banks were relatively rare and losses to depositors were even rarer. Even the panics themselves saw only modest losses to the banking system. The macro-prudential policies that we identify here – high cash requirements that fell most heavily on the most systemic banks, serious limits on real estate lending, effective public disclosures that supported market discipline – reinforced by competent supervision were key to creating this resilient banking system. As such, they provide important guidelines for today's debates about the value and potential effectiveness of macro-prudential policies.

References

Afonso, Gara, João A. C. Santos, and James Traina. (2014). "Do 'Too-Big-to-Fail' Banks Take on More Risk?" *Federal Reserve Bank of New York Economic Policy Review* 20(2):41–58.

Agarwal, Sumit, David Lucca, Amit Seru, and Francesco Trebbi. (2014). "Inconsistent Regulators: Evidence from Banking." *Quarterly Journal of Economics* 129(2):889–938.

Anginer, Deniz, Asli Demirguc-Kunt, and Min Zhu (2014). "How Does Deposit Insurance Affect Bank Risk? Evidence from the Recent Crisis." *Journal of Banking and Finance* 48(11):312–321.

Bernanke, Ben S., and Mark Gertler. (1989). "Agency Costs, Net Worth, and Business Fluctuations." *American Economic Review* 79(1):14–31.

Bernstein, Asaf, Eric Hughson, and Marc Weidenmier. (2010). "Identifying the Effects of a Lender of Last Resort on Financial Markets: Lessons from the Founding of the Fed." *Journal of Financial Economics* 98(1):40–53.

Bodenhorn, Howard. (2013). "Large Block Shareholders, Institutional Investors, Boards of Directors and Bank Value in the Nineteenth Century." Working Paper No. 18955, National Bureau of Economic Research.

Bodenhorn, Howard, and Eugene N. White. (2014). "The Evolution of Bank Boards of Directors in New York, 1840–1950." Working Paper No. 20078, National Bureau of Economic Research.

Borio, Claudio. (2012), "The Financial Cycle and Macroeconomics: What Have We Learnt?" Working Paper No. 395, Bank for International Settlements.

Bolles, Albert S. (1890). *The National Bank Act and Its Judicial Meaning*. New York: Homans Publishing Company.

Brown, Craig O., and I. Serdar Dinc. (2005). "The Politics of Bank Failures: Evidence from Emerging Markets." *Quarterly Journal of Economics* 120(4):1413–1444.

Brown, Craig O., and I. Serdar Dinc. (2011). "Too Many to Fail? Evidence of Regulatory Forbearance When the Banking Sector Is Weak." *Review of Financial Studies* 24(4): 1378–1405.

Calomiris, Charles W. (1989). "Deposit Insurance: Lessons from the Record." *Economic Perspectives, Federal Reserve Bank of Chicago* 30(3):10–30.

Calomiris, Charles W. (1990). "Is Deposit Insurance Necessary? A Historical Perspective." *Journal of Economic History* 50(2):283–295.

Calomiris, Charles W. (1992). "Do 'Vulnerable' Economies Need Deposit Insurance?: Lessons from the U.S. Agricultural Boom and Bust of the 1920s." In P. L. Brock (ed.), *If Texas Were Chile: A Primer on Banking Reform*, pp. 237–314, 319–328, 450–458. San Francisco: ICS Press.

Calomiris, Charles W. (2000). *U.S. Bank Deregulation in Historical Perspective*. New York: Cambridge University Press.

Calomiris, Charles W., and Mark Carlson. (2016a). "Corporate Governance and Risk Management at Unprotected Banks: National Banks in the 1890s." *Journal of Financial Economics* 119(3):512–532.

Calomiris, Charles W., and Mark Carlson. (2016b). "Interbank Networks in the National Banking Era: Their Purpose and Their Role in the Panic of 1893." BIS Working Paper No. 535.

Calomiris, Charles W., and Mark Carlson. (2016c). "The Predictive Content of National Bank Examiners' Loss Forecasts." Unpublished Working Paper.

Calomiris, Charles W., and Gary Gorton. (1991). "The Origins of Banking Panics: Models, Facts, and Bank Regulation." In R. G. Hubbard (ed.), *Financial Markets and Financial Crises*, pp. 109–173. Chicago: University of Chicago Press.

Calomiris, Charles W., and Stephen H. Haber. (2014). *Fragile by Design: The Political Origins of Banking Crises and Scarce Credit*. Princeton, NJ: Princeton University Press.

Calomiris, Charles W., Matthew Jaremski, Haelim Park, and Gary Richardson. (2015). "Liquidity Risk, Bank Networks, and the Value of Joining the Fed." Working Paper No. 21684, National Bureau of Economic Research.

Calomiris, Charles W., and Joseph R. Mason. (2003). "Fundamentals, Panics and Bank Distress during the Depression." *American Economic Review* 93(5):1615–1647.

Calomiris, Charles W., and Berry Wilson. (2004). "Bank Capital and Portfolio Management: The 1930s 'Capital Crunch' and Scramble to Shed Risk." *Journal of Business* 77(3):421–455.

Carlson, Mark. (2005). "Causes of Bank Suspensions in the Panic of 1893." *Explorations in Economic History* 42(1):56–80.

Carlson, Mark. (2015). "Lessons from the Historical Use of Reserve Requirements in the United State to Promote Bank Liquidity." *International Journal of Central Banking* 11(1):191–224.

Coffin, George M. (1891). *Handbook for National Bank Shareholders, Their Legal Rights and Liabilities Defined*. Washington, DC: H. L. McQueen.

Coffin, George M. (1896). *Handbook for Bank Officers*. Washington, DC: McGill and Wallace.

Crays, Dwight. (1941). *Bank Supervision in the United States*. Mimeo. Washington, DC: Board of Governors of the Federal Reserve.

Crockett, Andrew D. (2000). *Marrying the Micro- and Macro-prudential Dimensions of Financial Stability*. Remarks before the Eleventh International Conference of Banking Supervisors, Basel, 20–21 September, Bank for International Settlements. Retrieved from www.bis.org/speeches/sp000921.htm.

Davis, Lance E. (1965). "The Investment Market, 1870–1914: The Evolution of a National Market." *Journal of Economic History* 25(3):355–399.

Demirgüc-Kunt, Asli, and Enrica Detragiache. (2002). "Does Deposit Insurance Increase Banking System Stability? An Empirical Investigation." *Journal of Monetary Economics* 49(7):1373–1406.

Demirgüc-Kunt, Asli, Edward J. Kane, and Luc Laeven. (2008). "Adoption and Design of Deposit Insurance." In *Deposit Insurance around the World: Issues of Design and Implementation*, pp. 29–80. Cambridge, MA: MIT Press.

Drehmann, Mathias, Claudio Borio, and Kostas Tsatsaronis. (2012). "Characterising the Financial Cycle: Don't Lose Sight of the Medium Term!" Working Paper No. 380, Bank for International Settlements.

Hanes, Christopher, and Paul W. Rhode. (2013). "Harvests and Financial Crises in Gold Standard America." *Journal of Economic History* 73(1):201–246.

Hilt, Eric. (2008). "When did Ownership Separate from Control? Corporate Governance in the Early Nineteenth Century." *Journal of Economic History* 68(3):645–685.

International Monetary Fund. (2014). "Chapter 3: How Big Is the Implicit Subsidy for Banks Considered Too Important to Fail?" *Global Financial Stability Report*, April.

James, John A. (1976). "The Development of the National Money Market, 1893–1911." *Journal of Economic History* 36(4):878–897.

James, John A. (1978). *Money and Capital Markets in Postbellum America*. Princeton, NJ: Princeton University Press.

Jorda, Oscar, Moritz Schularick, and Alan M. Taylor. (2015). "Leveraged Bubbles." Working Paper No. 21486, National Bureau of Economic Research.

Kemmerer, Edwin W. (1911). *Seasonal Variations in Demands for Currency and Capital*. Washington, DC: National Monetary Commission.

Laeven, Luc, and Fabian Valencia. (2013). "Systemic Banking Crises Database." *IMF Economic Review* 61(2):225–270.

Lamoreaux, Naomi R. (1994). *Insider Lending: Banks, Personal Connections, and Economic Development in Industrial New England*. Cambridge: Cambridge University Press.

Lockhart, Oliver C. (1921). "The Development of Interbank Borrowing in the National System, 1869–1914." *Journal of Political Economy* 29(2):138–160.

Lunt, Edward C. (1922). *Surety Bonds: Nature, Functions, Underwriting Requirements*. New York: The Ronald Press Company.

Mankiw, N. Gregory, and Jeffrey A. Miron. (1987). "The Adjustment of Expectations to a Change in Regime: A Study of the Founding of the Federal Reserve." *American Economic Review* 77(3):358–374.

Miron, Jeffrey A. (1986). "Financial Panics, the Seasonality of the Nominal Interest Rate, and the Founding of the Fed." *American Economic Review* 76(1):125–140.

Mitchener, Kris J., and Gary Richardson. (2015). "Shadowy Banks and the Interbank Amplifier during the Great Depression." Working Paper, University of Warwick.

Moulton, H. G. (1918). "Commercial Banking and Capital Formation." *Journal of Political Economy* 26(7):705–731.

Odell, Kerry A. (1989). "The Integration of Regional and Interregional Capital Markets: Evidence from the Pacific Coast, 1883–1913." *Journal of Economic History* 49(2):297–310.

Office of the Comptroller of the Currency. (1890). *Annual Report of the Comptroller of the Currency*. Washington, DC: U.S. Government Printing Office.

Office of the Comptroller of the Currency. (1908). *Annual Report of the Comptroller of the Currency*. Washington, DC: U.S. Government Printing Office.

Paine, Willis. (1914). *The Laws of the United States Relating to National Banks*. New York: Baker, Voorhis, & Co.

Robertson, Ross. (1968). *The Comptroller and Bank Supervision, A Historical Appraisal*. Washington, DC: Office of the Comptroller of the Currency.

Shim, Ilhyock, Bilyana Bogdanova, Jimmy Shek, and Agne Subelyte. (2013). "Database for Policy Actions on Housing Markets." *BIS Quarterly Review* (September):83–95.

Smiley, Gene. (1975). "Interest Rate Movement in the United States, 1883–1913." *Journal of Economic History* 35(3):591–620.

Sylla, Richard. (1969). "Federal Policy, Banking Market Structure, and Capital Mobilization in the United States, 1863–1913." *Journal of Economic History* 29(4):657–686.

Tucker, George. (1839). *The Theory of Money and Banks Investigated*. Boston: Charles Little and James Brown.

White, Eugene N. (1983). *The Regulation and Reform of the American Banking System, 1900–1929*. Princeton, NJ: Princeton University Press.

White, Eugene N. (2001). "California Banking in the Nineteenth Century: The Art and Method of the Bank of A. Levy." *Business History Review* 75(2):297–324.

Index